Salesforce B2C Solution Architect's Handbook

Design scalable and cohesive business-to-consumer experiences with Salesforce Customer 360

Mike King

BIRMINGHAM—MUMBAI

Salesforce B2C Solution Architect's Handbook

Copyright © 2021 Packt Publishing

All rights reserved. No part of this book may be reproduced, stored in a retrieval system, or transmitted in any form or by any means, without the prior written permission of the publisher, except in the case of brief quotations embedded in critical articles or reviews.

Every effort has been made in the preparation of this book to ensure the accuracy of the information presented. However, the information contained in this book is sold without warranty, either express or implied. Neither the author, nor Packt Publishing or its dealers and distributors, will be held liable for any damages caused or alleged to have been caused directly or indirectly by this book.

Packt Publishing has endeavored to provide trademark information about all of the companies and products mentioned in this book by the appropriate use of capitals. However, Packt Publishing cannot guarantee the accuracy of this information.

Group Product Manager: Alok Dhuri
Publishing Product Manager: Alok Dhuri
Senior Editor: Storm Mann
Content Development Editor: Nithya Sadanandan
Technical Editor: Karan Solanki
Copy Editor: Safis Editing
Project Coordinator: Ajesh Devavaram
Proofreader: Safis Editing
Indexer: Subalakshmi Govindhan
Production Designer: Ponraj Dhandapani

First published: October 2021
Production reference: 1141021

Published by Packt Publishing Ltd.
Livery Place
35 Livery Street
Birmingham
B3 2PB, UK.

ISBN 978-1-80181-703-5

www.packt.com

To my wife, Martha Bellows, for her grace and support when I decided to take on yet another project. To my parents, Michael King Sr., Linda Rivers, and Joe Rivers, who have always put their children first. None of us would be who we are without you.

– Mike King

Contributors

About the author

Mike King has worked on the most complex B2C Commerce customer implementations, including multiple brands and geographies worldwide. Mike is also a certified Salesforce instructor, teaching the B2C Technical Architect certification preparation course.

In January 2019, Mike participated in the inaugural Salesforce cross-cloud academy. He has since worked with Salesforce on the B2C Solution Architect exam development team and in real-world B2C solution architecture implementations. Mike has also presented numerous times with Salesforce on the topic of B2C solution architecture, including at TrailheaDX and Dreamforce.

When not obsessing about Salesforce, commerce, and software architecture, Mike enjoys hiking, camping, and woodworking.

> *This project would not have been possible without the tremendous foundation set by the Salesforce Architect Success Program, especially Abraham Lloyd. Your presentations, training materials, solution kits, and countless phone calls helped me move out of my commerce comfort zone and into the big wide world of Salesforce. My sincere thanks also to Doug Midgley, my technical reviewer and B2C Solution Architect extraordinaire, for the countless hours spent making sure this book was the best it could be.*
>
> *I need to thank Slalom, especially Katie Dunlap and Shivani Majewski, who have been so supportive of this endeavor. Finally, I'd like to thank Tameem Bahri, for the encouragement and the introduction that ultimately led to this book.*

About the reviewer

Doug Midgley is an Amsterdam-based cross-product Salesforce architect working for Accenture. Originally from New Zealand, he has spent nearly a decade at various locations across Europe, with 6 years of this period spent implementing Salesforce solutions in a variety of industries.

His main focus is on the various marketing products offered by Salesforce. However, he also acts as a technical architect on Salesforce core implementations.

Having worked on multiple Marketing Cloud certifications, he was also involved in the creation of the Salesforce B2C Solution Architect certification.

Outside of his work life, he is an avid balcony gardener and passionate home chef.

Table of Contents

Preface

Section 1: Customer 360 Component Products

1
Demystifying Salesforce, Customer 360, and Digital 360

Learning the language – Salesforce, Customer 360, and Digital 360	**4**	Automation	18
		AppExchange	22
		Reports and dashboards	23
Lightning Platform	4	**Additional technology stacks**	**25**
Salesforce ecosystem	6	Salesforce Platform and beyond	26
Customer 360 evolution	6	Solution architecture methodology	27
Digital 360	8		
B2C solution architecture focus areas	8	**Acquisitions and legacy terminology**	**27**
Salesforce Platform (Force.com)	**9**	**Summary**	**28**
Salesforce orgs	10	**Questions**	**29**
Data model	10	**Further reading**	**29**
Security	16		
User experience customization	17		

2
Supporting Your Customers with Service Cloud

Service Cloud capabilities	**32**	Knowledge	41
Service Cloud editions	33	Service contracts and entitlements	42
Service Console	34	Computer Telephony Integration (CTI)	43
Customer support	34	Omni-Channel	43

Service Cloud data model — 45
Salesforce Platform data model review — 46
Additional objects — 46

Service Cloud APIs and integrations — 47
Available APIs — 47
Which API should I use? — 51
File-based integrations — 51
Data import and export capabilities — 52
Outgoing requests — 53

Service Cloud request limits and allocations — 54
Salesforce licenses and editions — 54
Capability capacity limitations — 55
Total API allocations — 55
API usage monitoring and enforcement — 56
API access and connected apps — 57
Feature allocation limits — 58
Data and file storage allocations — 58

Summary — 59
Questions — 60
Further reading — 61

3
Direct-to-Consumer Selling with Commerce Cloud B2C

B2C Commerce capabilities — 64
Customer experience options — 65
Roles and access — 69
Merchant tools — 69
Admin tools — 70

B2C Commerce data model — 71
Realms, instances, and sites — 71
Designing data sharing solutions — 74
System objects — 76
Custom objects — 77
Packt Gear B2C Commerce data model — 79

B2C Commerce APIs and integrations — 80
Feed-based integration support — 80
Job framework — 80
Account Manager — 81
Open Commerce API (OCAPI) — 82

Commerce APIs — 86
Integration points — 87

B2C Commerce quotas and governance — 88
API and object quotas overview — 88
Key solution design quotas — 89

B2C Commerce Marketplace — 90
Commerce Cloud product family — 91
Order Management — 91
Omni-Channel Inventory — 92
B2B Commerce — 92
Loyalty Management — 93
Commerce Payments — 93

Summary — 94
Questions — 95

4
Engaging Customers with Marketing Cloud

The Marketing Cloud component	98
Content Builder	100
Datorama	100
Google Analytics 360 connector	101
Journey Builder	101
Automation Studio	101
Interaction Studio	102
Email Studio	102
Mobile Studio	103
Advertising Studio	103
Social Studio	104
Salesforce CDP	104
Pardot	105

Marketing Cloud capabilities	105
Email management	106
Journey orchestration	107
Cloud Pages	107
Programmatic customization	108

Marketing Cloud data model	109
Lists	109
Data Extensions	109
Data Designer	110
Business Units	111
Suppression	112
Segmentation	112

Marketing Cloud APIs and integrations	115
Feed file-based integrations	115
API integrations	117
Productized integration	122
Importing data into a Data Extension	126
Marketing Cloud SDKs	126

Marketing Cloud design considerations	127
Marketing Cloud edition constraints	127
Data import volumes	128

Putting it all together	128
Summary	129
Questions	129
Answers	130

5
Salesforce Ecosystem – Building a Complete Solution

Experience Cloud and content management	132
Experience Cloud	132
Content Management System	135

OM, Payments, Loyalty Management, and B2B	136
Order Management	136
Salesforce Payments	138
Loyalty Management	139
Salesforce B2B Commerce Lightning	140

Enterprise CRM with Sales and CPQ and Billing	142

Sales Cloud	142	**MuleSoft and Heroku in**	
CPQ and Billing	143	**Customer 360**	**145**
Enterprise analytics with		MuleSoft in Customer 360	145
Tableau	**143**	Heroku in Customer 360	148
Tableau integration	144	**Packt Gear solution**	**149**
Tableau CRM	145	**Summary**	**150**
		Questions	**151**

Section 2: Architecture of Customer 360 Solutions

6
Role of a Solution Architect

Role of a B2C solution architect	**156**	Business case breakdown	170
Architect team responsibilities	157	**Architecture deliverables**	**172**
Stakeholders	**158**	System overview diagram	173
The full team	158	Data mapping	174
Alignment on goals	160	Sequence diagram	176
Stakeholder interviews	161	Technical specification documents	178
Project sequencing	**167**	**The Packt Gear team**	**180**
Building a firm foundation	167	**Summary**	**181**
Evaluating next steps	169	**Questions**	**182**

7
Integration Architecture Options

Cross-cloud application development life cycle	**184**	Integrated B2C solution application development life cycle	187
Service Cloud application development life cycle	185	**Point-to-point integrations**	**189**
		Prescriptive approach	191
B2C Commerce application development life cycle	186	Productized point-to-point integrations	192
Marketing Cloud application		B2C CRM Sync	193
development life cycle	187	Marketing Cloud Connect	198

Commerce and Marketing Connector 203
Integration middleware 210
When to explore integration middleware 212
Integration middleware and the point-to-point connectors 213
Advantages of MuleSoft 214
Leveraging MuleSoft in a B2C solution 219

Single source of truth 219
Incorporating a single source of truth 220
Leveraging Heroku 220

The Packt Gear approach 222
Summary 223
Questions 223
Further reading 224

8
Creating a 360° View of the Customer

Identifying the customer 226
Service Cloud customer identifiers 228
B2C Commerce customer identifiers 231
Marketing Cloud customer identifiers 235
Cross-cloud customer identification 237

Mastering customer data 241
Evaluating business needs 242
Cross-cloud customer data mapping 243
Data privacy and consent management 245
Handling legacy data 247

360° view of the customer 248
Experience delivery maturity 249
Recognizing customers as humans 250

Seamless identity 253
The Packt Gear approach 254
Summary 255
Questions 255
Further reading 256

9
Supporting Key Business Scenarios

Multi-cloud use case solution kits 258
Customer 360 Guide for Retail 258
Solution kits 260

Integrating chat bots and agent-supported chats 265
Supported use cases 265
Extending the chat solution architecture 268

Extending the chat workflow 271
Additional chat design considerations 272
Chat configuration extensions 273
Chat modifications for B2C CRM Sync 274

Capturing revenue with abandonment journeys 275
Abandoned cart workflow 277
Abandoned cart data model 278
Collect.js for abandonment scenarios 279

Guided hike abandonment tracking	282	Summary	284
Rebuilding the customer's cart	283	Questions	284

10
Enterprise Integration Strategies

Multi-org, realm, and BU scenarios	**286**	Aggregating data through services	308
Component product scopes and structures	287	**Integrations beyond Salesforce**	**312**
		External customer data sources	313
Solution design considerations	292	External system integration points	315
Enterprise data management	296	External integrations through middleware	318
Point-to-point integration impacts	**300**	**Monitoring the solution**	**319**
Multi-org with Marketing Cloud Connect	300	Log file aggregation	320
		Integration middleware	320
Implications for B2C CRM sync	301	Manual approaches	320
B2C Commerce and Marketing Cloud connector	304	Custom solution	321
Enterprise integration using middleware	**306**	**Summary**	**321**
		Questions	**322**
Virtualizing data access at scale	307	**Further reading**	**322**

Section 3: Salesforce-Certified B2C Solution Architect

11
Exam Preparation Tools and Techniques

Exam structure	**326**	Trailhead resources	333
Credential and target audience	327	Partner Learning Camp	333
Topic outline and weighting	330	**Hands-on experience**	**334**
Study materials	**332**	Broadening your perspective	335
Solution architecture guidebooks	332	Gaining product-specific knowledge	336

Getting started with Salesforce — 337
Summary — 338
Questions — 338

12
Prerequisite Certifications

Marketing Cloud Email Specialist exam overview — 340
Marketing Cloud Email Specialist topic overview — 341
Marketing Cloud Email Specialist study materials — 345

Platform App Builder exam overview — 346
Platform App Builder topic overview — 346

Platform App Builder study materials — 351
Integration Architecture Designer exam overview — 352
Integration Architecture Designer topic overview — 352
Integration Architecture Designer study materials — 356

Summary — 357
Questions — 357

13
Commerce and Integration

B2C Commerce Architect exam preparation topics — 360
The B2C Commerce Architect certification — 361
B2C Commerce supplemental topics — 367

Complementary component topics — 379
Overall solution design topics — 381
Summary — 382
Questions — 382

14
Certification Scenarios

Authentication and customer identity scenarios — 384
An example authentication and customer identity scenario — 385
Scenario solution development — 386
Evaluating system constraints — 388

Customer service scenarios — 389
Example customer service scenario — 389
Scenario solution development — 390
Evaluating system constraints — 395

Marketing-focused scenarios — 396

An example marketing scenario	397	An example data integration scenario	402
Scenario solution development	398	Scenario solution development	403
Evaluating system constraints	401	**Summary**	**406**
Data integration scenarios	**402**	**Questions**	**406**

Assessments

Other Books You May Enjoy

Index

Preface

Salesforce B2C solution architecture focuses on delivering business-to-consumer experiences using Salesforce products. This capability, and the Salesforce B2C Solution Architect certification, is in high demand because it truly takes a unified viewpoint and a broad understanding to get the most out of your Salesforce investment. You need to know the capabilities of the Salesforce products at a technical level, how they integrate, what their data model is, and how they fit into a larger enterprise technology landscape.

As a B2C Solution Architect, you need business domain knowledge, as well as strong organizational and communication skills, combined with deep technical expertise in a variety of areas. Make no mistake, this is challenging to achieve, but the rewards for an organization that truly understands their customer and provides them with a seamless experience are great.

A properly designed Customer 360 solution spanning B2C Commerce Cloud, Marketing Cloud, and Service Cloud on the Salesforce Platform provides the foundation for a single view of the customer, unique insight, and transformational capabilities. Incorporating products such as Order Management, Salesforce CDP, and MuleSoft can build a richer experience, while products such as Sales Cloud, B2B Commerce, and Pardot can stretch into the B2B solution world.

Who this book is for

This book is primarily aimed at Salesforce technical audiences familiar with one or more of the products in the Customer 360 suite (especially B2C Commerce, Marketing Cloud, and Service Cloud). With this book, you'll learn more about the capabilities of the complementary products in the tool suite and expand your capabilities.

For enterprise architects looking to learn more about the Salesforce ecosystem of products or for technology leaders in B2C organizations, this book will provide a valuable reference to help cut through the noise and form a solution. Here, you will learn how these products fit into your overall enterprise technology strategy, including data and integration.

Finally, if you're evaluating Salesforce for your organization, this book will serve as a roadmap for what you'll need to achieve your goals and how it all fits together. We're focused on the architect's viewpoint; we don't get into code-level detail or administration tasks.

What this book covers

Chapter 1, *Demystifying Salesforce, Customer 360, and Digital 360*, explains the core terminology used in the Salesforce space, including the difference between products, clouds, and platforms, as the first step in your journey. From there, we'll provide a foundational understanding of the Salesforce Platform on which so much of the solution is built.

Chapter 2, *Supporting Your Customers with Service Cloud*, covers Service Cloud's core functionality and goes deeper into the integration options and data model supported by the underlying Salesforce Platform.

Chapter 3, *Direct-to-Consumer Selling with Commerce Cloud B2C*, covers the strengths and limitations, core data model, and integration capabilities of B2C Commerce, which is the enterprise commerce engine used to power thousands of websites through the busiest shopping days of the year.

Chapter 4, *Engaging Customers with Marketing Cloud*, sets out how Marketing Cloud's core messaging and journeys platform supports marketing and transactional communications across a variety of channels, as well as marketing journey creation and more. We cover its capabilities, component products, data model, and integration options.

Chapter 5, *Salesforce Ecosystem – Building a Complete Solution*, focuses on a high-level review of additional Salesforce products, beyond the three pillars of the B2C solution architecture (B2C Commerce, Service Cloud, and Marketing Cloud), and where these products will have advantages in your solution.

Chapter 6, *Role of a Solution Architect*, teaches you how to assemble an appropriate team, how to structure a discovery, organize a project, and what the essential deliverables are for the B2C Solution Architect exam.

Chapter 7, *Integration Architecture Options*, goes into more detail about both point-to-point and middleware-based integration options. We'll also review cross-cloud development life cycles to help structure a team that can deliver on more than one workstream.

Chapter 8, *Creating a 360° View of the Customer*, explains how the heart of a successful B2C solution architecture is a complete and consistent picture of the customer. This means tying together commerce, marketing, service, and other experiences. We'll cover what a customer means in each system and how they all relate to one another.

Chapter 9, *Supporting Key Business Scenarios*, explores the Salesforce-provided solution kits that serve as a jumping-off point and then customizes and extends them for our fictional organization.

Chapter 10, *Enterprise Integration Strategies*, tackles topics such as multiple Salesforce orgs, B2C Commerce realms, and Marketing Cloud business units as we explore integration with other enterprise systems.

Chapter 11, *Exam Preparation Tools and Techniques*, serves as a quick reference for essential topics, study materials, and recommendations for how to get hands-on experience in these areas for those interested in the Salesforce B2C Solution Architect certification.

Chapter 12, *Prerequisite Certifications*, details how, before qualifying for the B2C Solution Architect exam, you'll need to achieve the three prerequisite certifications covered in this chapter. We'll provide a review of the topics, with an emphasis on the recommended order and which sections of this book to review for a refresher.

Chapter 13, *Commerce and Integration*, covers some essential topics and provides study recommendations for those interested in B2C Commerce technical architecture given that, although the Salesforce B2C *Commerce* Architect certification is not a prerequisite for the B2C *Solution* Architect certification, there are a lot of topics that will transfer across.

Chapter 14, *Certification Scenarios*, concludes by bringing everything together with four realistic example scenarios using our fictional Packt Enterprises company. For each scenario, we'll review possible options, shape a solution, and provide a recommended approach to help establish good habits that will transfer to the exam or real life.

To get the most out of this book

You should already have an understanding of concepts such as APIs, file exchanges, databases, and cloud software models. You should also understand high-level concepts in the **business-to-consumer** (**B2C**) domain, including customers, products, orders, marketing journeys, customer service cases, and order management. This book is a roadmap with links to a huge and ever-evolving set of Salesforce resources. You should get into the habit of using the links, bookmarking things, and reading further on your own..

While reading this book, it's helpful if you re-work the examples in a context that's meaningful to you. Think about your own organization or a client that you're working with. How is your situation similar or different? How would that impact your architectural decisions? What might you do differently and what questions would you ask to understand the situation?

This book is intended to be a roadmap to a way of thinking about architecture. It's a snapshot of the features and functionality available in a variety of software products at a point in time. That stuff will change, but the overall approach does not. Ask the right questions, figure out what tools you need and how they will work together, document your solution, and iterate.

Do not expect to use this book as a shortcut to pass the exam. There's no substitute for learning the materials and understanding how to apply them in various situations. Focus on the process, experiment, take your time, and only when you've truly locked in the information should you move on to certification.

Download the color images

We also provide a PDF file that has images of the screenshots and diagrams used in this book. You can download it here: `https://static.packt-cdn.com/downloads/9781801817035_ColorImages.pdf`

Conventions used

There are a number of text conventions used throughout this book.

`Code in text`: Indicates code words in text, database table names, folder names, filenames, file extensions, pathnames, dummy URLs, user input, and Twitter handles. Here is an example: "In addition to `access_token`, the authentication response also supplies the REST API and SOAP API access URLs and the token expiration time, which can be used to construct additional requests and to recreate the token before it expires."

A block of code is set as follows:

```
<script type="text/javascript">
    _etmc.push(["trackCart", {"clear_cart": true}]);
</script>
```

When we wish to draw your attention to a particular part of a code block, the relevant lines or items are set in bold:

```
<script type="text/javascript">
    _etmc.push(["trackCart", {"clear_cart": true}]);
</script>
```

Bold: Indicates a new term, an important word, or words that you see on screen. For instance, words in menus or dialog boxes appear in **bold**. Here is an example:

"The SFTP URL for a given Marketing Cloud instance can be found in the **FTP Accounts** section of **Setup**."

> **Tips or important notes**
> Appear like this.

Get in touch

Feedback from our readers is always welcome.

General feedback: If you have questions about any aspect of this book, email us at customercare@packtpub.com and mention the book title in the subject of your message.

Errata: Although we have taken every care to ensure the accuracy of our content, mistakes do happen. If you have found a mistake in this book, we would be grateful if you would report this to us. Please visit www.packtpub.com/support/errata and fill in the form.

Piracy: If you come across any illegal copies of our works in any form on the internet, we would be grateful if you would provide us with the location address or website name. Please contact us at copyright@packt.com with a link to the material.

If you are interested in becoming an author: If there is a topic that you have expertise in and you are interested in either writing or contributing to a book, please visit authors.packtpub.com.

Share Your Thoughts

Once you've read *Salesforce B2C Solution Architect's Handbook*, we'd love to hear your thoughts! Scan the QR code below to go straight to the Amazon review page for this book and share your feedback.

https://packt.link/r/1801817030

Your review is important to us and the tech community and will help us make sure we're delivering excellent quality content.

Section 1 Customer 360 Component Products

This section is about understanding the tools in your toolbox.

Before we worry about designing solutions that span products, we need to understand what products we need and how they work. We'll demystify concepts such as Customer 360 and Digital 360, clarify product and cloud boundaries, and then take each of the three primary component products in the Customer 360 ecosystem, reviewing their data models, integration options, and governance.

If you're already an expert in one of these areas, feel free to just skim through that particular chapter and focus on the areas that are newer or where you need a refresher. Everything in this book relies on understanding the capabilities of the component products covered here.

This section comprises the following chapters:

- *Chapter 1, Demystifying Salesforce, Customer 360, and Digital 360*
- *Chapter 2, Supporting Your Customers with Service Cloud*
- *Chapter 3, Direct-to-Consumer Selling with Commerce Cloud B2C*
- *Chapter 4, Engaging Customers with Marketing Cloud*
- *Chapter 5, Salesforce Ecosystem – Building a Complete Solution*

1
Demystifying Salesforce, Customer 360, and Digital 360

Salesforce, Customer 360, Digital 360, Customer 360 Audiences, Commerce Cloud, Service Cloud, Marketing, CRM, CMS, OMS…starting to feel a bit lost? Getting the terminology right is the first step in designing effective solutions that leverage the Salesforce ecosystem. That means knowing the difference between products built on the Salesforce **Customer Relationship Management** (**CRM**) platform, such as **Sales Cloud** and **Service Cloud**, and products built on separate technology platforms, such as **B2C Commerce** and most of **Marketing Cloud**.

In this chapter, we'll be untangling the key terms you'll encounter in marketing materials, sales cycles, and throughout the Salesforce product documentation so you can have meaningful conversations with clients or internal stakeholders. We'll then cover some things you need to know about the **Salesforce Platform**, before moving on to a few other critical technologies that have been added to the Salesforce family of products. The goal here isn't to go too deep into any of these technologies – we'll be covering several in more depth in the following chapters – but to refine our language and establish a firm foundational understanding that the rest of the book will build upon.

In this chapter, we're going to cover the following main topics:

- Learning the language – Salesforce, Customer 360, and Digital 360
- Salesforce Platform (Force.com)
- Additional technology stacks
- Acquisitions and legacy terminology

Throughout this journey, we'll be following along with **Packt Gear**, a fictional company that manufactures, markets, and sells outdoor supplies directly to the consumer. Packt Gear has been successful in recent years, but their home-grown technology stack is starting to hurt their ability to grow their business quickly. They've decided to transform their business by moving to Salesforce…they just need to figure out what that means. Fortunately, they have you to help!

Learning the language – Salesforce, Customer 360, and Digital 360

What do we mean when we say Salesforce? What does your client mean? What does your **Chief Marketing Officer (CMO)** mean? What do the other architects on your team mean?

This section is focused on clarifying the terminology you'll need in order to have effective conversations with all the stakeholders on projects that incorporate multiple Salesforce products.

First and foremost, Salesforce is the name of a software company. Their flagship product is the Lightning Platform, which supports many of their Salesforce-branded products, such as Sales Cloud and Service Cloud. In this section, we'll clarify the difference between Salesforce the company, the Lightning Platform CRM product, and the larger Salesforce ecosystem of products that use different underlying technology.

As a B2C solution architect working with Packt Gear, you know that the first thing to sort out is which Salesforce **products** are right for Packt Gear.

Lightning Platform

Over time, the term *Salesforce* has become synonymous with the CRM product, but using the name of the company to mean one specific product that the company sells can be confusing in real projects.

On top of the core Salesforce Platform, also known as **Core**, **Force.com**, or the **Lightning Platform**, Salesforce has built a variety of licensed products that extend the platform by adding use case specific features and functionality. The Lightning Platform-based CRM product sold by Salesforce is referred to as **Salesforce.com** (as opposed to just Salesforce, which indicates the company). Many, but not all, Salesforce products are built on the Salesforce Platform.

Salesforce Platform-based products can be divided into two broad categories: **function-specific** or **industry-specific**. These two categories have no *technical* significance; they are just ways for Salesforce to organize and sell features to customers. Function-specific products provide features that are organized around a specific use case but can be used across any industry.

The **function-specific** Salesforce Platform-based products include the following:

- Sales Cloud
- Service Cloud
- Work.com
- Employee Cloud
- Experience Cloud
- Order Management
- B2B Commerce
- Customer 360 Audiences

The **industry-specific** Salesforce Platform-based products include the following:

- Health Cloud
- Financial Services Cloud
- Government Cloud
- Manufacturing Cloud
- Media Cloud
- Nonprofit Cloud

> **Important note**
>
> The set of available Salesforce Platform-based products is constantly evolving, so this should not be considered an authoritative list. Many of these products are not relevant in B2C solutions; we'll be focusing on the ones that are.

Salesforce ecosystem

Other uses of Salesforce, including Salesforce Commerce Cloud and Salesforce Marketing Cloud, refer to hybrid offerings that include products on the core Salesforce Platform and products built on separate technology. They are owned by Salesforce the company, but they aren't built on the Salesforce Platform, at least not entirely.

Why does this matter? At its core, **B2C solution architecture** is about integration. When leveraging a variety of products that are all built on the Salesforce Platform, there's really no need for integration between them; they all share a **data model** and can work together. When including products that aren't built on the Salesforce Platform, however, the work becomes more complicated.

As you evaluate the products needed for Packt Gear, pay attention to which of the products in the overall solution are built on the Salesforce Platform and which are external and will have to be integrated.

Customer 360 evolution

As Salesforce evolved and grew from a pure CRM product company to an enterprise software vendor competing in a wide variety of industries, they needed a better way to describe the solution they bring when the entire toolset is applied. This concept became known as Customer 360.

Customer 360 concept

The heart of any successful business is its customers. Salesforce depicts this customer-centric focus with a concept called **Customer 360**. It's critical for you as a B2C solution architect to be able to separate the marketing message from the technology solution, however.

> **Tip**
>
> Customer 360 is **not** a product, it's a mindset. It means combining all of your Salesforce products together in service to a common understanding of your customers and their experiences with your brand.

Customer 360 component products for B2C solutions

While the term *Customer 360* refers to all the Salesforce products, this book is going to focus on a few key components that are the building blocks of a B2C solution:

- **Service Cloud** for customer service, often abbreviated to **SFSC**
- **B2C Commerce** for direct-to-consumer selling, often abbreviated to **SFCC** (though this more accurately refers to the *entire* **Salesforce Commerce Cloud**, *including* B2C Commerce as well as B2B Commerce and Order Management)
- **Marketing Cloud** for marketing and digital communication, often abbreviated to **SFMC**

Remember that we need to pay attention to which products are built on the Salesforce Platform and which are not. Service Cloud is built on the Salesforce Platform, whereas B2C Commerce and most of the components of Marketing Cloud are not.

In addition to these three key products, the following are often used in a B2C solution and will be covered at a higher level in later chapters:

- Salesforce Order Management for order management
- MuleSoft for integration

Customer 360 and Packt Gear

Packt Gear sells products online directly to the consumer, supports these consumers through customer service channels, and advertises online through a variety of digital channels, including email and social. Although there are many other operational considerations for making that happen, those are the core use cases for the initial digital transformation. So, a mix of B2C Commerce, Service Cloud, and Marketing Cloud sounds right! Remember that B2C Commerce is only one product in the Salesforce Commerce Cloud family of products.

We'll cover the rest in *Chapter 3, Direct-to-Consumer Selling with Commerce Cloud B2C*. We'll also evaluate integration options for pulling it all together in *Chapter 7, Integration Architecture Options*.

If your solution has other requirements, we'll be outlining the overall methodology for evaluating, understanding, and incorporating products into the solution so you can apply it to whatever tools you need in your unique business environment.

If Customer 360 means using the full power of Salesforce in service to your customer-centric vision, Digital 360 is focused on the customer experience portion of the solution.

Digital 360

The term **Digital 360** was coined in September 2020 to refer specifically to the following products within the Customer 360 ecosystem:

- Marketing Cloud
- Commerce Cloud
- Experience Cloud

In other words, these are the three products that are most likely to interface directly with the end customer rather than being tools you use to run your business.

As a rule, it's better to minimize the use of marketing terms such as Digital 360 since they really don't tell us much about the solution being discussed. Saying *Digital 360* isn't as clear as saying *Marketing Cloud, Commerce Cloud, and Experience Cloud* and it's subject to change over time.

B2C solution architecture focus areas

You can't buy licenses for Customer 360 and, as much as we'd like it to be otherwise, uniting these products under a common marketing umbrella does not make them an integrated solution. It's the job of the solution architect to make this vision a reality by understanding a few key aspects of every Salesforce product in a solution.

A B2C solution architect is responsible for the following aspects of an integrated solution:

- The **data strategy**, particularly customer data, focused on where data is stored and how it moves between products in support of the overall solution
- **Integration workflows** focused on when and how the various products in the solution communicate with each other (APIs, data feeds, event-based, middleware solutions, and transformations)
- Orchestration of **user workflows** that span between products, such as unified customer login or **Customer Service Representative (CSR)** ordering
- **Feature and functionality mapping** between products, ensuring that the best tool is used for any given job
- Overall solution **non-functional requirements**, such as performance, security, scalability, governance, monitoring, and total cost of ownership

A B2C solution architect is not responsible for the in-depth technical design of features and functionality specific to any single product in the overall solution.

Salesforce Platform (Force.com)

The Salesforce Platform is the core CRM technology and the original Salesforce product on which many other products are built. It is possible to purchase a license just for the Salesforce Platform and implement your own custom apps on top of that platform in much the same way Salesforce has done to implement standard products such as Service Cloud and Sales Cloud. In common use, when working on projects that span multiple products, Salesforce Platform-based products are frequently just referred to as **Core**. For consistency, we'll say *Salesforce Platform* in this book.

The Salesforce Platform uses a database behind the scenes and leverages many concepts, outlined in the following sections, that will feel familiar to anyone with a background in relational database design.

All apps built on the platform can leverage a set of capabilities, such as declarative automation, and a core data model, including objects such as Accounts and Contacts. *Figure 1.1* shows the way products built on the Salesforce Platform extend the core capabilities and data model:

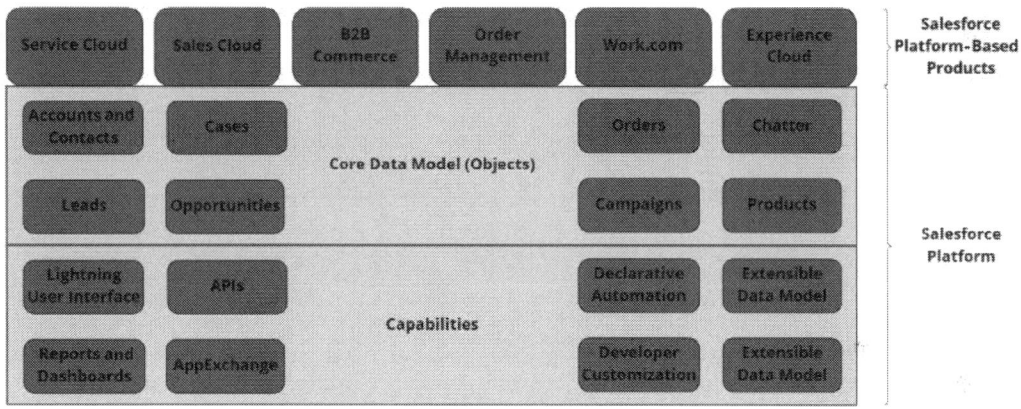

Figure 1.1 – Salesforce Platform and supported products

Since you're confident Packt Gear will be leveraging Service Cloud as part of their transformation, and you know that Service Cloud is built on top of the Salesforce Platform (unlike Marketing Cloud and B2C Commerce), we'll need to review some key aspects of how the Salesforce Platform operates.

Salesforce orgs

Each independent instance of the Salesforce Platform is called an **org**. A Salesforce org has a variety of licenses applied that unlock additional functionality, including product-specific licenses such as Service Cloud. A Salesforce org has a unique domain name, its own set of users, and an independent set of data.

Every Salesforce Platform license includes one **production** instance and some number of additional sandbox licenses. In addition to standard **sandboxes**, Salesforce has the concept of **scratch orgs**, which are ephemeral Salesforce orgs spun up based on a JSON configuration file as part of a source driven development workflow. They are used for a particular purpose, such as developing a feature, and then destroyed. A typical Salesforce Platform **DevOps** would leverage sandboxes or scratch orgs for feature development, integration, QA, and **User Acceptance Testing** (**UAT**) before moving to production.

> **Further reading**
>
> More information on Salesforce Platform editions and pricing can be found here: `https://sforce.co/3w6qcx1`.
>
> If you want to get your hands on a Salesforce org so you can follow along or dig deeper into any of the concepts we're talking about here, you can sign up for a free Developer Edition org here: `https://sforce.co/3vZ4riF`.

Data model

One of the key areas of concern for you as a solution architect is the design of a proper data model that spans the full solution and leverages each component product to store, expose, access, or synchronize data as appropriate. We'll cover cross-cloud data design in more detail in *Chapter 7, Integration Architecture Options*, and *Chapter 8, Creating a 360º View of the Customer*. Since it will provide a critical piece of the overall solution, we first need to establish the key considerations for the Salesforce Platform.

Objects and fields

The Salesforce Platform data model resembles a traditional relational database in that data is stored in tables (called **objects**) with multiple **records** for a given object, each of which includes numerous **fields**.

In the following figure, you can see a representation of a single object (**Account**) that has multiple fields (**Account Name**, **Account Number**, **Phone**, **Type**, and **Account Owner Alias**) and two records:

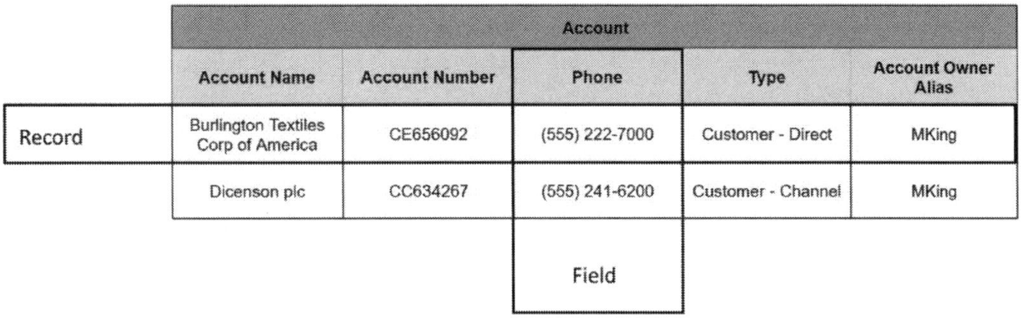

	Account				
	Account Name	Account Number	Phone	Type	Account Owner Alias
Record	Burlington Textiles Corp of America	CE656092	(555) 222-7000	Customer - Direct	MKing
	Dicenson plc	CC634267	(555) 241-6200	Customer - Channel	MKing

The Phone column is labeled as **Field**.

Figure 1.2 – Objects, records, and fields

The Salesforce Platform comes with several **standard objects** representing core CRM functionality, including **Accounts**, **Contacts**, **Leads**, **Opportunities**, and **Campaigns**. These standard objects are predefined by Salesforce and they cannot be removed, but access depends on the exact licenses purchased. Many of the licensed Salesforce products that are built on the Salesforce Platform also enable their own standard objects, such as the `UserServicePresence` standard object added by the **Service Cloud** product.

Each of the Salesforce-provided standard objects also comes with **standard fields**, which cannot be removed or modified. It is possible, however, to add additional **custom fields** to standard objects.

When creating a new custom field on any object (standard or custom), a variety of data types representing numerical, Boolean, date/time, and text values are available.

> **Tip**
> The critical thing for a solution architect to understand is that all data within the Salesforce Platform is stored as records in objects, which are like the rows in tables, and have strongly typed fields that can be defined declaratively to extend the data model.

Custom objects

Custom objects allow the Salesforce Platform to be extended by adding new data tables specific to your business needs. While the Core CRM use cases are covered by the Salesforce Platform, and your Service Cloud licenses will unlock additional customer service-specific functionality, every customer solution is unique, and customer-specific data will need to be added with custom objects.

One thing you know for sure, guided hikes are a huge aspect of the Packt Gear business. They don't just sell gear, they sell experiences, and they need to be able to allow customers to book hikes online, promote upcoming hikes with their customers, and change their bookings through customer service.

It sounds like you're going to need a way to track guided hikes in Salesforce! Enter custom objects.

You'll work with Packt Gear to understand what the key information for a typical hike is to decide how it should be represented in the Salesforce Platform.

Custom object name: `GuidedHike__c`

The following fields are found on the `GuidedHike__c` custom object:

Field Name	Data Type	Description
CreatedById	Lookup (User)	User who created this Hike Record
Name	Text(80)	Name of the Hike
LastModifiedById	Lookup (User)	User who last updated this Hike Record
OwnerId	Lookup (User, Group)	User or Group who owns this Record
StartTime__c	Date/Time	Date and time this Hike starts
Guide__c	Lookup (User)	The tour guide
StartPoint__c	Geolocation	Location where the Hike begins
Description__c	TextArea	Description of the Hike

Table 1.1 – GuidedHike__c custom object fields

In the preceding example, we can see a new custom object with the `GuidedHike__c` API name. It has the four standard fields that are exposed for every object, custom or standard, `CreatedById`, `Name`, `LastModifiedById`, and `OwnerId`, plus several additional custom fields. Additional standard fields may be created automatically behind the scenes.

> **Tip**
> All custom objects and custom fields are suffixed with two underscores and the letter c (__c) to indicate that they are custom.

We'll discuss the **Lookup** data types in the next section, but you can also see several other data types, including **Date/Time**, **Text**, **Geolocation**, and **TextArea** in use for the fields defined here.

Relationships

It's critical to understand not just how individual records are stored in objects, but also how those records relate to each other.

The Salesforce Platform record relationship types are as follows:

- **Lookup relationship**: A reference from one record to a related but independent record where each has its own security rules and owner.
- **Master-Detail relationship**: A parent-child relationship where the child object (the Detail) inherits the same security rules and owner as the parent. If the parent is deleted, the child is also deleted.
- **Many-to-many relationship**: A special case of Master-Detail where a junction object is created with two masters.
- **External lookup relationship**: A relationship linking a Salesforce standard or custom object to an **external object**, whose data is stored outside of Salesforce.

For Packt Gear, we've already decided that their new guided hike custom object will have a lookup relationship to the User object to reference the guide who will be conducting the hike. This type of relationship means that we'll be able to expose the hikes that a given guide is scheduled for and look up the guide record from the hike record, but otherwise, they're separate. We can change the guide associated with the hike if someone gets sick or leaves the company. We can also create hikes with no guide planned until we decide on the right person!

One other thing Packt Gear hikes need…hikers! Packt Gear wants to be able to keep track of which of their customers have signed up for a given hike. Since each hike will have multiple hikers, and hikers can go on multiple hikes, this sounds like a many-to-many relationship!

The following **Entity Relationship Diagram** (**ERD**) represents the proposed data model:

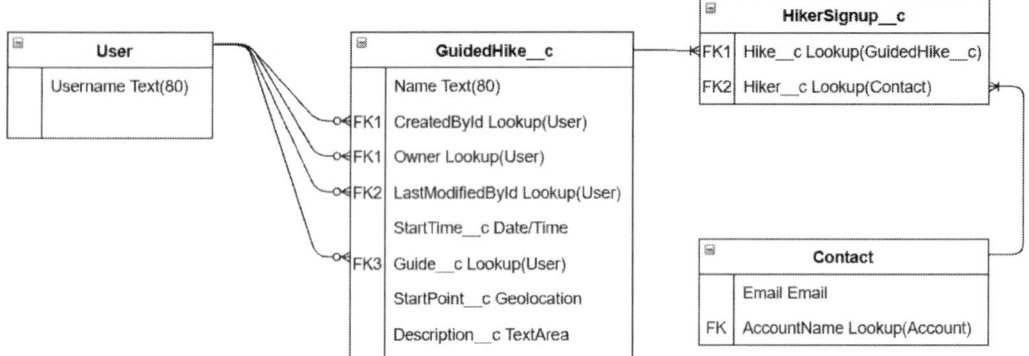

Figure 1.3 – ERD of GuidedHike__c signups

The previous ERD shows `GuidedHike__c` objects conducted by guides, represented by the `User` object, and attended by hikers, represented by the `Contact` object. Since many hikers can attend a hike and a hiker can attend many different hikes, a `HikerSignup__c` junction object is used to create a many-to-many relationship between `Contact` and `GuidedHike__c` record types.

The concept of a **record type** is important to understand as it relates to the Salesforce data model because it can impact the way that objects are tracked and exposed within the larger solution. Creating and applying a record type to a custom or standard object in Salesforce allows you to essentially describe multiple versions of the object for different purposes.

Sticking with our Packt Gear data model, we see that the preceding `HikerSignup__c` junction object describes `Account` records who are planning to attend a particular hike, represented by a `GuidedHike__c` record. It might at first glance seem like an odd choice to leverage `Account` for this purpose, since an `Account` record typically represents a business or organization whereas a `Contact` record typically represents an individual within that organization, and individuals go on hikes.

In B2C use cases, where we're typically selling to individuals rather than to businesses, it's common to use a special type of `Account` called a **Person Account**. A `Person Account` is a record type applied to the `Account` object that combines many of the fields typically associated with `Contact` and `Account`. At the database level, they're still stored as two records, but they're accessed and treated like one from a user experience viewpoint.

With Salesforce, you can define any record types you need on custom or standard objects. These record types control available picklist values, page layouts, and business processes associated with records. Ultimately, however, they're stored in the same way as other representations of the same object, so they don't require a separate object definition.

`Business Account` shows only fields from the `Account` record in Salesforce, while `Person Account` shows fields from both the `Account` and `Contact` records together. `Business Account` is associated with zero-or-more `Contact` records whereas `Person Account` has a one-to-one relationship with a specific `Contact` record:

Figure 1.4 – Business Account versus Person Account records

Figure 1.4 shows a **Business Account** and associated **Contact** record at the top and a **Person Account**, which is composed of a single **Account** and **Contact** record treated as a unit.

External objects

An **external object** is a special type of custom object that provides an interface to data stored in external systems. They are defined much like conventional custom objects but rely on an **external data source** configured with **Salesforce Connect**. External objects allow data from the external system to be mapped to fields defined on the Salesforce external object. They also support the creation of page layouts and search layouts to expose the external data in Salesforce. While there are some features of custom objects that aren't supported on external objects, it's important for you as a B2C solution architect to understand the capability to integrate outside data sources into Salesforce in this way.

> **Further reading**
>
> For additional reading on external objects, see `https://sforce.co/3vZtiTN`.

Security

As with many of the topics in this chapter, it's not possible to cover the Salesforce security model in its entirety in the scope of this book. Instead, we'll cover a few key aspects that are important to understand as they impact integrated solutions.

The Salesforce security model is composed of multiple layers of security, starting with the Salesforce instance or org, followed by an object within that instance, then a record of that object, and finally, at the individual field level within an object.

Access to an org, object, or field is controlled by a combination of a user's **profile** and **permission sets**. Permission sets and profiles also control what a given user is able to do functionally within a given Salesforce org.

Each user has exactly one profile assigned to them, which is associated with a particular Salesforce license and controls their default access and capabilities within Salesforce. Permission sets allow more granular additive permissions to be applied to a subset of users within a profile that requires additional privileges.

Access to specific records is controlled by **org-wide defaults** for that object, then by the user's **role** in the hierarchy of users (if enabled), then by **sharing rules**, and finally, by manual record sharing.

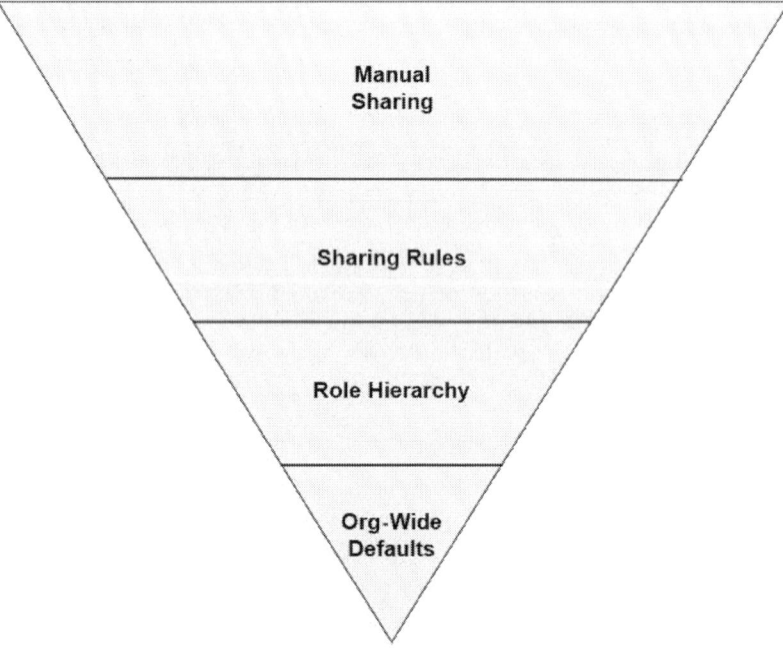

Figure 1.5 – Record access

As the preceding diagram illustrates, **Org Wide Defaults** establish the baseline access that all users have to records of a given object. From there, **Role Hierarchy**, **Sharing Rules**, and **Manual Sharing** can all grant access to additional records under specific conditions.

When designing Salesforce B2C solutions that include Salesforce Platform products such as Service Cloud, the details of the Salesforce security model will be handled by a platform specialist architect. Our goal here is to give you enough information to communicate effectively with the rest of your team with respect to Salesforce security.

> **Further reading**
> Start learning more about Salesforce data security topics here: `https://sforce.co/3wVv9ZW`.

For Packt Gear, you know from the preceding information that CSRs should have **Create, Read, Update, and Delete (CRUD)** access to the `Hiker_Signup__c` object, since they will be helping customers to sign up for hikes, but perhaps only store managers should be able to create, update, and delete `Guided_Hike__c` objects, since they are responsible for managing the planned hikes at their store.

User experience customization

A B2C solution architect generally won't be designing the experience within any product, unless they also happen to be playing the role of technical architect supporting that product, but it's important to understand the concepts in order to have a meaningful conversation.

Within the Salesforce Platform, the key concepts to understand are **apps** and **tabs**.

Apps

Every Salesforce org is composed of one or more apps that drive the user experience within the org. An app is a logical grouping of tabs that support a related use case.

For example, **Service** is an app that includes tabs for **Home**, **Chatter**, **Accounts**, **Contacts**, **Cases**, **Reports**, **Dashboards**, and **Knowledge**.

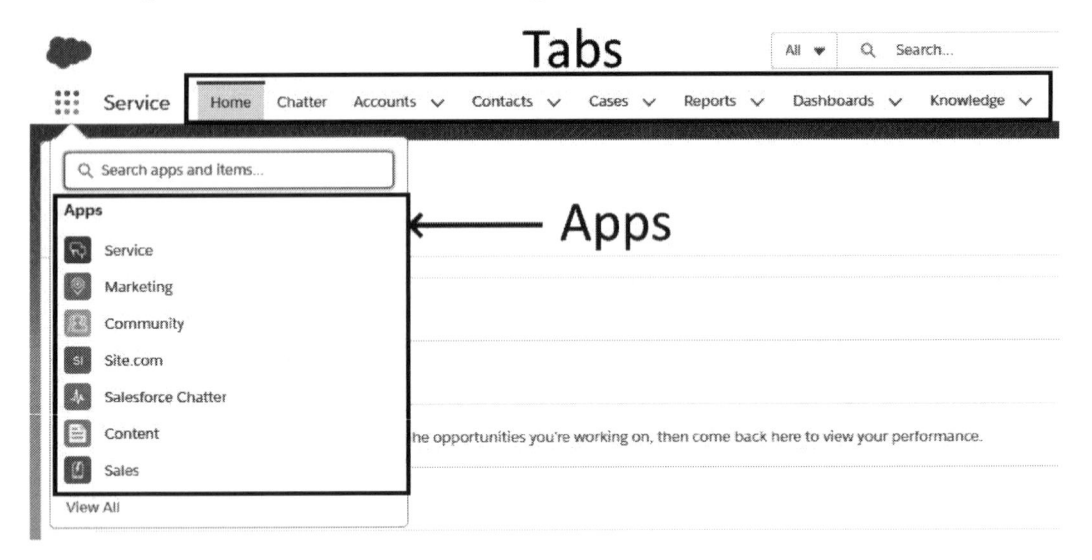

Figure 1.6 – Apps and tabs

Figure 1.6 shows how the Salesforce Platform is divided into apps, each of which has multiple tabs, which provide access to the data and functionality in the platform.

Tabs

Tabs are the primary container for a user experience within Salesforce and can represent an object, a **Lightning page**, or an outside website. Lightning Page tabs are a way of creating custom user experiences with code and are not in scope for this book. Tabs can be shared across any number of apps.

Automation

The Salesforce Platform, and, by extension, products such as Sales Cloud, Service Cloud, and Order Management, supports a variety of declarative automation options. Declarative automation options are ways of orchestrating work that would otherwise be done manually using no-code tools.

Examples of declarative automation include automatically sending an email to a sales lead when an opportunity crosses a certain value threshold, creating a task for a CSR if an order can't be fulfilled at the requested quantity, and requiring an approval step in order to issue a discount code to a customer in excess of a given amount.

Declarative automation tools can even be more robust user experience capabilities such as an interactive-style quiz displayed in an experience from **Experience Cloud**, allowing customers to describe their preferences. Much of the power of the Salesforce Platform comes from its low-code or no-code customization capabilities and declarative automation sits at the heart of that.

We'll give a high-level overview of the four declarative automation tools supported by Salesforce.

> **Further reading**
> For more information on choosing the right automation tool for a given task, see `https://sforce.co/3d6CnBw`.

> **Tip**
> For the B2C solution architect, understanding the declarative automation capabilities of the Salesforce Platform, especially flows, is an important part of leveraging the platform to its fullest extent. *Before turning to code, always evaluate declarative capabilities first.*

The four declarative automation tools available in the Salesforce Platform are as follows:

- **Workflows**
- **Processes**
- **Flows**
- **Approval processes**

We'll cover each of these four automation tools in the following sections.

When evaluating which tool to use, it's important to use the simplest tool that is capable of doing what you need. In the following sections, we'll review the capabilities and limitations of each declarative automation tool.

Because processes and flows are both parts of Lightning flows, we'll treat them together.

Workflows

Workflows are the most basic of the four declarative automation tools supported by the Salesforce Platform.

Workflow rules are only capable of four possible actions:

- Creating a **task**
- Sending an **email alert**
- Updating a field on the triggering record or its parent
- Sending an **outbound message**

Tasks are a type of object in the Salesforce Platform that track to-do items assigned to individual users. They're an appropriate way to queue up a manual action that needs to be taken in response to a record change. Email alerts leverage the Salesforce Platform-native email templates; they cannot be customized to use an outside email service such as Salesforce Marketing Cloud. Outbound messages are a Salesforce Platform capability that allows XML-based messages to be sent to a designated endpoint.

> **Tip**
> The only thing you can do with a workflow that you can't also do with a process or flow is send an outbound message.

Lightning flow

Lightning flow is an umbrella term for Salesforce automation that includes two of the four total declarative automation options: Process Builder-created processes and Flow Builder-created flows.

Processes and flows share the same underlying implementation and many of the same capabilities, but there are a few key differences that are important to understand when deciding which to leverage for a particular solution.

Process Builder-created processes

Processes, which are implemented with **Process Builder**, are more capable than workflows (except for the ability to send outbound messages), but simpler than flows. Processes consist of a series of simple If / Then / Else statements evaluated in order when a triggering event occurs. When the condition is satisfied, an action is taken, and the process either concludes or continues to evaluate the next condition (depending on the configuration).

Processes are triggered whenever a record is created or updated for the associated object, when explicitly called from another process, or when a **platform event** is received.

A process can do any of the following as a result of a triggering event:

- Execute **Apex** (custom code)
- Create a record
- Send an **email alert**
- Trigger a flow
- Post to **Chatter**
- Execute a process
- Invoke a **quick action**
- Interact with **Quip**
- Send a **custom notification**
- Submit a record for approval
- Update the triggering record or any related record

The only thing a process can do that a flow cannot is execute another process.

Processes do not have the capability to execute complex logical branching or loops or to interact directly with the user. For that, we need to leverage flows.

Flow Builder-created flows

Flows, which are implemented with Flow Builder, are the most robust automation tool available in the Salesforce Platform toolkit.

They can do all the things a process can do plus the following:

- Interact with the user through screens
- Execute complex logic
- Delete a record
- Update an unrelated record
- Send a non-alert email

> **Tip**
> At this point, you may be wondering, why don't I just use flows for everything? The Salesforce best practice is to do exactly that. Using flows by default is more consistent and easier to maintain.

Approval processes

The final category of declarative automation capabilities is an approval process. Approval processes allow individual records to be submitted to another user, often the manager of the record owner, for approval. Approval processes support all the same actions that workflows do as listed previously. Since approval processes are rarely a critical component of multi-product solution architecture scenarios, they are mentioned here for completeness only.

> **Further reading**
>
> You can learn more about approval processes here: `https://sforce.co/3cojwTj`.

As you work through some business cases for Packt Gear, or in your own project, be sure to look for ways to leverage declarative automation tools to minimize manual work and streamline operations!

AppExchange

Salesforce AppExchange is a marketplace of ready-to-use tools created by third parties or by Salesforce directly that can be integrated with any Salesforce org.

AppExchange solutions are divided into five categories:

- **Apps**: Full Salesforce apps that can be added to an existing org to support a new use case
- **Bolt solutions**: Industry-specific solutions that include broad functionality
- **Flow solutions**: Building blocks that can be added to any flow created in the org where they're installed
- **Lightning Data**: Datasets that are exposed to your org but maintained by a provider
- **Components**: Prebuilt drop in Lightning components that can be integrated into a Salesforce user experience built on Lightning

You, as a B2C solution architect, should be aware of AppExchange as the primary source of buy-not-build extensions for the Salesforce Platform and should evaluate potential AppExchange solutions for any use case that isn't supported by the Salesforce Platform natively or through declarative customization.

> **Important note**
> Salesforce AppExchange does *not* distribute extensions to Salesforce B2C Commerce; it only supports Salesforce Platform-based products. B2C Commerce runs on a separate technology. Some B2C Commerce extensions are *listed* on AppExchange for discoverability but installing them requires a developer and code changes.

Salesforce AppExchange is located at `https://appexchange.salesforce.com/`.

Reports and dashboards

The Salesforce Platform includes support for robust **reports** and **dashboards**. Reports are summary views of data drawn from one or more objects in Salesforce.

Reports

Reports and dashboards are a great way to gain insight into your B2C solution, but it's important to realize that they can only summarize data that is stored in the Salesforce Platform using objects or that is represented in the Salesforce Platform with an external object.

There are four types of reports in the Salesforce Platform:

- **Tabular reports**: Simple table of data, much like an Excel sheet
- **Summary reports**: Groups the source data by one or more rows
- **Matrix reports**: Groups the source data by one or more rows and columns
- **Joined reports**: Includes data from more than one report that shares a common field

Thinking back to the guided hikes you've modeled for Packt Gear, a summary report would be a great way to display the hikers who have signed up for upcoming hikes!

The following screenshot shows a sample summary report for the `GuidedHike__c` object grouped by hike name:

Hike: GuidedHike Name ↑	Account Name	Phone	Hiker Signup: Created Date
Hike the Grand Canyon (3)	Dolores Fortuin	555-123-1234	3/28/2021
	Melita Neil	555-543-3246	3/28/2021
	Pru Unruh	555-693-1295	3/28/2021
Subtotal			
Hike the Rockies (2)	Rolf Robin	-	3/28/2021
	Pru Unruh	555-693-1295	3/28/2021

Report: Accounts with Hike Signups and Hike
Guided Hikes

Total Records: 5

Figure 1.7 – Summary report

Dashboards

Dashboards roll up data from multiple reports in a visual format. Dashboards can contain up to 20 different reports and each report added to a dashboard can be represented by any of the following visual elements:

- Horizontal or vertical bar chart
- Horizontal or vertical stacked bar chart
- Line chart
- Donut chart
- Metric (single value)
- Gauge
- Funnel chart
- Scatter chart
- Lightning table

> **Further reading**
>
> Learn more about reports and dashboards here: `https://sforce.co/3m93Tm9`.

Additional technology stacks

The Salesforce ecosystem encompasses much more than just the Salesforce Platform, which is why we need an overall solution architect in the first place! This section provides a high-level overview of the Salesforce ecosystem, including how individual products are built on specific technology platforms, and how conceptual *clouds* – or families of products – can span across technologies.

The following figure depicts the multiple technology platforms on which a B2C solution is built:

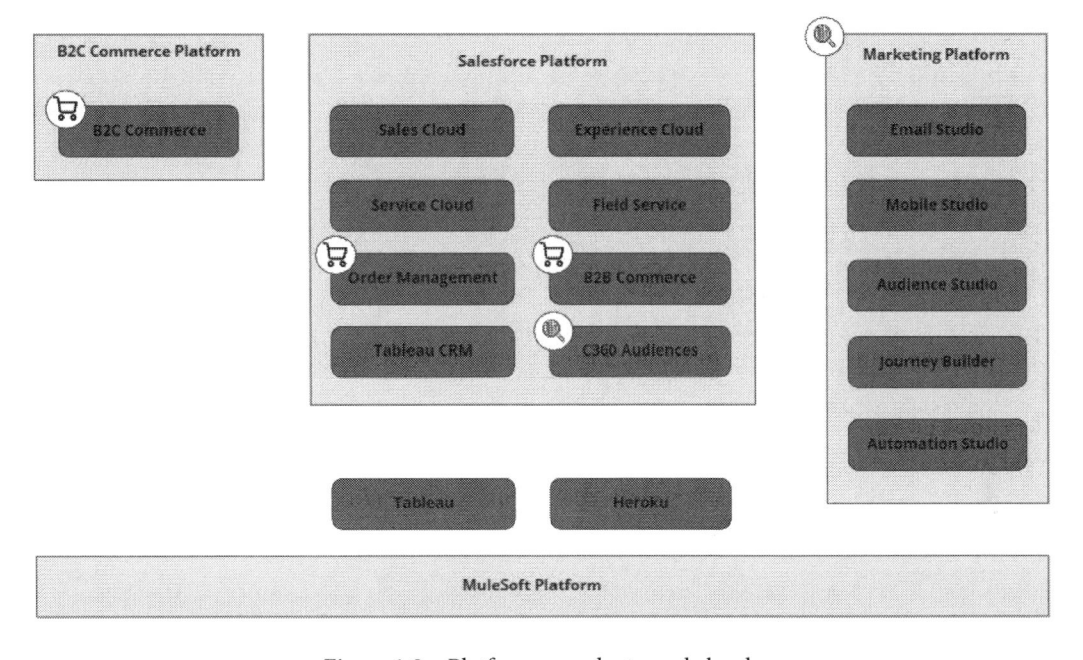

Figure 1.8 – Platforms, products, and clouds

In *Figure 1.8*, the shopping cart icon identifies products that are part of Salesforce Commerce Cloud and the magnifying glass icon identifies products that are part of Salesforce Marketing Cloud. This shows how clouds (such as Commerce Cloud) can be composed of products (such as **B2C Commerce** and **Order Management**) that are built on separate platforms (such as the **B2C Commerce Platform** and the **Salesforce Platform**).

Your job as a B2C solution architect is to design solutions that incorporate and integrate products across this ecosystem, regardless of their underlying technology, to create a cohesive solution.

Salesforce Platform and beyond

As described earlier, there are many Salesforce products built on top of the Salesforce Platform, but you should also understand that many are separate technologies. This is a vital difference to understand as a B2C solution architect since your job is to help your company or your clients to create an integrated experience that spans multiple products and clouds.

In the following sections, we'll touch on products beyond the Salesforce Platform and how they'll impact a B2C solution.

Core B2C solution technologies

For a B2C solution architect, the most important non-Salesforce Platform products to understand are the enterprise B2C Commerce product and the Marketing Cloud product. You may recall that the B2C Commerce product is part of Commerce Cloud, but that clouds in the Salesforce language don't necessarily represent specific technology, they just represent logical groupings of related components. The other products in Commerce Cloud, including Order Management and B2B Commerce, *are* built on the Salesforce Platform.

We'll be covering B2C Commerce and Marketing Cloud in detail during *Chapter 3*, *Direct-to-Consumer Selling with Commerce Cloud B2C*, and *Chapter 4*, *Engaging Customers with Marketing Cloud*, respectively.

Since you'll be helping Packt Gear migrate their commerce experience to Salesforce, you'll be thinking across all of these products throughout the process.

Integration-focused technologies

Beyond B2C Commerce and Marketing Cloud, it's helpful to understand the role of Salesforce products such as **MuleSoft** and **Heroku** in a B2C solution. These products serve the needs of enterprise integration scenarios and **Platform-as-a-Service** (**PaaS**) use cases. We'll be covering these two products in more detail during *Chapter 7*, *Integration Architecture Options*.

Out-of-scope technologies

Finally, there are many other products owned by Salesforce (the company) that are not part of the Salesforce Platform, such as **Salesforce Anywhere**, **Slack**, **Tableau**, and **myTrailhead**, but are not in the scope of this book since they aren't a core part of B2C solution use cases. That certainly doesn't mean you *can't* use these products in B2C solutions, you certainly can, but they are value-added rather than being a core component.

Solution architecture methodology

When you're integrating any product or technology into your overall solution, the approach is the same, whether it's another Salesforce technology, an in-house system, or a third party:

1. Review and understand the capabilities of the product and the role it will play in your overall solution; what gaps does it fill?
2. Review and understand the integration methodologies supported by the product.
3. Map your data across systems, determining what will reside in this new product and be accessed on-demand from other products and what will be synchronized.
4. Orchestrate your business use cases that include this new product across other products in the solution.

The next three chapters will cover *steps 1* and *2* as they relate to Service Cloud, B2C Commerce, and Marketing Cloud, respectively. *Chapter 8, Creating a 360° View of the Customer*, will be focused on *step 3* across the solution, and *Chapter 9, Supporting Key Business Scenarios*, will do the same for *step 4*. This will give you a clear methodology you can follow for any product or technology not explicitly covered in this book when you need to incorporate it into your solution.

In the next section, we'll cover some of the Salesforce acquisitions and legacy terminology you'll encounter in the B2C solution space.

Acquisitions and legacy terminology

When working with clients or researching more about the products covered in this chapter, you may occasionally come across terminology not used in this book. While I encourage you to always use the current names of products, Salesforce is notorious for changing and redefining product names frequently and it can be hard to keep up. Sometimes, you have to meet your clients where they are and use the language they are comfortable with in order to facilitate a meaningful conversation. Always anchor back to a solid understanding of exactly what is being proposed or implemented in terms of Salesforce-licensed products, the platforms they are built on, and the clouds they are a part of.

Since Salesforce is a company built largely through strategic acquisitions, many of the legacy names for products are the names of acquired companies.

Here are a few legacy product names you may encounter for awareness:

- **Demandware**: The enterprise **B2C Commerce** product that sits outside of the Salesforce Platform, often abbreviated to **SFCC** (though this more accurately refers to the *entire* Salesforce Commerce Cloud, including B2C Commerce)
- **ExactTarget**: The core of Marketing Cloud, including Marketing Cloud Email Studio, which also sits outside of the Salesforce Platform
- **CloudCraze**: The original B2B Commerce product built on the Salesforce Platform
- **Community Cloud**: Now called Experience Cloud, built on the Salesforce Platform

> **Tip**
> It's always best to use the most current and accurate name when possible. Language is incredibly important when describing a solution to ensure a common understanding. Once you're moving into the solution phase, move away from the marketing terms and talk about what you're building.

Summary

To recap on what we've learned in this chapter, Salesforce is a company, and Customer 360 is the idea of leveraging your Salesforce products in service to a common understanding of a customer. Furthermore, clouds are logical groupings of one or more products that meet the needs of a particular use case or industry vertical, while products are built on a variety of technology platforms but are always licensed and usable tools that unlock specific use cases.

The Salesforce Platform, or Force.com, is the core underlying technology that supports Salesforce.com, the original CRM product from Salesforce, as well as many other Salesforce Platform-based products. Digital 360 is a marketing term that represents Marketing Cloud, Commerce Cloud, and Experience Cloud used together in a solution.

Equipped with this knowledge, you should be able to have a meaningful conversation about an appropriate solution that meets the needs of direct-to-consumer selling online, including marketing and support components, within the Salesforce ecosystem. You should be able to help coordinate between stakeholders and platform specialist architects, who will be handling the individual components.

In the next chapter, we're going to cover the specific role of Service Cloud in this solution so that you'll understand the role it plays in the larger solution.

Questions

1. Which of the following Salesforce products are built on the Salesforce Platform: B2C Commerce, Marketing Cloud, or Service Cloud?
2. True or False: A Salesforce object represents a single record in the underlying database table.
3. True or False: When looking to add a feature to B2C Commerce that isn't supported natively, you should first evaluate solutions from the AppExchange.
4. When extending the Salesforce Platform data model, what is the difference between a custom object and an external object?
5. You'd like to be able to query a list of the Salesforce Platform account records created in the past 90 days and display them in a table. Which Salesforce Platform tool would best support that need?
6. Building on the data model you've started for Packt Gear, you determine that the guide for a hike should receive an email alert every time a new hiker registers for their hike. What's the simplest declarative automation tool that will meet this need?
7. CSRs need to go through a series of steps whenever they generate a new coupon code for a customer. Each of these steps is displayed on a different screen and each builds upon the previous. Which of the following best meets that need: Process Builder, Flow Builder, custom Apex code, or an AppExchange solution?
8. When reviewing some promotional materials at a trade show, you find some interesting capabilities attributed to *Digital 360* – which Salesforce products is this referring to?

Further reading

There are many books dedicated to learning about the Salesforce Platform in all its depth. In fact, two of the three prerequisite certifications for the B2C solution architect certification are focused entirely on the Salesforce Platform: **Platform App Developer** and **Integration Architecture Designer** (the third is **Marketing Cloud Email Specialist**).

> **Important note**
> This book does not attempt to cover any of the Salesforce Platform topics in sufficient depth to take and pass the prerequisite certifications. This book is focused on the topics that are essential for B2C Solution Architecture and builds upon that prerequisite knowledge.

For additional reading on the Salesforce Platform, the following Packt titles are recommended:

- Sharif Shaalan, *Salesforce for Beginners*
- Paul Goodey, *Salesforce Platform App Builder Certification Guide*
- Andrew Fawcett, *Force.com Enterprise Architecture*
- Tameem Bahri, *Becoming a Salesforce Certified Technical Architect*

2
Supporting Your Customers with Service Cloud

Service Cloud, along with B2C Commerce and Marketing Cloud, is a component of the Customer 360 ecosystem and a major subject of the B2C Solution Architect certification. In this chapter, we'll cover the key capabilities of Service Cloud and how it builds upon the Salesforce Platform capabilities we discussed in *Chapter 1*, *Demystifying Salesforce, Customer 360, and Digital 360*. Since Service Cloud is a Salesforce Platform-based product, everything we discussed as a capability of the Salesforce Platform is also available with Service Cloud and then some. The first part of this chapter focuses on the capabilities an organization gains by adding Service Cloud to their overall solution.

As you'll see in *Chapter 8*, *Creating a 360° View of the Customer*, Service Cloud and the underlying Salesforce Platform are the central repository for many categories of data in the B2C solution. In the second part of this chapter, we'll take a closer look at the Service Cloud data model and how it supports B2C use cases.

To design and build an integrated solution, you must understand the integration options available for each component product. To that end, we'll cover the Salesforce Platform API integration options that will be used to integrate Service Cloud, as well as the design considerations that will help shape the integration architecture. Finally, we'll cover the critical-to-understand licensing constraints around Service Cloud to ensure a secure and scalable solution.

Packt Gear knows they have customer service challenges.

Their current system relies on agents knowing everything there is to know about Packt Gear, or knowing who to ask, which makes it hard to onboard new team members. They also find that their agents spend most of their time helping with a few common problems, such as resetting a password or checking on the status of their orders. Finally, their primary means of support is still the good old-fashioned telephone call, which takes a lot of agent time and doesn't meet the needs of today's fast-paced mobile consumer.

Throughout this chapter, we'll look at ways you can leverage Service Cloud to help Packt Gear revolutionize its customer service experience.

In this chapter, we're going to cover the following main topics:

- Service Cloud capabilities
- Service Cloud data model
- Service Cloud APIs and integrations
- Service Cloud request limits

Service Cloud capabilities

Service Cloud adds everything you need to turn the world's #1 CRM into the hub of an optimum customer service experience. As a B2C solution architect, you'll need to understand what capabilities a base Service Cloud license adds to the Salesforce Platform, where additional licenses can be added to unlock additional features, and how it supports your overall B2C solution.

The most important Service Cloud capabilities in this context include robust case management tools, chat support, knowledge management, service contracts and entitlements, **Computer Telephony Integration (CTI)**, and **Omni-Channel routing**.

Service Cloud editions

Service Cloud, like most Salesforce Platform-based products, is available in multiple editions. The four options for Service Cloud editions are as follows:

1. **Essentials**
2. **Professional**
3. **Enterprise**
4. **Unlimited**

Of the capabilities outlined in this chapter, most are available in either Enterprise or Unlimited. The available features in Essentials and Professional vary and should be verified when evaluating either of these lower-cost options. As we discussed in *Chapter 1, Demystifying Salesforce, Customer 360, and Digital 360*, it is also possible to sign up for a free Developer Edition org (including Service Cloud) and I highly encourage you to do that so you can follow along.

> **Further reading**
> The signup for Salesforce Developer Edition can be found here:
> `https://sforce.co/3vZ4riF`.
>
> The pricing and features of each Service Cloud edition are outlined here:
> `https://sforce.co/3fnKqg6`.

> **Important note**
> Only Enterprise and Unlimited support API-based integrations are essential for integrating Service Cloud into your overall B2C solution. Essentials and Professional are therefore not appropriate choices for use in a larger connected ecosystem.

The primary difference between Enterprise and Unlimited is that the Unlimited edition comes with 24/7 support from Salesforce, including phone and live chat, as well as expert coaching for making the most of the product. While that may be vital to your business, it's not a factor in designing a B2C solution.

Since you know Packt Gear is going to be integrating Service Cloud with B2C Commerce and Marketing Cloud, they'll need an Enterprise or Unlimited edition of Salesforce.

Service Console

The command center for the CSR experience in Service Cloud is the **Service Console**. The Service Console is an additional app that's made available with Service Cloud licenses. It streamlines the service agent's daily interactions with customers. If you think of the **Service app** as the place where customer service managers oversee the daily operations of a support center, the Service Console app is where the frontline agents work with the customer.

The Service Console allows agents to have multiple tabs open at the same time with different cases, accounts, chat sessions, and more. Knowing that Packt Gear's customer support is currently bottlenecked because they can only support one customer at a time, this ability to jump between working logged cases and providing real-time support via chat or phone calls is going to make a big difference!

The Service Console is also important to understand as a B2C solution architect because jumping between systems is the enemy of productivity. Your job is to understand what data and tools the service agents need to do their work, as well as to ensure they are at the agent's fingertips within the Service Console experience, regardless of what system provides that feature!

For example, CSRs need to be able to help customers with their online basket when they call in because a coupon code isn't working as expected. Sure, the agent could log into the commerce system and try to figure it out while jumping back and forth with Service Cloud to manage the customer case, but that's not a connected experience! As soon as a customer initiates a chat session from the website, the agent should have the full customer context available and be able to jump right in and help, without leaving the Service Console. To make that happen, the systems need to be integrated.

Similarly, if an agent needs to resend an order confirmation email from Marketing Cloud, they shouldn't have to jump over and trigger it manually!

> **Tip**
> We'll focus on how to enable connected business cases like the preceding one in *Chapter 9, Supporting Key Business Scenarios*. For now, we just want to establish that Service Cloud is the hub of the agent experience.

Customer support

The core of an effective service experience is customer support, and there are three main channels by which Service Cloud facilitates direct customer support: case management tools, chat support, and **Digital Engagement** (for social messaging channels).

As with each of the component products in this book, the purpose here is not to make you an expert in Service Cloud; it's to give you sufficient understanding so that you can design a solution that makes appropriate use of Service Cloud as a component product, as well as to give you the language to have conversations with more specialized architects who are focused on the Service Cloud component of the larger solution.

There are many excellent resources available to learn more about Service Cloud, but one of the most valuable tools in the Salesforce ecosystem is **Trailhead**. If you're not familiar with Trailhead, it's a huge library of free training materials provided by Salesforce covering all sorts of topics, including Salesforce products. You can also create as many test environments to experiment with concepts as you like, which I highly encourage you to do.

The following Trailhead Trails will help you learn more about Service Cloud:

- *Get Started with Service Cloud for Lightning Experience*: `https://sforce.co/3ryGP0S`
- *Expand Service Cloud with Digital Engagement*: `https://sforce.co/3mcIclb`

> **Further reading**
> The authoritative source for Service Cloud help can be found here: `https://sforce.co/3czINdj`.

Case management tools

One of the things that can be a bit confusing when evaluating Service Cloud is why you need it. After all, the Salesforce Platform includes cases, accounts, contacts, and several other capabilities that provide the foundation of a customer service experience. The answer is that Service Cloud takes all those things and makes them smarter and more efficient while adding significantly to the toolset.

> **Tip**
> A **case** is the fundamental way of tracking customer questions or concerns that agents are working on. Each case record represents a discreet issue or interaction that's created through a variety of **channels**, routed via **assignment rules** and **Omni-Channel routing** to **users** or **queues**, and that are ultimately worked on by agents in the Service Console.

Case auto-assignment

Case assignment rules control how cases are assigned to users and queues in your unique customer service workflow. Cases can be created manually by agents, automatically using **Web-to-Case** or **Email-to-Case**, or through a variety of other means. Regardless of how a case is initially created, assignment rules in Service Cloud control what happens next. A Service Cloud administrator can configure a series of criteria, evaluated in sequence, and a user or queue to assign the case to when the criteria are matched. A queue is a structure for holding work items that are pending assignment to a specific pool of agents.

This example shows a Case Assignment Rule dividing incoming cases between domestic and international premium and standard support teams:

Action	Order	Criteria	Assign To	Email
Edit | Del	1	(Account: Billing Country EQUALS US,USA,United States,United States of America) AND (Account: SLA EQUALS Gold,Platinum) AND (Account: Type CONTAINS Customer)	Domestic Premium Support Queue	
Edit | Del	2	(Account: Billing Country EQUALS US,USA,United States,United States of America) AND (Account: SLA EQUALS Silver,Bronze) AND (Account: Type CONTAINS Customer)	Domestic Standard Support Queue	
Edit | Del	3	(Account: Billing Country NOT EQUAL TO US,USA,United States,United States of America) AND (Account: SLA EQUALS Gold,Platinum) AND (Account: Type CONTAINS Customer)	International Premium Support Queue	
Edit | Del	4	(Account: Billing Country NOT EQUAL TO US,USA,United States,United States of America) AND (Account: SLA EQUALS Silver,Bronze) AND (Account: Type CONTAINS Customer)	International Standard Support Queue	
Edit | Del	5	Account: Type CONTAINS Partner	Mike King	

Figure 2.1 – Case assignment rules

> **Tip**
> Only one Case Assignment Rule can be active at a time, though it can contain multiple criteria.

Web and email-to-case tools

Email-to-Case capabilities allow customers to email a support address and have cases created in Service Cloud automatically. Agents can then email updates back to customers as they work directly on the case, all while maintaining the optimum Service Console context for the agent with a convenient channel for the customer.

While Email-to-Case is an important feature of Service Cloud, it's not a focus area for the B2C solution architect since it's not part of the larger integration landscape.

In contrast, Web-to-Case is a way of embedding a contact us-like experience into another site to allow customers to create cases in Service Cloud from the commerce storefront (for example). This is a critical component of a B2C solution's design since it provides a native way to expose Service Cloud functionality within B2C Commerce. Web-to-Case supports custom case fields, which can be populated either from user-entered data on the storefront form or hidden fields.

> **Tip**
> Hidden fields on the **Web-to-Case** form are a great way to capture B2C Commerce customer data on the automatically created Service Cloud case to ensure the agent has the full context when addressing the customer's concern.

Chapter 8, *Creating a 360° View of the Customer*, will focus on the details of identifying customers across Salesforce products, but we'll give a sneak preview here!

When a customer on your storefront decides to contact you through the form on the website, it's appropriate to ask for some basic information:

- Email address
- The subject of the case
- Case description

What's important to know as a B2C solution architect is that this isn't enough information for looking up that customer in B2C Commerce. For the agent to properly handle this case, they'll need to be able to retrieve the customer record in B2C Commerce, and that requires a few additional pieces of information:

- Customer ID
- Customer Number
- Customer List ID
- Site ID

These aren't pieces of information that the customer is going to know themselves or be able to populate in a web form, but they're readily available when *building* the web form on the commerce storefront so that they can be embedded in hidden form fields. These will then be sent over to Service Cloud when the form is submitted by the user. This will allow the Service Cloud Web-to-Case functionality to map these values to Custom Fields on the Case record so that the agent can retrieve all the details they need about this customer.

> **Important note**
> If you're not sure what these B2C Commerce identifiers represent, don't worry – we'll cover that in the next chapter on B2C Commerce and go much deeper on their role in an integrated B2C solution during *Chapter 8, Creating a 360° View of the Customer*.

Case email auto-response

Case auto-response rules allow Service Cloud administrators to configure templatized email responses to be sent to the case originator when a new case is received. Like assignment rules, only one case auto-response rule can be active at a time in Service Cloud, but that rule can have many rule entries that specify conditions and associated email templates.

Case escalation rules and queues

Case escalation rules build upon queues and email templates. In Service Cloud, escalation rules are set up to automatically escalate cases based on configurable criteria. Within Service Cloud, you can configure up to five actions that execute on escalation, including reassigning the case to another user or queue and sending emails to the case owner, other users, or other recipients by email.

Chat support

Embedding chat into your commerce storefront is a great way to get closer to your customers and reduce the friction of any interaction points. Service Cloud provides a guided setup flow that can be accessed from Service Setup to streamline setting up Omni-Channel routing, generating a snippet for embedding chat in your website, configuring records associated with chat, and enabling offline support.

Incoming chats are placed in a provided queue and routed to the best available agent to support based on configurable routing rules. Agents take and manage the default chat experience within the Service Console app.

Much like a Web-to-Case form, Service Cloud supports a pre-chat form for gathering relevant customer information before initiating the agent chat session. You can customize the pre-chat form provided by Service Cloud to capture additional information from the commerce storefront to super-charge the chat experience.

Finally, the chat can either be *reactive* or *proactive*. Reactive chat is always available but waits for the customer to click on it to begin an interaction. Proactive chat can be configured to automatically offer a chat session when there's some indication the customer is confused or needs help, such as repeatedly navigating to the cart and leaving, or searching but not finding results.

Foundational chat experience

At its most basic, chat support means leveraging Service Cloud's native chat capabilities to embed a **Chat Now** option within the commerce storefront, which automatically falls back on case creation during off hours or when no agents are available. When a customer initiates a chat session, use the pre-chat form to gather information, such as subject, email address, or order number, that's relevant to their question. From there, leverage Service Cloud Omni-Channel routing for chats to get the incoming chat request to the most qualified available agent who can work with the customer to understand their issue and, hopefully, resolve it.

The challenge with this approach is that the agent is reliant on the customer providing the data they need to get to the bottom of the issue. The agent may also have to log into the B2C Commerce backend (**Business Manager**) to research the issue or assist the customer more directly.

Improved chat experience

You should enhance the pre-chat form so that it includes additional attributes, such as the customer identifiers mentioned under Web-to-Case (customer ID, customer number, site ID, and customer list ID), as well as the customer's storefront session cookies (`dwsid` and `dwsecuretoken`). Customize the B2C Commerce storefront to transparently annotate the pre-chat form with this enhanced data using **JavaScript** from within the storefront experience.

On the Service Cloud side, you should enhance the chat experience to leverage the additional customer data, which will allow you to pull real-time data from B2C Commerce into the Service Console and empower the agent to take over the customer's storefront basket to directly assist with issues.

Intelligent chat experience

You should leverage Einstein Bots within Service Cloud to automate routine tasks such as resetting the B2C Commerce password, resending emails from Marketing Cloud, or fetching the current order status. This reduces the demand for agent time and allows customers to resolve more issues themselves.

> **Tip**
> We'll be providing a much deeper dive into integrated chat experiences with chatbots in *Chapter 9, Supporting Key Business Scenarios*.

Planning your approach

For Packt Gear, you know just having the ability for customers to chat with an agent directly from the storefront, as well as for the agent to work on multiple chat requests at a time, is a huge improvement over the current phone-based system. Knowing it's important to build the right customer data foundation, you decide to enrich the pre-chat variables with the additional customer descriptors mentioned previously so that the agent will know who they're working with right away and be better equipped to help.

While you know Einstein Bots are a powerful feature, they can be gradually added over time, so you decide to start with the Intelligent Chat Experience and save bots for a future phase.

Digital Engagement addition

The optional additional cost of a Digital Engagement purchase extends Service Cloud to support messaging with customers through social channels such as SMS, WhatsApp, and Facebook Messenger. These conversations can be either live agent or bot supported in the same way that other chat sessions can, as described previously.

The important distinction for the B2C solution architect to keep in mind is that Digital Engagement channels can't embed pre-chat data enriched by the B2C Commerce storefront, so you can't assume you'll always have that data.

In *Chapter 8, Creating a 360° View of the Customer*, we're going to cover creating a unified view of your customer in much more detail. With the right infrastructure in place, you'll be able to look up your customer in Service Cloud and find the corresponding B2C Commerce identifiers needed to create the connected experience.

Knowledge

Salesforce Knowledge, as part of Service Cloud, extends the Salesforce Platform by adding support for knowledge articles that can be written by experts within your organization. These articles can cover a variety of topics, including answers to common customer support questions such as how to reset a password or check your order status. Knowledge articles can also serve as internal run books explaining agent scenarios, such as how to place an order through B2C Commerce or how to update a customer's email preferences as they relate to Marketing Cloud.

Tracking solutions with Knowledge

Like many Service Cloud capabilities, Knowledge includes a helpful setup wizard available from Service Setup. Although this guided setup workflow is helpful, it's also important to understand how you'll be leveraging knowledge in your overall solution. Have a plan for who will create knowledge articles, what topics will be covered, and how they'll be incorporated into other channels.

Record types can be applied to knowledge articles to differentiate between articles that are intended to be public-facing, perhaps exposed through an experience created with **Experience Cloud**, from internal knowledge articles that will be visible to agents only. This will allow different page layouts, including different fields as well as different business processes such as including a marketing review of articles, to become part of the public site before publication.

Customizing your case's auto-response rules to include suggested knowledge articles that are exposed through your public help center is a great way to get your customers the help they need faster, as well as to take some of the load off your agent team.

This sounds perfect for Packt Gear! Sharing common knowledge articles, and then publishing them for the public commerce storefront under a FAQ section, would allow customers to self-service quickly and effectively without having to contact customer support at all. This would also allow agents to focus on unique challenges that truly require their time.

How would this work? We'll discuss Service Cloud APIs and integrations later in this chapter, but leveraging a Record type for knowledge articles intended to be public-facing would allow them to be separated from internal agent-supported articles. From B2C Commerce, the Service Cloud API could be used to retrieve relevant knowledge articles and store them as **Content Assets** in B2C Commerce, where they can easily be displayed on the storefront. A background job that runs once a day could fetch the latest articles and update the existing ones, keeping the B2C Commerce storefront in sync with the latest and greatest without the service agent ever having to leave Service Cloud.

> **Tip**
>
> Einstein Article Recommendations can be used to leverage **machine learning** (**ML**) to automatically scan incoming cases for keywords, phrases, or other characteristics and recommend appropriate knowledge articles to help the agent resolve the issue efficiently.

Service contracts and entitlements

Service contracts and entitlements are less common in the B2C world than in the B2B world, but we'll mention them here for completeness. Service contracts are a way of tracking and describing a (usually paid) contract between an organization and a customer. They describe an enforceable **Service-Level Agreement** (**SLA**).

Service contracts work closely with entitlements, which describe what support channels a particular customer can leverage. For example, customer A has paid for platinum support (Service contract) and is *entitled* to 24/7 phone support. Customer B is a gold-tier customer and is *entitled* to a response to their case, which was submitted by web or email within 24 hours but does not have phone support. Customer C has not paid for a Service contract and can only leverage the company's public knowledge base or customer community in a self-service manner.

In the B2C world, Service contracts may be appropriate for high-value products such as appliances or electronics. The ability to sell a Service contract, with a selectable term and service level, on your B2C Commerce channel, which is tracked in Service Cloud and grants the purchaser support entitlements, is an example of a B2C solution *business case* that would require integrating multiple products.

> **Tip**
>
> We'll provide several in-depth examples of exactly how to design and build this type of integration in *Chapter 9, Supporting Key Business Scenarios*. This chapter is focused on the capabilities of Service Cloud as they relate to B2C use cases.

Computer Telephony Integration (CTI)

To support call center service scenarios, Service Cloud provides a JavaScript API called **Open CTI** that can be leveraged to integrate **computer-telephony integration** (**CTI**) systems with your **Salesforce Call Center**. Open CTI requires development effort to integrate but creates a seamless, browser-based means of leveraging a softphone to handle incoming and outgoing calls, as supported by your CTI system. Salesforce Call Center, including Open CTI, allows agents to provide phone support and track outcomes against cases, associate contacts, and accounts; leverage knowledge articles; and essentially take advantage of all the features of the Service Console. Many telephony providers offer AppExchange solutions that provide feature-rich integrations and experiences with a low implementation effort.

Omni-Channel

Omni-Channel in Service Cloud refers to the capability to intelligently route incoming work, including cases and chats, to the most qualified available representative using configurable rules.

> **Important note**
> In B2C commerce, Omni-Channel generally refers to the ability to transact commerce in a channel-agnostic way, including online, in store, or through marketplaces. This is not related to the Service Cloud Omni-Channel capability.

Omni-Channel routing

Omni-Channel routing has two primary configurable components:

- Presence configuration
- Routing configuration

The presence configuration allows agents to control their current status, which impacts their ability to accept cases. The default options are *Available*, *On Break*, and *Busy*. Additional statuses can be configured and made available to agents by a Service Cloud administrator. The presence's status is displayed in the utility bar of the Service Console, so it's always available to agents.

The following diagram shows a basic Omni-Channel routing flow:

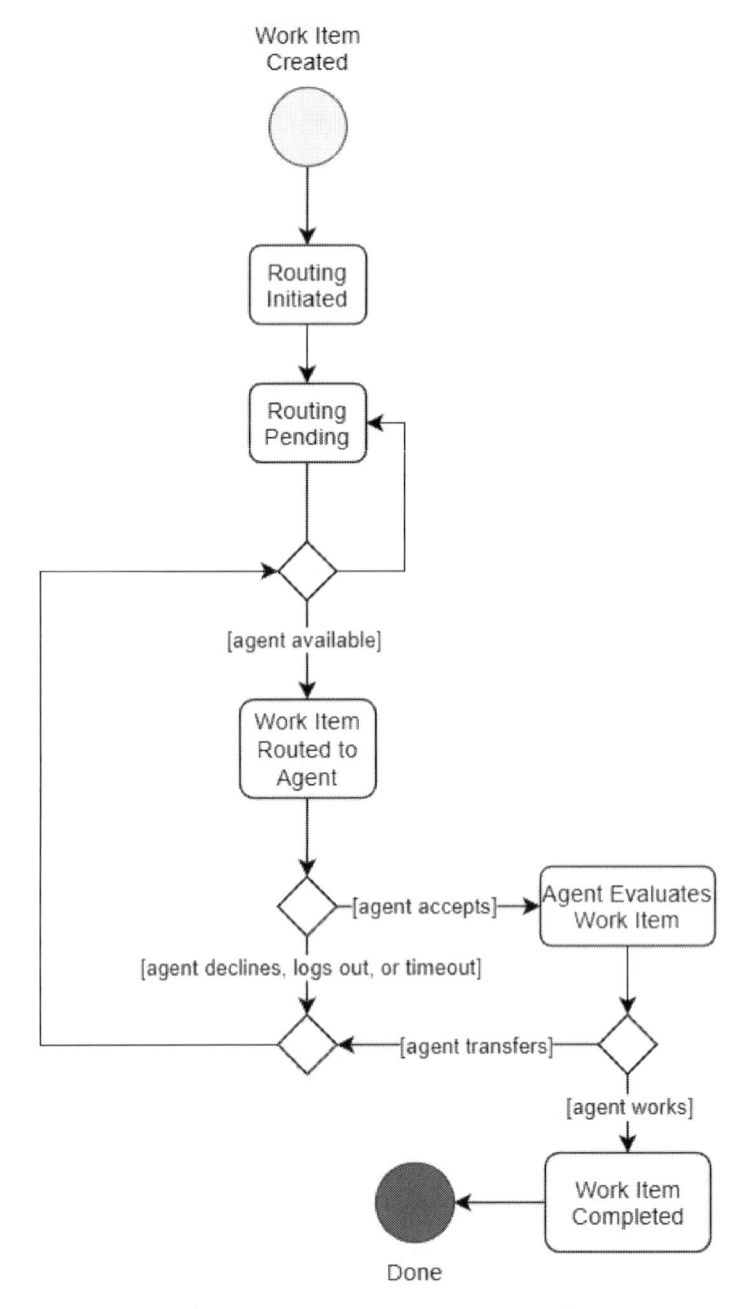

Figure 2.2 – Omni-Channel routing workflow

As the preceding diagram shows, the Service Cloud Omni-Channel routing capability supports agent workflows, allowing work to be distributed according to capacity within the Service Console.

Routing configurations place incoming **work items**, such as cases and chats, into queues based on rules that are configured with Process Builder. Queues are available in the Salesforce Platform without Service Cloud, but Service Cloud adds the ability to intelligently route work into queues based on presence status, service contracts, entitlements, agent assigned skills, and work priority.

Omni-Channel Supervisor

Omni-Channel Supervisor allows CSR managers to oversee the work in a support center at a higher level. Specifically, supervisors can monitor agent work statuses routed by Omni-Channel, review and monitor Service Cloud voice transcripts and chat messages, and message agents in real time to help them with cases. Agents can also flag work in progress as requiring assistance from a supervisor to ensure visibility and draw attention. Now that you understand the capabilities of Service Cloud, we'll cover the overall Service Cloud data model.

Service Cloud data model

The Service Cloud data model builds on the Salesforce Platform data model. The core CRM object types available in the platform are also available with Service Cloud, plus several additions. Cross-cloud data modeling is one of the primary responsibilities of a B2C Solution Architect, so it's critical to know not just how the Salesforce data model works in general (as discussed in *Chapter 1, Demystifying Salesforce, Customer 360, and Digital 360*) but the specific objects in that data model and what they represent. Storing the right data in the right place, making it available as needed, and synchronizing the critical components are all part of the B2C Solution Architect's responsibility.

In this chapter, we're going to focus on Service Cloud. In the next two chapters, we'll take a similar look at the B2C Commerce and Marketing Cloud data models before bringing it all together.

> **Tip**
> The concepts we've discussed here for Service Cloud can be applied to any Salesforce Platform-based product, such as Experience Cloud or Order Management, but the specific objects that are used may differ.

Salesforce Platform data model review

As a refresher, the Salesforce Platform stores data in conceptual tables called objects. Each object has strongly typed fields, analogous to columns in a spreadsheet, which can be either standard (system-defined) or custom. Individual instances of that object are called records, which are analogous to rows in a spreadsheet.

The most important objects to understand in Service Cloud for B2C solutions are accounts and contacts, which are standard Salesforce Platform objects that we covered in *Chapter 1, Demystifying Salesforce, Customer 360, and Digital 360*. We're not going to cover them again here but if you need a refresher, be sure to review that chapter because accounts and contacts will be the foundation of much of the cross-cloud work we'll cover in later chapters.

Additional objects

Salesforce enables several additional standard objects for the data model when Service Cloud is enabled in your org. In this section, we'll look at some of the important additional objects you'll need to be familiar with as part of the larger B2C solution context.

Many additional objects and relationships are relevant for designing the complete Service Cloud solution, but this is outside the scope of this book:

- **Agent Work** (`AgentWork`): This represents a work assignment that's been routed to an agent.
- **Chat Session** (`LiveAgentSession`): Tracks agent chat sessions, which can consist of multiple chat transcripts.
- **Chat Transcript** (`LiveChatTranscript`): Describes the details of a single customer's interaction via chat. This is an appropriate place to annotate session-specific information from the initiating system, such as B2C Commerce session identifiers.
- **Chat Visitor** (`LiveChatVisitor`): This represents a single customer who has initiated a live chat session.

> **Further reading**
> The complete Service Cloud data model is described here: `https://sforce.co/2R1kWef`.

To leverage the Service Cloud data model from outside systems, you also need to understand the Service Cloud APIs and integration options.

Service Cloud APIs and integrations

The Service Cloud APIs are the Salesforce Platform APIs; everything covered in this section applies to all Salesforce Platform-based products equally, although all of them require permissions configuration to be enabled. You can think of the Service Cloud APIs as interfaces to the product for outside systems.

As with any integration scenario, understanding the options for interfacing with a system programmatically is the foundation of a proper design. Native Service Cloud features such as Web-to-Case and Live Chat simplify integration by supporting direct integration without the use of APIs or custom code, but there are other scenarios where custom code will be required, so it's important to understand these capabilities.

Salesforce has a lot of APIs available, which can be overwhelming at first, but there are a few key options that will be leveraged in the majority of B2C integration scenarios.

Available APIs

The following screenshot is of the Salesforce documentation. It shows all the available Salesforce Platform API options:

API NAME	PROTOCOL	DATA FORMAT	COMMUNICATION
REST API	REST	JSON, XML	Synchronous
SOAP API	SOAP (WSDL)	XML	Synchronous
Connect REST API	REST	JSON, XML	Synchronous (photos are processed asynchronously)
User Interface API	REST	JSON	Synchronous
Analytics REST API	REST	JSON, XML	Synchronous
Bulk API	REST	CSV, JSON, XML	Asynchronous
Metadata API	SOAP (WSDL)	XML	Asynchronous
Streaming API	Bayeux	JSON	Asynchronous (stream of data)
Apex REST API	REST	JSON, XML, Custom	Synchronous
Apex SOAP API	SOAP (WSDL)	XML	Synchronous
Tooling API	REST or SOAP (WSDL)	JSON, XML, Custom	Synchronous

Figure 2.3 – Salesforce API Options. Documentation reference: `https://sforce.co/3dlUcN2`

As you can see, each API is described by the protocol, data format, and communication mechanism it supports. The protocol and data format are helpful in selecting an API option that aligns with the capabilities of the client application or programming language. The communication mechanism is helpful in choosing an API that has the appropriate performance characteristics. Most importantly, however, you'll need to understand the functionality supported by each of these API options.

> **Tip**
> Additional examples of how to leverage Salesforce Platform APIs to meet specific use cases within a B2C solution architecture are provided in *Chapter 8, Creating a 360° View of the Customer*, and *Chapter 9, Supporting Key Business Scenarios*.

The following sections will cover protocols, data formats, communication mechanisms, and capabilities in more detail.

Protocols

The **REST** and **SOAP** protocols are standard web service protocols supported by most enterprise applications and commonly used languages. The **Streaming API** leverages the transport-independent **Bayeux protocol**, which allows **CometD**-enabled clients to receive near-real-time updates when records change in Salesforce.

> **Important note**
> While the Streaming API may sound like a great option, neither B2C Commerce nor Marketing Cloud support CometD, so they cannot communicate with this mechanism.

Data formats

The data format is an important consideration, depending on the capabilities of the source platform, since B2C Commerce custom code is an **ECMAScript** implementation that supports some ES6 constructs, **JavaScript Object Notation (JSON)** is the most convenient format to use when interacting from the B2C Commerce side.

Marketing Cloud supports multiple native scripting languages (see *Chapter 4, Engaging Customers with Marketing Cloud*, for details). **AMPscript**, one of the native scripting languages used in Marketing Cloud, supports XML natively, while **server-side JavaScript (SSJS)** supports JSON. A similar evaluation could be made from any connecting system, but it may be most consistent to assume JSON since this is widely supported and less verbose than XML.

Communication mechanisms

Finally, the communication column (**synchronous** or **asynchronous**) describes how data is processed within the Salesforce Platform in response to a received call. Asynchronous APIs, such as the Bulk API, return a result to the calling system immediately and enqueue the actual work to process separately. If the calling system needs to know the outcome of that work, a polling solution is required to check on the status of the work in progress. For small data volumes, a synchronous communication mechanism is preferable.

Capabilities

The **REST API** and **SOAP API** both focus on low-volume data manipulation, including **Create**, **Read**, **Update**, and **Delete** (**CRUD**) operations and query operations. Use these APIs to interact with a small number of records, such as by updating a single contact record based on changes in another system. The choice of REST or SOAP is purely one of convenience, so use whichever your source system supports most easily.

The **Connect REST API** is primarily focused on providing programmatic access to content that's exposed via **Salesforce Content Management System (CMS)**, **Experience Cloud**, **B2B Commerce Lightning**, **Chatter**, and its related elements. These are all Salesforce Platform products that focus on creating *externally facing* experiences, and the Connect REST API supports this user experience layer.

For Packt Gear, you might use the Connect REST API to pull content from the Salesforce CMS for use in an in-store kiosk about upcoming Guided Hikes. This will help the look and feel stays consistent with the CMS-based content that's leveraged in a public Experience and syndicated to B2C Commerce and Marketing Cloud, which can both receive content from CMS natively.

The **User Interface API** is intended to support use cases where a version of the Salesforce internal user experience is being replicated off-platform, such as in a custom native mobile app.

> Tip
> The Connect REST API is focused on Salesforce *external* experiences (for customers), while the User Interface API is focused on Salesforce *internal* user experiences (for employees).

The **Analytics REST API** is for the **Salesforce Analytics** product, now called **Tableau CRM**, which provides advanced AI and analytics capabilities on top of Salesforce. It's not a primary use case in B2C solutions unless that product is a component.

The **Bulk API** is ideal for working with large data volumes asynchronously. It can be used to submit a query or insert, update, or delete many records and leverage a polling mechanism to monitor the status from the calling application. The Bulk API is ideal for bulk loading customer records from an ERP into Salesforce or performing nightly updates from a third-party loyalty system, which ensures the contact records have the proper loyalty tier. This may grant them additional service entitlements.

The **Metadata API** is used to manage the customization and configuration of your org from an outside system and is most useful in **DevOps** workflows or for supporting **Interactive Development Editor (IDE)** tooling, such as **Salesforce Extensions for Visual Studio Code**.

You only need to leverage the **Streaming API** with clients that support CometD, as mentioned previously, and that rules out B2C Commerce and Marketing Cloud. The Streaming API would be a great option to leverage for an application monitoring solution such as **AppDynamics**. Key aspects of the overall business flow, such as initiated chat sessions and their outcome, can be streamed to the monitoring solution in near-real-time with low overhead.

The **Tooling API** is similar to the Metadata API but provides more fine-grained access to the org's metadata. The Tooling API supports the **Salesforce Object Query Language (SOQL)** for many metadata types, which allows calling applications to retrieve smaller pieces of metadata than the Metadata API supports. Ultimately, these two APIs overlap in terms of functionality, and both are intended to support the implementation of development tools and workflows.

Finally, The **Apex REST API** and the **Apex SOAP API** are for custom web services that have been implemented with **Apex** in the Salesforce Platform. Apex is the Salesforce server-side programming language and can be used to implement custom services to support business needs, which are then exposed over one or the other of these API channels. An example of a custom web service that's built into Service Cloud to support a B2C use case is an identity matching service that accepts a variety of customer identifiers, such as email, phone number, address, and social handle, and returns a contact and an account ID to match them against. Since this would require some custom logic in the query, the raw REST API wouldn't be appropriate (unless the logic was being implemented in the calling system), so a custom service would be preferable.

Which API should I use?

For most common B2C solution integration use cases of using point-to-point integrations, you should use the REST API. Many middleware solutions, however, prefer SOAP because the **Web Service Definition Language** (**WSDL**) provided by SOAP streamlines API client setup.

The Bulk API is a better choice for interacting with large numbers of records at a time.

The Connect REST API is useful for creating custom user experiences that have a consistent look and feel with CMS or Experience Cloud-based experiences.

It's less likely you'll need to use any of the other Salesforce APIs in your B2C solution architecture, but you should now be aware of what they are.

> **Further reading**
>
> To learn more about any of the available Salesforce Platform API options, start with the Salesforce help article called *Which API Do I Use?* here: https://sforce.co/3dlUcN2.

File-based integrations

One important thing to know about the Salesforce Platform is that it has no native support for file/feed-based integrations. Both B2C Commerce and Marketing Cloud have excellent support for sending a CSV or XML file through an SFTP server and importing it into the target system on a scheduled basis, but this capability does not exist in the Salesforce Platform without the use of third-party tools.

The best alternative to file-based integrations for large data volumes is the Bulk API, as discussed in the previous section. An integration-focused solution such as **MuleSoft** or a custom application in **Heroku** can also offload this capability. With the introduction of **Salesforce Functions** in the Spring 2021 release, Salesforce provided the ability to build serverless functions that run on Kubernetes within the context of the Salesforce Platform, which would be the closest thing to a native solution for file-based integrations.

> **Further reading**
>
> You can learn more about Salesforce serverless functions here: https://sforce.co/3bXotSy.

We'll explore integration options in more detail in *Chapter 7, Integration Architecture Options*.

Data import and export capabilities

Data import and export are not integration options, with the possible exception of the Data Loader **command-line interface** (**CLI**), but these capabilities are an important part of designing an overall solution that incorporates the Salesforce platform. There will be times during the solution build where you need to get records into and out of Salesforce, and these are the tools to do it.

Data Import Wizard

The **Data Import Wizard** is exposed from within the Salesforce org through the **Setup** section. As its name suggests, the Data Import Wizard supports imports *only* and has a limit of 50k records at a time. Data Import Wizard also supports only a subset of the platform standard objects (and all custom objects).

The primary advantage of the Data Import Wizard is that it allows the user to bypass processes and workflows that would otherwise be triggered based on record creation or updates. This can be especially useful when bulk importing legacy data from another system that would otherwise meet the criteria for something such as automated alerts.

Data Loader

Data Loader is a desktop client application available for Windows and Mac. It can be installed directly from the **Data Loader** section in **Setup** within your Salesforce org. Data Loader supports up to 5 million records per batch and supports record deletion as well as data export. Data Loader also supports all standard and custom objects, making it the most powerful choice for moving data into and out of a Salesforce org.

Data Loader provides both a point-and-click user experience and a command-line interface that can be used to automated scheduled imports and exports.

The disadvantages of Data Loader are the fact that it needs to be installed as a separate piece of software, as well as the fact that it cannot avoid triggering workflows and processes in your org for records that are added or changed, so these features will need to be disabled in advance by an administrator if needed. This limitation can, in large part, be mitigated by adding custom logic to automations to avoid executing during bulk data load via Data Loader, but this is not supported natively.

The Data Loader command-line interface, combined with some custom scripting, would be a reasonable solution for supporting a feed-based integration with the Salesforce Platform. A pattern such as the one shown in the following diagram could be scheduled to execute daily, hourly, or every few minutes to support a system that does not natively provide web service integrations. The following diagram shows a simple SFTP to API integration component hosted in Heroku:

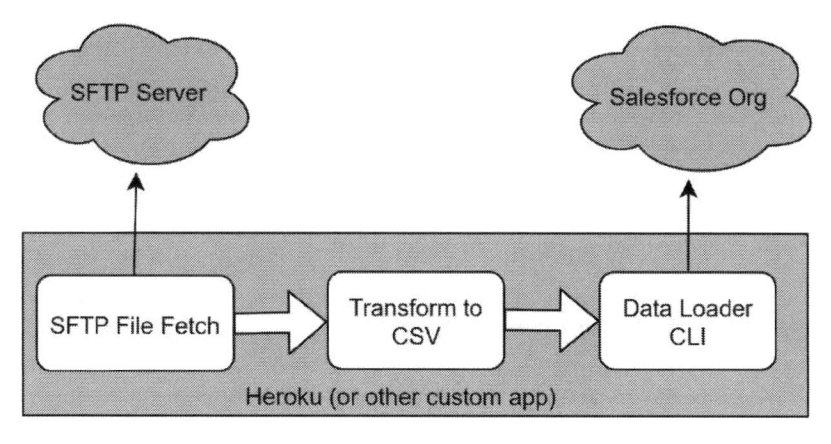

Figure 2.4 – Data Loader-based feed integration pattern

Report export

It is also possible to generate tabular reports in any Salesforce Platform-based product, including Service Cloud, and then save those reports as an Excel or CSV file. Since this doesn't support large data volumes, scheduling, or automated delivery, it is of limited use in integration scenarios. It can, however, be a good way to explore data and experiment with mapping, transforming, and loading during the solution design phase of a project.

Outgoing requests

As we mentioned previously, the Salesforce Platform does not natively support sending or receiving file transfers. All integrations initiated by the Salesforce Platform must use real-time API calls, most commonly using Apex callouts. An Apex callout allows Salesforce Apex to invoke an external web service or make an HTTP request and process the result in custom code. This type of integration can support SOAP- or REST-based APIs and can also support making asynchronous callouts for long-running web service calls.

Apex callouts are used extensively in typical Service Cloud and B2C Commerce point-to-point connections to allow Service Cloud to update B2C Commerce as customer data changes or based on CSR interactions. For more information on this pattern, see *Chapter 7, Integration Architecture Options*.

To integrate using any of the options presented in this section, you should also know and consider Salesforce Platform's limitations, which we will cover in the next section.

Service Cloud request limits and allocations

Now that we've explored the capabilities, data model, and integrations of Service Cloud as part of a larger B2C solution, we need to consider its limitations to avoid designing a solution that will not scale or run afoul of licensing constraints. The origin of the Salesforce Platform, as discussed in *Chapter 1, Demystifying Salesforce, Customer 360, and Digital 360*, is as a CRM supporting sales teams. As such, it was not designed to handle extremely high-volume use cases. Salesforce also resides on a multi-tenant architecture, which means your org is sharing resources with the orgs of other businesses, and Salesforce has limitations in place to prevent one customer from monopolizing those resources.

There's a world of difference between thousands of sales team members logging into Salesforce to manage their accounts, contacts, leads, and opportunities and handling 10k orders per hour as B2C Commerce does or sending millions of emails a day as Marketing Cloud does. Because of this, there are some use cases where the Salesforce Platform is still not an appropriate solution at scale. The rest of this section will outline design constraints that, if respected, can help ensure that your solution meets the needs of the business for years to come.

> **Important note**
> Using the Salesforce Platform as your system of record for data for high volume use cases can quickly exceed allowed request limits, causing your solution to fail under load.

Salesforce licenses and editions

To evaluate your API request limits, you must start with your **Salesforce Edition** (Sandbox, Developer, Enterprise, Performance, or Unlimited). As we discussed at the beginning of this chapter, the Essentials and Professional editions don't support API-based integration by default. If API access is purchased for the Professional edition, it has the same limitations as the Enterprise edition.

Once you have your edition, the second consideration is the number and type of licenses you have for your org. This book does not cover Salesforce license design in depth, but there are a variety of licenses you can use at various costs that enable various capabilities within an org. Licenses are associated with Salesforce Profiles, which are then applied to users, to grant capabilities.

Capability capacity limitations

Certain non-API-based integration points that we discussed previously in this chapter, namely Email-to-Case and Web-to-Case, have their own limitations that should be considered when incorporating them into a connected solution.

Email-to-Case comes in two flavors – locally installed agent and on-demand Email-to-Case. The On-Demand Email-to-Case capability provided by Salesforce, which does not require installing an agent on a physical device, limits email attachments to under 25 MB and allows a maximum of 1,000 emails to be converted into cases, x the total number of user licenses, to a maximum of 1,000,000. The locally installed version supports attachments over 25 MB but allows a maximum of 2,500 emails to be converted to cases per day.

With Web-to-Case, a maximum of 5,000 cases can be created through this channel every 24 hours. This limit can be increased by Salesforce support, but it's important to ensure that anti-spam measures such as reCAPTCHA are in place to prevent malicious traffic from creating excessive cases. If cases over this limit are created, a maximum of 50,000 cases are enqueued and created when the 5,000/24-hour limit refreshes.

Total API allocations

If you followed the instructions in *Chapter 1, Demystifying Salesforce, Customer 360, and Digital 360*, to create your own Developer Edition org, you can find the licenses that have been applied by navigating to **Company Information** in **Setup**. The following screenshot shows the available licenses in a Developer Edition org:

User Licenses

Name	Status	Total Licenses
Salesforce	Active	2
Salesforce Platform	Active	3
Customer Community Login	Active	5
XOrg Proxy User	Active	2
Work.com Only	Active	3
Customer Portal Manager Custom	Active	5
Identity	Active	110
Customer Community Plus	Active	5
Silver Partner	Active	2
Gold Partner	Active	3

Figure 2.5 – User licenses

While a Developer Edition org always has a fixed limit of 15,000 total API calls every 24 hours, we can use this license set as a reference and assume this is an Enterprise Edition org for the sake of calculation.

An Enterprise Edition org starts with 100,000 total API calls every 24 hours. From there, we add the following:

- 1,000 API calls for each **Salesforce** license (2 x 1,000 = 2,000)
- 1,000 API calls for each **Salesforce Platform** license (3 x 1,000 = 3,000)
- 200 API calls for each **Customer Community Plus** license (5 x 200 = 1,000)

Not all license types grant additional API calls, and this is only a subset of the licenses available in an org that are used to demonstrate the concept.

Regarding the preceding example, the total number of API calls per 24 hours would be as follows:

100,000 + 2,000 + 3,000 + 1,000 = 106,000

Anything over that and you run the risk of Salesforce disabling or blocking further requests. While it is possible to purchase additional API calls, you should ensure your solution is making optimal use of the existing capabilities.

> **Further reading**
>
> You can find the details of API request allocations here: `https://sforce.co/2OkTqYc`.

API usage monitoring and enforcement

As described in the Salesforce help document mentioned previously, you can manually monitor your API usage in the following places:

- The **API Usage** section of the **System Overview** page in **Setup**.
- The **API Requests, Last 24 Hours** item in the **Organization Detail** section of the **System Overview** page in **Setup**.
- The **API Request Limit per Month** usage-based entitlement from the **Company Information** page in **Setup**.

Perhaps more usefully in solution design, you can monitor your API usage and limits programmatically using the following:

- The `Sforce-Limit-Info` response header for all REST APIs
- The `<type>API REQUESTS</type>` element in SOAP API response bodies
- The `/limits` call in the REST API

> **Tip**
> The preceding API-based methods for monitoring your platform's API limits are not appropriate for *avoiding* these limits without a robust fallback plan, but they are a useful way to incorporate API utilization into an overall solution monitoring tool.

API access and connected apps

Access to Salesforce APIs is controlled from the Salesforce org using **Connected apps**. A Connected app is used to manage identity and access control whenever the Salesforce Platform is interacting with an outside system, including other Salesforce products that aren't running on the Salesforce Platform.

The four main use cases for a Connected app are as follows:

1. Providing access to the Salesforce API for external applications, such as allowing B2C Commerce to update contact and account records using the REST API when the commerce customer profile is updated on the storefront.
2. Using the Salesforce Platform as an identity provider for outside systems, such as supporting **single sign-on** (**SSO**) across public experiences built on Experience Cloud and the B2C Commerce storefront.
3. Managing access to third-party apps installed within your org, such as Marketing Cloud Distributed Marketing.
4. Serving as an authorization provider for external API gateways such as MuleSoft's Anypoint Platform.

Connected apps utilize industry-standard protocols for authentication. For API authentication (option 1), a Connected app uses **OAuth 2.0** to allow outside systems to authenticate with the Salesforce Platform with a token exchange. For SSO scenarios (option 2) the Salesforce Platform supports **SAML 2.0** and **OpenID Connect**.

> **Important note**
> This book does not cover these industry-standard protocols in depth, though later chapters will provide additional examples of API-based authentication between systems (option 1 in the preceding list) as this is a key B2C solution architecture use case.

Feature allocation limits

In addition to API and integration constraints, Salesforce places certain allocation limits on features that are used within the platform. These allocation limits vary by Salesforce edition used and impact many aspects of the platform, including user interface elements such as tabs, data management tools like sharing rules, and the allowed number of processes and flows. All limits are per org and many are within a 24-hour rolling period, much like the API usage limits discussed previously.

In most cases, the B2C solution architect can rely on a Salesforce Platform or Service Cloud technical architect to review and understand the implementation details of this nature within the Salesforce Platform. The B2C solution architect should focus on knowing and understanding feature constraints that impact interaction with external systems, such as the maximum allowable cases that can be created through Web-to-Case, as discussed in the *Capability capacity limitations* section.

> **Further reading**
> The full list of feature allocation limits is documented here: `https://sforce.co/3xn5ucb`.

Data and file storage allocations

Understanding limitations on data storage is a critical part of designing solutions that span multiple products. Storage limits, especially data storage limits, can be the deciding factor between moving data between systems and accessing them on demand. *Chapter 7, Integration Architecture Options*, discusses these tradeoffs in more detail.

Salesforce divides storage allocations into Data Storage (information contained in Salesforce Records) and File Storage (static files used to support capabilities such as attachments and PDFs uploaded to the org). Both types of storage are calculated asynchronously, so they may not be 100% up to date at all time, and both types of storage include a base allocation based on the Salesforce edition being used and an additional allocation for each user license that's been purchased. The third category of storage, Big Object storage, is fixed at 1,000,000 records per org and can only be updated through Salesforce support.

The following table outlines the storage allocation limits per org for each category described previously:

Edition	Data Storage Minimum	Data Storage per License	File Storage Minimum	File Storage per License
Contact Manager	10 GB	20 MB	10 GB	612 MB
Group				
Professional				
Enterprise				2 GB
Performance		120 MB		
Unlimited		20 MB for Lightning Platform Starter User		
Developer	5 MB	N/A	20 MB	N/A
Personal	20 MB			
Essentials	10 GB		1 GB	

Table 2.1 – Edition storage constraints

As you can see, an org running Professional edition with 10 users would have 10.2 GB of available data storage (10 GB base + 20 MB * 10 users = 10.2 GB).

With the information covered in this section, you should understand the APIs, features, and data limitations that govern the implementation of the Salesforce Platform. Since Service Cloud runs on top of the Salesforce Platform, all of these design constraints apply to Service Cloud and should be considered when designing a B2C solution architecture.

Summary

Now that you've read this chapter and *Chapter 1, Demystifying Salesforce, Customer 360, and Digital 360*, you should understand and be able to articulate the way Service Cloud extends and builds upon the Salesforce Platform as part of a B2C solution. When selecting a Service Cloud edition, you should understand the tradeoffs and recognize that Enterprise and Ultimate Edition are the best choices to support API-based integrations.

As part of a complete B2C solution, you'll now be able to explain what role Service Cloud serves both independently and in conjunction with other products. Specifically, you should be able to design solutions around the Service Console, the home base for agents working in Service Cloud every day. Capabilities such as chat management, Digital Engagement, and Omni-Channel routing can be integrated with outside systems, including B2C Commerce, to ensure the right agent can help your customer the first time around.

To support customer service and agent education, you should feel comfortable designing a solution that leverages capabilities such as knowledge articles, Service contracts, and entitlements integrated with self-service help and prioritized queues.

When creating a cross-cloud data model, you'll now be able to map data to not only the core Salesforce Platform objects but the extended object set provided by Service Cloud. Perhaps most importantly, you have the foundational understanding to evaluate the various Salesforce Platform API and integration options to make the right decisions about data formats, integration methodologies and use cases when integrating with external systems while respecting the platform limitations.

In the next chapter, we'll provide an overview of B2C Commerce by covering its capabilities, integration options, and constraints in much the same way we did here for Service Cloud.

Questions

1. During early discussions with a potential customer, they mention that they are currently using Service Cloud Professional Edition and that they want to integrate it with their B2C Commerce storefront. What concerns should you, as a B2C Solution Architect, raise?

2. When reviewing integrated solution requirements with your client, you note that they need the ability to resend order confirmation emails from Marketing Cloud when a customer contacts support. Should this capability be added to the Service app or the Service Console app in Service Cloud?

3. What Service Cloud capability allows incoming work items such as chat requests and cases to be routed to the most qualified agent based on schedules, in-progress work, and availability?

4. Service agents often need to walk customers through a series of manual steps when troubleshooting product-specific issues over the phone. What Service Cloud tool would allow agents to have that information at hand when working on a product support case?

5. When a customer initiates a chat request from the B2C Commerce storefront, what's the best way to enrich the Service Cloud chat transcript with additional data points to allow the agent full access to the customer's profile in B2C Commerce?
6. What are the most important Salesforce Platform APIs to know about when designing a B2C solution architecture, and what use cases do they support?
7. To create a complete picture of the customer, your client would like to update a custom object in Service Cloud every time any customer views a **Product Detail Page** (**PDP**) on the commerce storefront. What are some potential concerns with this approach?
8. What needs to be created in Service Cloud to allow outside system access to a Salesforce Platform API or to allow someone to use the Salesforce Platform as an identity provider for an SSO solution?
9. The Packt Gear internal accounting system sits behind a corporate firewall and only supports sending flat files to a **Secure FTP** (**SFTP**); it cannot send or receive real-time web service requests. Despite that, it's important this accounting system provides vital data regarding customer invoice payments that need to be updated in Service Cloud. What are some options to get this file-based data into the Salesforce Platform?

Further reading

- *Sales and Service Cloud Pricing*: https://www.salesforce.com/editions-pricing/sales-and-service-cloud/
- *Service Cloud Editions*: https://www.salesforce.com/editions-pricing/service-cloud/
- *Service Cloud Capabilities*: https://www.salesforce.com/content/dam/web/en_us/www/documents/pricing/salesforce-service-cloud-pricing-editions.pdf
- *API Request Limits and Allocations Quick Reference*: https://developer.salesforce.com/docs/atlas.en-us.salesforce_app_limits_cheatsheet.meta/salesforce_app_limits_cheatsheet/salesforce_app_limits_platform_api.htm

3
Direct-to-Consumer Selling with Commerce Cloud B2C

Salesforce Commerce Cloud is the umbrella term for the family of products designed to support commerce transactions, regardless of the channel. One of the products in the Salesforce Commerce Cloud is **B2C Commerce**, formerly called Demandware. It's a standalone SaaS product designed to support the needs of the world's largest organizations across a variety of industries selling products direct to consumers online, in store, through social channels, marketplaces, and more.

B2C Commerce includes robust product and catalog management, pricing and promotion support, inventory tracking, customer data management, personalized AI recommendations powered by Commerce Cloud Einstein, and more. This chapter will focus on outlining the primary features of B2C Commerce within a larger B2C solution so that you, as the solution architect, can understand what role this product plays and what the integration points and best practices are.

Just like with our coverage of the core Salesforce Platform, Service Cloud, and Marketing Cloud, this chapter is *not* intended to make you an expert on Salesforce Commerce Cloud or B2C Commerce. The goal of this chapter is to equip you with the tools you need to design a solution that leverages B2C Commerce and to communicate effectively with the platform specialists, including a B2C Commerce architect, who will be focused on this component of the solution in depth.

The other products in Salesforce Commerce Cloud, at the time of writing, include Order Management and B2B Commerce. There are also several complementary products from Salesforce that work together with the core Commerce Cloud products, including Loyalty and Payments. These Salesforce Commerce Cloud products, beyond B2C Commerce, will be covered in the last section of this chapter.

In this chapter, we're going to cover the following main topics:

- B2C Commerce capabilities
- B2C Commerce data model
- B2C Commerce APIs and integrations
- B2C Commerce quotas and governance
- B2C Commerce Marketplace
- Commerce Cloud product family

B2C Commerce capabilities

The primary difference between B2C Commerce and the Salesforce B2B Commerce product is their capabilities. The B2C Commerce product, which is the focus of this chapter, supports extremely high-volume transactional selling, including guest channels. The B2C product also supports far more robust campaigns and promotions, as well as personalized recommendations with Commerce Cloud Einstein.

The B2B product, however, supports robust tiered account structures, customizable product pricing, and a more flexible user experience layer. The B2B product also benefits from being built on the core Salesforce Platform, so it shares a common data model with products such as Service Cloud.

B2C Commerce is not intended to be the system of record for order data in the long term; it's intended to take the order and export it to an **Order Management System** (**OMS**) for allocation, fulfillment, tracking, and support. B2C Commerce is also not an appropriate solution for primary customer service capabilities, though it will play a role.

Customer experience options

At its heart, the B2C Commerce product is a transactional commerce engine. That means it's focused on being able to take orders at scale, ensuring that payments are processed, inventory is updated, and the right prices and promotions are applied. The way that the Commerce engine is exposed to the end customer, however, can vary depending on the implementation.

There are two primary ways of implementing commerce experiences with B2C Commerce: **Storefront Reference Architecture** (**SFRA**) and **headless**.

Storefront Reference Architecture (SFRA)

Salesforce provides a complete implementation of a fully functional commerce storefront that leverages all the features of its enterprise B2C Commerce platform. This custom storefront supports shopping, search, account management, ordering, content, and everything else you'd expect from a storefront. Nearly all B2C Commerce implementations that leverage the platform for the frontend are built from the **Storefront Reference Architecture** (**SFRA**) or its predecessor, **SiteGenesis**.

SiteGenesis is an older version of the reference storefront, but the underlying B2C Commerce platform is the same, as are all of the APIs and integration points. As a B2C solution architect, the differences between these two versions of the storefront are not particularly impactful. Work with a B2C Commerce-specific technical architect on the details of the storefront integration points required by your overall B2C solution architecture.

SFRA-based sites are enhanced and adapted to meet the needs of each merchant running on the platform, including all the custom functionality and integrations they require. It's important to understand that SFRA is not a template that can be tweaked by changing a couple of icons, fonts, and colors; it's a working code sample. Customizations are built on top of it with essentially no limitations. SFRA also supports a robust declarative user experience building feature called **Page Designer**, which looks and feels very much like **Experience Builder** in Salesforce Experience Cloud. Experience Builder is also the foundation of B2B Commerce.

What does that mean? It means content setup in Salesforce CMS can be leveraged on B2B Commerce storefronts, custom experiences from Experience Cloud, and Page Designer-based pages on the B2C Commerce storefront to maintain a consistent brand experience.

Headless commerce

For customers who want the maximum amount of flexibility with their commerce experiences and are willing to pay a premium in terms of implementation cost and complexity, Salesforce provides a couple of options for headless commerce experiences built on top of the B2C Commerce engine. All headless experiences on B2C Commerce leverage the B2C Commerce REST APIs for integration (as discussed in the *B2C Commerce APIs and integrations* section, later in this chapter).

Custom headless

The first option for a headless experience on B2C Commerce is to build something fully custom using the Salesforce REST APIs. Salesforce has provided a **NodeJS SDK** that wraps the Commerce APIs to support exactly this use case, along with a sample application leveraging **GraphQL** and Apollo to expose a custom **backend for frontend** (**BFF**) layer between the storefront and the B2C Commerce raw APIs.

This pattern of leveraging a BFF or some type of middleware between the custom head and the Commerce APIs is a best practice; it supports the implementation of custom business logic and external integrations.

Fully custom headless implementations require significant additional planning and expertise to design scalable and secure solutions, since much of the infrastructure will now sit outside of the B2C Commerce platform. In this case, you, as the customer or partner, are responsible for managing things such as the cloud hosting provider, custom database, in-memory caching, autoscaling, and leveraging a **Content Delivery Network** (**CDN**). All of this is handled automatically and at no additional cost when leveraging an on-platform SFRA-based storefront, but there is a trade-off in terms of control.

The following diagram shows a basic headless architecture, leveraging the Salesforce NodeJS Commerce SDK in a public cloud hosting solution:

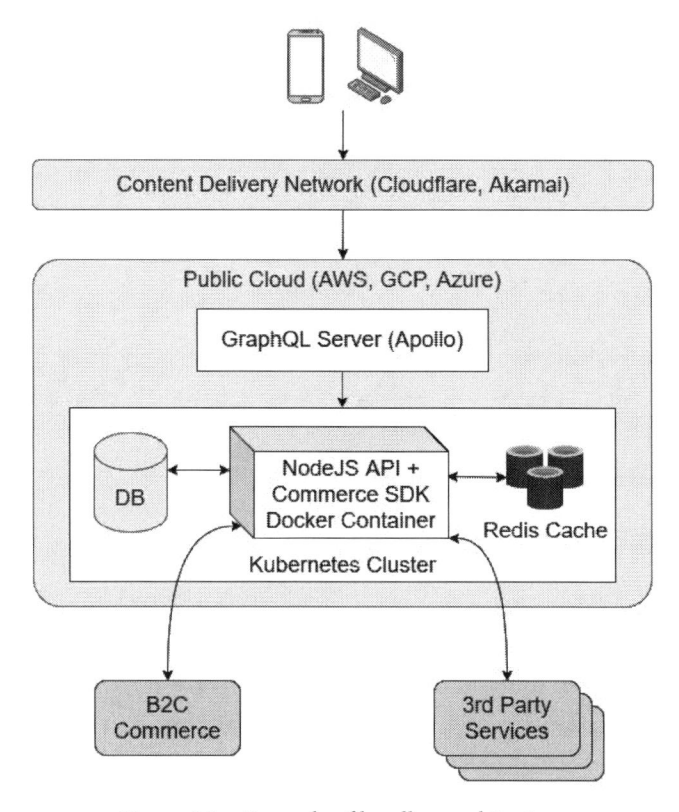

Figure 3.1 – Example of headless architecture

In this example architecture, you can see that there is a significant amount of infrastructure the customer will be responsible for designing and maintaining outside of the **B2C Commerce** engine shown at the bottom left. Some type of CDN is recommended here. The overall solution needs to be hosted, and having a scaling solution that uses a combination of caches and horizontal scaling while leveraging a solution such as **Docker**, in combination with **Kubernetes**, is advised.

PWA Kit and Managed Runtime

For a middle ground between fully headless and an SFRA-based storefront, Salesforce offers a solution called **PWA Kit and Managed Runtime**. This option decouples the frontend, now built with a custom **Progressive Web SDK** leveraging **React**-based components. This app-like web experience is referred to as a **Progressive Web App** (**PWA**) and can offer limited offline capabilities, similar to a native mobile app, but is still delivered in a browser.

As a customer, you have complete control over this frontend experience and can update/deploy independently of the core B2C Commerce platform code. The primary advantage of leveraging PWA Kit and Managed Runtime versus the fully custom headless approach is that the Managed Runtime provides a scalable and secure infrastructure to host your integration layer (BFF) and storefront code. The PWA Kit also provides a starting point for building your storefront.

PWA Kit and Managed Runtime is still significantly more complex and costly to implement than leveraging SFRA on the B2C Commerce platform to power a modern, mobile-first web experience.

Hybrid approaches

Many B2C Commerce customers leverage some combination of the previously mentioned approaches. Most commonly, the commerce storefront leverages an on-platform SFRA-based approach for a performant mobile-first experience, and REST APIs are used to support additional experiences such as mobile apps, in-store kiosks, or conversational commerce.

Additionally, some customers choose to hybridize their primary storefront delivery by hosting some portions of the shop flow in a more flexible, content-focused tool such as Salesforce Experience Cloud and the core cart through checkout flow in B2C Commerce. This type of solution requires routing each request at the DNS layer based on the intended destination and leveraging a **single sign-on** (**SSO**) approach to create seamless authentication for the customer. We'll cover that approach in *Chapter 8, Creating a 360° View of the Customer*.

Packt Gear

Knowing they'll always have the option to build additional headless experiences using OCAPI, or even the Commerce APIs, in the future means Packt Gear can be confident that getting their new commerce experience live using SFRA is the right choice. This will let them start delivering value quickly, without spending a lot of time and money on infrastructure dependencies, but it won't limit their long-term flexibility. Someday, they know they'll want a native mobile app experience and a **point-of-sale** (**POS**) integration, which will allow their store associates to order products they don't have in stock from the website and ship them to the customer's home, but first things first!

Roles and access

B2C Commerce leverages a tool called **Account Manager** to control all access to the backend management tool, known as **Business Manager**, as well as to the REST APIs. In the past, it was common for merchants to log in to Business Manager directly, but that approach has been deprecated. Now, using a unified authentication mechanism through Account Manager is the new standard since this facilitates centralized administration of user access control and granular permissions, a key requirement for **Payment Card Industry (PCI)** compliance.

Your account administrator will provision users in Account Manager and assign instance access from there. Within each instance (Production, Staging, Development, or Sandboxes), users have much more granular access to individual Business Manager modules and functions.

It is also possible to link your Account Manager instance to a Salesforce Platform org to use as an identity provider, allowing business users to log in to Service Cloud and transparently gain access to their B2C Commerce instances at the same time.

> **Important note**
> Unlike with a Salesforce Org, there is no way to get a B2C Commerce instance to learn or experiment with without being part of the B2C Commerce partner program. If you'd like access to a B2C Commerce environment, you'll have to work with your Salesforce Partner Account Manager or Customer Success Manager (depending on whether you're a partner or customer).

Merchant tools

Merchants running their business on B2C Commerce have a variety of tools at their disposal. In this chapter, we're only going to cover the core capabilities that relate to the larger B2C solution and are likely to interact with outside systems. As with each component, platform specialists will be responsible for the details of the B2C Commerce portion of the implementation.

In most B2C solution architectures, merchants will leverage Business Manager to directly interact with the following capabilities:

- **Catalogs and Products**: Used to categorize and enrich products, which are typically fed from a **Product Information Management (PIM)** system into B2C Commerce before they are displayed on the storefront.

- **Content, campaigns, and promotions**: In most cases, this data will be managed directly within B2C Commerce via Business Manager, though it is also possible to leverage integrations to external systems such as a **Content Management System** (**CMS**).

- **Customers**: B2C Commerce relies on its internal customer records for tracking profile data and managing authentication. While it is not possible to leverage an outside customer data store in place of the B2C Commerce native customer records, it is possible to integrate with an outside system (such as Service Cloud) to ensure these records stay in sync. This is the focus of *Chapter 8, Creating a 360° View of the Customer*.

- **Orders**: Once orders are taken in B2C Commerce (generally only after payment is authorized), they remain in B2C Commerce for a configurable amount of time to allow for customer or CSR cancellation before being exported to a downstream system, typically an OMS. After that point, the order in B2C Commerce should no longer be referenced as the authoritative source of order information as it will quickly become out of date.

- **Reporting and Analytics**: B2C Commerce's native analytics provide robust insight into both technical system performance characteristics and storefront performance.

Admin tools

IT users or administrators of B2C Commerce are going to leverage a separate section of Business Manager that's geared primarily toward their use cases, including creating and managing sites, controlling users and role-based permissions, and scheduling instance backups.

B2C Commerce supports daily scheduled backups on each instance with configurable data included. This is not considered a disaster recovery solution but a data integrity solution. If an accidental change is made or an import overwrites something important, up to five backups are available to revert the change.

In the next section, we'll cover the B2C Commerce data model, which underlies all of the capabilities we've discussed so far.

B2C Commerce data model

The first thing to understand about the B2C Commerce data model is simply the structure of the system itself. With Salesforce Platform orgs, you will have one Production org, which serves as the system of record for nearly all code, configuration, and metadata changes. In addition, you'll have a number of **Sandboxes** (depending on the Salesforce edition) that can synchronize and copy both data and metadata from Production to support development, integration, and testing.

With B2C Commerce, each customer has at least one realm hosting exactly three primary instances and a larger pool of Sandboxes, each of which contains one or more sites. In the next section, we'll cover the role of realms, instances, and sites in B2C Commerce since all data will be stored in these structures. After that, we'll cover the data model's design considerations and options for extending it within B2C Commerce.

Realms, instances, and sites

A B2C Commerce realm is a collection of three **Primary Instance Group** (**PIG**) instances and a pool of **Secondary Instance Group** (**SIG**) instances, also known as Sandboxes. Each instance in a realm is exclusively used by one client, although multiple realms share the same underlying infrastructure in what Salesforce refers to as a **Point of Delivery** (**POD**). The multi-tenant nature of a B2C Commerce POD is an important consideration when reviewing quotas and governance, which will be covered later in this chapter.

The following diagram shows a POD containing multiple realms, each with PIG and SIG instances:

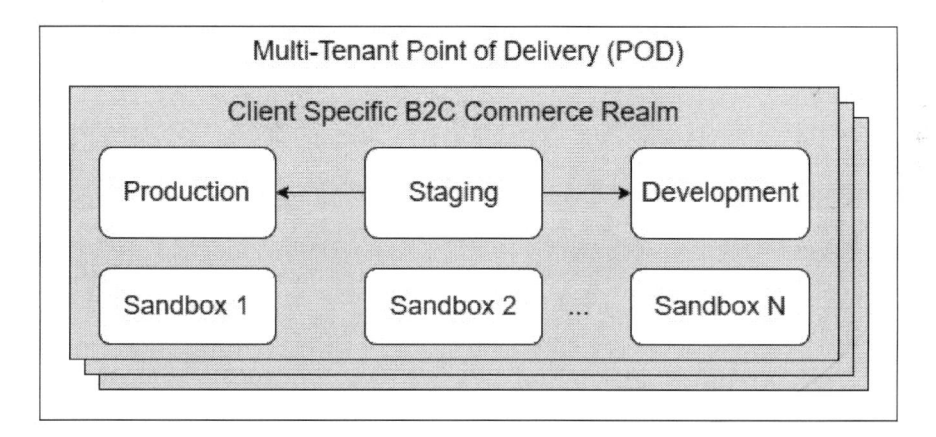

Figure 3.2 – POD, realm, and instances

Note that each instance shown here could also contain any number of sites.

Within a given realm, the three PIG instances each serve a specific role:

- **Staging**: This is the source of truth for most data, including products, catalogs, content, pricing, promotions, and configuration.
- **Production**: This is the source of truth for customer, inventory, and order data only; it is a transactional system where live customers make purchases and from which orders are sent to an **Order Management System** (**OMS**).
- **Development**: This is a production-like testing environment.

A given client may have multiple realms, typically to support different regions of the world or legally distinct business units that cannot share data. Each realm is completely independent, so any integration between them would require custom development.

There are a few additional considerations you'll need to understand concerning how data moves within a B2C Commerce realm. The next few sections will cover where data and configurations are loaded and how they are moved between instances, the roles of Sandboxes, and how sites are managed within each instance.

Merchandising and replication

The Staging instance is where the merchandising team will spend the bulk of their time setting up their site, scheduling campaigns and promotions, organizing products into categories, managing searches, and otherwise running their business. Changes that are made to Staging are then replicated, when ready, to the Production instance to become part of the live site experience. Staging can also replicate down to Development to create an environment that mirrors Production for testing purposes.

> **Tip**
> B2C Commerce replications are from Staging to Development or Production *only*. It is not possible to initiate a replication from any other instance, nor is it possible to replicate *to* Staging. Moving data between any other instances requires an import/export workflow.

Secondary Instance Group (SIG) or Sandboxes

Sandbox environments are created on demand, consume a pool of available credits every hour they are running for, and have a limited lifetime. Sandbox environments are used primarily for development and **continuous integration** (**CI**). Once code has been integrated and is ready for pre-release testing, it typically moves to the Development instance and from there, to Staging for **User Acceptance Testing** (**UAT**).

B2C Commerce sites

Each instance in a realm contains one or more sites, each representing a unique storefront that's exposed to the end customer, either with an SFRA-based web storefront or an off-platform frontend integrated with headless APIs. Typically, B2C Commerce customers leverage sites for separate brands or for separate regions that are either geographically proximate (such as the United States and Canada) or where the cost of an additional local realm is not justified (such as a European merchant experimenting with a separate site for US customers).

While we've already learned that Packt Gear has ambitions for expansion overseas in Europe, for now, they're focusing on their flagship US site launch, so one site and realm will be ideal. An additional site can be added to the existing realm for Canada, and another in the future for Europe. There's no limit regarding the number of sites a customer can have on a B2C Commerce realm. If business is booming in Europe, there may come a time when having a realm that's closer to their customers might be worth the expense for performance reasons, but that's still years away.

Role in a B2C solution architecture

With the Salesforce Platform, the integration point of the final solution will always be a production org. With B2C Commerce, the situation is a bit more complicated.

The following diagram shows a simplified system overview diagram depicting the integration points for different types of data within a B2C Commerce Realm versus the single integration point used for the Salesforce Platform (in this case, Service Cloud):

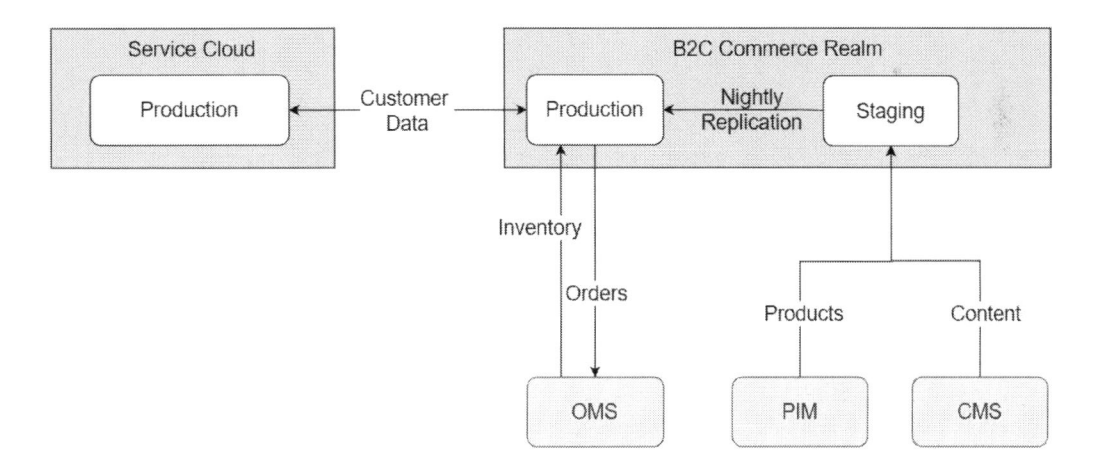

Figure 3.3 – System overview diagram

As you can see, you, as a solution architect, need to consider that B2C Commerce integrations will either be targeting the Staging instance (source of truth for things such as products, content, and promotions) or the Production instance (source of truth for things such as customer data, inventory, and orders). If you were to implement an integration that updated product information directly in Production, it would get wiped out each night when new products were replicated from Staging!

Within each instance, you also need to be cognizant of which site you're targeting to ensure that the right updates are made in the right place.

Designing data sharing solutions

In some instances, there are certain data structures that you'll need to understand as a B2C solution architect. Some data will be scoped to a particular site, meaning it cannot be shared between multiple sites in an instance, but other data will be explicitly assigned to a site or retrieved dynamically and can therefore be shared across sites.

The following are the shared data structures in a B2C Commerce instance:

- **Customer list**: Stores a set of customers associated with one or more sites
- **Catalog**: Stores a set of products or categories associated with one or more sites
- **Inventory list**: Stores the inventory for the purchasable SKUs associated with one or more sites or with individual stores
- **Price book**: Stores a set of prices for a given product associated with one or more sites
- **Content library**: Stores a collection of content resources, including static content such as images, JavaScript, and CSS, as well as dynamic content such as HTML blocks associated with one or more sites

Of these options, the fact that customer lists store customer records, which are, in turn, associated with one or more sites, is important in understanding customer profile synchronization, which is the foundation of a successful B2C solution.

It's a best practice to store product data that's been fed from a PIM solution in a catalog, referred to as a master catalog, and to separately assign those products to categories in a catalog referred to as a storefront catalog, which is then assigned to a site. The terms master catalog and storefront catalog are just conventions; there is no technical difference between them, but following this pattern facilitates sharing product data between sites that have different taxonomies.

The following diagram shows product master catalogs being fed into Staging from PIM, where the products are assigned to categories in a storefront catalog, which is, in turn, assigned to a site:

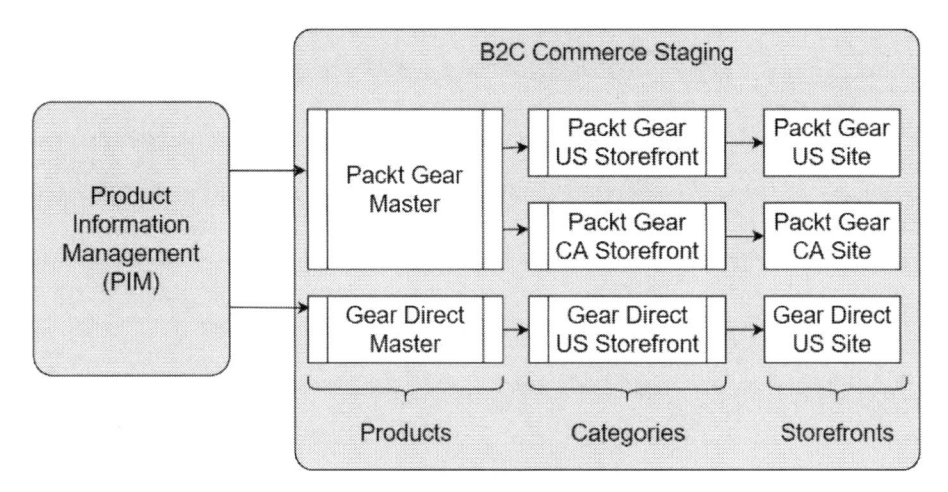

Figure 3.4 – Master and storefront catalogs

Here, the Packt Gear storefronts in the US and Canada share the same product assortment, but Gear Direct has a separate set of products.

Inventory lists and their sharing rules are important topics when designing a solution that includes Order Management and the related Omni-Channel Inventory Service. These products are not part of B2C Commerce but part of the larger Commerce Cloud family of products. When you leverage these products together, it is possible to track inventory centrally and leverage it across both B2C Commerce and Order Management, as well as additional outside systems, using API-based integration.

Price books track product prices and can support a variety of options, such as time based (scheduled) prices and tiered prices based on quantities purchased. It is common to have at least two price books assigned to a given site: a list price and a sale price book. All price books are currency-specific, so supporting multiple currencies in a single site requires having price books for each currency, and then dynamically assigning the correct currency-based price book to the current user session on the storefront.

Finally, content libraries allow a brand with multiple local sites in different geographies to share common content. The content library is also the data store that's used by Page Designer and the synchronization point for the Salesforce CMS, which is also used by Experience Cloud and B2B Commerce.

System objects

The B2C Commerce data model is far less flexible than the Salesforce Platform data model. This is in large part by design, since the B2C Commerce system is designed to be a highly efficient, secure, and scalable transactional commerce engine. Customers building on the B2C Commerce platform are intentionally deterred from making changes that would threaten the performance and stability of their sites and realms, or those of other customers on the same PoD. That's not to say it's *impossible* to design and build a system that doesn't perform well; it certainly is, but Salesforce has taken steps to reduce the likelihood of that happening.

Understanding System object access and inheritance, as well as the options for extending System objects with custom attributes, can help ensure the right data is modeled in the right place within B2C Commerce.

System object access

In B2C Commerce, there is no direct database access, nor is there an arbitrary query language such as SOQL for the Salesforce Platform that's an equivalent of the **Data Manipulation Language** (**DML**). Instead, B2C Commerce operates on a set of System objects representing common commerce concepts such as `Product`, `Customer`, `Catalog`, `Site`, `Promotion`, `PriceBook`, or `Basket`.

These System objects can be created, retrieved, updated, and deleted through one of three methods:

1. B2C Commerce **Script API**
2. **Open Commerce API (OCAPI)**
3. **Commerce APIs**

The B2C Commerce Script API is the ECMAScript-based API that's used on the B2C Commerce platform to build custom business logic, server-side controllers, backend jobs, and any other programmatic customization. As of February 2021, the B2C Commerce Script API supports some ECMAScript 6 language constructs.

OCAPI and the Commerce APIs are both REST-based APIs that support external integrations and will be covered later in this chapter.

> **Further reading**
>
> You can learn more about B2C Commerce Script APIs here: `https://sforce.co/3g9tCYI`.

System object inheritance

All System objects provided by Salesforce inherit from a root class called `Object`; all System objects that can be stored and retrieved inherit from a sub-class of Object called `PersistentObject`; and all System objects that can be annotated with additional custom attribution inherit from a subclass of `PersistentObject` called `ExtensibleObject`.

Since the vast majority of B2C Commerce System objects are `ExtensibleObject` subclasses, it's possible to decorate most with additional custom attributes to represent business-specific data.

Extending system objects with custom attributes

One example of extending the B2C Commerce data model is adding custom attributes to the B2C Commerce Customer Profile System object with the corresponding identifiers for that customer in Service Cloud (Account ID and Contact ID) and Marketing Cloud (Subscriber Key). We'll cover this in detail in *Chapter 8, Creating a 360° View of the Customer*.

Another important difference between custom attributes that are added to B2C Commerce System objects and custom fields that are added to Salesforce Platform Objects is that it is not possible to enforce uniqueness on B2C Commerce custom attributes, index them at the database level, or create a formula or roll up summary fields. Each custom attribute is simply a place to store a piece of data. While it is possible to query System objects based on custom attributes (for example, query Customers by Contact ID), the performance is comparatively poor due to the lack of database-level indexing.

Custom objects

When the custom attributes that have been added to System objects are not sufficient, such as when an entirely new concept needs to be represented and persisted, the only option within the B2C Commerce platform is **Custom objects**.

Custom Objects in B2C Commerce are conceptually similar to Custom Objects in the Salesforce Platform; both behave like a custom database table containing structured data with custom fields added. B2C Commerce Custom Objects have some important differences, however.

First, B2C Commerce Custom Objects come in two flavors: **replicable** and **non-replicable**. As we discussed earlier, most data in B2C Commerce is managed in Staging and replicated to Production either on demand or on a schedule. Custom Objects that fall into this pattern should be created as replicable Custom Objects. Data that's related to live customers, inventory, or orders, however, is managed directly in Production. This is represented by a non-replicable Custom Object. Replicable Custom Objects can only be created or changed by REST APIs, manually in Business Manager, or by the Script API running in the context of a job (basically, just not from the storefront). Non-replicable Custom Objects, on the other hand, can be created and updated from the storefront but cannot be moved between instances.

To give an example of each, if you were designing a Custom Object to store the configuration for Packt Gear's custom backpack selector quiz (questions, options, steps, and so on) and the intent was for a merchandiser to be able to set up the quiz in Staging, experiment with different configurations, and then release it to Production when ready, this would be represented by a replicable Custom Object.

If you wanted to store the results of completing the quiz for a particular customer for a brief period until it could be synchronized to an outside system, that would be a non-replicable Custom Object. It's created from the storefront by customer activity and should never be moved between Staging and Production.

Importantly, Custom Objects in B2C Commerce have hard caps on the total number of records you can create in an instance (400,000 each for replicable and non-replicable) across all sites. For this reason, it would *not* be a good design to store quiz results in Custom Objects *indefinitely*, since you would eventually reach this limit and additional attempts to save the results would fail. It is, however, a common practice to store Custom Objects temporarily until a scheduled job can push the data to another system and delete the object.

An alternative approach would be to integrate the storefront directly with an external API, without storing any data in B2C Commerce, but this can slow down the performance of the storefront and does not provide an elegant fallback in case the external service is temporarily unavailable. The B2C Commerce platform also limits storefront requests to making no more than eight external API calls per storefront request (generally, a page view), which can be another reason to minimize third-party calls made directly from the storefront.

The more durable and performant pattern is to leverage a Custom Object as a temporary store and then process it using a job in the background.

Packt Gear B2C Commerce data model

As you are working with your client, Packt Gear, you realize that their US and Canadian operations are separate from a business perspective. They have a similar look and feel and they share the same set of customers, but they operate in different currencies (USD versus CAD). In addition, the US site ships products from a central warehouse near Chicago, while the Canadian site ships from a separate warehouse in the Toronto area.

Based on this, it sounds like Pack Gear should be sharing a content library, as well as a customer list, but they should be separate sites to allow different business units to operate independently. Having separate sites will also allow the US site to have an inventory list assigned to it that stores inventory from the Chicago warehouse, where the Canadian site would have a separate inventory list associated with the Toronto warehouse. Separate price books should also be used to allow for US and Canadian dollar pricing.

Since Packt Gear sells the same products on both sites, one shared master catalog containing the product definitions will be fed nightly from the PIM, but each site will have its own storefront catalog where those products are categorized. This will allow the different teams to experiment with different structures as the seasons change and priorities shift.

Beyond the base B2C Commerce data model, you know that Packt Gear will want to allow customers to register for their Guided Hikes on the commerce storefront. You discuss this with the B2C Commerce platform architect and agree that the available `GuidedHike__c` records should be queried from Service Cloud in real time using the REST API, and then cached for 15 minutes so they can be displayed on the B2C Commerce storefront. When customers register for a hike, you decide to leverage a transient, non-replicable custom object to store that registration information and build a background job to process those objects. You then use the Service Cloud REST API to create the `HikerSignup__c` junction record on the Service Cloud to relate the customer's Contact and chosen `GuidedHike__c` record (see *Figure 1.3* in *Chapter 1*, *Demystifying Salesforce, Customer 360, and Digital 360*, for further details). The Custom Object in B2C Commerce will be promptly deleted by the job after the record is created in Service Cloud to permanently store the registration.

To leverage the data model we reviewed in this section, you'll need to understand the options for integrating with B2C Commerce from outside systems. We will cover this in the next section.

B2C Commerce APIs and integrations

As is true with any integration scenario, successfully integrating B2C Commerce into the larger B2C solution architecture is a function of understanding the available integration options. It does little good to understand the underlying data model if you don't know how to access it from another system!

Unlike the Salesforce Platform, B2C Commerce implementations still traditionally make heavy use of file-based integrations for data feeds, though API options are available. We'll cover both file-based integrations and API options in the following sections.

Feed-based integration support

B2C Commerce has native support for the FTP, SFTP, and WebDAV server integrations. Of the three, WebDAV is the only type that B2C Commerce can host natively. All files that are sent to or retrieved from a B2C Commerce instance must use WebDAV.

Despite that, the most common pattern by far is to leverage an outside SFTP server to host files being transferred to or from B2C Commerce. From there, a backend job running in B2C Commerce retrieves the file, performs any necessary pre-processing, and then imports it into the B2C Commerce instance. It is a best practice to import and export files from B2C Commerce using the B2C Commerce native XML format.

> **Further reading**
>
> You can find the B2C Commerce XML schemas here: `https://sforce.co/2PUkzC3`.

Since the Salesforce Platform does not support file-based integrations, this is not a commonly leveraged pattern for integration with Service Cloud. Marketing Cloud, however, has excellent support for CSV import and export (as we'll cover in the next chapter), so we do commonly see bulk data transfer between B2C Commerce and Marketing Cloud via files passed through an SFTP server.

Job framework

B2C Commerce supports backend job scheduling and execution within each PIG instance. B2C Commerce jobs are created from modular components called **Job Steps**. Each Job Step is implemented as a Script API function and exposed through a JSON registry, including input and output variables. Within a job configuration, these steps can be combined and chained together to handle any bulk processing tasks, including processing import/export files. This is a common alternative to performing resource-intensive processing tasks on the storefront, where it would impact the user experience.

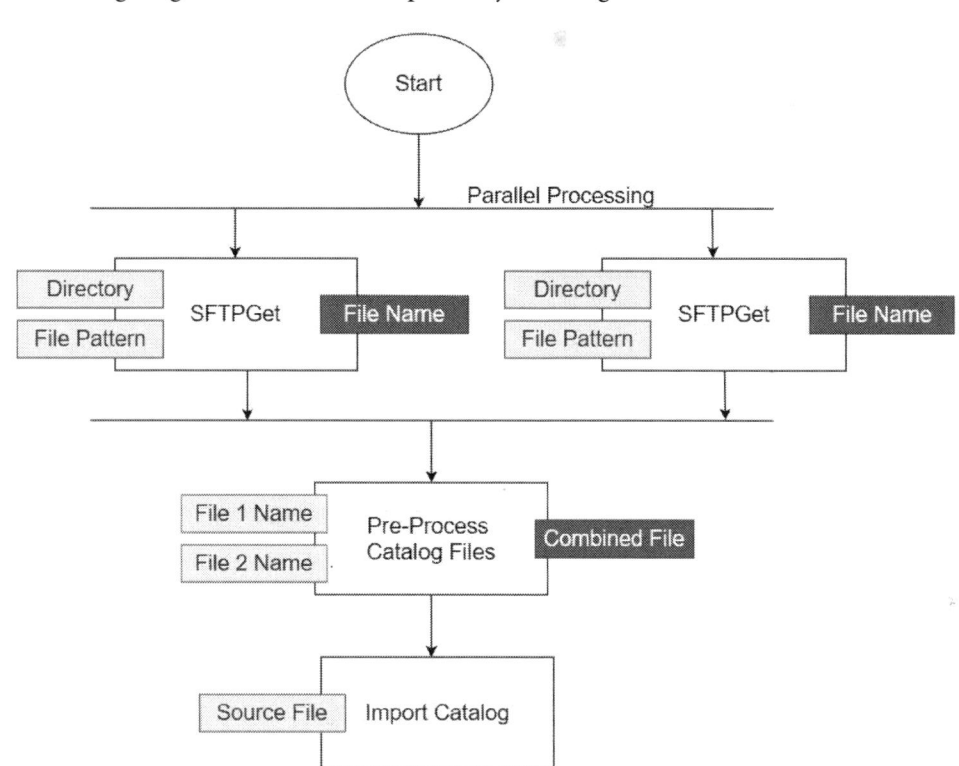

The following diagram shows an example of a job configuration:

Figure 3.5 – Job setup

In the preceding example job, two files are being retrieved from SFTP servers using the `SFTPGet` Job Step. These files can be retrieved in parallel since they have no dependency on each other. Each job step takes a `Directory` and `File Pattern` as input parameters and returns `File Name` as an output parameter. Once the two files are retrieved, a pre-processing step takes both as input parameters and outputs a `Combined File`. This `Combined File` is then passed into the `Source File` input parameter on the `Import Catalog` job step, which will import the new catalog data into the current B2C Commerce instance.

Account Manager

Account Manager is used to provision an API Client ID, which is required for all types of API access to a B2C Commerce instance. This API Client ID takes the form of a GUID and, depending on whether you're using the **Open Commerce API (OCAPI)** or the newer Commerce APIs, it may be associated with API roles at the time of creation, specifying the actions allowed to be taken with this Client ID.

> **Tip**
> As a best practice, always provision a unique Client ID for every client application and instance combination, making sure to keep Production and non-Production IDs separate. This helps with managing security and access control and allows a given ID to be deactivated if it's compromised, without it impacting other integrations.

Open Commerce API (OCAPI)

The original REST API for the B2C Commerce product is called the **Open Commerce API**, or just **OCAPI**. OCAPI has robust support for both data management and shopper interaction; it's used to support thousands of mobile apps and off-platform headless experiences powered by B2C Commerce.

The following sections cover the fundamentals of OCAPI, including security and access control, sub-categories of APIs, authentication mechanisms, and the concepts of resources, documents, and hooks.

Access control

In addition to provisioning a Client ID in Account Manager, as described previously, OCAPI permissions must also be configured in each instance through Business Manager. Account Manager controls access at the level of the customer account overall, while Business Manager is specific to a given instance within that account (Staging, Production, Development, or Sandboxes).

Access to OCAPI is configured using a JSON document that specifies what resources and HTTP methods a particular Client ID is allowed to use, as well as what origins it's allowed to initiate requests from.

The following is an example of a simple OCAPI JSON configuration allowing access to search for products and authenticate as a customer:

```
{
    "_v": "21.3",
    "clients": [{
        "allowed_origins": ["https://www.mysite.com"],
        "client_id": "[your_own_client_id]",
        "resources": [{
            "resource_id": "/product_search",
            "methods": ["get"],
```

```
                "read_attributes": "(**)",
                "write_attributes": "(**)",
                "cache_time": 900
            },
            {
                "resource_id": "/customers/auth",
                "methods": ["post"],
                "read_attributes": "(**)",
                "write_attributes": "(**)"
            }
        ]
    }]
}
```

OCAPI API categories (Shop, Data, Metadata)

OCAPI is three distinct categories of API bundled together, each with its own slightly different feature set and authentication mechanisms:

- **Shop API**: All API resources required to emulate shopper behavior on the storefront
- **Data API**: All API resources required to emulate merchandiser behavior on the backend, perform administrative functions, or move data in and out of the system
- **Meta API**: An API describing the available OCAPI resources and their expected document formats (to support OCAPI consumer client discovery)

The Shop API and Data API are by far the most commonly used in integration scenarios because they're the only ones directly able to affect the target instance.

Authentication

The mechanism that's used to authenticate with OCAPI is different, depending on which of the three API categories you're going to be interacting with. To emulate shopper behavior, such as creating a mobile app where an individual customer can browse products and make purchases, you'll retrieve a **JSON Web Token (JWT)** using the /customers/auth resource. This can either be a guest token, equivalent to accessing storefront without logging in, or an authenticated user token, equivalent to logging in to a merchant's website.

With that JWT, it's possible to programmatically access any Shop API resource that your Client ID is enabled for.

Alternatively, to access the Shop API as a Business Manager user (employee of the merchant organization) and act on behalf of a customer, you can authenticate using **OAuth 2.0** using the `/dw/oauth2/access_token` resource with a mechanism called *Business Manager user grant*. This mechanism requires valid Business Manager user credentials, as well as a valid Client ID, but it supports more than the JWT-based authentication for the Shop API, such as applying price adjustments to the basket. This is the appropriate authentication mechanism to leverage when allowing CSRs to act on behalf of a customer from Service Cloud and adjust the B2C Commerce basket.

Finally, in situations where API interactions happen directly from server to server with no user involved (customer or agent), OCAPI supports OAuth 2.0 through a *client credentials grant*. A client credentials grant requires a Client ID and a **Client Secret** (also generated in Account Manager), which must be kept secure within the calling system. This type of authentication is appropriate for direct data synchronization between Service Cloud and B2C Commerce, where an agent is not using their credentials to initiate the session.

> **Further reading**
>
> For additional details on OCAPI, including authentication, see *Getting Started with OCAPI* in the B2C Commerce documentation here: `https://sforce.co/3fVF5gd`.

Resources and documents

OCAPI REST API endpoints are referred to as resources. Resources are also the level of granularity at which OCAPI permissions are specified via JSON, as described previously.

A full OCAPI URL to retrieve a product might look like this:

`https://www.test.com/s/mysite/dw/shop/v21_03/products/p123`

Breaking this URL down into its parts, the structure is as follows:

`https://{host_server}/s/{site_id}/dw/{api_type}/{api_version}/{resource}`

Let's look at these parts in more detail:

- `host_server`: The HTTP hostname of the target instance
- `site_id`: The ID of the site in the target instance
- `api_type`: Either shop or data

- **api_version**: Target version of OCAPI (for backward compatibility)
- **resource**: The target resource, which must be enabled for the client ID that was passed in the request header

The full set of supported Shop API and Data API resources is available in the OCAPI documentation linked previously.

When retrieving results from an OCAPI resource or using HTTP POST to push updates to a resource, the JSON or XML data that's exchanged is referred to as a document and follows a particular schema, which can be extended to support custom attributes as needed.

Examples of OCAPI documents include `ProductResult`, `CustomerRegistration`, `CouponItem`, and `ContentSearchResult`.

The following is an example `Customer` document response from a POST to `/customers/auth` to initiate a guest customer session:

```
{
    "_v": "20.10",
    "_type": "customer",
    "auth_type": "guest",
    "customer_id": "bd7GZS7Q9gkZav2uv39gVmbPTu",
    "preferred_locale": "en_US",
    "visit_id": "a5abcaf18b5c7980a70f4d4487"
}
```

Hooks

Aside from supporting more capabilities, the primary advantage that OCAPI holds over the newer Commerce APIs is the ability to implement custom functionality with **OCAPI hooks**. Hooks allow custom logic to be attached either before or after the platform provided implementation fires to trigger custom business logic or even call other APIs off platform.

OCAPI hooks would, for example, allow us to update the Service Cloud contact record when the Shop API is used to update a B2C Commerce customer record in the same way we would if the user logged in on the storefront and made an update through the **My Account** section. Considering where to integrate custom functionality like this is an important part of designing headless solutions.

Commerce APIs

The Commerce APIs are a newer set of REST APIs for B2C Commerce that are implemented on top of the MuleSoft platform with more of a microservice architecture. While OCAPI is intended to expose existing platform functionality via web services, the Commerce APIs are architecturally different and sometimes expose different capabilities, but ultimately resolve to the same core B2C Commerce dataset and commerce engine. You can safely mix and match OCAPI and Commerce APIs-based integrations alongside an SFRA storefront in whatever way makes sense for your business.

Because they are more modern and, in the case of the Shopper APIs, performance-focused, the Commerce APIs are primarily targeted at fully headless commerce use.

The documentation for the Commerce APIs is not stored in the B2C Commerce InfoCenter with the OCAPI and Script API documentation; it's in a separate Commerce Cloud Developer Center here: `https://bit.ly/3uIAqSO`.

Authentication

Like OCAPI, the Commerce APIs require a Client ID to be created through Account Manager to access the APIs. Unlike OCAPI, however, the permissions for that Client ID are provisioned with a simpler set of scopes in Account Manager when the Client ID is created. There is no JSON document specifying resources to allow or disallow for each instance.

When a client authenticates with the Commerce APIs, they also pass the OAuth scopes they will require for the session being initiated during the authentication process. These OAuth scopes must be included in the scopes allowed for the Client ID when it was created. The returned OAuth token or JWT is only allowed to access features that fall into these authorized scopes.

API categories (customer and backend)

The Commerce APIs are also divided into multiple categories: **Shopper** and **backend**. These are roughly analogous to the Shop and Data APIs used by OCAPI. The Shopper APIs are high performance and mimic storefront functionality, whereas the Data APIs require a higher level of security, have no performance guarantees, and can manipulate backend data outside of the context of an individual customer.

Commerce API families

Where OCAPI has resources (endpoints) and documents (datasets that are exchanged), the Commerce APIs have broader API families that map to the OAuth scopes that can be assigned to Client IDs. API families cover broad sets of functionality such as campaigns, catalogs, CDN zones, and products. API families that are part of the Shopper API category start with Shopper in the name (for example, Shopper Customers versus Customers).

Integration points

Commerce APIs do not have the equivalent of OCAPI hooks, which allow custom business logic to be injected into the execution flow; they expose B2C Commerce platform functionality only. This is one reason why a middleware layer that wraps the raw Commerce APIs is essential in any headless implementation relying on this set of APIs.

Since B2C Commerce doesn't expose any event-driven actions, such as the ability to run custom code or a process where a record changes, it is necessary to inject custom code into the triggering event.

The following table shows the integration points for data changes that require an update to be made to an outside system:

Interaction Via	Integration Point	Used For
On-platform web storefront	Custom code included storefront implementation	Any updates made by the customer through the B2C Commerce web experience such as updating their preferences in the My Account section of the commerce site.
OCAPI	OCAPI before / after hooks	External system integrating with B2C Commerce through OCAPI REST APIs to support things like mobile apps or API based data loading.
Commerce APIs	Custom middleware wrapping raw Commerce APIs	External system integrating with B2C Commerce through Commerce APIs to support things like mobile apps or API based data loading.
File Based Import / Export	Custom code included in job implementation	Typically, batch file-based integrations processing data import / export that need to be reflected in outside systems.
Business Manager	*None supported*	Manual changes to B2C Commerce data through Business Manager by an authorized user; there is not way to trigger custom code in this situation so real-time updates to outside systems are not possible.

Table 3.1 – B2C Commerce integration points

Like the Salesforce Platform, B2C Commerce is a multi-tenant environment and Salesforce enforces certain constraints to protect the system and help ensure performance. The next section covers these constraints, which are an important part of designing a system that can be integrated with B2C Commerce.

B2C Commerce quotas and governance

B2C Commerce, like the Salesforce Platform, is a shared architecture hosting multiple customers. Like the Salesforce Platform, B2C Commerce also has specific limitations enforced to prevent one customer from monopolizing shared resources or destabilizing the system. Understanding and respecting platform governance also helps ensure the overall solution is performant and scales well under load.

There are three levels of severity of B2C Commerce quotas:

- **Enforced**: The B2C Commerce platform will throw an exception if quotas of this type are violated, preventing the operation from completing and likely causing errors in the implementation. Violations of this severity must be addressed immediately.
- **Not Enforced**: These quotas trigger a warning and may be enforced in the future; they can have serious impacts on the performance and stability of the storefront but won't cause immediate failures. Violations of this severity should be addressed in normal maintenance cycles in a timely fashion.
- **Informational**: These quotas represent Salesforce's internal monitoring. They may be upgraded in the future, but no action is required at this time.

API and object quotas overview

The B2C Commerce quotas are divided into two broad categories: **API quotas** and **object quotas**. API quotas describe what you're allowed to do with the B2C Commerce APIs, and they're typically divided into storefront behavior and job behavior. APIs of this type are important for designing solutions that manipulate data or interact with outside systems, especially from the storefront.

As an example, we'll review the API quota known as `api.pipelet.RemoveCustomer`:

- **Storefront Limit**: Maximum of two customer deletions for a given storefront request (typically a page load)
- **Job Context Limit**: None

The second category of quotas is object quotas, which describes the limits on the numbers of certain objects, typically per B2C Commerce instance. For example, the `object.CustomerGroupImpl` quota limits the maximum number of Customer Groups on a given instance to 500. Since Customer Groups are the primary way B2C Commerce segments and targets customers on the storefront, this could be an important constraint if you're considering synchronizing customer segmentation from Marketing Cloud into B2C Commerce to drive experiences.

> **Further reading**
>
> The full details of the B2C Commerce API and object quotas are available here: `https://sforce.co/3mFvtHW`.

You can review the status of quota violations of your instance at any time by navigating to **Administration | Operations | Quota Status**.

Key solution design quotas

When designing solutions that incorporate the B2C Commerce product, there are a handful of quotas that come into play. All quotas should be respected, and you should review the statuses of your quotas on test instances before any new code changes are released, but during the solution design phase, the following should be at the top of your mind:

- `api.dw.object.CustomObjectMgr`: It is not possible to create or remove more than 10 instances of a Custom Object during any single storefront request.
- `api.dw.io.File`: It is not possible to create, zip, unzip, rename, or write to a local file from the storefront; this is only possible in backend jobs. Reading from files is allowed, with limits on volume.
- `api.dw.net`: It is not possible to access an FTP, SFTP, or WebDAV server from the storefront, only from jobs, and external web service calls are limited to a maximum of eight requests for every storefront request.
- `api.pipelet.ImportExport`: It is not possible to import or export data from the storefront, only from jobs.
- **Non-Replicable and Replicable Custom Objects**: A maximum of 400,000 Custom Object records of each type can be created across all sites in an instance.

> **Tip**
>
> The 400,000 Custom Object record quota applies to the total number of records, not to the number of Custom Object definitions.

In the next two sections of this chapter, we'll cover options for extending or supplementing the B2C Commerce product using third-party solutions from the B2C Commerce Marketplace or other Salesforce products in the Commerce Cloud family.

B2C Commerce Marketplace

Whereas the Salesforce Platform has AppExchange, B2C Commerce has the **Commerce Cloud Partner Marketplace**. B2C Commerce **Independent Software Vendor (ISV)** partners create extensions to the core B2C Commerce product, often to integrate with their own cloud-hosted solution. These ISV partners offer services covering everything from tax and payments to loyalty, to content management, and more. All ISV partners wishing to list a solution in the B2C Commerce Partner Marketplace must have their solution, called a **B2C Commerce cartridge**, certified by Salesforce. B2C Commerce cartridges are also frequently called **LINK cartridges**, a reference to older terminology.

There are a few important differences between AppExchange solutions and B2C Commerce cartridges. First, B2C Commerce cartridges are always distributed as source code with documentation. They must be integrated into the customer's B2C Commerce solution code base by following the documentation provided by the vendor. There is no click and deploy option available for B2C Commerce. Since B2C Commerce cartridges are deployed as source code, there is also no option to automatically update cartridges in the future. They must be manually updated by the customer when a new version is desired.

Finally, in large part because of the limitations listed previously, B2C Commerce cartridges are never sold or licensed on their own; they're always distributed free of charge. This means that nearly all B2C Commerce cartridges in the marketplace serve to connect your B2C Commerce implementation to an external SaaS solution, which is a paid service. For example, a popular **payment gateway** such as Cybersource invests in creating a B2C Commerce cartridge and getting it certified and listed in the marketplace – not to sell the cartridge itself, but to make it easier for B2C Commerce customers to integrate their (paid) tax service into their solution.

> **Further reading**
>
> The full B2C Commerce Marketplace can be found here: `https://sforce.co/3s4ZC4o`.

In cases where B2C Commerce alone does not meet the needs of an organization, you, as a B2C solution architect, should be familiar with the other products in the Commerce Cloud family.

Commerce Cloud product family

Aside from B2C Commerce and the related marketplace, there are several other products in the **Salesforce Commerce Cloud family** that can play a useful role in a B2C Commerce solution, and that you should evaluate as a B2C solution architect. These complementary products can fill gaps that would otherwise require a third party or custom development.

Importantly, while the following products are part of the Commerce Cloud family, they are licensed separately and built on separate technology, so they should be evaluated like separate product purchases that still need to be integrated into the overall solution. Where Salesforce has provided productized integrations to streamline this work, I will mention this accordingly.

Order Management

Salesforce **Order Management** takes over where B2C Commerce ends, supporting post-purchase order handling requirements. B2C Commerce is a transaction processor, but it does not handle things such as order allocation and fulfillment, which are the province of Order Management.

Order Management supports order allocation across multiple distribution centers or stores based on configurable rules such as inventory availability or proximity to the shipping destination. Orders can be fed into Order Management either from B2C Commerce, B2B Commerce, or from other sources via API integrations.

Salesforce Order Management also works closely with Salesforce Service Cloud to allow CSRs direct access to orders placed on the storefront for cancellation, modification, returns, and exchanges. Order allocation rules, escalations, and exception handling are modeled in Order Management primarily with flows, a declarative automation technology that we covered in detail in *Chapter 1, Demystifying Salesforce, Customer 360, and Digital 360*.

Since Salesforce Order Management is built on the Salesforce Platform, it supports all the same core capabilities and integration points that the platform supports. In addition, there is a productized integration between B2C Commerce and Salesforce Order Management that allows customers who leverage both products to integrate them with configuration rather than code. Orders taken in B2C Commerce are automatically pushed to Order Management for downstream processing in near-real time, without the need for a feed or API-based integration. The primary challenge of integrating these two products is in ensuring that all custom attributes that are attached to order objects in B2C Commerce are properly mapped to Order Management Object Custom Attributes.

> **Further reading**
> You can learn more about Order Management here: `https://sforce.co/3dUR2jE`.

Omni-Channel Inventory

Omni-Channel Inventory is a Salesforce product offering that provides a robust, real-time inventory tracking and management solution that's accessible natively to both B2C Commerce and Order Management, within the Salesforce Platform. Omni-Channel Inventory administration, such as creating inventory locations and managing stock reserve levels, is performed using the Omni-Channel Inventory Console within the Salesforce Platform. You can retrieve, reserve, and update the available inventory using Omni-Channel Inventory Service endpoints, which are part of the Commerce APIs. Omni-Channel Inventory Locations and Location Groups can be mapped directly to B2C Commerce inventory lists with configuration in Business Manager, not custom code.

> **Further reading**
> You can learn more about Omni-Channel Inventory here: `https://sforce.co/2Qj5BW2`.

B2B Commerce

While this book focuses on the B2C solution architecture and designing systems of software that support B2C use cases, it's still important to know that Salesforce has a dedicated product within the larger Commerce cloud family for **Business-to-Business** (**B2B**) Commerce. The **B2B Commerce** product is built on the Salesforce Platform, like Order Management and Service Cloud, and has no productized integration with the B2C Commerce product.

> **Important note**
> Customers who choose to leverage both B2C Commerce and B2B Commerce must implement the two products separately, and then manually integrate them using the Salesforce Platform and B2C Commerce REST APIs.

B2B Commerce is primarily differentiated by a more robust capability to support tiered account structures and delegated purchasing authority within a customer organization, which are not required in B2C use cases. The B2B Commerce product also supports more flexible pricing and quoting models and bulk purchasing capabilities.

On the other hand, the B2C Commerce product has a much more flexible user experience layer and more robust support for campaigns and promotions. The B2C Commerce product is also designed to handle much higher order volumes than the B2B Commerce product.

> **Further reading**
>
> You can learn more about B2B Commerce here: `https://sforce.co/3ddUHtO`.

> **Tip**
>
> The B2B Commerce documentation is divided into two sections: *B2B Commerce for Visualforce* (formerly known as **CloudCraze**) and *Commerce on Lightning Experience*. The Lightning Experience version is the latest and the only version used for new implementations moving forward.

Loyalty Management

Salesforce **Loyalty Management** provides a robust and customizable set of features to support B2B and B2C loyalty programs on top of the Salesforce Platform. Loyalty Management adds many new object definitions and capabilities that integrate natively with **Customer 360 audiences** and Marketing Cloud, using Marketing Cloud Connect. Because B2B Commerce is also built on the Salesforce Platform, it can share most of the same data elements that Loyalty Management uses.

Integrating B2C Commerce with Loyalty Management requires some custom development currently. Loyalty Management exposes new REST API resources within the Salesforce Platform REST API to support member benefits administration and voucher redemption within a loyalty context.

> **Further reading**
>
> You can learn more about Loyalty Management here: `https://sforce.co/2OJJKqh`.

Commerce Payments

Commerce Payments is a bit different from the other products mentioned here because it's not a separate Salesforce product to be purchased but a direct integration to the Stripe platform as a payment provider. This productized integration allows you to connect with an existing Stripe account or create a new Stripe account directly from Business Manager, within B2C Commerce.

Stripe is a global payment processing platform that supports a robust feature set, including deffered payments, credit cards, and regional payment methods. However, only credit card processing is supported by the B2C Commerce integration natively.

Once a Stripe account has been created, it is still managed through the Stripe dashboard as normal. Since the B2C Commerce storefront is entirely managed through custom code, a new code component is available from Salesforce's GitHub that customers can add to their storefront code base to expose Commerce Payment's functionality.

This is a good choice for customers who are already using Stripe or who do not have a preferred payment partner, and who are looking for the easiest available payment integration for B2C Commerce.

> **Further reading**
>
> You can learn more about Commerce Payments here: `https://sforce.co/3wUyvNc`.

Summary

After reading this chapter, you should be well-equipped to discuss the role of B2C Commerce in a larger solution, including its capabilities, integration points, and possible complementary products in the Commerce Cloud family.

You should be able to work with your client or your organization to evaluate options for building a user experience on the B2C Commerce platform using SFRA or mixing-and-matching headless experiences that are delivered with the B2C Commerce REST API options. You should also have a basic understanding of what a merchant can manage in B2C Commerce as it relates to other products in the solution.

When designing solutions that leverage customization built on B2C Commerce, you should have an understanding of the possible data model extension points and the limitations of Custom Objects. You should also be familiar with the two REST API integration options, OCAPI and Commerce APIs, as well as the design considerations and authentication mechanisms for each.

Finally, you should be familiar with other products in the Salesforce Commerce Cloud family or third-party integrations available through the Commerce Marketplace so that you can leverage the right tool for the situation at hand.

In *Chapter 4, Engaging Customers with Marketing Cloud*, we'll cover the third and final core product in the B2C solution space in Marketing Cloud.

Questions

1. Packt Gear wants to get their new commerce experience up and running as quickly as possible, and it's important that it has a mobile-optimized, high-performance experience. Should they leverage SFRA, PWA Kit and Managed Runtime, or a custom headless experience for their site build?

2. One of the requirements for your client's new implementation is for customer service representatives to be able to access orders and perform refunds, returns, or adjustments on behalf of customers. What products would you recommend to meet this use case?

3. Your client's service agents are logging in to Business Manager using Salesforce Identity through Account Manager and are making changes to content because some messaging references an out-of-date promotion, but every morning the old messaging is back! What is the most likely issue here?

4. When a customer makes a change to their profile information in B2C Commerce, you want to push those changes to the Contact record in Service Cloud. It's important that this code fire for both the storefront and for updates made through the mobile app, which uses Commerce APIs. Where will a developer need to implement these code changes?

5. You have a use case that allows customers to fill out a form on the B2C Commerce storefront to initiate a **Return Merchandise Authorization** (**RMA**) process. This data needs to be pushed to a custom in-house web service that is notoriously unreliable. The longest it would be unavailable for is a few minutes, but this happens frequently. How could you ensure that customers are always able to submit this form and the results reliably make it to the service, even if it's not in real time?

6. Which API options would you consider for implementing an in-store kiosk experience that requires access to the same B2C Commerce data that an anonymous user browsing the storefront would see?

7. To keep B2C Commerce customer data in sync with the latest loyalty data, including in-store purchases, your client would like to send a nightly feed with each customer's current computed tier from their internal systems. What are the options for retrieving files with B2C Commerce and which instance should this feed be sent to?

8. Your client needs a way to retrieve the most current product data available from B2C Commerce, including a computed value for the available ship date that is based on the inventory's availability and other factors within B2C Commerce. This additional attribute should be added to the API response before it is sent back to the client application, and your client is not leveraging any middleware solution at this time. Which B2C Commerce REST API option is appropriate here?

4
Engaging Customers with Marketing Cloud

Salesforce Marketing Cloud, along with Service Cloud and Commerce Cloud, forms the foundation of a B2C solution. Marketing Cloud adds the ability to better understand and communicate with your customer through a variety of channels, including email, social, SMS, and push notifications.

In this chapter, we'll review the components of the Marketing Cloud product and how they work together. We'll then focus on the core capabilities Marketing Cloud brings to a Customer 360 solution, the Marketing Cloud data model, and review the integration options available. Finally, we'll conclude with a review of Marketing Cloud solution design considerations.

Building upon our Packt Gear example, we'll look at how Marketing Cloud can allow Packt Gear to build customer journeys that align with common business scenarios, re-targeting customers who build a shopping cart but don't proceed through checkout (abandoned cart).

In this chapter, we're going to cover the following topics:

- The Marketing Cloud component
- Marketing Cloud capabilities
- The Marketing Cloud data model
- Marketing Cloud APIs and integrations
- Marketing Cloud design considerations

By the end of this chapter, you'll understand the various component products of the Marketing Cloud ecosystem and their roles in a B2C solution architecture. You'll also be able to incorporate the Marketing Cloud data model into a larger B2C solution and integrate with Marketing Cloud using file transfer and API options, all while keeping Marketing Cloud design constraints for a scalable solution in mind.

The Marketing Cloud component

Marketing Cloud is composed of several different products built on a variety of technologies. Many of the core messaging and journey-building components reside on the core Marketing Cloud platform, but newer products that have been added to the portfolio such as **Datorama**, **Salesforce CDP**, and **Interaction Studio** are entirely separate. This hybrid approach to technology means that fully leveraging Marketing Cloud and understanding its role in a B2C solution means understanding the Salesforce Platform, as well as the various technologies within the Marketing Cloud ecosystem.

> Tip
>
> The core Marketing Cloud platform refers to the product formerly known as **ExactTarget**, acquired by Salesforce in 2013 and rebranded as **Marketing Cloud**. This core platform includes contact management, email messaging, social communication, journey orchestration, and the flexible Data Extension capability. This is the product that's most often referred to in a B2C solution context, and is the product that's integrated with the Salesforce Platform using *Marketing Cloud Connect*. In the context of this book, Marketing Cloud refers to that core messaging and journeys solution, unless otherwise specified.

Marketing Cloud, unlike B2C Commerce and the Salesforce Platform, does not have separate instances that are used for development and testing. There is only one Marketing Cloud instance per client, known as Production, and data is organized within that instance using **business units (BUs)**. BUs allow some data segregation within a Marketing Cloud instance but less than you'd achieve with separate Salesforce orgs or B2C Commerce realms. We'll cover Marketing Cloud BUs in more detail in the *Marketing Cloud data model* section, later in this chapter.

Unfortunately, it is also not generally possible to get access to a real Marketing Cloud instance to use for training purposes, unless you have access to one through a partnership agreement or are a current Salesforce Marketing Cloud customer.

The following diagram shows the Marketing Cloud component products and the underlying platform technology that supports them:

```
┌─────────────────────────┐      ┌─────────────────────────┐   ┌─────────────────┐
│   Salesforce Platform   │      │ Marketing Cloud Platform│   │   Data Studio   │
│  ┌───────────────────┐  │                                    └─────────────────┘
│  │  Salesforce CDP   │  │  Marketing    ┌───────────────┐    ┌─────────────────┐
│  └───────────────────┘  │    Cloud      │Journey Builder│    │    Datorama     │
│                         │   Connect     └───────────────┘    └─────────────────┘
│  ┌───────────────────┐  │   <───>       ┌───────────────┐    ┌─────────────────┐
│  │  Pardot Lightning │  │               │ Email Studio  │    │   Interaction   │
│  └───────────────────┘  │               └───────────────┘    │     Studio      │
│                         │               ┌───────────────┐    └─────────────────┘
│                         │               │ Mobile Studio │    ┌─────────────────┐
│                         │               └───────────────┘    │   Advertising   │
│                         │               ┌───────────────┐    │     Studio      │
│                         │               │Automation Stud│    └─────────────────┘
│                         │               └───────────────┘    ┌─────────────────┐
│                         │               ┌───────────────┐    │  Social Studio  │
│                         │               │Content Builder│    └─────────────────┘
│                         │               └───────────────┘
│                         │               ┌───────────────┐
│                         │               │    GA 360     │
│                         │               └───────────────┘
└─────────────────────────┘      └─────────────────────────┘
```

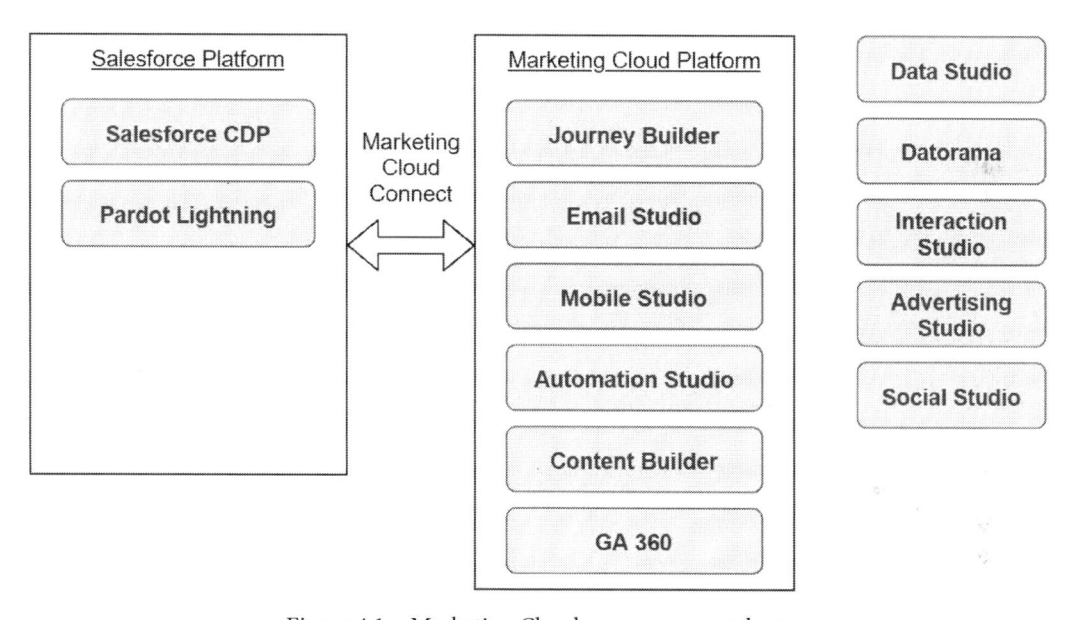

Figure 4.1 – Marketing Cloud component products

The following sections will outline the individual components of Marketing Cloud and how they work together to meet customer needs. As the preceding diagram shows, many of the components of Marketing Cloud are on the core Marketing Cloud platform, some are built on the Salesforce Platform, and others are completely separate technology under the general umbrella of Marketing Cloud.

When designing solutions that incorporate Marketing Cloud, it's also important to understand that the available components are determined by the Marketing Cloud edition you license, with several advanced features being additional cost options.

The available Marketing Cloud editions are **Basic**, **Pro**, **Corporate**, and **Enterprise**. Only **Pro** and above support API calls as part of the base package, which means **Basic** is not an appropriate choice for integrated multi-cloud scenarios.

> **Further reading**
> Detailed information about Marketing Cloud capabilities by edition is available here: `https://sforce.co/32k81qg`.

Content Builder

To deliver a consistent branded experience to customers, your content must be consistent. **Content Builder** is the component of Marketing Cloud that's focused on creating reusable content assets from simple imagery to HTML blocks, to reusable headers and footers. These content blocks can be used directly in SFMC messages, including Email Studio, or accessed from other systems.

In a fully integrated B2C solution, a more fully featured **Content Management System (CMS)** such as Salesforce CMS could be used to push content into Marketing Cloud, as well as B2C Commerce and Experience Cloud. It is possible, but not common, to leverage content created in Marketing Cloud's Content Builder in other systems, such as B2C Commerce.

> **Important note**
> Content Builder is included in all Marketing Cloud editions and is part of the core Marketing Cloud platform.

Datorama

Datorama is a robust data analytics, visualization, and reporting engine designed to create a cohesive view and understanding of your marketing data from multiple sources. Datorama can be incorporated into a solution to enhance and augment single-channel analytics or improve upon manually generated reports and additional insights.

> **Important note**
> Datorama is a separately purchased product and is not included with any Marketing Cloud editions.

Google Analytics 360 connector

The **Google Analytics 360** connector integrates Marketing Cloud with Google's analytics and marketing tools, including Google Analytics site tagging. This connection allows customer behavior across content, website, and email touchpoints to be understood together.

This connection is bi-directional, allowing insights into Marketing Cloud data to be leveraged within Google Marketing Platform, as well as allowing insights from Google Analytics to be leveraged in Marketing Cloud journeys.

> **Important note**
>
> Google Analytics 360 integration and Google Marketing Platform are separately purchased products that are not included with any Marketing Cloud edition. If purchased, Google Analytics 360 integration works with the core Marketing Cloud platform.

Journey Builder

Journey Builder is a declarative visual solution for orchestrating customer interactions across both time and devices. A journey could begin when a customer makes a purchase, waits until an event indicates that the product has been shipped, and sends an email soliciting feedback a week later. Journeys created in Journey Builder can branch based on a variety of conditions. For example, a post-purchase journey might suppress feedback requests if a customer service case was opened by the user after the purchase.

Journey Builder leverages data from various other Marketing Cloud component products to orchestrate the customer touchpoints that are delivered through tools such as Email Studio or Mobile Studio.

> **Important note**
>
> Journey Builder is included in the Marketing Cloud Corporate and Enterprise editions only. It is available at an extra cost as an addition to the Professional edition but is not available with Basic. If available, Journey Builder is part of the core Marketing Cloud platform.

Automation Studio

Automation Studio is conceptually similar to Journey Builder and can be found in the **Journey Builder** section of the Marketing Cloud navigation. Where Journey Builder supports building a planned sequence of steps for customers to go through with automated touchpoints along the way based on actions and decisions, Automation Studio creates automated workflows that execute within Marketing Cloud.

Automation Studio automations are initiated either based on a defined schedule or when a file is received in Marketing Cloud's integrated **SSH File Transfer Protocol** (**SFTP**) server. From there, a sequence of steps, including extracting data, importing files, creating or refreshing groups, executing SQL queries, sending notifications, and more, can be configured.

> **Tip**
> Automations created with Automation Studio are a common means of supporting feed file-based integrations to and from Marketing Cloud via SFTP.

> **Important note**
> Automation Studio is part of the core Marketing Cloud platform.

Interaction Studio

Where Journey Builder is a tool for orchestrating customer interactions over time based on conditions, **Interaction Studio** is a tool for understanding and adapting their experiences across touchpoints. Interaction Studio allows marketers to visualize and manage customer experiences in real time based on customer behavioral data, such as the products that customers engaged with on site and the interactions that they've had with your call center.

Journey Builder can do things such as send an email or trigger an SMS message based on certain conditions, whereas Interaction Studio can be used to build a tailored site experience on B2C Commerce based on the path a customer took to get there and what they might be most interested in seeing.

> **Important note**
> Interaction Studio is a separately purchased product and is not included with any Marketing Cloud edition.

Email Studio

With **Email Studio**, Marketing Cloud can send tailored marketing emails to subscribers or unique transactional emails to customers. Email Studio allows marketers to create consistent brand experiences with consistent email templates, personalized content pulled from subscriber data, and advanced email capabilities such as forms that support graceful degradation for incompatible clients.

Email Studio supports both drag-and-drop visual editing and HTML-based email creation, as well as the Marketing Cloud proprietary scripting language, **AMPscript**, which can be used within email templates to generate content dynamically.

Beyond individual emails, Email Studio can also be used for planning, timing, and targeting email campaigns, as well as measuring impact for both positive measures (open rate and click rate) and negative measures (unsubscribes, soft-, and hard-bounce rates).

> **Important note**
> Email Studio is included with all Marketing Cloud editions and is part of the core Marketing Cloud platform.

Mobile Studio

Mobile Studio is a partner product to Email Studio that supports functionality targeted at SMS, push notifications, and social messaging on mobile devices. Careful use of mobile interactions for critical or timely communications can augment a marketer's email campaign strategy and advertising campaign strategy. Mobile Studio includes **MobileConnect** (for SMS and MMS communications), **MobilePush** (for native mobile app push notification support), and **GroupConnect** (for chat app messaging).

Using a Journey Builder, marketers could escalate to an SMS reminder if a customer who has opted in to such communications does not respond to an email regarding an open service case within a given time.

> **Important note**
> Mobile Studio is included in Corporate and Enterprise editions of Marketing Cloud only. If available, it is part of the core Marketing Cloud platform.

Advertising Studio

Advertising Studio powers advertising campaigns across digital channels, including Google, Facebook, LinkedIn, Twitter, and Pinterest. Advertising Studio can ingest data from journeys or Marketing Cloud data extensions.

As an example, leveraging Advertising Studio to target ads at customers who have *emotionally unsubscribed* (stopped opening) emails sent using Email Studio is an effective way to reengage customers by meeting them where they are. On the other hand, using B2C Commerce data to suppress advertising for specific products to customers who have already purchased them helps marketers make better use of their advertising budgets.

> **Important note**
> Advertising Studio is a separately purchased product not available with any Marketing Cloud edition.

Social Studio

With **Social Studio**, marketers can more effectively integrate social channels and understand brand sentiment through customer conversations and online interactions. Social Studio is a tool for engaging with customers, either directly or using AI-powered automation, in a consistent way across marketing and service touchpoints.

In an integrated B2C solution, Social Studio would be the tool that allows service and marketing teams to proactively resolve customer concerns directly in social conversations, before they escalate to negative reviews or cases.

> **Important note**
> Social Studio is a separately purchased product not included in any Marketing Cloud edition.

Salesforce CDP

Salesforce CDP, formerly known as **Customer 360 Audiences (C360 Audiences)**, supports ingesting customer data from all of your sources and mapping to a common **Cloud Information Model (CIM)**. This allows data from disparate systems such as CRM data, marketing data, third-party data, commerce data, loyalty data, and more to be reconciled to a single representation of an individual, thus creating a more complete understanding.

Salesforce CDP uses a declarative data mapping methodology with AI-driven attribute mapping recommendations to allow source data to be mapped into the CIM easily and consistently. Once data is ingested, deduplicated, and represented in a common format, Salesforce CDP allows the marketer to build sophisticated audience models representing various segments of their customer base, such as men over 40 in urban areas, likely new parents, price-sensitive fashion shoppers, and so on. These audiences can be simulated with the known dataset to determine the reach and depth before being piped out to marketing content delivery and advertising systems, or used natively in other Marketing Cloud products.

By leveraging audiences built on Salesforce CDP, marketers can create much more sophisticated journeys with Journey Builder or tailor experiences with Interaction Studio.

> **Important note**
> Salesforce CDP is not included in any Marketing Cloud edition. Salesforce CDP is also available in three editions: Corporate, Enterprise, and Enterprise Plus.

Pardot

The latest version of **Pardot** is also built on the Salesforce Platform, not the core Marketing Cloud platform, so it can take advantage of the Salesforce Platform CRM functionality we outlined in *Chapter 1, Demystifying Salesforce, Customer 360, and Digital 360*.

Pardot is a marketing automation engine designed to help marketers build leads and nurture relationships in the B2B space. While Pardot is a powerful tool for B2B marketing, it is unlikely to play a role in a B2C solution.

> **Important note**
> Pardot is a separately purchased product not available with any Marketing Cloud edition.

At this point, you should understand the various components and products in the Marketing Cloud ecosystem, including those that are built on the core Marketing Cloud platform that support messaging and journey orchestration. For the rest of this chapter, we will focus on the core Marketing Cloud messaging and journey products as part of a B2C solution.

In the next section, we'll cover the core capabilities these Marketing Cloud components bring to a B2C solution.

Marketing Cloud capabilities

Understanding the capabilities of Marketing Cloud, especially as it relates to a B2C solution, requires taking a step back and evaluating it more holistically than the product-by-product review we did in the previous section. Fortunately, the capabilities required by most direct-to-consumer sellers in the retail or consumer goods space are available with a **Marketing Cloud Corporate** or **Enterprise edition** license, which we'll assume as the baseline for this discussion.

Salesforce CDP is also worth evaluating, for an additional cost, if robust audience segmentation and a 360 view of the customer is required in the marketing space. Other products should be evaluated on an as-needed basis.

For Packt Gear, a careful review of the capabilities of each Marketing Cloud product leads you to believe that a **Marketing Cloud Corporate** edition license will be the right starting point. This provides access to helpful tools such as Journey Builder, mobile and in-app messaging, push notifications, rich messaging, and Einstein AI-powered recommendations for the web and copywriting. Additional products can be added as needed once you've established the foundation of your B2C solution.

Email management

By far the most common use of Marketing Cloud in a B2C solution is to build, send, and track emails. This includes both marketing emails, which require consent and are covered by legislation such as **CAN-SPAM**, and transactional emails, which are sent in response to a customer action and do not require additional consent.

In Marketing Cloud, reusable content is created with Content Builder and structured into emails using **Email Studio**, which allows the specific content to be personalized using *AMPscript* or declarative rules based on the recipient or send conditions (such as products included). Journey Builder will most often be used to orchestrate email sends and other interactions across channels.

For transactional emails, such as sending an order confirmation email after a storefront purchase, the client system can trigger them directly using **Marketing Cloud APIs**.

While it is possible to send a transactional email from B2C Commerce when an order has been placed, or directly from Service Cloud in response to an open case, there are two primary advantages to leveraging Marketing Cloud for all email communication with customers:

- Leveraging Marketing Cloud for email engagement maintains brand consistency through the reuse of assets and templates.
- Communicating through Marketing Cloud for various touchpoints facilitates more robust journeys that consider communications outside of the marketing workstream.

To leverage email-based communications at the right time based on customer behavior, we can leverage Marketing Cloud Journey Builder for journey orchestration.

Journey orchestration

When leveraging data and events from B2C Commerce, Service Cloud, and other systems, Marketing Cloud will be responsible for understanding customer behavior and guiding the customer through carefully orchestrated communications and touchpoints to nurture the relationship. Leveraging Journey Builder to send emails, SMS messages, and push notifications allows for a more robust experience than simply firing off single messages in isolation.

A marketer building a journey around post-purchase reviews can gently remind customers to submit a review through different channels at different times with suppression based on service channels. An abandoned cart journey can make decisions based on user segmentation data to incentivize with a coupon, for price-conscious customers, or offer expedited shipping for those judged to be more impulse-driven.

Customers can be placed into journeys that have been created with Journey Builder in a variety of ways:

- **Data Extension**: This is Marketing's Cloud extensible data store. It will be covered in the *Marketing Cloud data model* section, later in this chapter.
- **API Event**: An event that's triggered by other code or an external system REST API call.
- **CloudPages**: Marketing Cloud's lightweight web page, primarily used to capture subscriber information.
- **Salesforce Data**: Data that's stored or changed in the Salesforce Platform, including Service Cloud data.
- **Audience Studio**: Enter a journey based on an audience that's been created with Audience Studio. Once a customer enters a journey, marketers can use components such as message activities (email, SMS, and push notifications), advertising activities, flow control activities (split, join, and wait), customer updates, and Sales and Service Cloud activities (update CRM data).

Cloud Pages

Cloud Pages, supported in **Marketing Cloud Professional** edition and above, allows marketers to create public-facing landing pages using the same Content Builder components used to create emails and templates. These pages can capture subscriber information and serve as an easy marketing vehicle.

For Packt Gear, you've learned that a European expansion is on the 3-year plan. The brand has a small but loyal following among outdoor enthusiasts in Europe who are eager to know when they'll be able to buy their favorite brand without crossing the ocean. One option would be to stand up an additional site on B2C Commerce to serve as a landing page and capture interest, but it's comparatively expensive and you don't need commerce at this stage. Instead, you can create a **cloud page** through **Marketing Cloud** that provides the latest information on the planned expansion and allows interested customers to sign up for updates!

Programmatic customization

Marketing Cloud supports programmatic customization using two scripting languages: **AMPscript** and **server-side JavaScript** (**SSJS**). Both are primarily focused on personalizing content. Both execute within Marketing Cloud at the time that a message is sent or a page is rendered to ensure the result is unique to the recipient. Both are high-performance languages that are suitable for large-scale communications.

AMPscript is a comparatively simple language with a shallower learning curve that is ideally suited for injecting custom content or handling simple conditions inline. It's used in emails, CloudPages, SMS messages, and push notifications.

SSJS is based on the well-known JavaScript language, which is used in nearly all web development scenarios. Increasingly, libraries such as Node.js are using JavaScript for server-side development instead of client (browser) execution, and this is also the use case for SSJS. Since SSJS supports most JavaScript capabilities, it's a robust programming language that can handle more complex tasks requiring data structures, branching conditions, loops, and libraries.

Leverage SSJS for complex tasks that require more capabilities than AMPscript provides.

Finally, Marketing Cloud also supports the **Guide Template Language** (**GTL**), or simply **Guide** for short. GTL is a templating language based on the Handlebars and Mustache templating languages with additional functionality specific to Marketing Cloud, such as access to Data Extensions and contact attributes to personalize messages.

Whereas AMPscript and SSJS are used to inject logic into HTML or SMS messages, GTL is an alternative structure that builds personalized content into the message format directly. It's not commonly used but may be encountered in some implementations.

What underlies all the capabilities of Marketing Cloud is its data model, which will be covered in the next section.

Marketing Cloud data model

Marketing Cloud supports two methods for storing customer-specific data: **lists** and **Data Extensions**. Within a given Marketing Cloud instance, data access and permissions can also be sub-divided into **BUs** to reflect separate brands, geographies, or corporate entities that should not have access to shared data. BUs are only included in Marketing Cloud Enterprise edition, though they can be purchased for an extra cost in other editions.

In this section, we will cover the Marketing Cloud concepts of lists, Data Extensions, data relationships, BUs, suppression, and segmentation. These concepts together form the basis of the Marketing Cloud data model.

Lists

A **list** is the simpler of the two and is used exclusively to store collections of subscribers to target communications. Within Marketing Cloud, you can create as many lists as you need within a Marketing Cloud instance and can include subscriber attributes such as postal code, favorite color, and last purchase date. It is not possible to store data in lists without it being tied to a specific subscriber, however. In addition, lists have a maximum capacity of 500,000 entries each.

Lists generally do not import or process as quickly as Data Extensions, and they do not support external access with REST APIs, nor do they support Triggered Sends, making them of limited use in integrated B2C solutions.

One special list in Marketing Cloud is the **All Subscribers** list, which is the master list of subscribers associated with a given Marketing Cloud instance. Any subscriber that's added to any list is automatically also added to the **All Subscribers** list. In addition, any subscriber that is contacted from a sendable Data Extension is also automatically added to the **All Subscribers** list when the first communication is sent. The **All Subscribers** list is used to track consent management centrally for subscribers.

Data Extensions

A **Data Extension** is conceptually similar to a database table. It's the Marketing Cloud equivalent of a custom object in the Salesforce Platform or B2C Commerce. Data Extensions support more than 500,000 entries per Data Extension and can store arbitrary structured data, such as purchase history, product catalogs, and service case data. Data Extensions are faster to import and support API access, as well as Triggered Sends.

While a Data Extension may sound superior, this added power comes with additional complexity. To create a new Data Extension, you must fully describe the data model, including each field and its data type, before the new Data Extension can be used. Data Extension fields can be any of the following data types: **Text**, **Number**, **Date**, **Boolean**, **EmailAddress**, **Phone**, or **Decimal**.

You must also indicate whether you want the new Data Extension to be sendable. Only a Data Extension that is marked as sendable can have messages sent to it with tools such as Email Studio. It is also not possible to manually add records to a Data Extension like you can with a list; we'll cover the options for importing data into a Data Extension in the next section.

Since a Data Extension can be used to store any data, not strictly subscriber data, it is necessary to link a sendable Data Extension to the Email Studio **All Subscribers** list by specifying a field in the Data Extension that relates to a primary key on the **All Subscribers** list (often, this will be **Email Address** or **Contact ID**). This allows for common consent management related to that subscriber across lists and Data Extensions. If a subscriber opts out of communications, they are removed from all the lists and sendable Data Extensions until they explicitly opt in again.

> **Important note**
> Using an email address as the primary key in the **All Subscribers** list is not recommended and can cause extensive rework to support integration to the Salesforce Platform. See *Chapter 8, Creating a 360° View of the Customer*, for additional details.

Data Designer

Data Designer is a tool in Contact Builder that's used to review and define data relationships for contacts within your Marketing Cloud instance. With Data Designer, you can define a link between a contact and any data extension by defining both the related attribute and the cardinality of the relationship. Essentially, you're defining a primary and foreign key relationship.

Data Designer relationships can be one-to-one, population, one-to-many, or many-to-many. One-to-one relationships can be used to link a Marketing Cloud contact record to supplementary information regarding the contact that was pulled from another system, such as a profile from a loyalty system, where there would only be exactly one entry for that contact.

An example of a data relationship might be relating a customer to their preferred store based on a **Store ID** field, which can be found in both the Customers and the Stores Data Extensions; the following diagram illustrates this relationship:

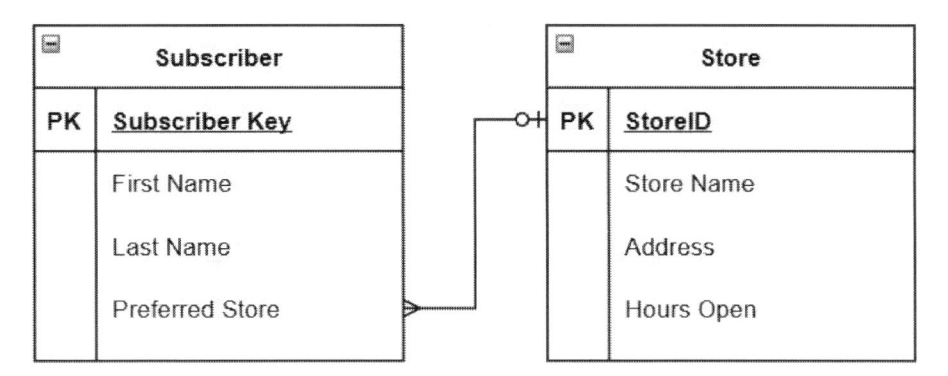

Figure 4.2 – Marketing Cloud data relationship

In the preceding diagram, the **Subscriber** record has a reference to a record in the **Store** Data Extension, which contains details about the preferred store. A **subscriber** can have, at most, one **preferred store**, while zero or many **subscribers** could have the same **preferred store**. This is an example of a one-to-many relationship.

Data Designer also provides one place to review all data related to a single contact, including linked data from lists and Data Extensions.

Business Units

Business Units are hierarchical structures that are used to align data access within Marketing Cloud to an organization's needs. Users are assigned to a Business Unit and can only access data associated with that Business Unit. The exception to this Business Unit partitioning is the **All Subscribers** list, which is always accessible to all Business Units, regardless of how the instance is configured. Content and subscribers can be shared between Business Units by placing them in a shared items folder.

Separate Business Units can also be leveraged to segregate test data for use with lower environments (such as B2C Commerce staging or a Service Cloud sandbox) from production data used with live client environments (B2C Commerce or Service Cloud production). To preserve this segregation in an integrated B2C solution where Marketing Cloud Connect is used to synchronize Salesforce Platform contact data into Marketing Cloud, contacts in the Salesforce Platform also need to be segregated; otherwise, their consent status will be tracked centrally for all.

As you continue to think about the needs of Packt Gear, you realize that they probably don't need separate Business Units at this phase. We'll examine some of the complexities and considerations we must make when supporting multiple Business Units in *Chapter 10, Enterprise Integration Strategies*.

Suppression

In Marketing Cloud, there are a few different ways to help ensure that only valid contacts who have opted in receive your messages. We will have a look at them in the following subsections.

Suppression lists

Suppression lists are used with guided, user-initiated, and triggered email sends. A suppression list is a list of subscribers that you don't want to receive communications from. By adding an email address to a suppression list, that email address will not receive any communications from your account. This is typically done to block addresses with a history of spam complaints or known fraud or problem addresses.

Publication lists

Publication lists are complementary to suppression lists and are used when sending email or SMS messages to a sendable data extension. Publication lists are channel-specific and support granular opt-out capabilities. If a customer receives a communication from a category of communications associated with a publication list, they have the option of unsubscribing from just that publication list rather than from all communications.

Exclusion lists

Exclusion lists are the final category of suppression. Exclusion lists are valid subscribers who have opted into communication but who you don't want to include in a message. An example of this category would be an email sent to a list that contains some subscribers who have already received a similar message from a different email send event. In this case, you can exclude the customers from the original list in the new send event without impacting their overall consent tracking.

Segmentation

Getting the right message to the right subscribers at the right time requires segmenting the available data based on characteristics. This can be done using robust AI-powered insights derived from large data volumes using products such as Salesforce CDP to create audiences, but it can also be done using native Marketing Cloud functionality for simpler scenarios.

Segmentation can be accomplished on the data itself, meaning lists and Data Extensions, or it can be accomplished in the context of a particular journey using decision splits and journey filters. Finally, Salesforce CDP-based audiences can be used to drive Marketing Cloud-based experiences.

Data segmentation

While conceptually similar, the methods of segmentation that are used for lists and Data Extensions are slightly different.

Segmenting lists

Lists can be segmented using a **Data Filter**.

A Data Filter allows a marketer to assign criteria for inclusion using a visual interface based on subscribe attributes. The primary advantage of creating and leveraging a Data Filter, over just applying a filter to a list directly, is that the Data Filter exists independently of the list and can be reused with other lists or Data Extensions in the future.

For example, a Data Filter could be used to find all the subscribers who have expressed an interest in mountain climbing. Once perfected, that Data Filter could be used on a list of all subscribers, or a separate list that is used for in-store shoppers in the Boulder area, or for a list of customers who have expressed interest in adventure travel.

Segmenting Data Extensions

One way to segment Data Extensions is by leveraging Data Filters, as we discussed in the previous section for lists.

In addition to Data Filters, Data Extensions also support executing **queries** directly using **Structured Query Language** (**SQL**). To use queries against a Data Extension, you must create an additional Data Extension that the results of the query will be placed in. The resulting Data Extension must be created with the appropriate fields with matching data types based on the query being executed.

From there, SQL can be used to craft and execute the query using the SQL query activity in Automation Studio, placing the results into the new Data Extension. This is the most complex option, and it requires an understanding of SQL, but it provides virtually unlimited potential to analyze and extract segments from the data available in Marketing Cloud.

Journey segmentation

Increasingly, Marketing Cloud-based communication and experience delivery is orchestrated by Journey Builder. Within the context of a journey, the goal is to ensure that each contact receives the right experience at the right time. This can be accomplished using decision splits and journey filters.

A decision split is one of the native activities available within Marketing Cloud Journey Builder. By adding a decision split to a journey, contacts can be sent down different paths in the journey based on defined criteria. Each decision split offers multiple criteria, each of which corresponds to a different exit path, and are evaluated in order.

You can either use attributes and comparisons directly or by leveraging journey filters. Journey filters can be used in a couple of different ways within the context of a journey. First, they can be used to control which contacts enter a journey in the first place. Second, they can be used to support decision splits. Finally, they can be used to control which contacts in the journey meet a given goal.

Filters are configured with multiple conditions and comparisons that have been assigned to attributes and used in combination. Filter statements can be grouped using `And` and `Or` logic to create more complex statements than are possible using raw attribute evaluation, which is supported by decision splits without filters.

You can read more about Marketing Cloud decision splits here: `https://sforce.co/3qZRfbq`.

You can read more about Marketing Cloud journey filters here: `https://sforce.co/3r55viV`.

Salesforce CDP

The most robust option for segmenting contacts in a Marketing Cloud journey is to leverage Salesforce CDP. As described earlier in this chapter, Salesforce CDP allows marketers to generate audiences based on a variety of data attributes associated with their customers. Audiences generated with Salesforce CDP can be shared by using the **Audience data extension entry source** in Journey Builder.

By connecting Salesforce CDP audiences to Journey Builder using an Entry Source as new contacts are added to an audience or new audiences are discovered, it's simple to design experiences geared specifically to that audience.

> **Further reading**
> To learn more about Salesforce CDP and Journey Builder, especially some notes around consent management, review the Salesforce documentation here: `https://sforce.co/3k7a0Z1`.

To leverage the various components and capabilities of Marketing Cloud, or to integrate with the data model, you'll also need to understand the APIs and integrations that allow external systems to integrate with Marketing Cloud.

Marketing Cloud APIs and integrations

Successfully incorporating Marketing Cloud into a larger B2C solution depends on understanding the available APIs and integration points. Like B2C Commerce, Marketing Cloud supports both API and feed-based integrations, so you, as the solution architect, are expected to know the strengths and drawbacks of each option.

In addition, like the Salesforce Platform, Marketing Cloud has both a SOAP API and a REST API, which cover overlapping but not identical functionality.

> **Tip**
> It may be necessary to leverage a mix of feed files, REST API-, and SOAP API-based integrations to Marketing Cloud within one solution.

Finally, Marketing Cloud supports productized integrations to the Salesforce Platform, including Service Cloud and Sales Cloud. Productized integrations are integrations that are available *out of the box* and require no custom development on your part to take advantage of. The primary example of a productized integration is the **Marketing Cloud Connect** product, which synchronizes data between Marketing Cloud and the Salesforce Platform.

Feed file-based integrations

Marketing Cloud uses **SFTP** for all file-based integrations. Simple FTP is not secure and is no longer supported under any circumstances. Marketing Cloud provides an integrated SFTP server but can also connect to externally hosted SFTP servers if necessary.

The SFTP URL for a given Marketing Cloud instance can be found in the **FTP Accounts** section of **Setup**. To access and manage the Marketing Cloud SFTP server, a Marketing Cloud SFTP account must be created by navigating to **FTP Accounts** under **Setup | Data Management**. The Marketing Cloud SFTP user will default to using the **Member ID** (**MID**) as the first username. You can create up to two additional usernames for a total of three, which are generated by appending _2 and _3 to the MID.

The following additional security configurations must be made when creating a Marketing Cloud SFTP user:

- Initial password
- Read-only or full access
- Allowed IPs
- Authentication options (password and/or SSH key)

With the Marketing Cloud SFTP user, you can use any SFTP client to access the SFTP server.

Marketing Cloud automatically creates the following folders on the SFTP server, which should not be deleted:

- `Import`: Source for all files to be imported into Marketing Cloud
- `Export`: Location of all files to be exported from Marketing Cloud
- `Reports`: Location of any reports generated by Marketing Cloud

Use the SFTP server to import data into Data Extensions or lists, and to export data that's been extracted from Marketing Cloud for consumption by other systems. To trigger imports automatically when a file is added to the `Import` folder, or on a recurring schedule, use Automation Studio to create an automation that retrieves data from the SFTP server.

In addition to the integrated or external SFTP servers, a Marketing Cloud admin can also configure Marketing Cloud to retrieve data files from a **safehouse** or **Amazon Simple Storage Service (S3)**.

A safehouse is a high-availability and highly redundant Marketing Cloud data store accessible only to authenticated users. Here, decrypted files can be stored to avoid having them stored on the SFTP server, even temporarily. When using a safehouse, encrypted files are transferred to the Marketing Cloud SFTP server. The File Transfer activity is used to decrypt them to the safehouse, and then the Import activity is used to import them from the safehouse directly into Marketing Cloud.

Knowing Packt Gear is going to be integrating B2C Commerce with Marketing Cloud, we know that an SFTP-based integration will be the best way to synchronize non-customer data such as products and content into Marketing Cloud for use in commerce emails.

> **Further reading**
> You can learn more about Marketing Cloud file transfer options here: `https://sforce.co/3x7DgTu`.

API integrations

Marketing Cloud supports real-time API integrations using a SOAP API and a REST API, collectively called **Marketing Cloud APIs**, similar to the Salesforce Platform. The SOAP API is the original Marketing Cloud API and still has the most comprehensive support for Email Studio products and their related functionality. The REST API overlaps with the SOAP API but is more modern and provides more comprehensive support for other Marketing Cloud products outside of Email Studio.

> **Tip**
> Because the REST and SOAP APIs do not cover the same functionality, it may be necessary to mix both in the same Marketing Cloud solution.

Both the Marketing Cloud APIs use an **OAuth API** token that's retrieved using a client ID, which requires an **Installed Package** in Marketing Cloud. These two APIs can share the same token, which makes it easier to mix and match their functionality to create a complete solution.

We'll cover API authentication first, since it's common to both the SOAP API and the REST API, and then we'll cover each of those APIs separately.

API authentication

To authenticate with the Marketing Cloud APIs, you must create an Installed Package in Marketing Cloud to allow API access for a particular client. This is conceptually similar to creating a connected app in a Salesforce Platform org or creating a new API client in B2C Commerce Account Manager.

Creating a new Installed Package can be done by going to **Setup | Apps | Installed Packages** in Marketing Cloud.

When adding a new API Integration component, you'll have the option of either supporting **server-to-server integrations** using the **Client Credentials Grant type** or **web and public app integrations** using the **Authorization Code Grant type**.

The installed package must also specify the allowed scopes for the API client, which controls what Marketing Cloud functionality the client is permitted to access.

Server-to-server integrations

Server-to-server integrations are appropriate for automated integrations between systems, such as synchronizing data from B2C Commerce into Marketing Cloud in real time. This type of integration requires requesting an API token using the client ID and secret that Marketing Cloud supplies when the Installed Package is created. The API token can then be used to access the Marketing Cloud API resources that are included in the token request.

The following is an example of an authentication request being used to retrieve an API access token in a server-to-server integration scenario, to support reading and writing to a Data Extension:

```
Host: https://YOUR_SUBDOMAIN.auth.marketingcloudapis.com
POST /v2/token
Content-Type: application/json
{
    "grant_type": "client_credentials",
    "client_id": "8c2h39terosecuet39e8ih49",
    "client_secret": "469873165695432168",
    "scope": "data_extensions_write data_extensions_read",
    "account_id": "65237"
}
```

The preceding request, if successful, would return a response similar to the following:

```
HTTP / 1.1 200 OK
{
    "access_token": "{excerpted}",
    "expires_in": 1080,
    "token_type": "Bearer",
    "rest_instance_url": "mcett49o8et52met9
       hov93he8gm.rest.marketingcloudapis.com",
    "soap_instance_url": "mcett49o8et52met9-
       hov93he8gm.soap.marketingcloudapis.com",
    "scope": "data_extensions_write data_extensions_read"
}
```

Note that in the preceding example, `access_token` has been removed for clarity, but this token is the key to accessing the relevant APIs and should be treated as a credential and kept secure. In addition to `access_token`, the authentication response also supplies the REST API and SOAP API access URLs and the token expiration time, which can be used to construct additional requests and recreate the token before it expires.

If the credentials included in the request are not valid, an error message is returned instead with a `401 Unauthorized` response, similar to the following:

```
HTTP/1.1 401 Unauthorized
{
    "error": "invalid_client",
    "error_description": "Invalid client ID. Use the client ID in
      Marketing Cloud Installed Packages.",
    "error_uri": "https://developer.salesforce.com/docs"
}
```

> **Further reading**
>
> For additional details, see the Marketing Cloud documentation under *Access Token for Server-to-Server Integrations* here: `https://sforce.co/3ndRpdh`.

Web and public app integrations

Web and public app integrations rely on a user to physically enter their credentials to authenticate with Marketing Cloud. In the client application, the user would be redirected to Marketing Cloud in their browser, with the client ID for the Installed Package appended as a query string to the URL, along with a redirect URL. If the user successfully authenticates, an authorization code is returned on the redirect response, which can then be used to request an access token.

The following sequence diagram shows a user authenticating through Marketing Cloud to access an external app:

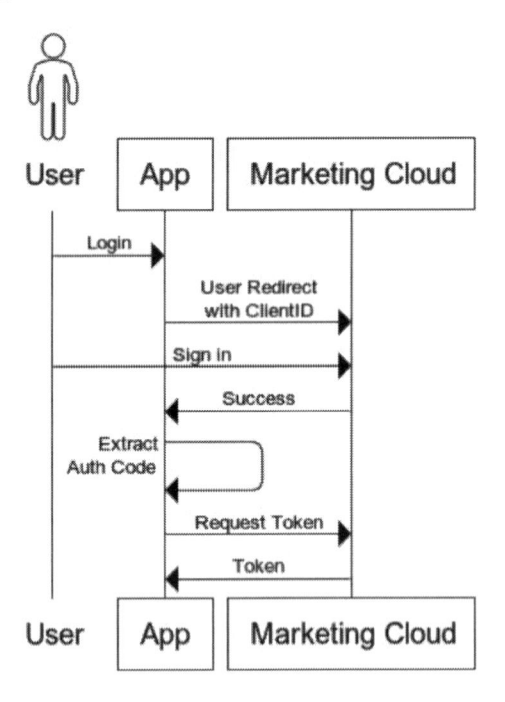

Figure 4.3 – Web and public app authentication

This shows the workflow, including user interaction, that is required to authenticate using web and public app integration.

> **Tip**
> Since web and public app integrations rely on user interaction, they're less likely to be used in integrated B2C solutions than server-to-server integrations, but they are helpful to be aware of as an option.

SOAP API

The SOAP API supports the following Marketing Cloud features:

- Automation Studio
- Classic content (not Content Builder)
- Subscribers and list management
- Tracking

- Triggered Sends
- Email Studio

In addition to the aforementioned features, which are all features focused on creating, sending, and tracking emails, the SOAP API can be used to update account information for external application management. Like all SOAP APIs, the Marketing Cloud SOAP API relies on a set of **Web Service Definition Language (WSDL)** files that define the allowed format for supported objects, such as **Account** and **Email**.

SOAP is an XML-based syntax and works naturally with tools and languages that have robust support for integrated XML manipulation, such as Microsoft's C#. SOAP also supports both synchronous and asynchronous operations, so it can be a good choice for more batch integrations where a large dataset needs to be processed and the results are not needed immediately.

In general, the SOAP API is the best choice for Email Studio-related functionality.

REST API

The REST API supports the following Marketing Cloud features:

- Contact Builder
- Content Builder
- GroupConnect
- Journey Builder
- MobileConnect
- MobilePush
- Personalization Builder
- Transactional messages
- Triggered Sends
- Campaign Management

The REST API works via JSON request bodies and responses, which makes it a natural choice for languages and environments based on JavaScript, such as Node.js or the B2C Commerce script API. All requests that are processed via the REST API are processed synchronously and support a maximum of 4 MB per request.

The REST API should be the default choice for new integrations that require the feature sets it supports.

One important feature of the REST API is the ability to call the **Transactional Messaging API**. The Transactional Messaging API can be used to immediately send email or SMS messages that are non-promotional. Examples of transactional messages include order confirmation emails, ship notifications, and case updates from Service Cloud.

This capability is like the Triggered Send capability supported by the SOAP API, but it has several advantages over that older technology approach:

- The Transactional Messaging API scales and performs better than Triggered Sends.
- The Transactional Messaging API always sends as quickly as possible; it does not rely on email priorities that have been configured in a send definition.
- The Transactional Messaging API provides improved message tracking using the `messageKey` attribute.

The SOAP API and REST API options we've discussed in this section both support custom integrations built by a development team to be integrated with Marketing Cloud. In some cases, custom development is not required, and productized integrations provided by Salesforce can be leveraged.

Productized integration

In addition to the API- and file-based integrations, which both require custom development, Marketing Cloud supports a productized out-of-the-box integration to the Salesforce Platform. These integrations can be enabled and configured within the respective products, without the need to involve a development team, and are designed to operate at a high scale.

Productized integrations are supported by Salesforce support, unlike some of the enablement frameworks we'll cover in later chapters. These two factors together mean the productized integrations we'll cover in the subsequent sections should be preferred to custom integration wherever possible.

Marketing Cloud Connect

MC Connect is a managed package provided by Salesforce through AppExchange (managed packages and AppExchange were covered in *Chapter 1, Demystifying Salesforce, Customer 360, and Digital 360*). MC Connect integrates a single Marketing Cloud instance with one or more Salesforce orgs. This is the primary connection point to the Salesforce Platform, including Service Cloud and Marketing Cloud. It's also a critical component of any B2C solution that includes these products.

For Packt Gear, you can be certain that this will be the primary connection point between their Salesforce Platform-based products and Marketing Cloud.

> **Tip**
> In most cases, MC Connect will be the only integration point needed between Service Cloud and Marketing Cloud, avoiding custom development entirely.

Since MC Connect plays such an important role in B2C solutions, we'll cover it in some detail here, including its prerequisites, how it's integrated, and the features it supports.

MC Connect prerequisites

The single most important thing to understand about MC Connect is that it requires the Subscriber Key in Marketing Cloud, which uniquely identifies the subscriber in the **All Subscribers** list, to match **Contact ID**, **Lead ID**, or **User ID** in the Salesforce Platform. This is the foundation of building a successful customer data strategy across platforms and will be explored in much more detail in *Chapter 8, Creating a 360 View of the Customer*.

This can be an issue for customers that have an existing integration between B2C Commerce and Marketing Cloud because it is common, though not recommended, to use the email address as the Subscriber Key in that scenario.

If your Marketing Cloud instance is not currently using a Subscriber Key or the Subscriber Key does not match the Salesforce Platform contact ID, you will need to work with Marketing Cloud professional services to perform what is called a **subscriber key migration** before MC Connect can be enabled.

Aside from that, MC Connect requires a valid license for Service Cloud and Marketing Cloud, and your Marketing Cloud instance must be enabled for **Marketing Cloud Connect** by Marketing Cloud Professional Services.

> **Further reading**
> Detailed prerequisites and installation instructions are available here:
> `https://sforce.co/3eqv1Jz`.

MC Connect integration

MC Connect, once installed and configured, allows users to log in once and access both Marketing Cloud and Service Cloud functionality through MC Connect. MC Connect uses a Connected App for authentication (covered in *Chapter 2, Supporting Your Customers with Service Cloud*). When using MC Connect, the Salesforce Platform's REST and SOAP API request limits are not impacted, which can be an important design consideration. The Bulk API limits still apply as normal, however.

MC Connect also supports declarative attribute mapping from Salesforce Platform CRM objects such as **Contact**, **Lead**, and **User** to **Marketing Cloud subscriber** profile attributes. This mapping can be handled from the Marketing Cloud side by selecting the corresponding Salesforce attribute for any profile attribute under **Profile Management** in **Email Studio**.

> **Important note**
> Work with a Marketing Cloud technical architect specialist when designing the data mapping between the Salesforce Platform and Marketing Cloud to ensure all use cases and sequences are considered. Declarative mapping cannot be relied upon when contacts are initially created via email sends rather than via the Marketing Cloud Connect sync process from Salesforce. Leveraging the Data Extension synchronization process described here is more reliable.

If you have multiple Marketing Cloud Business Units, you can select which are integrated with the Salesforce Platform by navigating to **Manage Business Units** under **Configure Marketing Cloud Connector** in the **Marketing Cloud** tab of your Sales or Service Cloud app.

MC Connect features

When using MC Connect, Service Cloud users can send emails from Marketing Cloud to Contact, Lead, or Person account records. The first time this feature is used, the corresponding entry is automatically added to the Marketing Cloud **All Subscribers** list. This allows centralized tracking of email preferences and history. It is also possible to send emails from Service Cloud using Marketing Cloud to a campaign or report if it contains a **Contact ID** or **Lead ID** field, which will map to the Marketing Cloud Subscriber Key.

MC Connect replicates a subset of the Marketing Cloud tracking and analytics data to the Salesforce Platform for convenience. This data can be used as a quick reference to understand communications to individuals (**Contact** or **Person accounts**) or more aggregate statistics. This feature can be used, for example, to see whether an order confirmation email from B2C Commerce successfully fired for a customer when they contacted an agent in the customer service center.

In addition to mapping subscriber profile attributes to CRM object attributes, it is possible to synchronize Marketing Cloud Data Extensions to Salesforce Platform objects for custom data. As noted earlier, this process is more reliable than directly mapping attributes between the Salesforce Platform record and the Marketing Cloud record, since it does not depend on the contact being originally created via the MC Connect sync process.

Marketing Cloud Connect also provides support for triggered emails, automation, and Journey Builder, including adding Salesforce Platform-based journey entry events and activities. On the Salesforce Platform side, MC Connect adds support for using Marketing Cloud-derived segmentation in campaigns and reports created in the Salesforce Platform.

> **Further reading**
> The full set of MC Connect features is documented here: `https://sforce.co/3xfAaNj`.

Distributed Marketing

Distributed Marketing is a less commonly used mechanism for providing Marketing Cloud functionality in the Salesforce Platform that may be appropriate in specific use cases. Distributed Marketing is designed to support sending branded emails from Marketing Cloud from Sales or Service Cloud using templates controlled in Marketing Cloud.

Distributed Marketing is intended for users who have access to the Salesforce Platform but not Marketing Cloud, and is primarily useful with semi-independent relationships that need to maintain a centralized branding. An example of this would be insurance agents operating independently but communicating using a brand template.

Both Marketing Cloud Connect and Distributed Marketing support sending emails from Marketing Cloud to contacts and leads, but Distributed Marketing specifically focuses on that use case. Distributed Marketing is designed to allow agents to customize specific components of an email while remaining within a branded template.

> **Tip**
> Marketing Cloud Connect is a more fully featured integration and should be preferred in most B2C integration solutions.

Importing data into a Data Extension

The primary ways to import data into a Data Extension are as follows:

- Use the **Import Wizard** from the Data Extension view.
- Use the **Import activity** within Automation Studio to import data on a schedule.
- Use the **Marketing Cloud API** to import data.

The Import Wizard is a natural choice for one-time imports such as loading historical data or test data into an environment. The Import Wizard walks you through retrieving a file either from the local machine or an FTP server, specifying the file delimiter and format, mapping columns in the import file to fields in the Data Extension, and then importing them.

Marketing Cloud provides an integrated SFTP server, and an **Import activity** can be used to automate retrieving and importing a comma- or tab-delimited file from an SFTP into a Data Extension, which creates a remarkably simple-to-configure and scalable pattern that's used in integrated solutions.

Leveraging the B2C Commerce and Marketing Cloud connector, which will be discussed in more detail in *Chapter 7, Integration Architecture Options*, B2C Commerce creates CSV files containing product and category data, which are then posted to the Marketing Cloud SFTP server, and then retrieved and imported into Data Extensions in Marketing Cloud daily or more frequently. This pattern is also used for customer data, content, coupons, and order data.

Marketing Cloud SDKs

To facilitate integration with Marketing Cloud from common development environments and languages, Salesforce provides several **Software Development Kits** (**SDKs**) that wrap the raw Marketing Cloud APIs and provide example integrations covering everything from authentication to data manipulation.

Leveraging an SDK as a starting point can be a great way to jump-start your integration, but it will still integrate with Marketing Cloud using the APIs we discussed in the *API integrations* section. You, as the B2C solution architect, still need to understand Marketing Cloud integration best practices to design a secure, functional, and scalable solution.

The following free and community-supported SDKs are available from GitHub:

- **C# SDK**: https://sforce.co/2QM1t0N
- **Java SDK**: https://sforce.co/3dzpQYO

- **Node SDK:** https://bit.ly/3xEXh3S
- **Python SDK:** https://sforce.co/3sCdSBO
- **Ruby SDK:** https://sforce.co/3dyxXVs

> **Important note**
> The Marketing Cloud SDKs from Salesforce are not part of the product and are intended as development accelerators. They may have known issues that will need to be addressed by the user and they are not eligible for support from Salesforce.

In the next section, we're going to review the design considerations that should be at the top of your mind when creating a solution that leverages Marketing Cloud as a component.

Marketing Cloud design considerations

Just as with Service Cloud and B2C Commerce, there are a few Marketing Cloud constraints that you'll need to be aware of when designing solutions that incorporate this suite of products. In the following sections, we'll cover Marketing Cloud design constraints based on edition and data import volume guidelines.

Marketing Cloud edition constraints

In addition to controlling which features you have access to within Marketing Cloud, as described in the *Marketing Cloud capabilities* section, the edition of Marketing Cloud also sets certain constraints, as shown in the following table:

Edition	Basic	Pro	Corporate	Enterprise
API Calls Per Year	$	2M	6M	200M
Automations	$	15k	45k	100k
Contacts	–	15k	45k	500k
Data Extension Storage	1 GB	15GB	45GB	100GB
SMS Messages	–	$	1k	1k
Users	5	15	45	100
Business Units	$	$	$	5

Table 4.1 – Marketing Cloud editions

The preceding table shows the included events or objects of each type by **Marketing Cloud** edition (if any). Cells marked with a **$** indicate capabilities available for an extra cost. Capabilities marked with a – indicate capabilities not available with the given edition. For any cells with an included allocation, additional units can be purchased for a fee.

Packt Gear plans to synchronize their existing loyalty database from in-store purchases through the Salesforce Platform as Contact records. This will allow them to send a marketing email through Marketing Cloud via MC Connect, announcing their new website. All those loyal customers will have a Contact record created and synchronized to Marketing Cloud. After some investigation, you learn that Packt Gear has over 250k loyalty customers in their database! That means they'll need an Enterprise license of Marketing Cloud; otherwise, they'll have to pay for additional contact capacity.

Data import volumes

By leveraging Data Extensions, Marketing Cloud can import around 1 million rows in about 10 minutes. For scenarios where high data volumes are anticipated, leveraging Data Extensions is highly recommended.

Import speeds are based on the Marketing Cloud lists versus Data Extensions documentation here: `https://sforce.co/3gimN8X`.

Now that we've covered the most important design constraints for Marketing Cloud, we'll use the next section to bring it all together in support of the Packt Gear solution.

Putting it all together

Returning to our example client, Packt Gear, let's review how everything we learned in this chapter can support their needs. So far, we've determined that they'll be leveraging Service Cloud and B2C Commerce, but Marketing Cloud is a more nuanced conversation. We know that Packt Gear will need the core Marketing Cloud platform to support messaging and journeys, especially email communication. This is the heart of their customer communication strategy.

Since only Marketing Cloud Professional edition and above support API-based integrations, we'll need that at least. With Marketing Cloud Professional edition, Packt Gear will have access to Email Studio and Content Builder; however, Journey Builder and Mobile Studio are only available with Corporate edition and above. Since designing engaging customer journeys is such a core part of their business, moving to Corporate edition is advisable and rounds out the key features that are required of the core Marketing Cloud platform.

Packt Gear can also evaluate other complimentary products under the Marketing Cloud umbrella, such as Salesforce CDP and Interaction Studio, but these products don't need to be incorporated into the core B2C solution architecture and can be layered on top of a well-designed solution in a later phase.

Summary

Based on the information in this chapter, you should be prepared to explain the role of Marketing Cloud in a B2C solution, including how it interacts with other components of the solution, such as B2C Commerce and Service Cloud. You should also understand the way Marketing Cloud is composed of multiple components, and which of those components are most important in an integrated solution.

When designing a cross-cloud data model in a B2C solution, you should know how to leverage Marketing Cloud lists and Data Extensions and the capabilities and constraints of each. You should also be able to work with a dedicated Marketing Cloud technical architect to design a strategy for customer data synchronization, which you can do using Marketing Cloud Connect between the Salesforce Platform and Marketing Cloud.

Now that you've had a chance to review the capabilities of the Marketing Cloud REST and SOAP APIs, you should be able to make an appropriate choice or design an integration that utilizes a combination of both, including an authentication strategy, for API-based integrations that are not productized, such as real-time interaction with B2C Commerce.

Knowing that Marketing Cloud supports **SFTP** and fast imports/exports of large volumes of data using Data Extensions, you should be able to explain how to synchronize non-customer data such as a product catalog from B2C Commerce into Marketing Cloud so that it can be used to generate product recommendations via Email Studio.

Finally, you'll be able to help your organization or customer select the optimum Marketing Cloud edition by considering the capabilities of each, as well as the constraints they impose on things such as total API requests per year or user count.

In the next chapter, *Chapter 5*, *Salesforce Ecosystem – Building a Complete Solution*, we'll move beyond the three core products in a B2C solution architecture and review other Salesforce solution components that may complement the overall solution.

Questions

1. Of the following three Marketing Cloud component products, which is built on top of the Salesforce Platform: Email Studio, Automation Studio, or Salesforce CDP?
2. What Marketing Cloud tool would you recommend to a customer looking to add SMS marketing capabilities to their existing email marketing?
3. What is the simplest tool you can use to add programmatic customization to Marketing Cloud emails and CloudPages?
4. You know your solution requires storing hundreds of thousands of product data records in Marketing Cloud, which will be fed on a nightly basis from B2C Commerce. What is the appropriate storage mechanism in Marketing Cloud?

5. You're working with a customer that currently uses Marketing Cloud to send emails from B2C Commerce and they're looking to add Service Cloud. Are there any potential concerns you should address early on?

6. True or False: The Marketing Cloud REST API is a newer API and should be used exclusively for new implementations; the SOAP API should only be used to support existing legacy clients.

7. When designing a solution to synchronize contacts, leads, and accounts from the Salesforce Platform to Marketing Cloud, what's the most appropriate tool to leverage?

8. Your organization is evaluating Marketing Cloud and is considering starting with the Basic edition to test the role of Marketing Cloud in an integrated B2C solution before investing more heavily. What caveats should be discussed?

Answers

1. Salesforce CDP.
2. Mobile Studio.
3. AMPscript supports simple programmatic customization of emails and Cloud Pages.
4. Marketing Cloud Data Extensions support data volumes and, unlike lists, do not require an associated subscriber for records.
5. Without a Salesforce Platform-based product, such as Service Cloud, in the solution, the customer is likely using their email address as their Subscriber Key, which is not compatible with Marketing Cloud Connect. This will necessitate a subscriber key migration, which is performed by Marketing Cloud professional services.
6. False. While it's true that the REST API is newer and should be preferred where it meets a customer's needs, the SOAP API and the REST API support different feature sets, so both may be needed in new implementations to meet all use cases.
7. Marketing Cloud Connect is the productized integration between the Salesforce Platform and Marketing Cloud and supports several use cases, including synchronizing contacts, leads, and accounts with Marketing Cloud Subscribers.
8. Marketing Cloud Basic does not support Marketing Cloud Connect for contact synchronization and does not provide API calls without extra costs.

5
Salesforce Ecosystem – Building a Complete Solution

Service Cloud, **B2C Commerce**, and **Marketing Cloud** are the three pillars of a successful B2C solution on Salesforce. That being said, there's a whole lot more involved in successful direct-to-consumer selling than that!

This chapter covers some of the many Salesforce products that can complement the core solution. While it's certainly not necessary to build your entire B2C solution on Salesforce products, there are often advantages to using Salesforce products where possible. For example, you don't have to use Salesforce **Order Management** (**OM**) for order processing, but if you do, your B2C Commerce orders will automatically be sent to OM when they're ready for exporting on the storefront, saving you potentially significant integration effort.

Many of the products mentioned in this chapter, such as MuleSoft and Tableau, are built on completely different technology platforms than any of the products we've discussed so far. They have their own capabilities, API and integration methodologies, object models, and design constraints. Obviously, since we've spent a chapter each on Marketing Cloud, B2C Commerce, and Service Cloud to cover those topics, we won't be able to reach the same depth for the products covered in this chapter.

For each product in this chapter, we'll cover the high-level capabilities, the role in a B2C solution, the benefits of the Salesforce option, and important design constraints.

In this chapter, we're going to cover the following main topics:

- Experience Cloud and content management
- OM, Payments, Loyalty Management, and B2B
- Enterprise CRM with Sales and CPQ and Billing
- Enterprise analytics with Tableau
- MuleSoft and Heroku in Customer 360

By the end of this chapter, as the B2C solution architect for Packt Gear, you'll be prepared to evaluate options for value-added products that could be incorporated into the initial implementation and the long-term roadmap. You'll also understand where customizing an existing product makes sense and where a separate product would be a better fit.

Experience Cloud and content management

Salesforce Experience Cloud, formerly known as **Community Cloud**, is a Salesforce Platform-based product that is used to build public-facing websites (or experiences). A classic use case for Experience Cloud is creating customer portals that allow for self-service support and collaboration with forums or knowledge sharing.

The Salesforce **Content Management System** (**CMS**) is also built on the Salesforce Platform and is used to create branded consistent content components that can be leveraged in a variety of channels, including B2C Commerce, and Experience Cloud. In the subsequent sections, we will learn about Experience Cloud and CMS.

Experience Cloud

Experience Cloud shares the same underlying data model used by all Salesforce Platform-based products, including Service Cloud, CMS, B2B Commerce, and OM (see *Chapter 1, DeMystifying Salesforce, Customer 360, and Digital 360*, for the complete list). This allows public-facing experiences built with Experience Cloud to directly interact with or expose the underlying Salesforce Platform data without requiring integration to access or synchronize data (subject to certain licensing constraints).

Features of Experience Cloud

So far in this book, we've discussed three different ways of creating public-facing web pages or sites: B2C Commerce with SFRA, Marketing Cloud CloudPages, and now Experience Cloud. One of the challenges of successful solution design in Salesforce is realizing that there are often multiple different ways of accomplishing the same goal, but that some ways are better than others.

CloudPages, for example, primarily provides simple static pages that allow for Marketing Cloud data collection or for managing subscription and profile data. B2C Commerce with SFRA can be used to create extremely high-scale commerce experiences that are dynamic and personalized with access to underlying product and customer data, but the user experience is less flexible than an experience built with Experience Cloud.

The primary reason to add Experience Cloud to a B2C solution is to deliver content-focused experiences that are easily changed and have minimal dependency on commerce data. If you're looking to add a blog where brand stylists and trusted influencers can publish content describing their favorite outfits, and you want customers to be able to comment and discuss, Experience Cloud is a great choice.

Experience Cloud pages are built with drag-and-drop declarative editors that are much easier to update on the fly than traditional B2C Commerce storefront pages. A hybrid solution including Experience Cloud-based content pages, editorial experiences, and account management combined with B2C Commerce-based product list pages, search pages, **Product Detail Pages** (**PDPs**), and checkout would be a best of both worlds' scenario.

> Tip
> B2C Commerce offers a feature called **Page Designer** that allows select content pages to be controlled with a visual editor designed to look and feel like the Experience Cloud Experience Builder. Experience Cloud offers this experience for *every* page.

Experience Cloud differentiators

There are many ways to add dynamic, flexible, content-focused experiences to a commerce storefront. Some customers leverage an open source CMS such as **Drupal** or even an enterprise **Digital Asset Management** (**DAM**)/CMS combo such as **Adobe Experience Manager** to serve a portion of their storefront. This approach is sometimes referred to as **hybrid headless** and is discussed in *Chapter 3, Direct-to-Consumer Selling with Commerce Cloud B2C*.

Using Experience Cloud in your solution offers some advantages that can streamline the implementation, although you should always review the specific features you require against the capabilities offered by a software package before making an investment. Because Experience Cloud is a Salesforce product, Salesforce provides a clear set of instructions for creating a seamless customer login experience with B2C Commerce and Experience Cloud. While you can certainly build something similar with other technology, this can save substantial time and help protect the quality of the result.

More importantly, Experience Cloud shares the underlying data model with Salesforce Platform products such as Service Cloud, so no integration at all is required there. Customers can initiate a service chat, file a case, review their status, read knowledge articles, and support each other all without needing to access an outside system.

> **Further reading**
> Read more about building seamless customer experiences with Experience Cloud and B2C Commerce here: `https://sforce.co/3etpKRx`.

Experience Cloud design constraints

Although Salesforce provides a clear **point-of-view** (**POV**) and target architecture for creating a seamless identity with B2C Commerce, it is still a separate technology, so there is custom work required to tie these two together. First, B2C Commerce needs to be configured to use **Salesforce Identity** as an **OAuth2** provider. Second, Experience Cloud needs to be customized to both serve as the identity provider for B2C Commerce and link the required User record created to give registered customers access to the experience with the Contact record representing the customer in the CRM.

> **Important note**
> Service Cloud uses the Contact record in the Salesforce Platform to represent a customer. Experience Cloud requires a separate User record, which must be linked to the Contact record. Review *Chapter 1, Demystifying Salesforce, Customer 360, and Digital 360*, in the *Customer 360 component products for B2C solutions* section, for more information on Contact and User objects.

Content Management System

The **Salesforce CMS** centralizes the production and maintenance of content assets including everything from individual images to blocks of content corresponding to specific promotions or campaigns. This feature sounds a bit like Content Builder in Marketing Cloud, and it is, but it's a standalone product that can be used across B2C Commerce, Experience Cloud, and external systems via API integration.

Salesforce CMS features

Salesforce CMS supports core CMS use cases such as content authoring, publication, asset tagging, and distribution using a **Content Delivery Network** (**CDN**). This is really focused on creating consistently branded assets for use in both Salesforce and non-Salesforce channels such as mobile apps, display ads, and social channels.

Salesforce CMS differentiators

The primary reason to use Salesforce CMS over any of the many competing products in this space is that it comes pre-integrated with B2C Commerce Page Designer, as well as Experience Cloud experiences. This covers a significant number of customer touchpoints essentially out of the box where custom integration would otherwise be required.

Since Salesforce CMS is built on the Salesforce Platform, it allows employees to manage CMS content in the same system they use to build experiences and review service cases. The Salesforce Platform also provides seamless login to B2C Commerce Business Manager and the Marketing Cloud admin portal.

Salesforce CMS design constraints

The Salesforce CMS is not intended to create standalone experiences; it must be paired with Experience Cloud for that. The integration with B2C Commerce storefronts also relies on Page Designer, which is not in use for a significant number of storefronts, so custom development may be required to implement Page Designer before being able to take advantage of CMS content. B2C Commerce Page Designer is also not used on all pages of the B2C Commerce site, so additional effort may be required to leverage CMS content on pages that aren't traditionally built on Page Designer, such as the PDP.

As you can see, adding additional products to the Salesforce Platform org that is used to host Service Cloud in order to support public-facing customer experiences and centralized content management can add significant capabilities to the B2C solution.

In the next section, we'll review some additional Commerce Cloud components beyond B2C Commerce that can be helpful in B2C solution architecture.

OM, Payments, Loyalty Management, and B2B

As we discussed in *Chapter 3, Direct-to-Consumer Selling with Commerce Cloud B2C*, Commerce Cloud is a lot more than just B2C Commerce. Creating a complete commerce solution requires additional components, including OM and Payments, which are also available from Salesforce. Features such as loyalty might be a value-added consideration and if your business also sells B2B, evaluating B2B Commerce is worthwhile.

Each of these is a separate product with its own licensing cost and each should be evaluated like any purchasing decision. In this section, we'll provide a very high-level overview of these products to illustrate why they may or may not be the right fit for your business.

> **Tip**
> B2C solutions will always be a mix of Salesforce and non-Salesforce products working together. The important thing is to make the right choice for your business.

Order Management

Salesforce OM provides support for downstream order handling after the initial commerce transaction. Where B2C Commerce leaves off, OM picks up.

OM features

OM can ingest orders from a variety of sources, not just B2C Commerce, and handle the allocation of those orders based on available inventory across a variety of locations such as warehouses or stores. OM also supports features such as split shipments, order returns, cancellations, and post-purchase order manipulation. OM works together with Service Cloud to allow agents to find and, if necessary, manipulate orders after they've been placed on the storefront.

Order processing in OM is primarily controlled using **flows** created with **Flow Builder**, making it easy to see, understand, and revise without custom code. Where code is required, such as for external integrations such as tax calculation or payment processing, **invocable Apex** can be used and dropped into an existing flow.

The following figure shows an example OM screen flow, used for guiding a service agent through returning an item:

OM, Payments, Loyalty Management, and B2B   137

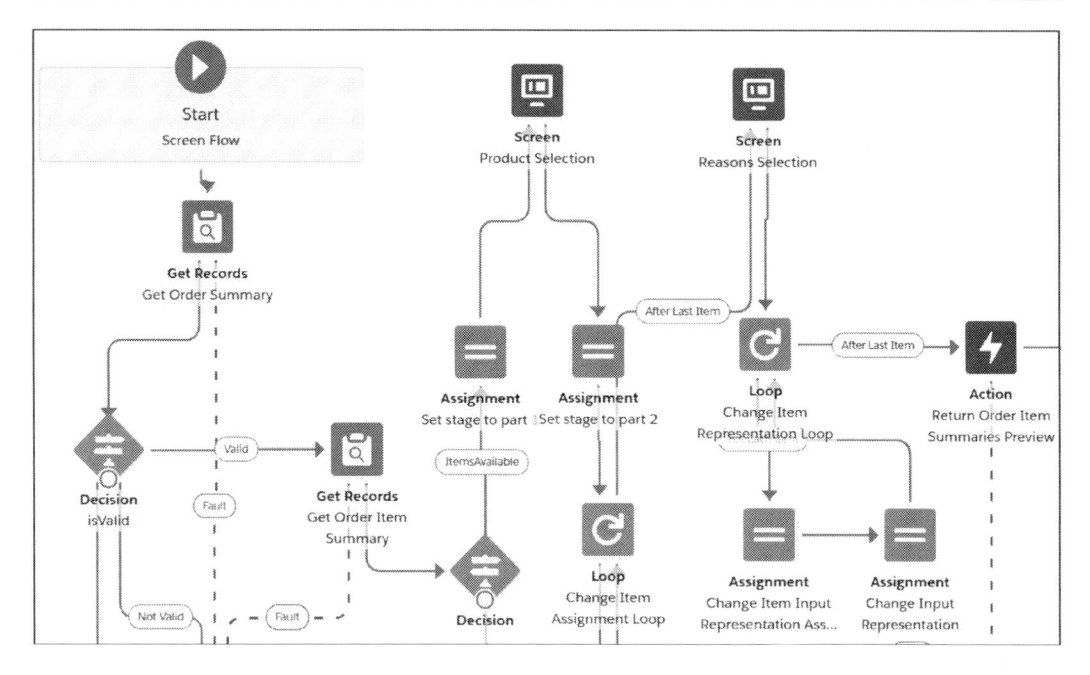

Figure 5.1 – Return item flow

As you can see in the figure, flows can be complex and can involve multiple interaction screens. In this example, the agent selects the products to be returned and the reasons for the return on successive screens. From there, looping and branching logic is used to process the selections before executing the return processing.

OM has a usage-based licensing model, so customers pay for each order processed depending on the package purchased.

OM differentiators

As with most of the products in this chapter, the primary advantage of using Salesforce OM over competing OM products is the strength of its prebuilt integrations with other components of a Salesforce B2C solution.

Specifically, orders placed through B2C Commerce are automatically sent to OM for processing with no custom integration required. There may be some work required to map custom attributes between the two systems, but this is a small incremental effort compared to fully custom OMS integrations. In addition, SFRA comes with several prebuilt components that pull the order status from OM to display on the storefront when a customer logs in to check their order history/status or manage their orders.

When agents are using Service Cloud, they are in the same system as OM and can directly see and work with orders placed by customers, regardless of the channel. Finally, by leveraging the Salesforce Omnichannel Inventory Service, OM can share the same high-scale view of inventory across locations as B2C Commerce, helping to avoid over or undersell situations with multiple systems separately tracking inventory.

OM design constraints

OM is a newer product from Salesforce, at least at the time of writing, and is rapidly evolving. For many basic OM scenarios, it may be exactly what's needed, but for complex or custom use cases, a careful evaluation of features is recommended compared to competing products.

As with all Salesforce Platform-based products, API request limits and other platform design constraints should be considered as described in *Chapter 2, Supporting Your Customers with Service Cloud*.

Salesforce Payments

In September 2020, Salesforce announced a partnership with **Stripe** called **Salesforce Payments**. With the initial launch, the product is pre-integrated with B2C Commerce, allowing B2C Commerce customers to register for a Stripe account or link an existing Stripe account directly from Business Manager. Salesforce Payments supports a wide variety of payment instruments (credit card, bank transfer, SOFORT, and so on) and can be configured with multiple or separate **Merchant Identification Numbers** (**MIDs**) based on either the currency used or country.

In a typical credit card-driven B2C workflow, a payment partner has at least two touchpoints. It will be leveraged by the storefront (B2C Commerce) to authorize payment for a transaction in real time before the transaction is finalized, and then it will be leveraged again in the OMS or **Enterprise Resource Planning** (**ERP**) system to capture funds when the order is shipped to the customer. There are times, especially when a custom-made non-returnable product is being purchased, where capturing funds at the time of the sale is appropriate as well. Finally, the payment partner will be used to process any refunds or adjustments made after the purchase.

Salesforce Payments is a great option to consider if you're already using Stripe or don't have an existing payment partner. As Salesforce continues to invest in Salesforce Payments, it's likely additional prebuilt integrations to products such as OM and B2B Commerce will become available, but for now, those components still need to be integrated into Stripe using existing **Stripe public APIs**.

Loyalty Management

Loyalty Management, released in January 2021, is focused on creating a deeper and more durable connection between you and your customers. Loyalty Management generally means keeping track of customer purchases, referrals, social sharing, product reviews, and other brand touchpoints and rewarding the customer for their engagement.

Salesforce Loyalty Management is a comprehensive solution supporting far more than the traditional B2C loyalty scenarios. It can also be used for ongoing customer engagements such as airlines and hotels, which may have many more ways of accruing value (points) and earning rewards. Customers can also accrue value and earn rewards through third parties using Loyalty Management (think of an airline partnership with a ride-sharing service as an example).

Loyalty Management supports rewards in the form of status tiers, which can be linked to entitlements such as priority support or free shipping, and vouchers that can be redeemed for things such as discounts on purchases or free gifts. Creating a successful loyalty program not only rewards your customers, but also builds brand loyalty and customer understanding and increases customer **Total Lifetime Value (TLV)**.

> Tip
> Loyalty Management integrates natively with Salesforce CDP, also built on the Salesforce Platform, expanding the view of CDP audiences with loyalty data.

Loyalty Management is built on the Salesforce Platform and requires custom integration with B2C Commerce and Marketing Cloud to provide a consistent experience across those touchpoints.

Salesforce B2B Commerce Lightning

Salesforce B2B Solution Architect is the companion certification to Salesforce B2C Solution Architect, to which this book is targeted. Significant additional learning will be needed to be prepared to design and build solutions on top of the Salesforce B2B Commerce product. In this section, as is true in most of this chapter, we're just scratching the surface to ensure that you know where to look if you need additional components to complement the core B2C solution.

B2B Commerce is built on the Salesforce Platform, which means it shares none of the same underlying technology as B2C Commerce. B2B Commerce is, specifically, built on top of Experience Cloud (discussed earlier in this chapter), which gives it a much more flexible user experience and more robust declarative automation capabilities than B2C Commerce. B2B Commerce supports several concepts that are central to B2B selling, such as tiered account structures, account-specific product assortments and pricing, and lines of credit. If any of these requirements come up during requirements gathering, the B2B Commerce product may be a better fit since B2C Commerce does not do these things natively and may not be flexible enough to accommodate at scale.

What B2B Commerce does not do, however, is support the same volume and scale of transactions as the B2C Commerce product. B2C Commerce can easily support thousands or tens of thousands of orders per hour with correspondingly large page view numbers and can natively support guest shopping. It's designed to be SEO-optimized, completely customizable on the frontend, and high-scale. The B2C Commerce promotion engine is also geared toward B2C use cases (think buy-one-get-one style promotions), whereas B2B Commerce tends toward higher-order volumes where this isn't appropriate.

In the following figure, you can see that an **OrderSummary** object represents the result of a series of **Order** objects representing changes applied to an initial **Order** representing the customer's transaction. When an order is fulfilled, one or more **FulfillmentOrder** objects are generated, representing shipments associated with the **OrderSummary** object.

> **Further reading**
>
> Review the full OM **Entity Relationship Diagram (ERD)** here: `https://sforce.co/2UG9Flc`.

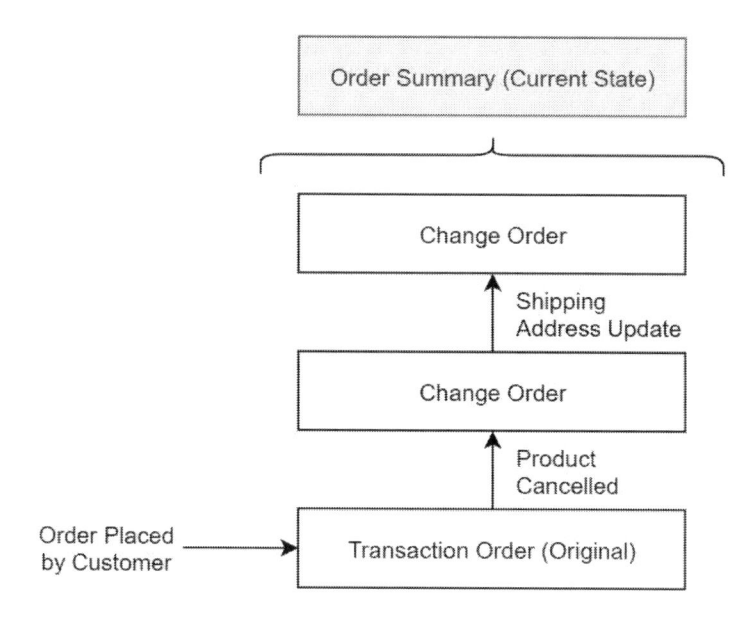

Figure 5.2 – OrderSummary object

As you learn more about Packt Gear's business model, you learn that the bulk of their business is direct-to-consumer sales (B2C), but they do also sell customized versions of their products in bulk to corporations that want high-quality branded apparel and gear. In the future, B2B Commerce would be a good option to explore since it could allow interested companies to specially order larger quantities of a product, supply a logo or message, customize the color and fabric options, and work with a sales rep to secure an individual quote invoiced to a purchase order.

This workflow is, of course, very different from an end customer making a purchase on the storefront with a credit card.

As for Packt Gear, and many B2C Commerce customers, OM and Payments solutions fill a gap for organizations that don't already have a solution in place. Their prebuilt integrations with B2C Commerce allow for a faster and less expensive initial implementation. Loyalty management from Salesforce can be a more significant investment in time and cost to implement but is a great way to build customer connections long term. Finally, B2B Commerce allows an organization to sell through wholesale channels at scale.

In the next section, we'll review other Salesforce Platform-based products that are only tangentially involved in B2C solutions. As a B2C solution architect, you should be aware of these products, but will be less likely to be designing solutions that leverage them.

Enterprise CRM with Sales and CPQ and Billing

The Salesforce Platform is host to a wide variety of products, including Service Cloud, Experience Cloud, CMS, OM, Loyalty Management, and B2B Commerce, covered earlier in this chapter. The last two Salesforce Platform-based products that we'll consider in this section are Sales Cloud and Revenue Cloud.

Sales Cloud

Sales Cloud is a sales management and automation product focused on gathering leads, converting them into Accounts, Contacts, and Opportunities, and nurturing relationships to lead to new deals. Sales Cloud includes sophisticated tools for forecasting sales and managing sales funnels with guidance for representatives at each stage of an opportunity tailored to the opportunity.

In general, this type of sales has less of a role in B2C solutions, which relies more on marketing efforts to reach a larger audience and drive business. While Sales Cloud might be used in a B2B scenario to acquire new clients and support a small number of large opportunities, it would be impractical to track every potential customer who might buy a backpack on your B2C site in Sales Cloud.

The parallel for B2C is using something such as Marketing Cloud to build audiences or segments based on customer persona or behavioral data, create marketing journeys to nurture them as they learn more about the products and pricing, and then encourage additional purchases and brand loyalty. Where Sales Cloud gives every opportunity individual attention, Marketing Cloud works at scale.

That's not to say that the Salesforce Platform in general won't be the system of record for customer data in a B2C solution architecture; it will, it's just more likely to be used for customer service agents using Service Cloud than sales executives using Sales Cloud. Read more about the overall customer data strategy and related approaches in *Chapter 8, Creating a 360° View of the Customer*.

As a B2C solution architect, you probably won't be designing solutions that leverage Sales Cloud, but you should have a basic understanding of it when the org that hosts Service Cloud or OM also hosts Sales Cloud. Specifically, the Account and Contact model used in typical B2B sales does not map as well to B2C use cases, where the Person Account model is a more natural fit.

Account and Contact versus Person Account considerations are discussed in detail in *Chapter 1, DeMystifying Salesforce, Customer 360, and Digital 360*, so review that section for more information. Just know that if Sales Cloud is in play in the org where you're integrating, this will be a consideration.

CPQ and Billing

Configure, Price, Quote (CPQ) and Billing from Salesforce supplement products such as B2B Commerce and Sales Cloud to support more complex pricing and billing scenarios. CPQ refers to the process of creating individual quotes for unique order scenarios, often including customized products or bundles and large order volumes. Because this type of pricing can be labor-intensive and requires human intervention, it's less likely to be used in B2C scenarios where customers are typically ordering existing products from a pool of available inventory.

The Billing part of the CPQ and Billing offering helps automate and streamline the alignment of billing and revenue with order delivery to streamline invoicing, also typically in B2B scenarios. This set of products is also frequently referred to as **quote-to-cash**, since it supports the life cycle from building an offer, setting a competitive price that protects margins, building a quote for that configuration and price point, and then realizing revenue from the sale.

This seems like a natural fit for Packt Gear's custom branded gear sales in their B2B channel! As an architect, you should always be considering the current needs and implementation approach as well as the long-term roadmap. Knowing that Packt Gear will explore B2B Commerce and CPQ after their B2C solution launches can help inform the data model for the Salesforce org long term.

Enterprise analytics with Tableau

Salesforce acquired **Tableau** in August 2019 and we've just seen the beginning of the impact this will have on the Salesforce ecosystem. Tableau elevates the data visualization and analysis capabilities of the Salesforce ecosystem, something nearly every component product can benefit from. For now, integrating with Tableau from component products is still mostly a manual effort requiring data to be synchronized into Tableau from other products such as B2C Commerce and Service Cloud, where it can be aggregated and analyzed to help inform business decisions.

Where products such as Customer 360 Audiences, part of Marketing Cloud, provide a special purpose view of data (customer segmentation and audience building), a product such as Tableau is data-agnostic. It can ingest data from all sources throughout your enterprise and mine for insight that can be used to drive strategy across many channels and technologies.

The following figure shows three categories of data visualization, including single-system; multi-system, single-purpose, multi-system, and general-purpose:

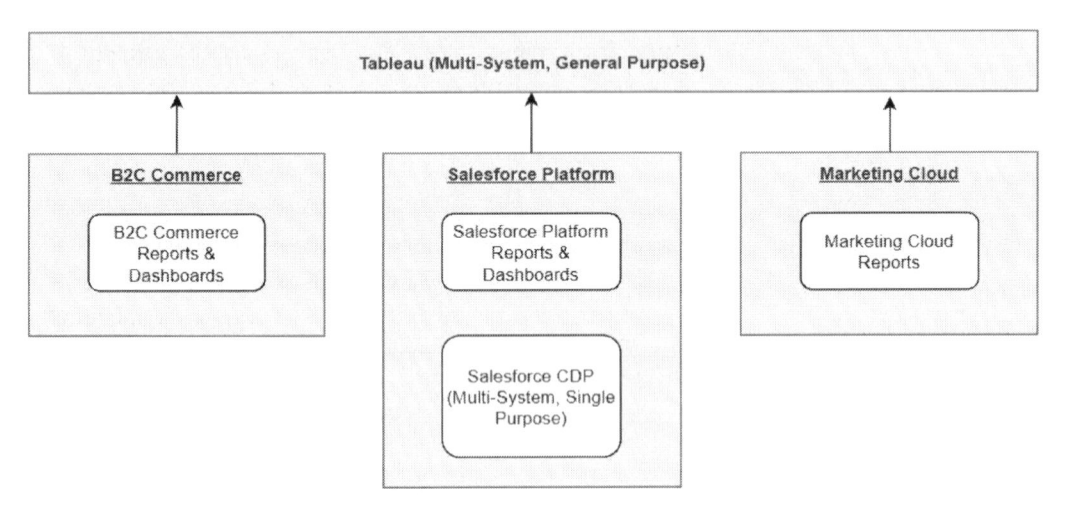

Figure 5.3 – Data visualization

In this view, you can see that each system has an integrated tool for creating reports on data specific to that platform (B2C Commerce, Salesforce, or Marketing Cloud). Tools such as Salesforce CDP can provide a multi-system view of data, but it's specifically regarding audience segmentation and insight for customer data. In contrast, a dedicated data and analytics tool such as Tableau provides a multi-system view of data that's general-purposed and can be used to derive insight into any type of data you can integrate.

Tableau integration

The entire purpose of Tableau is to pull together, aggregate, and analyze data from different systems. It has many available prebuilt native connectors for popular data sources. At the time of writing, Tableau lists 85 supported connectors out of the box. Connectors include loosely structured data sources such as text files and JSON, a wide variety of databases including SQL and NoSQL, and CRM data sources including Salesforce.

When evaluating this integration, however, note that when Tableau lists Salesforce as a supported connector, they specifically mean the Salesforce Platform. This won't help pull in data from B2C Commerce or Marketing Cloud, unless it's first synchronized to the core platform using some other mechanism. A custom connector to Tableau could need to be implemented to use either of these products as a direct data source for Tableau.

Tableau CRM

Despite the similar name, **Tableau CRM** is a different product built directly on the core Salesforce Platform. Tableau CRM was formerly known as **Einstein Analytics**, but was renamed after the Tableau acquisition to better align with the overall vision of Tableau being the data visualization solution.

Although Tableau has a native connector to extract Salesforce Platform data to inform visualizations and insights, it's still a separate system and there's no easy way to weave those insights into the day-to-day actions of sales and service teams using Salesforce. Tableau CRM fills that gap, bringing the visualization and insight capabilities of Tableau directly into the Salesforce Platform so it can be leveraged within the workflows of users.

The next section introduces MuleSoft and Heroku, which will be discussed in more detail in *Chapter 7, Integration Architecture Options*.

MuleSoft and Heroku in Customer 360

MuleSoft and Heroku are Salesforce acquisitions that are not part of the core Salesforce Platform. Despite that, or perhaps because of it, they can play a unique role in a B2C solution, especially for larger enterprises with more complex data and integration needs.

MuleSoft in Customer 360

MuleSoft is an integration and API platform designed to form the backbone of a larger enterprise integration strategy. When properly leveraged, a solution such as MuleSoft can significantly reduce the time and cost of integration work at scale by creating consistent APIs across disparate technology solutions. In principle, when leveraging MuleSoft in an integrated solution instead of integrating each component point to point, each would be integrated with MuleSoft and MuleSoft would handle the orchestration between them.

MuleSoft value proposition

It may at first seem counterintuitive to say that adding an additional product to the solution could simplify integration, but the key is realizing that the number of new point-to-point integrations required when adding a new product to an existing solution grows exponentially based on the size of the existing solution (assuming every product integrates with every other).

The following figure shows a conceptual integration map with point-to-point integrations between components of a solution:

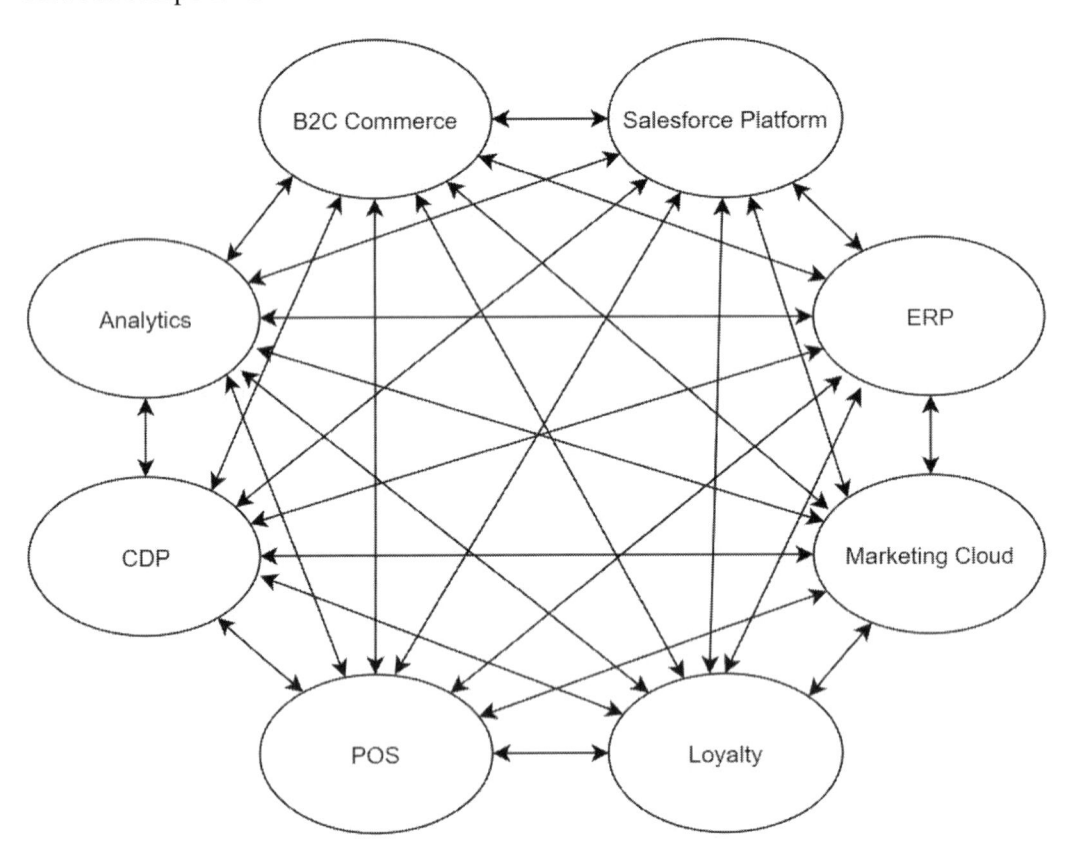

Figure 5.4 – Point-to-point integrations

As we can see in the following figure, by leveraging MuleSoft, only one new connection is needed for each new component product:

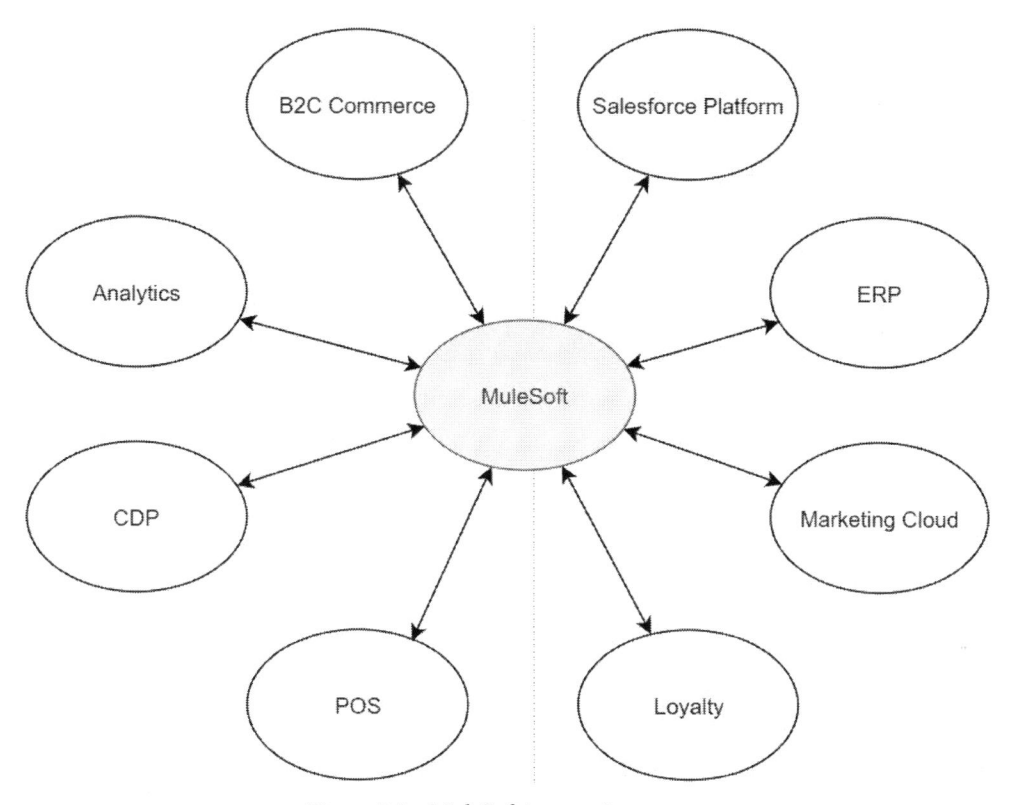

Figure 5.5 – MuleSoft integration pattern

Obviously, not every system needs to talk to every other, and integrations are not all created equal, but it's still helpful to consolidate this logic in one place.

MuleSoft can also handle API non-functional requirements such as security, logging, monitoring, documentation, and discoverability, making it simpler and more consistent to leverage APIs across your organization.

We'll review the role of MuleSoft specifically in a B2C solution architecture in *Chapter 7*, *Integration Architecture Options*.

MuleSoft Composer

For customers who use both the Salesforce Platform and MuleSoft, Salesforce has created **MuleSoft Composer**. MuleSoft Composer is a Salesforce Platform app that allows non-developers to orchestrate integration workflows using declarative tools creating workflows that run on the MuleSoft Anypoint Platform. MuleSoft Composer is not an alternative to or a lightweight version of MuleSoft, nor is it built entirely on the Salesforce Platform; it's a simpler way to create MuleSoft-based integrations to and from the Salesforce Platform without having to leave that product.

With MuleSoft Composer, Salesforce administrators can leverage prebuilt integration components to connect with data sources such as NetSuite, Google Sheets, Slack, Tableau, or Workday. These components can be strung together dynamically and used to move data into the Salesforce Platform, where it can further kick-off other Salesforce declarative automation capabilities such as Lightning flows.

At this time, MuleSoft Composer offers a limited set of features compared to the full capabilities of MuleSoft and the Salesforce Platform for integration, but it may be of interest to customers that are looking to empower their teams to have flexible access to select data sources. For mission-critical integrations supporting a B2C solution, however, a carefully designed and implemented solution that is well tested will be essential.

Heroku in Customer 360

Heroku is the Salesforce **Platform-as-a-Service** (**PaaS**) offering. Essentially, that means that Heroku provides the platform on which to build fully custom applications at scale without having to completely design your own cloud-hosted solution. Under the covers, Heroku is built on top of **Amazon Web Services** (**AWS**) and provides a layer of abstraction over concepts such as compute instances, load balancing, auto-scaling, and networking. This allows developers to focus on creating applications using the tools they're familiar with.

Designing a truly enterprise-scale solution built on Heroku will absolutely require a dedicated team and a Heroku specialist architect, but it can require a much lower level of effort than a fully custom solution that includes cloud hosting.

In a B2C solution, Heroku can be a potential solution for certain design constraints for the other component products we discussed in earlier chapters. Heroku has a productized integration to the Salesforce Platform called **Heroku Connect** that can create a bi-directional synchronization between the Salesforce Platform and a PostgreSQL database hosted in Heroku. For situations where Salesforce Platform API limits are a constraint, especially for read-only access, this can provide near real-time access to Salesforce Platform data without impacting your org API limits.

Like MuleSoft, we'll explore the potential role of Heroku in B2C solutions in more detail in *Chapter 7, Integration Architecture Options*.

By this point, you should have enough of an awareness of MuleSoft and Heroku to discuss their potential roles in a B2C solution, though additional reading will be required to design solutions that incorporate them.

In the following section, we take into account the various Salesforce products that could complement the solution and apply them to the Packt Gear solution we've been developing so far.

Packt Gear solution

In previous chapters, we decided Packt Gear's B2C solution will include B2C Commerce, Service Cloud, and the core Marketing Cloud solution to support messaging and journeys. You also know Packt Gear wants to create robust social experiences where outdoor enthusiasts can interact, discuss their favorite hikes, the weather in their area, great spots for fishing, and the best gear for the activities they like. This is a natural fit for Experience Cloud, which would be supported by Salesforce CMS to maintain a consistent look and feel with B2C Commerce. Customization will also be required to implement a seamless identity management solution across B2C Commerce and Experience Cloud, so customers do not have to log in to separate systems.

Finally, since Packt Gear is in the market for a new OM solution anyway, Salesforce OM is a good fit and will require minimal customization for their use cases. In a future phase, building out a loyalty solution or a B2B Commerce capability may also make sense, but the work done for this initial implementation will support that goal.

The following diagram shows the proposed solution space for Packt Gear, based on everything we know so far:

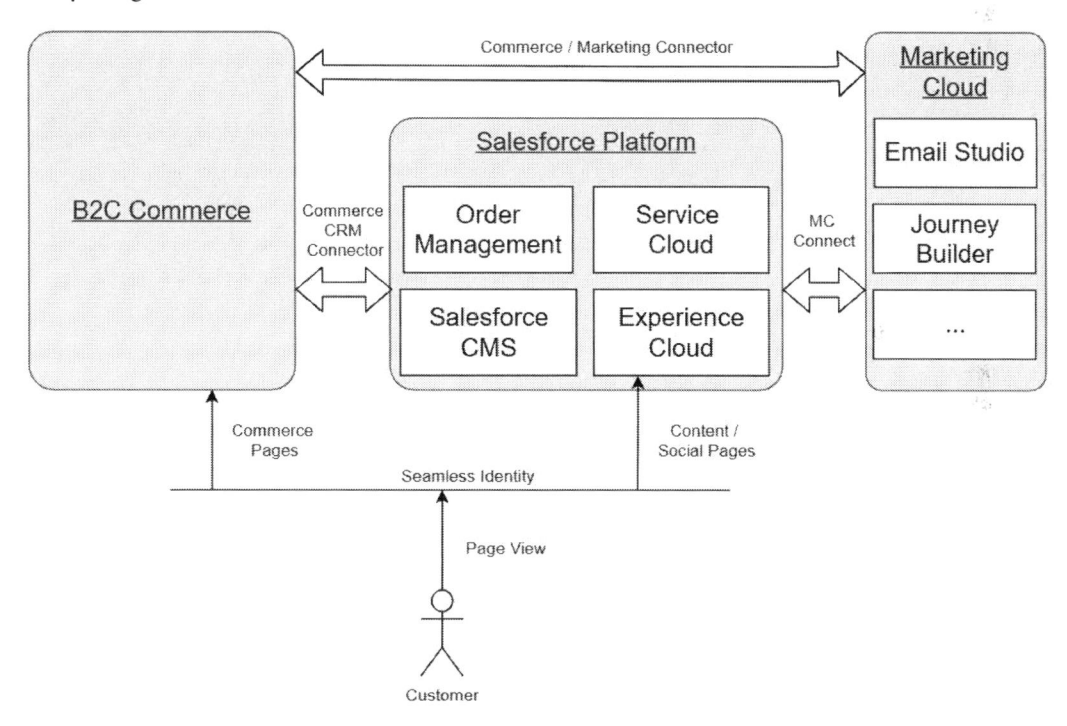

Figure 5.6 – Packt Gear proposed solution

The preceding solution shows how a customer accessing a web page on the Packt Gear public solution would be directed to either B2C Commerce or Experience Cloud, depending on the type of page they are trying to view. In this view, Experience Cloud (leveraging Salesforce Identity) is set up as an identity provider for B2C Commerce, allowing a customer to log in once and navigate both experiences seamlessly.

In addition, we can see that OM, Service Cloud, and Salesforce CMS are hosted in the Salesforce Platform org that hosts Experience Cloud. Both B2C Commerce and the Salesforce Platform are integrated with Marketing Cloud to share relevant data points and functionality as part of the emerging B2C solution architecture.

Summary

After reading this chapter, you should understand and be able to evaluate a variety of potential value-added products to fill gaps in your B2C solution architecture beyond the core Service, Marketing, and B2C Commerce components. This will help you make informed decisions about what products and licenses are required to meet the needs of a specific organization based on their unique requirements.

Now that you have a broader understanding of the Salesforce ecosystem, you should also be able to start thinking about both immediate priorities and longer-term roadmap items that would support an organization's goals.

When reviewing potential Salesforce products, you should understand which are built on the Salesforce Platform and which require some type of integration effort. For products that are built on separate technology and require some integration, you should also understand what advantages and considerations there are to leveraging the Salesforce option in place of third-party competitor offerings that may have similar capabilities.

The most likely components to use in a B2C solution design from this chapter are Experience Cloud and Salesforce CMS. Experience Cloud supports customizable content-driven experiences, and paired with Salesforce CMS creates a consistent branded experience across touchpoints including Commerce, Marketing, and Service. To add additional functionality to the B2C solution, products such as OM, Payments, and Loyalty Management should be considered. Related products that would be more appropriate in a B2B solution include components such as B2B Commerce, Sales, CPQ, and Billing.

In the following chapters, we'll cover how to design a solution that incorporates all these products cohesively. We'll start with *Chapter 6, Role of a Solution Architect*, where we will discuss putting together the right team to support you as you embark on your B2C solution design.

Questions

1. Packt Gear has a vision for an online experience where their customers can not only shop for gear but also discuss the best outdoor experiences and trails in their area, post reviews, and interact with each other around their shared love of the outdoors. Packt Gear wants to be able to tag appropriate products to hikes or excursions to allow shopping within the same experience, but much of the site will be content- and user-driven. What Salesforce product(s) should you explore to supplement the core B2C Commerce component?

2. When reviewing an organization's requirements for their new B2C solution, you find the following requirements:

    a) The ability for customers to cancel their own order from the storefront within 15 minutes of placing the order

    b) The ability for customer service agents to cancel a customer's order on their behalf any time before it is fulfilled

    c) The ability for customers to review their own order history including an up-to-date fulfillment status

    d) The ability for agents to return or refund orders that have been fulfilled on behalf of a customer

    What product or combination of products would be needed to meet these requirements?

3. If an organization is looking to build a custom data lake and is evaluating various options, what are the advantages of using Heroku, assuming the CRM data from the Salesforce Platform will need to be synchronized into the data lake?

4. Your organization sells footwear and apparel directly to the consumer using B2C Commerce from inventory stocked in a central warehouse. In addition, custom orders are occasionally taken from corporations who want to create branded versions of your standard running shoes to give to sponsored athletes. These orders are generally high value and high in quantity and require custom pricing based on a variety of factors with some flexibility for the sales rep to adjust to win the deal. Is B2C Commerce the right solution for this additional site? If not, what would be a better choice?

5. Recent surveys have found that your customers find the experience between your mobile app, commerce storefront, marketing emails, and social channels inconsistent. The content, branding, and imagery are managed by separate teams and while they do follow the same style guide, the various interpretations are jarring to the customer, not to mention the wasted work of re-creating similar content. What's the right Salesforce tool to evaluate in this situation?

6. As Packt Gear gets up and running with their new B2C solution, they're finding great insights from the reports and dashboards in B2C Commerce and Service Cloud as well as customer insights from C360 Audiences, but they're having trouble getting the *big picture*, including data from a third-party loyalty system, product manufacturing costs, logistics data, and more. What's the appropriate Salesforce tool to evaluate for general-purpose data visualization and analytics including a wide variety of input sources?

Section 2: Architecture of Customer 360 Solutions

This is the heart of B2C solution architecture. This section takes what we learned about the various Salesforce products in the ecosystem and starts to draw it all together. We'll start by focusing on how to build a successful team, structure discovery, analyze requirements, and document a technical solution. We'll cover integration options, including Salesforce productized connectors and integration accelerators, as well as middleware-based integration solutions. We'll also cover customer data architecture best practices and business scenarios established on the Customer 360 ecosystem. Finally, the complexities introduced by larger enterprises will form the basis of the last chapter of this section.

The role of a solution architect requires making informed integration decisions, and getting the important things right upfront to add business value through use cases.

This section comprises the following chapters:

- *Chapter 6, Role of a Solution Architect*
- *Chapter 7, Integration Architecture Options*
- *Chapter 8, Creating a 360° View of the Customer*
- *Chapter 9, Supporting Key Business Scenarios*
- *Chapter 10, Enterprise Integration Strategies*

6
Role of a Solution Architect

It takes a team to successfully design and implement a B2C solution that spans multiple products, provides a comprehensive view of customer data, allows seamless experiences for both customers and employees, and meets business stakeholder needs. No one person should be expected to know enough about these different components to design in-depth solutions on each, nor would one person ever have sufficient time to do so. The job of the B2C solution architect is to provide a unified vision across technology to bring this solution to life, working closely with a larger team.

In this chapter, we're going to examine what it truly means to be a B2C solution architect. Somewhere between platform technical architects, the ultimate specialist, and enterprise architects, who focus on the interaction between systems rather than the details of a particular component, sits the B2C solution architect. In this role, you're expected to understand the Salesforce products that are relevant in this space, covered in the first five chapters of this book, and the best practices for integrating them together, covered in the next four chapters of this book.

Without question, the B2C solution architect is a leadership role and will be relied on to not only help define the technical solution but to help define the team required to design and implement that solution. In this chapter, we'll cover the team structure required and provide some recommendations for running an integrated project, including the types of deliverables you should expect to produce.

We're going to cover the following main topics in this chapter:

- Role of a B2C solution architect
- Key stakeholders
- Project sequencing
- Architecture deliverables

Role of a B2C solution architect

The role of a B2C solution architect is a demanding one. Regardless of your background, you're expected to have a working knowledge of several different products both at a functional and a technical level. You'll need to understand the Salesforce products that are most commonly leveraged in B2C solutions and how they work together, and be familiar with most of the rest of the Salesforce ecosystem in enough detail to recognize when it might be worth bringing up or learning more about. While it doesn't mean you're an expert in everything, it means having more than just a casual understanding.

For Service Cloud, B2C Commerce, and Marketing Cloud, you should have a working knowledge of the following (covered in *Chapter 2*, *Supporting Your Customers with Service Cloud*, *Chapter 3*, *Direct-to-Consumer Selling with Commerce Cloud B2C*, and *Chapter 4*, *Engaging Customers with Marketing Cloud*, respectively):

- Functional capabilities of the product, the business needs that the product addresses, and how it serves the customer
- Best practices and capabilities for integrating with the product from outside systems (Salesforce or otherwise)
- Governance limits or quotas that should be considered when designing a solution that incorporates that product
- Productized integrations from Salesforce that can lead to a faster, more performant integration

For each of the other products in the Salesforce ecosystem covered in *Chapter 5*, *Salesforce Ecosystem – Building a Complete Solution*, you should know what role it serves and why it might be an advantage to leverage over third-party products.

In addition to the aforementioned product-specific knowledge, a B2C solution architect is expected to understand the Salesforce best practices for integrating and leveraging their products together in service to a common solution. This is the heart of the Customer 360 concept. The next three chapters cover this in more detail.

The good news is you won't have to do everything on your own!

Architect team responsibilities

A successful B2C project will require multiple architects, each specializing in one of the component products, with the B2C solution architect providing direction on the points of integration. In practice, even though you'll be serving the role of a solution architect on a project, you're likely to have a background in one of the component products that may allow you to also serve as the technical architect for that component.

Throughout this chapter, we'll follow a simple five-phase process for discovery on a B2C solution architecture project:

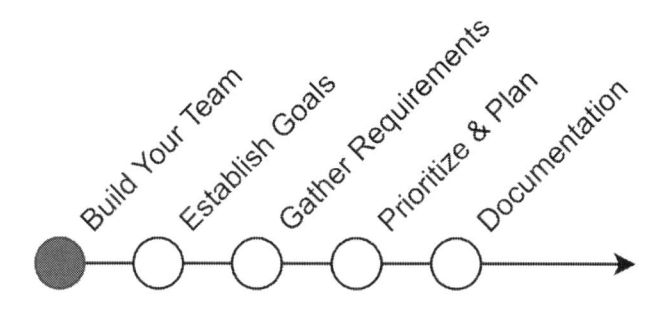

Figure 6.1 – Building your team

In this model, we'll start by assembling the right team, then align the whole team on high-level project goals, then gather requirements, prioritize, and build the appropriate architectural documentation.

> **Important note**
> There are many ways to structure a project or a team that can lead to a successful outcome. The approach outlined in this chapter is intended to illustrate the components of a successful project, but the exact team structure and methodology used will vary by organization.

As the solution architect, you'll be responsible for the customer data strategy, the flow of information between systems, the overall data model, the design of workflows and experiences that cross between systems, and the overall solution architecture.

Your B2C Commerce partner architect will be responsible for the B2C Commerce-specific data model. They'll also be responsible for B2C Commerce-specific integrations such as tax calculations and payments as well as customizations to the B2C Commerce product such as a custom product designer.

The Service Cloud architect will be responsible for the design of the Salesforce Platform user roles and hierarchy, sharing and permissions, overall org data model, and much more. Your job will be to figure out how a customer registering on the B2C Commerce storefront shows up in Service Cloud for service agents to find and then in Marketing Cloud so that you can design a welcome journey to introduce your new customer to the brand.

In addition, you'll be responsible for the final solution that meets the needs of the business. That means avoiding complex and hard-to-maintain solutions, organizational or data silos, technical debt, and quick-fix solutions. You'll have to work closely with the other architects and stakeholders throughout the design and implementation of the solution, knowing what to listen for, when to get involved, and what should be handled by others.

Stakeholders

In the real world, solutions are a lot more than architecture and technology. They must meet the needs of a business and its customers. As a B2C solution architect, you should have a clear understanding of how to use and integrate products, especially Salesforce products, in a solution. What you can't know in advance, however, is what a specific business needs from that solution. To find that out, you'll need to conduct stakeholder interviews. Stakeholder interviews allow you to discuss needs with representatives from various levels and groups within the impacted parts of the business.

As important as the role of the B2C solution architect is, you also won't be going at it alone. You'll need the right team to support you. In the following sections, we'll cover what an architect team looks like, how you can align the team on common goals, and how to conduct stakeholder interviews to identify the business needs that will drive the solution.

The full team

In your role as the B2C solution architect, you'll be working closely with the platform or product-specific technical architects focused on individual pieces of the larger solution. You'll also need to work with enterprise architects, who are responsible for the overall technology architecture of an organization of which the B2C solution may only be a part. The following diagram gives an overview of the typical architecture roles, although in some cases one person could play multiple roles:

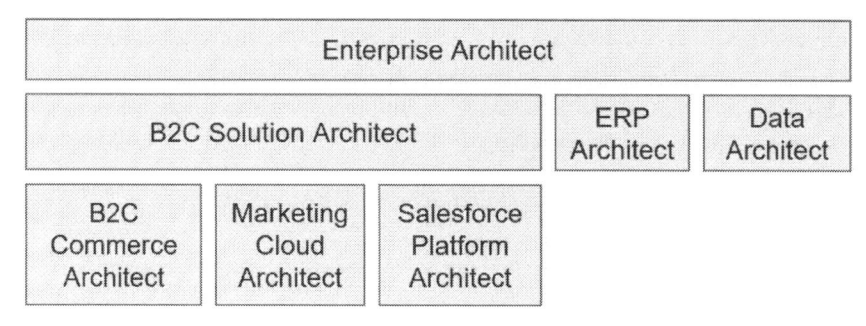

Figure 6.2 – Types of architects

The preceding figure shows how an enterprise architect owns the overall technical solution for an organization while more specialized technical architects focus on individual products or aspects of the business. The B2C solution architect sits between these two broad categories.

In addition to complementary architects, the following roles will typically be required on a B2C solution implementation project:

- **Executive sponsor**: Provides high-level direction to the project in alignment with a larger business strategy. They are also responsible for allocating appropriate resources and budget.
- **Product owner**: Responsible for ensuring the business needs and use cases are going to be met by the solution designed and documented by the business analyst and architects.
- **Project manager**: Responsible for coordinating the project, tracking the timeline and budget, scheduling meetings, and overall project health.
- **Business analyst**: Designs and documents the functional requirements of the solution and how it should operate from the user's perspective, and works very closely with their architecture peers.
- **Technical leads**: Translate architecture deliverables into a successful implementation on each component product.
- **Development team**: Handles code and complex declarative customization on each component product under the direction of a technical lead.
- **Quality assurance**: Ensures the resulting product meets the agreed-upon specifications and gracefully handles anticipated error conditions.

Depending on the complexity and needs of your specific project, you may need some or all of these roles at the level of specific products, across multiple products, or across the entire solution. If you're working in a consulting environment, you may also need some of these roles on both the client and service provider side of the joint team.

Discuss each as you build out a project org chart and make sure each role is accounted for, regardless of the job title associated with the individual doing the work. In some organizations, a project manager may be called a **program manager**, or a technical lead may be a **senior developer**; ultimately, what matters is that the responsibilities are accounted for within the team.

Alignment on goals

Creating an integrated solution that meets the needs of a unique organization requires some degree of up-front alignment, so everyone is moving in the same direction. This isn't about being prescriptive in terms of technology or business processes, it's about being deliberate in how team members communicate and coordinate.

This is phase 2 of the discovery process; with the team assembled, it's time to make sure everyone is working toward the same outcome:

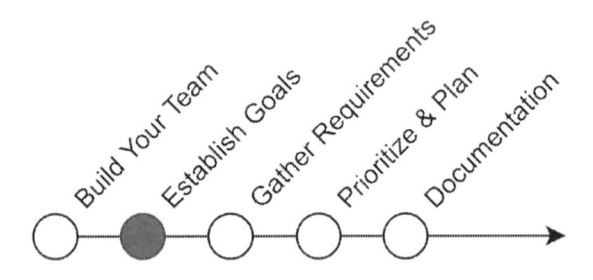

Figure 6.3 – Establishing goals

For a project that spans organizational boundaries to be successful, you'll need a sponsor that is at a high enough level in the organization that everyone involved reports to. In most organizations, that means having someone at the executive level who sets the tone and direction for their teams.

An example of an executive-level project goal would be the following:

Break down organizational silos and ensure that all customer data is available to the marketing team, to better target potential customers, and to the service team to better support existing customers.

As you work through the project, any time there's a discussion around customer data, everyone needs to stop and think whether it refers back to the project goal.

In addition to pointing the ship in the right direction, the team should agree on some ground rules.

Some example rules of engagement for an integrated product might include the following:

- Include a representative from the customer service team in any conversation around customer interaction.
- Include the solution architect in any decisions around data modeling.
- Be proactive about raising questions if you don't understand something, even if it's not in your area.
- When designing experiences, ask how this could impact other workstreams.

Based on the rules of engagement you establish for your project, you can start working together to understand the business needs through stakeholder interviews.

Stakeholder interviews

To ensure that your technical solutions produce the right business outcomes, the first step is to ensure you understand what those outcomes are. That means interviewing the people or teams responsible for each customer touchpoint. The goal is to find out what they need from the final solution so it can be considered as a unified whole.

This is the beginning of phase 3 of the discovery process, gathering requirements:

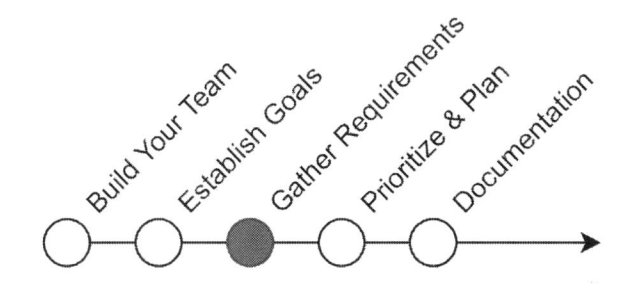

Figure 6.4 – Gathering requirements

At a minimum, look to schedule interviews with stakeholders from the following areas:

- Customer service
- Commerce
- Marketing
- Client IT

For each stakeholder interview, you'll start by creating a set of interview questions to guide the conversation, then review and assess the results of the conversation, and finally map the business needs not covered to technical solutions required to meet those needs.

Interview questions

For each area, you should aim to get a cross-section of roles and responsibilities, including leadership, management, and the people working day to day with your customers. People working at different levels of an organization will have different priorities and may be exposed to different points of friction or frustration, but they're all important to consider.

With executive leadership, ask questions such as the following:

- What is your highest priority for this project?
- How will the success of this project be measured (KPIs)?
- How well do you understand the health of your business?
- What data and analytics tools do you need to get the big picture?
- What areas of friction are slowing down your teams?
- What takes up the largest amount of your time?
- How well do you understand your customers and their interactions with your brand?
- Are you open to adapting your business processes to minimize customization?

With project leaders, ask questions such as the following:

- What are the main frustrations you hear from your teams?
- What mistakes do you see most commonly in day-to-day activities and how could we avoid them?
- What types of escalations are you receiving from customers?
- How well do you understand the work your teams are doing?
- How do you measure the success of your teams?

For the people working with your customers day to day, ask questions such as the following:

- What are the concerns most raised by customers every day?
- What takes up the largest portion of your time?
- Are there any tasks you do that feel repetitive and low value?

- How many different systems do you have to access to do your job?
- What portion of your time do you spend working on something new proactively versus reacting to concerns?
- How well do you understand how your work impacts other parts of a customer's experience with your company?
- How well do you understand how your work impacts your co-workers in other parts of the company?

Before conducting interviews, learn as much as you can about the company, the business they're in, the customers they serve, and the values that motivate them. Include additional questions to the preceding list that are more specific or relevant in each area and tailor the language to the industry. If an interview takes an unexpected turn, don't be afraid to explore it. If it seems productive, you may find valuable information.

> **Tip**
> Learn the language and culture of your client, make sure to understand their industry so you can have informed conversations.

If you work for a healthcare company, it's more appropriate to say *patient* instead of *customer*, and you may also need to expand your conversations to including *billing* and *patient services*. The important thing is to have a structured conversation in which you're listening for business problems you can solve with technology.

To continue with the Packt Gear example, a comment during stakeholder interviews could be, "Each store currently tracks their own guided hikes. When a customer has a question, we have to call the store to help them."

By asking additional questions, this could be turned into a user story format:

As a customer service representative, I want the ability to view and update customers' guided hike registrations on their behalf so that I can more effectively assist our customers.

We will return to this example throughout the chapter as we gradually build it into a requirement.

Assessing the results

Based on the conversations you have across the business, you're likely to notice some patterns starting to emerge. To be successful in a digital transformation and create a truly customer-centric organization, it's possible that more than just the technology will have to change.

The three primary requirements for a successful digital transformation are the following:

- **People**:
  - Do you have the right people in the right positions?
  - Are they motivated and measured in ways that support collaboration?
  - Is everyone aligned on the same goals regardless of organizational structure?
- **Processes**:
  - Does your organization promote collaboration, share data by default, consider impacts on other workstreams and systems, measure success collectively, and plan holistically?
- **Technology**:
  - Do you have an integrated solution allowing all the components to work together in service to a common goal?

While this book is focused on *technology*, the first two requirements of the list are equally important. During your conversations with stakeholders, some elements of **Organizational Change Management (OCM)** are going to arise that can't be solved with architecture.

If your customer service team is measured based on call volume and your commerce team is measured based on conversion and revenue, who is incentivized to deflect customer service cases by exposing knowledge articles on the commerce site to allow customers to find their own solutions? If the commerce team has their own graphics department working on the website, how will you convince them to use the assets in the new CMS being rolled out by the marketing team?

Document these non-technical challenges and ensure they're part of the plan for the overall solution. You probably won't be the one solving them, but someone must. There's little point in putting technology in place if no one knows how or wants to use it.

For the final category, technology, you absolutely *can* make a difference!

Thinking about our user story regarding guided hike sign-ups, we can clearly see that the way Packt Gear schedules hikes and keeps track of hiker registrations is going to change. This is going to affect the local store employees who plan the hikes (people), the way that hikers are signed up and tracked (process), and the systems that store that information (technology).

Without a plan to address all three, the new system is unlikely to be successful.

Mapping business needs to technology solutions

Your goal, as you sort through all the feedback from your interviews, is to figure out which concerns impact the technical solution and plan for how to accommodate them. Not everything needs to be part of the initial solution, so implementing a **Minimum Viable Product** (**MVP**) and creating a prioritized roadmap is recommended. To determine what goes in an MVP, you need to understand the difference between foundational decisions that you absolutely must get right out of the gate and incremental improvements you can layer on to a solution down the road.

The key things you should be listening for that inform technology decisions are the following:

- Repetitious or low-value work
- No or inadequate access to data and insights
- Need to work across multiple systems to complete tasks
- Customers needing help with basic tasks
- Operating in a reactive mode

As you identify business needs, start to organize them into the following categories based on what you know so far: single system, foundational multi-system, and incremental multi-system.

Single-system changes impact one system only; for example, a streamlined checkout process or a better cadence of welcome emails.

Single-system changes may be important, even transformative, but they aren't the province of the overall solution architect. You should coordinate handing these insights off to the individual product teams to pursue, always leaving open the option to pull you back in if unexpected dependencies arise.

Foundational multi-system changes are required in multiple systems that will have a significant long-term impact on the solution or that will be hard to change later once a direction is chosen.

Foundational multi-system changes are issues such as not having a consistent view of customer data across systems, separate customer or employee logins required across systems, or no integrations between systems at all. These types of changes are going to form the basis of the long-term connected solution; every future touchpoint is likely to involve customer data, authentication, or some type of integration (file or API based). These should be the initial focus of the architectural solution to safeguard the long-term solution.

Incremental multi-system changes are required in multiple systems that add value but have minimal impact on other features and that can be implemented and adjusted later.

The Packt Gear example regarding guided hike sign-up and tracking is an example of an incremental multi-system requirement. It touches more than just Service Cloud, sign-ups have to happen through the B2C Commerce storefront and marketing communications related to sign-ups go through Marketing Cloud, but it could be added to a solution without fundamentally changing the approach.

Categorizing features

You're going to uncover lots of value-added features such as exposing knowledge articles across systems, more consistent brand experience with content, ability to trigger abandoned cart email journeys, or ability to suppress marketing emails to customers with open service cases. Features such as these, while potentially very impactful for a business, can be built on top of the initial solution and prioritized in essentially any sequence.

Once your business needs are properly categorized and your architectural focus areas are determined, you can begin mapping these to technology solutions. First, determine what out-of-the-box product capabilities will support the business goal, including data storage capabilities and customer-facing features. Reviewing the features of each in-scope product in the first part of this book may help.

Next, if there are significant gaps, evaluate additional product options that may be needed to support the capability. *Chapter 5, Salesforce Ecosystem – Building a Complete Solution,* may be particularly helpful here, though you may also need to look outside of Salesforce at AppExchange solutions or other third parties.

Finally, determine what customization will be required in component products and work with product-specific technical architects to confirm that the changes can be supported. From there, knowing the features required to support the business case are available and can be supported, you can focus on the integration methods and data flow between systems that will be required to bring it all together.

Chapter 9, Supporting Key Business Scenarios, will review several examples of breaking down business scenarios to technical needs and designing a solution to meet those needs.

Having gotten a team aligned and gathered requirements through stakeholder interviews, then mapped those requirements to specific technology solutions, the next step is determining the optimum sequence for rolling out changes.

Project sequencing

There are many ways to prioritize and sequence work based on business priority. You might decide to implement the features that will build upon your existing technology footprint before investing in new technology. You might choose to work on the most impactful components first, the ones that are going to have the biggest effect on revenue or customer satisfaction. Maybe your business is coming up to the end of a software contract and the most important thing is to get your customer service team up and running on Service Cloud before the old system expires.

No matter what method of prioritizing outcomes is appropriate for your situation, there are a few things you'll need to get right out of the gate.

Building a firm foundation

Your job as the B2C solution architect is to make sure that any foundational decisions around data strategy or integration are properly thought through and accounted for. There will always be incremental improvements to make in the future, but there are a few things that you must get right out of the gate to avoid costly rework.

Breaking the requirements down into steps, prioritizing the critical up-front decisions, and building a plane is phase 4 of the discovery process:

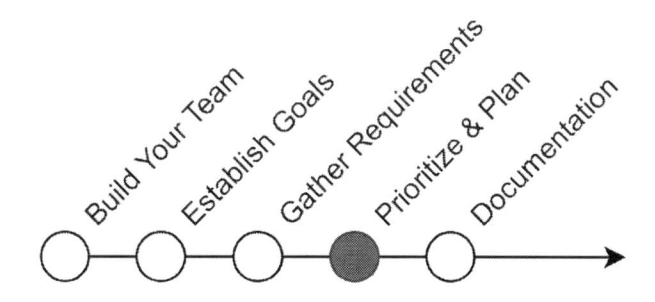

Figure 6.5 – Prioritizing and planning

Out of the gate, focus on identifying architectural decisions that will establish the foundation of the work to come. The next two chapters are dedicated to building the right foundation of integration and customer data to support the business cases discussed in *Chapter 9, Supporting Key Business Scenarios*.

In particular, the following decisions should be made carefully up front because they're harder to reverse course on later:

- What is the system of record for customer data and how will it be accessed from or shared with other systems?
- How will different systems authenticate with each other and what mechanisms will be used for integration?
- What component products do you know will be part of the solution, now or in the future, that should be planned for?

The first point in the list is perhaps the most important. There's more than one right answer – the next chapter covers this in detail – but it's still a foundational decision because once you have a solution in place, changing it will impact nearly every aspect of the rest of the solution. Be mindful of who needs access to what data and under what circumstances; also, consider regulatory concerns around customer data storage and customer consent. In some parts of the world, most notably Europe under GDPR but increasingly in other areas, improper storage of customer data can have serious ramifications for a business.

With the second point, it's not necessary to decide upon every API endpoint, resource, and use case you'll ever need up front. You can build upon that as you develop the solution incrementally. It is important to understand the integration mechanisms you'll be leveraging, how the various systems will authenticate with each other, and how you'll keep credentials secure.

If you're building an integrated solution that relies on APIs to communicate between components, are you going to build with integration middleware or point to point? Will you use a mix of both? This decision can have a significant impact on the way your solution evolves and is challenging to unwind if a different approach is needed later. We'll cover these options in more detail in *Chapter 7, Integration Architecture Options*.

Finally, having an idea of the component products in a solution can help to shape that solution. You will never know this perfectly; the world changes too fast and new solutions will be needed in the future but try to define at least the core of a solution. Integrating B2C Commerce with Marketing Cloud and trying to add Service Cloud in a later phase is going to cause significant rework. If you know that Service Cloud is going to be used eventually, it's far better to leverage an inexpensive license for the Salesforce Platform to serve as the customer data repository and then integrate that to Marketing Cloud. This sets the stage to build out Service Cloud when an organization is ready without rework.

> **Tip**
> We'll expand upon why integrating B2C Commerce with Marketing directly can cause rework in *Chapter 8, Creating a 360° View of the Customer*.

Since we know that the requirement to track and manage guided hike sign-ups in a system that customer service representatives have access to is an incremental, multi-system requirement, it doesn't need to be part of the MVP deployment, but we'll keep it in mind for the next phase.

Evaluating next steps

At this point in the design process, you'll have documented your business use cases and identified the things you absolutely must get right out of the gate. Now you'll have a lot more flexibility in how you sequence improvements. It's important to keep in mind that there is no one correct B2C solution architecture.

Every business is unique and has unique needs.

Here are a few considerations that you might use to prioritize the remaining work:

- Address customer pain points based on surveys/feedback.
- Consolidate systems to reduce technology costs.
- Focus on revenue-driving initiatives such as abandoned cart.
- Leverage the most mature parts of the organization first while you build the infrastructure for the next phase.
- Strengthen your brand consistency through content and communications.
- Prioritize data and analytics gaps to help inform the next wave of changes.
- Pick out *quick wins* that have a comparatively low cost to implement.

Regardless of the method you choose, review the business needs identified earlier and score them from 1 to 10. Look for common themes among the pieces, things that would logically be done together because they impact the same parts of the technology of the experience, and group them. Identify any dependencies or prerequisites among the business cases and make sure those are respected. You can't build intelligent chatbots if you don't have chat capability, for example.

As you work through this exercise of prioritization and share it with stakeholders, a natural roadmap will begin to emerge. If you're working in an agile environment and just building to capacity, great, populate your backlog and get moving!

If you're working in a consulting environment and creating a **Scope of Work** (**SOW**), you may need to estimate the cost and time to do the work overall at this stage. Work methodically through each business case, estimating the effort required to make the underlying technical changes. This is also a good time to evaluate the sequencing of work across different systems to ensure that changes are executed in a coordinated fashion.

Business case breakdown

Let's take an example: the business case you're trying to unlock is to allow customer service agents working in Service Cloud to view a customer's B2C Commerce wish list when they are helping the customer with an issue via live chat. The business value is that this might allow an agent to suggest upsells or substitutions if the customer has concerns with a product that they ordered but perhaps something on their wish list is comparable and could be offered at a discount.

Evaluating the technical changes required to unlock this business case, you decide that three things are required:

1. The agent needs to know who they're interacting with (**ContactID**).
2. B2C Commerce needs to expose the customer's wish list to Service Cloud.
3. Service Cloud needs to retrieve and display the wish list in the Service Console.

Once you establish the right foundation of customer identity as described in detail in *Chapter 8, Creating a 360° View of the Customer*, the first item will be in place. You'll also have the corresponding identifiers for the B2C Commerce customer record: **Customer Number**, **Customer ID**, **Customer List ID**, and **Site ID**.

For the second item in the preceding list, the required B2C Commerce information is available via the OCAPI Shop API through the `Customers` resource:

```
GET /customers/{customer_id}/product_lists
```

Details of this API resource are available at `https://sforce.co/2SwqnT3`.

Based on this, there should be no need to customize B2C Commerce, you can just configure the **Client ID** used by Service Cloud to allow access to this resource.

> **Tip**
> If you need a refresher on the B2C Commerce API options, review *Chapter 3, Direct-to-Consumer Selling with Commerce Cloud B2C*.

For the final piece, exposing that information in Service Cloud, there are a variety of options available depending on the integration method you're using (see *Chapter 7, Integration Architecture Options*). However, the simplest solution would be to create a new **Lightning Web Component** (**LWC**) in Service Cloud that can be added to the **Page Layout** for the **Contact** record in the Service Console. When the **Contact** is opened by an agent working on a case, this LWC can query B2C Commerce for the customer's current wish list information (stored in a product list) and display it for the agent.

While it's possible to store that information in Service Cloud using a new custom object linked to the **Contact** record, you decide this information isn't needed outside of this one specific context so there's no need to fetch and store it in advance.

This is an appropriate level of detail for a B2C solution architect to reach with the solution design. The required products have been determined, the integration method has been specified, the specific resources or endpoints identified, and the required customization or configuration in each system to support the use case is clear.

A Service Cloud-specialized architect or technical lead can take this direction, refine or clarify it if needed, and provide a design spec and estimate for the work to be done. This method, repeated for each desired business case, is the fundamental methodology used for designing multi-system solutions.

For the Packt Gear guided hike example, we've already discussed an approach for building the data model to support this in Service Cloud. Once the data is in Service Cloud, it can be retrieved and updated from B2C Commerce via REST APIs, and hike sign-ups can be pushed to Marketing Cloud using Marketing Cloud Connect.

Next, we'll review the ways these design decisions are documented and communicated through architecture deliverables.

Architecture deliverables

As a B2C solution architect, your primary role in a project is to design the overall technical solution to support business needs regardless of the component products. The way that you'll distill and communicate that design is through a set of architectural deliverables.

Creating the architectural documentation, based on the foundational decisions and requirements gathered, is the last phase of the discovery process before moving into implementation:

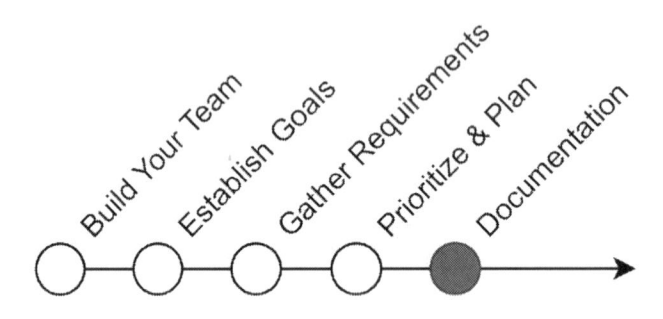

Figure 6.6 – Documentation

Architectural deliverables are any work product that is intended to document and communicate the design of the solution to other stakeholders, including the implementation team. These can be documents, presentations, diagrams, spreadsheets, wiki pages, or anything else that helps to take the solution from the theoretical to the concrete. Your role is to take those business needs, such as the ability to pull up a customer's order history when they start a live chat session, and turn them into implementation details needed to create that experience across technologies.

In the following sections, we'll cover the most important architectural diagrams you'll use to document and guide your B2C solution architecture: the system overview diagram, data mapping diagram, and sequence diagram. We'll also cover what constitutes a complete **technical specification document** (**TSD**).

These are the key artifacts of a well-designed B2C solution architecture.

System overview diagram

The most important artifact you'll be responsible for is a system overview diagram showing how each of the component products fits together in a B2C solution and what ties them together. This will be built in conjunction with your enterprise architect counterparts, who will be able to contribute more information about how the overall architecture interacts with other parts of the business technology landscape.

The following system overview diagram shows a simple integration scenario with the Salesforce Platform, B2C Commerce, and Marketing Cloud:

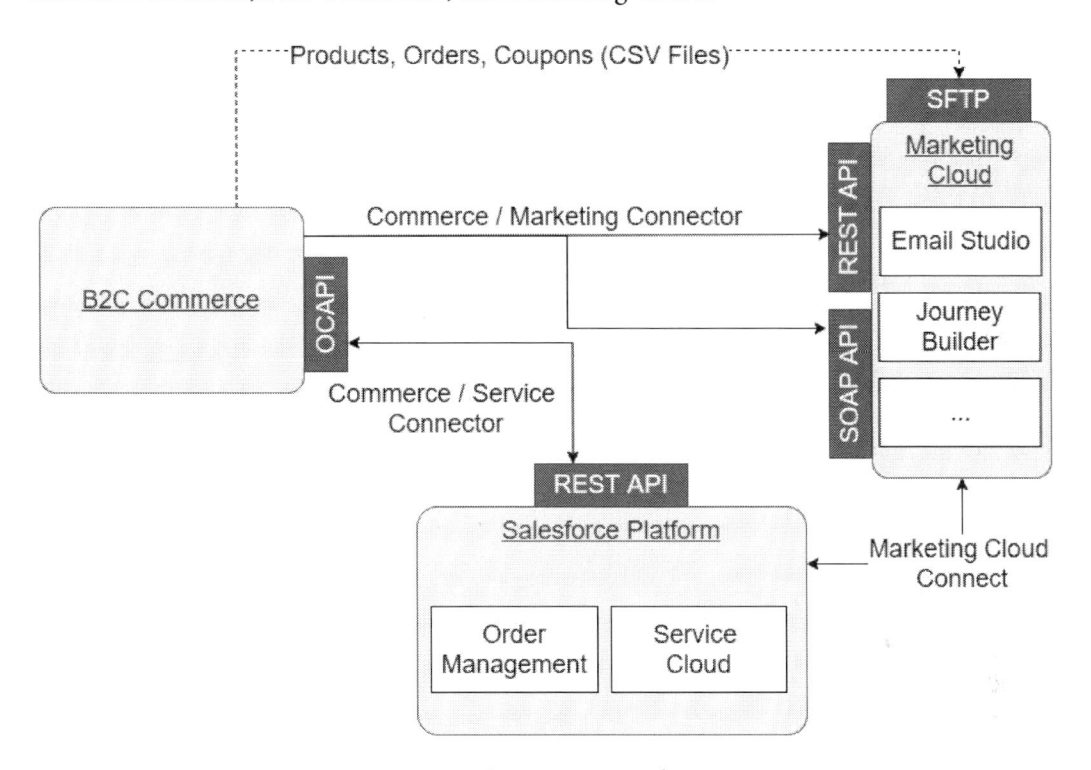

Figure 6.7 – System overview diagram

In the preceding diagram, you can see visually that the Salesforce Platform is host to two component products that are part of this solution: **Order Management** and **Service Cloud**. We can also see that we're leveraging **Email Studio** and **Journey Builder** within **Marketing Cloud**. In a real system overview diagram, we'd likely have additional Marketing Cloud components to list here. We'll cover each of these component integration accelerator options in detail in *Chapter 7, Integration Architecture Options*.

In addition to the products involved, we can also see how the systems are integrated. Specifically, you can see that **B2C Commerce** and the **Salesforce Platform** are integrated with a **Commerce / Service Connector**, which is built on top of **OCAPI** on the **B2C Commerce** side and the **Salesforce Platform REST API**. We can also see that Commerce is integrated with Marketing Cloud using a **Commerce / Marketing Connector**, which is one-directional from B2C Commerce to Marketing Cloud using both the **REST API** and **SOAP API**. In addition to the real-time calls via API integration, we can see that **Product**, **Order**, and **Coupon** data is being sent using **CSV** files to the **Marketing Cloud SFTP** server in batch mode.

In the bottom right of the diagram, it's clear that the Salesforce Platform and Marketing Cloud are connected using something called **Marketing Cloud Connect**. Because Marketing Cloud Connect is a productized solution from Salesforce rather than custom code built on top of the APIs, it's shown to the side, but it does leverage the same APIs used by custom solutions behind the scenes.

While all this information can certainly be described with text, it's far more consumable as a diagram. Creating and maintaining a system overview diagram like this is the responsibility of the B2C solution architect. As the solution evolves, it will grow to include additional platforms and products and you might expand upon the data being moved between systems.

Data mapping

There are a variety of ways that data can be accessed from and moved between systems, and a variety of data points you might consider, but for anything that's going to be synchronized between different systems, you'll need to define the data mapping between them. In the example we outlined earlier in this chapter, wish list data was accessed on demand, so there was no synchronization that needed to take place and, therefore, no data mapping but that won't always be the case.

The fundamental data mapping exercise is going to be for customer data, something we'll focus on extensively in *Chapter 8, Creating a 360° View of the Customer*. In most solutions, customer data *will* be synchronized between systems so the way that data will be represented in each system needs to be established up front.

In the following example, we're showing an example B2C Commerce Customer profile, Service Cloud Account and Contact records, and a Marketing Cloud Subscriber profile along with a subset of attributes stored in each that we need to map together:

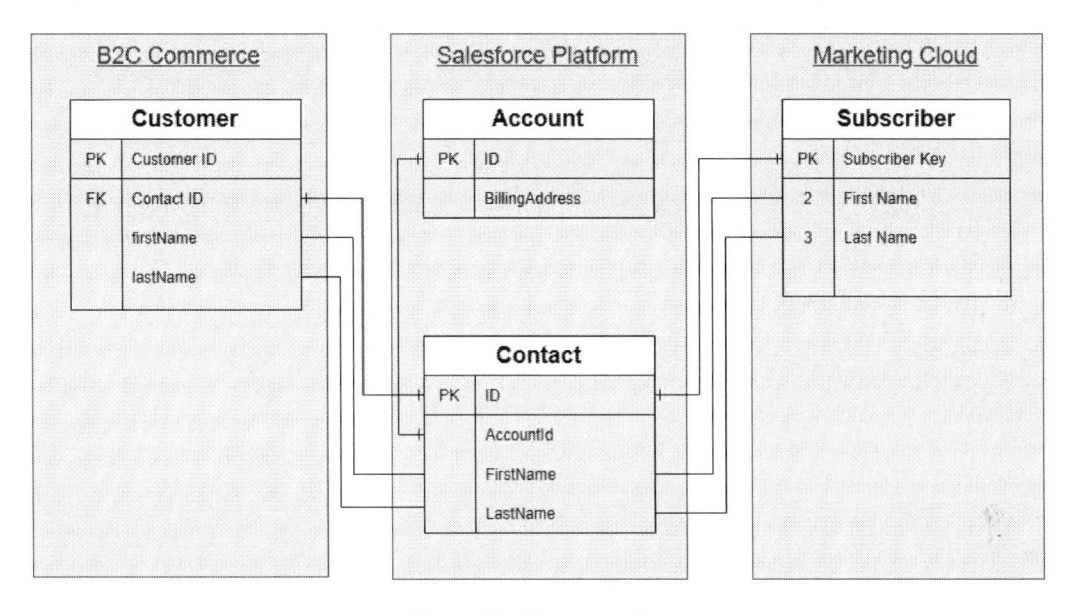

Figure 6.8 – Data mapping

The preceding diagram shows a simple example of customer data stored in three different systems: **B2C Commerce**, the **Salesforce Platform** (for example, Service Cloud), and **Marketing Cloud**. In each system, the representation of a customer is slightly different. In B2C Commerce, a **Customer** record is used with **Customer ID** as its **Primary Key** (**PK**) and attributes for firstName and lastName. In the Salesforce Platform, two related objects are used together to represent a person: Account and Contact, each with their own PK ID. Although there are two objects involved, when using Person accounts, they are treated as a unit with data describing the individual shared across both. Finally, in Marketing Cloud, the representation of the same individual is the Contact identified by a Contact Key.

This diagram also shows that the B2C Commerce Customer record has been extended with a **Contact ID** field that matches the ID of the **Contact** record in the Salesforce platform corresponding to this customer. In turn, the Marketing Cloud Contact Key is also the Contact ID value, linking all three records together despite being in different systems. Since these records represent the same individual, they all store that person's first and last name, but they use different fields to do so. This diagram shows the representation of first name and last name in each system and relates them together.

For large datasets, this can also be expressed in a tabular format as follows:

Field	Type	B2C Commerce	Salesforce Platform	Marketing Cloud
Contact ID	string	contactID	Contact.ID*	Subscriber Key
Customer ID	string	customerID*	B2CCustomer__c	B2C Customer ID
Customer No	string	customerNo*	B2CCustomerNo__c	B2C Customer ID
First Name	string	firstName	FirstName	First Name
Last Name	string	lastName	LastName	Last Name

Figure 6.9 – Data mapping table

In the tabular view shown, we're expressing essentially the same information as we showed in the data mapping diagram in *Figure 6.8* by showing how each data point is stored in each component system. The bold identifiers with an asterisk denote the source system for a given identifier. This format can support much larger datasets.

You should plan to create tables or diagrams like this for all data points that will be synchronized or accessed between systems as another architectural deliverable.

Sequence diagram

With a system overview diagram in place to describe the overall interaction between component products, and a data mapping relating synchronized data storage between systems, it's time to turn our attention to mapping out specific interactions to support business cases. The best way to represent this type of interaction is using a sequence diagram.

The example sequence diagram shows a simplified live chat sequence involving B2C Commerce and Service Cloud:

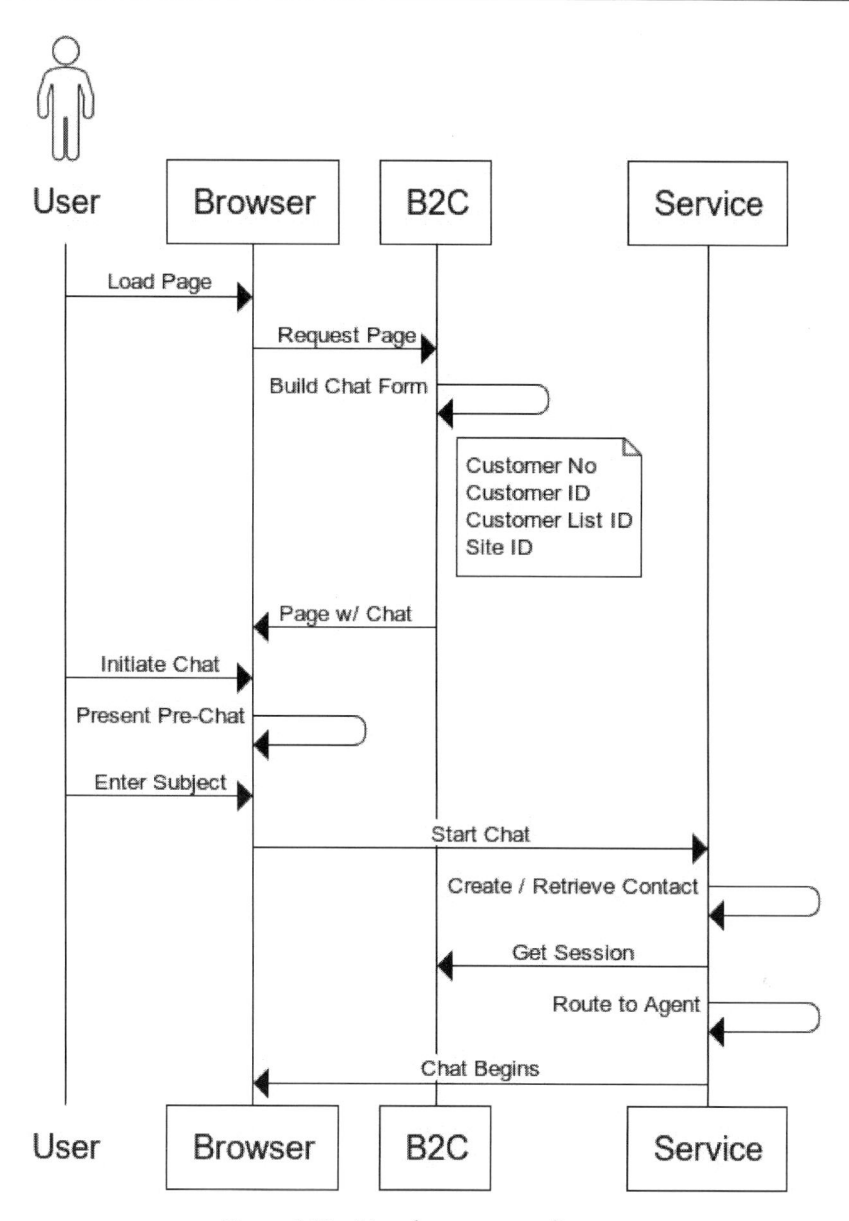

Figure 6.10 – Live chat sequence diagram

This sequence diagram depicts the involved actor (the user) and systems (browser, B2C Commerce, and Service Cloud). It shows the sequence of events from top to bottom as well as the actions taken by each system involved. We can clearly see that B2C Commerce is responsible for building the chat form including the **Customer Number**, **Customer ID**, **Customer List ID**, and **Site ID**.

The user must populate a pre-chat form with a subject, then the browser calls Service Cloud to initiate the chat session. Service Cloud will find or create a corresponding Contact record and retrieve the B2C Commerce session information before routing to an agent to start the chat. At this point, the agent has the full context on the customer, including their current basket state in B2C Commerce.

A sequence diagram like this, created for each use case, clearly identifies the role of each system in the overall solution and can help to coordinate implementation and testing on complex multi-system workflows.

Technical specification documents

A **TSD** translates between business requirements and technical details required for implementation. It serves two primary purposes; it helps ensure a correct implementation and it serves as long-term documentation of the solution. Therefore, it's just as important to *maintain* your TSDs as an implementation evolves as it is to create a quality TSD in the first place. The first time you have to wake up in the middle of the night to fix a problem with a system you didn't build, you'll appreciate good-quality documentation!

A well-written TSD clearly describes how a particular component of a solution will be built, including where the data will reside, how it will be accessed, how systems will interface with each other, and the order in which it will happen. The TSD can incorporate each of the architectural deliverables described earlier in this section along with sufficient descriptive text to explain the solution.

In general, a TSD should start with a high-level description of the use case being addressed. For example, implement context-aware live chat between B2C Commerce and Service Cloud allowing a CSR to have access to the full B2C Commerce customer profile and session information while assisting a customer when that customer initiates a chat session from the B2C Commerce storefront.

From there, it should peel back the layers from the general to the specific, describing more detail at each level with plenty of supporting diagrams or tables.

Building upon our example, the next level of detail might be to explain that the **Live Chat** form will be rendered by the B2C Commerce server with each page view in the footer.

The **Live Chat** form should include four hidden pre-chat header variables and one customer entered one for the subject field as follows:

Value	Pre-Chat Header Field	B2C Commerce Source
Customer ID	customerID	`customer.ID`
Customer Number	customerNo	`customer.profile.customerNo`
Customer List ID	customerList	`CustomerMgr.siteCustomerList.ID`
Site ID	siteID	`Site.current.ID`
Subject	Subject	`<Customer Entered>`

Figure 6.11 – Pre-chat header fields

The preceding mapping shows not just what variables to include in the rendered form, but also where to retrieve those values in B2C Commerce. From here, this mapping needs to be carried through to the Service Cloud side where the values are used to retrieve customer information from B2C Commerce and stored on the `Chat Transcript` object.

In addition to tracking data through systems, a TSD also needs to specify non-functional requirements of a system, including the following:

- Expected performance characteristics and timeouts
- Error handling and fallback/retry mechanisms
- Security and encryption
- System accessibility
- Legal compliance and consent
- Data cleanup and retention
- Usability and maintenance
- Troubleshooting guidelines

As you work through the technical design, think about all the ways that things could go wrong and how the system should handle them. If you're making a real-time call from B2C Commerce to Service Cloud during account creation to create/update the **Contact** record, what happens if that call times out? Do we now just have a forever-orphaned B2C Commerce profile with no **contact ID**? That won't work, you'll need to have a way to retry that call in the background when Service Cloud is back up or the issue is resolved.

What happens if a call to Marketing Cloud to trigger an order confirmation email fails? Can the customer contact support and can they manually trigger another? Can the customer resend it themselves from their order history page? Will B2C Commerce automatically retry later? Any of these solutions would work, depending on the business need; the point is to ensure that these cases are thought through and accounted for.

Your TSD is complete when there's no ambiguity regarding how the proposed solution will be implemented from a technology perspective. The involved systems are clearly identified, data storage is mapped out down to the field level, including the system of residency and any synchronization requirements, all interfaces between systems are described, the sequence of interactions and dependencies are clear, required customizations within each system are noted, and expected error handling is noted.

Examples of Salesforce recommended documentation deliverables for B2C architects are available at `https://sforce.co/33zJuhB`.

The Packt Gear team

Working in the role of B2C solution architect for Packt Gear, you know you'll need a lot of support to design and implement the best solution for the business. Your responsibility will be understanding and creating the documentation to support the overall technical integration, data mapping, and workflow between products in the solution to support the business needs.

We used a couple of simple examples of cross-cloud requirements in this chapter. A real-life solution will have many more, but the process doesn't need to change. Listen for pain points during interviews that can be turned into user stories. Map the user stories to technology solutions and prioritize them as either foundational or incremental. Finally, create the technical documentation to deliver the solution.

From there, you'll need the support of platform-specific technical architects to design and document the implementation details for B2C Commerce, Marketing Cloud, Service Cloud, and Order Management. You'll also need business representatives and product owners to keep everyone aligned on the anticipated outcomes and usability. You'll need functional architects and business analysts to document the solution and design an experience that meets the needs of both internal users and customers.

You'll need technical leads and developers to build the solution, quality assurance engineers to test not only the component parts but also the solution, and a project manager to keep it all on track. It's not going to be easy, but with the right team and a solid plan, you're ready to get started!

Summary

After reading this chapter, you should be able to explain where you as a B2C solution architect fit into a larger team. You should also feel comfortable helping to shape a program team that can lead to successful outcomes and articulating the need for each role. Once the team is assembled, you'll be able to work with your executive sponsor to align the team on the overall program goals that each group will be working toward.

With the right team assembled, you can identify required stakeholder interviews and the appropriate questions to ask at each level to understand business needs. You'll also be able to work with your platform-specific technical architects and business analyst counterparts to assess the results of stakeholder interviews and map the requirements back to technical solutions. At this stage, you should clearly understand what changes are needed, the involved systems, and the technical solution required to implement the capabilities.

As your work with your team and business stakeholders, you should be able to separate foundational architectural decisions that need to be made up front and will be difficult to change from incremental changes that can be scheduled later. Once you get the foundation in place, you can prioritize ongoing work according to business impact, quick wins, anticipated ROI, or other factors.

With your roadmap in place, you should know what deliverables are required from you as a B2C solution architect and from the other platform-specific technical architects on your team to ensure a successful outcome. You'll be able to document the overall solution in a system overview diagram, document the data storage in each system and how they relate with a data mapping diagram, and use sequence diagrams to show visually the way users and systems interact in specific use cases.

Finally, you'll be able to pull together all of this with a TSD that provides sufficient detail for the implementation team to bring the business vision to life.

In the next chapter, we'll go through a detailed review of integration options and the tools provided by Salesforce to support each.

Questions

1. True or false? An enterprise architect provides platform-specific technical expertise to support the B2C solution architect.
2. What is the purpose of conducting stakeholder interviews when shaping a B2C solution?
3. Which diagram is used to express high-level products and their interaction points within a B2C solution architecture?
4. When is it appropriate to defer foundational components of the implementation and focus on high-value quick wins?
5. Why is it important to break down business cases into technology solutions after the stakeholder interview phase?
6. True or false? When mapping data between systems, it's important to get all the way to the field level.

7
Integration Architecture Options

With a firm understanding of the products that will be leveraged in the overall solution, and the right team assembled with alignment on project goals, it's time to start evaluating options for bringing it all together. In this chapter, we'll cover three main strategies for integration, including point-to-point integrations, integrations through a middleware layer, and building around a single source of truth. In most solutions, elements of each of these integration patterns will be leveraged to create the right solution for a given organization.

In *Chapter 6*, *Role of a Solution Architect*, we covered some of the other architects you'll be working with as part of an integrated solution, including enterprise and product-specific technical architects. The decisions around integration architecture and patterns are where you'll be coordinating most heavily with the enterprise architect, who likely has a larger vision for how integration should work within the organization. Product technical architects can provide valuable insight into capabilities and constraints for each component as well.

For each of the three patterns covered, we'll review some reasons to incorporate elements of that pattern into the overall solution as well as considerations for when it may not be the right choice. Considerations such as organizational technical maturity, enterprise architecture landscape, budget, timeline, and long-term plans can all play a role in choosing the right target state integration architecture.

In this chapter, we're going to cover the following main topics:

- Cross-cloud application development life cycle
- Point-to-point integrations
- Integration middleware
- Single source of truth
- Monitoring the solution

After reading this chapter, you'll have the skills needed to make informed decisions about Salesforce B2C solution architecture integration strategies. You'll understand the capabilities and role of the Salesforce point-to-point connectors and where integration middleware adds value. When an organization is organized around or striving toward a single source of truth solution, you'll be able to explain what that means and how it interacts with a Salesforce B2C solution architecture.

Cross-cloud application development life cycle

To implement an integrated solution, it's necessary to not only understand the way instances and environments are structured in each component product, but the way instances in one product relate to instances in another product. Salesforce orgs are different from B2C Commerce realms, and both are different from Marketing Cloud instances, but all must work together not just in a production environment but to support a full application development and testing life cycle.

Having covered each product in isolation, this section discusses how they fit together, not just in a final state architecture, but during the application development life cycle.

> **Tip**
> For a refresher on the instances and environments supported by each product, review *Chapter 2, Supporting Your Customers with Service Cloud*; *Chapter 3, Direct-to-Consumer Selling with Commerce Cloud B2C*; or *Chapter 4, Engaging Customers with Marketing Cloud*.

The following sections touch briefly on each product's development life cycle before suggesting an integrated approach that brings them all together.

Service Cloud application development life cycle

With Service Cloud, and all Salesforce Platform-based products, there are many different workflows used to support application development life cycles. Different Service Cloud Edition licenses also support different types of Sandbox instances, but the following diagram is one example:

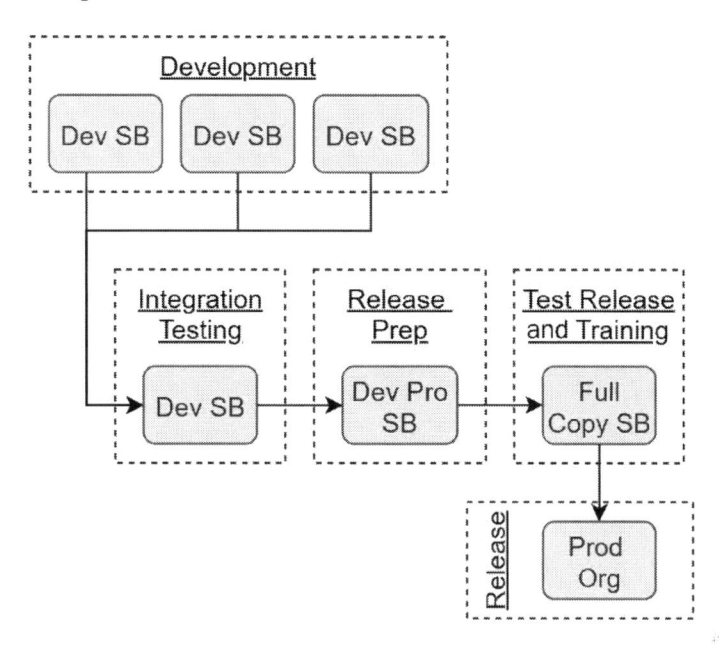

Figure 7.1 – Example Salesforce Platform application development life cycle

In *Figure 7.1*, we can see that developers use **Developer Sandbox (Dev SB)** instances for implementing specific features. Once a feature is complete, it is moved to a dedicated **Dev SB** for integration testing (where work from multiple developers is combined). After that, a **Developer Pro Sandbox (Dev Pro SB)** is used for release prep and final testing before a test deployment is made to a **Full Copy Sandbox (Full Copy SB)**. The **Full Copy SB** can be used for training and performance testing on production data volumes. As a final step, the **Production Org (Prod Org)** is updated with the fully tested deployment. For teams leveraging SFDX, Scratch Orgs may replace Dev SBs, but a similar workflow exists.

B2C Commerce application development life cycle

In B2C Commerce, Sandboxes are used for feature development and sometimes integration testing. QA testing would happen on the Development instance, and UAT would happen on the Staging instance before code is ultimately released to production. The following diagram depicts this application development life cycle using B2C Commerce instances:

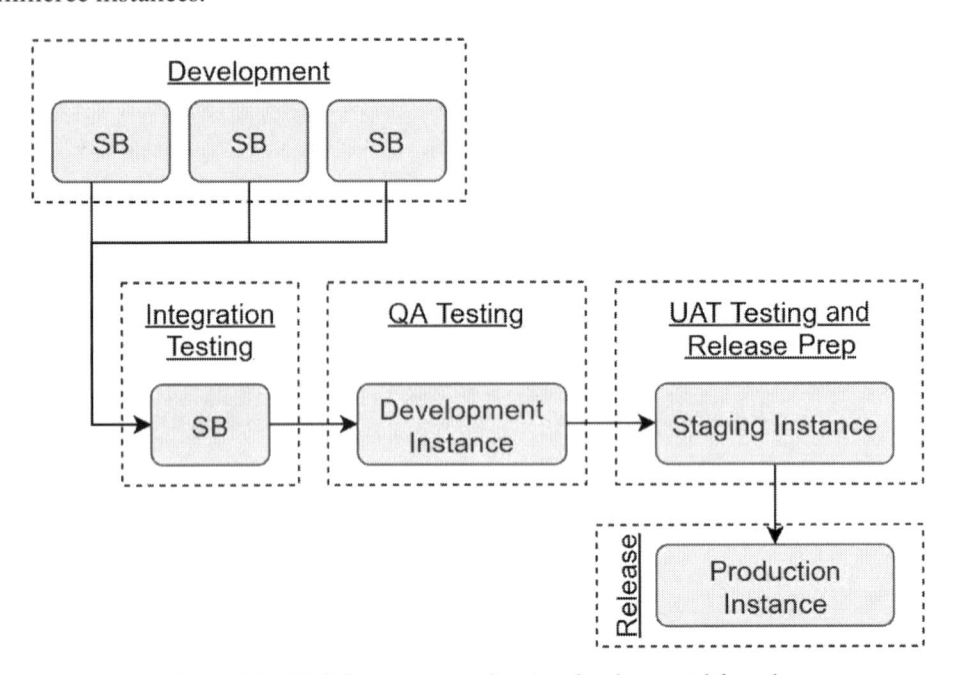

Figure 7.2 – B2C Commerce application development life cycle

As the preceding diagram shows, a similar workflow to the one depicted for the Salesforce Platform can be achieved with B2C Commerce instances. The primary difference is that the B2C Commerce workflow is less flexible. Each B2C Commerce realm has exactly one instance each of Development, Staging, and Production, and each has a specific role in the application development life cycle. Review *Chapter 3, Direct-to-Consumer Selling with Commerce Cloud B2C,* for more information on B2C Commerce instance structures.

Marketing Cloud application development life cycle

Finally, in Marketing Cloud, there is only one instance per customer – production. No similar development life cycle is possible with Marketing Cloud. It is possible to segment test data from production data to some extent using **Business Units (BUs)**, but all changes take place on the production instance.

This can be managed in a variety of ways, depending on the needs of your organization. One simple approach is to leverage test versions of each Marketing Cloud component. For example, create an *Order Confirmation TEST* email to correspond to your *Order Confirmation* email. Ensure that only test emails are included in test data extensions and manually migrate changes to your real components when they are tested and approved. This is the simplest and least expensive option but is also the most manual and error-prone.

Another option is to purchase and leverage separate test BUs segregated from your production BUs. This requires an Enterprise 2.0 instance of Marketing Cloud and has an associated cost for purchasing BUs. It's a more affordable option than purchasing an entirely separate Marketing Cloud instance and has better support for sharing components, but it does not fully partition data. All subscriber data from test business units will also be added to **All Subscribers** and **All Contacts**.

It is also possible to purchase an entirely separate Marketing Cloud instance, but there is no mechanism to migrate or share components between them, making this an expensive option and of limited use as a test and staging tool.

Integrated B2C solution application development life cycle

The instance and environment structures, as well as the application development life cycles, are important to consider when designing solutions that require changes in multiple products to succeed. It is easy to draw a diagram showing B2C Commerce and Service Cloud passing customer data back and forth, but this solution requires development and testing in both systems so changes must be coordinated to ensure they are active in the same instances at the same time. This may require coordinating release cycles between product teams or leveraging feature switches and techniques such as mocked APIs to minimize dependencies.

The following diagram shows a coordinated application development life cycle across different products for implementing features that require changes in both:

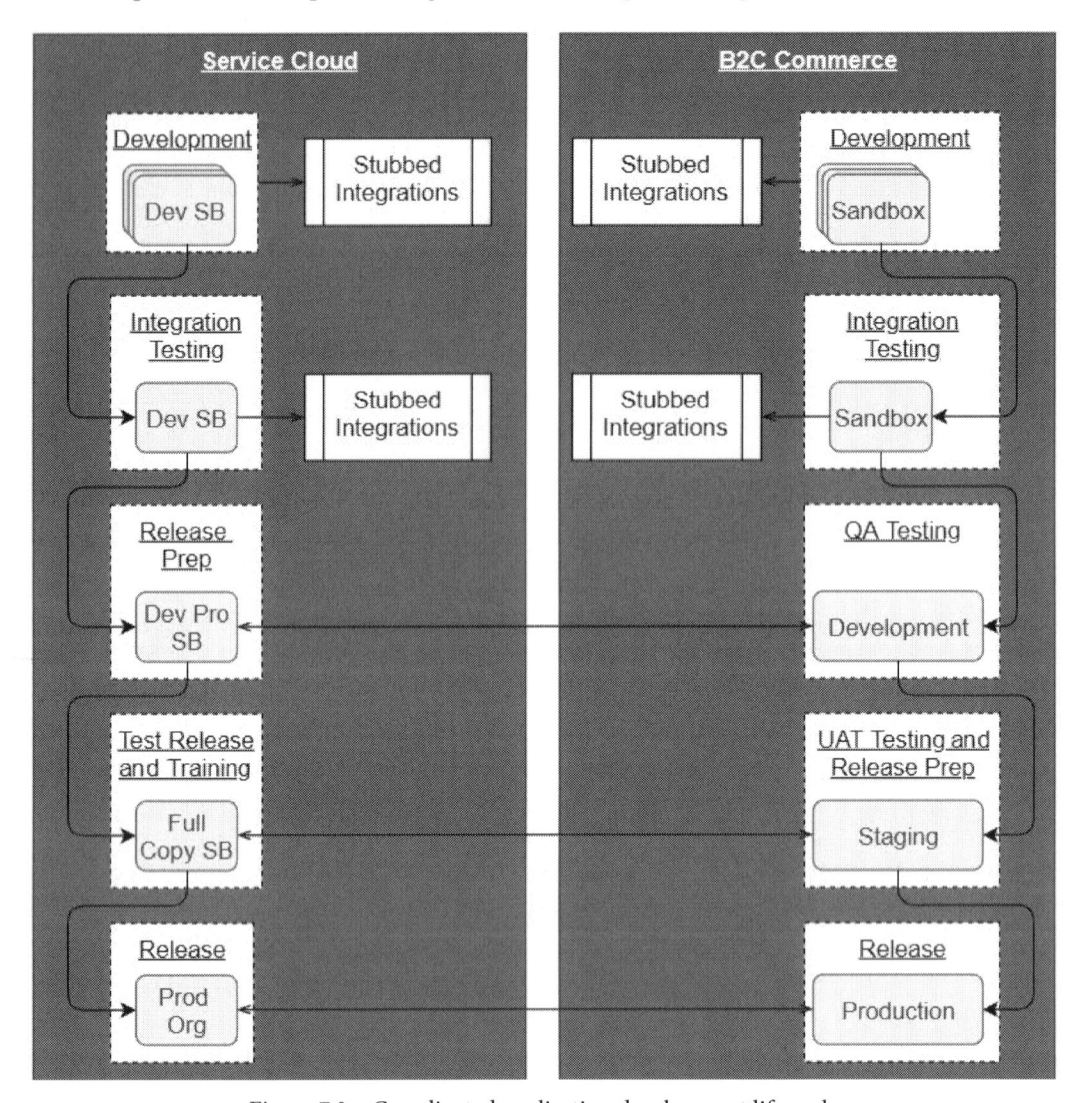

Figure 7.3 – Coordinated application development life cycle

This is one potential solution for integrating environments between Service Cloud and B2C Commerce to support each stage of the development life cycle. This requires releases with interdependent features to be coordinated and tested at the same time, starting with release prep to ensure a full end-to-end experience is testable.

Where Marketing Cloud is in the picture, since it has only one instance, changes are generally made in advance of required integration by external systems, so they are ready when needed. For example, if a B2C Commerce instance needs to trigger an order confirmation email from Marketing Cloud, the appropriate transactional email would first be implemented in Marketing Cloud and then B2C Commerce would be updated to use it. In many cases, if a test BU is being leveraged, the changes will first be made here and tested from integrated environments before being deployed to the production BU.

Now that we've established a method for moving changes through environments, let's review the various ways of integrating component products in a B2C solution. In the rest of this chapter, we'll discuss accelerator solutions provided by Salesforce, productized integrations, custom development options, and integration middleware options that can all be used to create a seamlessly integrated solution.

Point-to-point integrations

Point-to-point integrations are any connections between the component systems of a solution where the express purpose of the component is something other than an integration layer. Making a SOAP API call from B2C Commerce to Marketing Cloud to trigger an order confirmation email after a customer places an order through the storefront is an example of a point-to-point integration. Fetching customer data from MuleSoft, which in turn retrieves data from other systems, is not point-to-point.

Point-to-point integrations are sometimes viewed as an anti-pattern as integration middleware solutions such as MuleSoft, Dell Boomi, Talend, and Jitterbit grow in popularity. Indeed, an architecture built on a well-structured integration solution has significant advantages, which will be discussed in the next section. Despite that, there are still many situations where point-to-point integrations are the best choice or even required.

The following diagram represents the canonical retail solution architecture integration diagram from Salesforce:

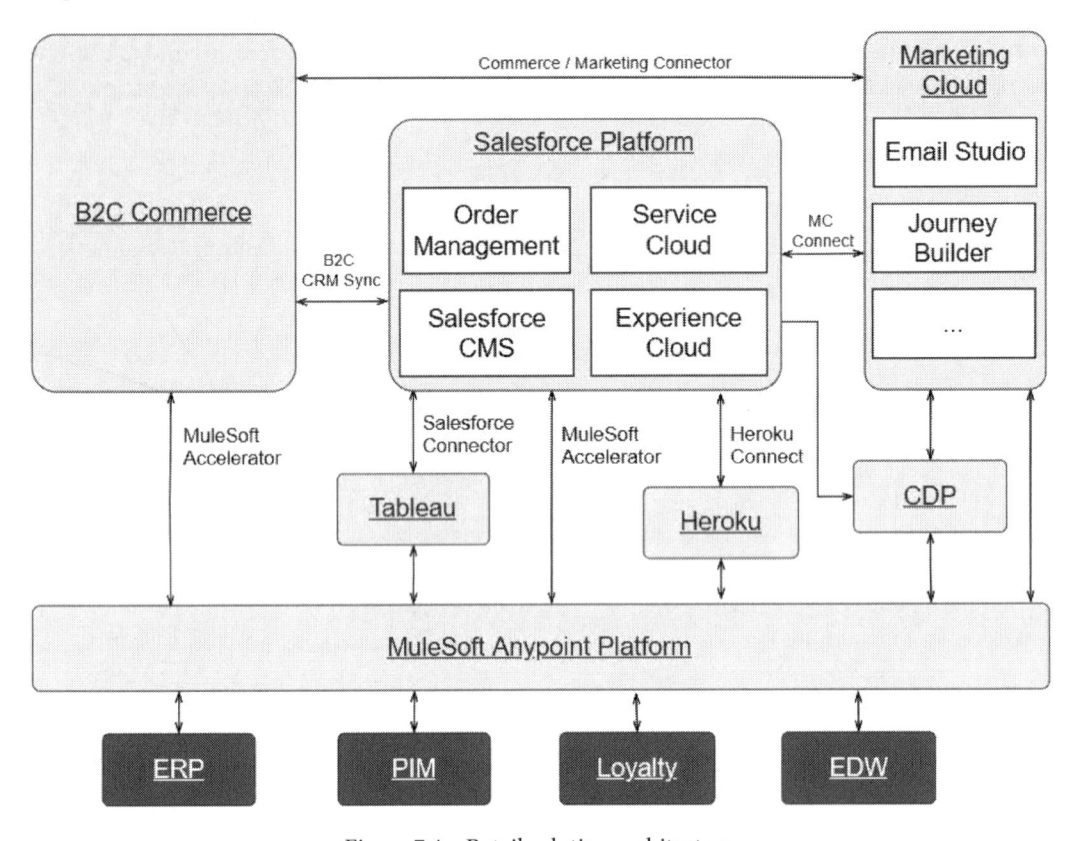

Figure 7.4 – Retail solution architecture

This diagram is one every B2C solution architect should be intimately familiar with. It depicts the three core technology platforms that make up a B2C solution on Salesforce: **B2C Commerce**, **Salesforce Platform**, and the **Marketing Cloud** core messaging and journeys platform. In this diagram, we're also showing the four Salesforce Platform products we'll be using for Packt Gear: **Order Management**, **Service Cloud**, **Salesforce CMS**, and **Experience Cloud**. There are many other Salesforce Platform-based products that could occupy that central box for different clients. Marketing Cloud, on the right, shows the core components that are enabled based on the Marketing Cloud edition we've determined is appropriate for Packt Gear.

On the lower part of this diagram, we can also see several products that are not required for a B2C solution architecture, but often play a role. These include **Tableau**, **MuleSoft**, **Heroku**, and **Salesforce CDP**. All these products have been covered in some depth in earlier chapters so we will not be re-hashing that information here. Instead, we'll talk about the role of MuleSoft and Heroku as integration solutions later in this chapter.

The original retail solution architecture diagram with supporting documentation is available at `https://sforce.co/2U0fQQP`.

First, however, we're going to talk about the arrows *between* the products. These represent point-to-point connections that are used to integrate the component products of a B2C solution.

In the rest of this section, we'll cover the three most important point-to-point enablement solutions that will appear in nearly all B2C solutions: **B2C CRM Sync**, **Marketing Cloud Connect**, and the **Commerce and Marketing Connector**.

Prescriptive approach

The guidance from Salesforce for using point-to-point connectors with B2C Commerce, Marketing, and Service Cloud focuses on customer data synchronization use cases. In short, the default approach should be to leverage the connectors between these three products detailed in the rest of this section to synchronize customer data, with the Salesforce Platform Account and Contact records being the system of record for customer data.

B2C CRM Sync is used to keep B2C Commerce and the Salesforce Platform synchronized, and Marketing Cloud Connect is used to keep the Account and Contact record in the Salesforce Platform synchronized with the Marketing Cloud subscriber records. This synchronization only handles the data records; additional metadata or capabilities must be integrated separately. The connection between B2C Commerce and Marketing Cloud using the Commerce and Marketing Connector is only used for non-customer data such as products and coupon codes.

This approach has several advantages, most importantly, allowing the core CRM solution to be the authoritative source for customer data and optimizing use of the productized Marketing Cloud Connect solution for moving data into Marketing Cloud. Since the Salesforce Platform hosts many Salesforce products, not just Service Cloud, this also puts additional products, such as Order Management, Experience Cloud, and more, on the same system as the primary customer record.

Finally, this approach facilitates integration with external systems for customer data by consolidating to one primary touchpoint: the CRM.

When aligning the approaches outlined here with the Salesforce Integration Patterns and Practices catalog, the point-to-point connectors leverage a mix of integration patterns for various scenarios, as outlined in the following table:

Connector	Pattern	Scenario
B2C CRM Sync	Remote Process Invocation – Request and Reply	Update B2C Commerce when Contact or Account data changes in the Salesforce Platform.
	Remote Call-In	Receive updates from B2C Commerce when customer profile data changes in B2C Commerce.
	Data Virtualization	Retrieve customer address or Wishlist information from B2C Commerce to display in the Service Console on demand.
Marketing Cloud Connect	Productized Integration	Marketing Cloud Connect (MC Connect) leverages a variety of techniques under the covers but encapsulates functionality in a managed package that cannot be modified or viewed by customers.
Commerce and Marketing Connector	Remote Process Invocation – Fire and Forget	Collect.js is used on the B2C Commerce storefront to provide streaming updates regarding shopper behavior to Marketing Cloud to power messaging and journeys.
	Remote Process Invocation – Request and Reply	Triggered send via SOAP API is used to send a transactional email.
	Batch Data Synchronization	CSV files generated by B2C Commerce job with Product, Order, Content, and Coupon data and posted to the Marketing Cloud SFTP server to be ingested with Automation Studio and stored in Marketing Cloud Data Extensions on a recurring schedule.

Table 7.1 – Point-to-point connector integration patterns

Detailed coverage of the Salesforce standard integration patterns and practices is not in the scope of this book, but it is important for the Integration Architecture Designer certification. This B2C solution architect prerequisite certification is discussed in more detail in *Chapter 12, Prerequisite Certifications*.

More information on the Salesforce Integration Patterns and Practices is available at `https://sforce.co/3xxN5JZ`.

We'll cover each of the three point-to-point connectors in the following sections.

Productized point-to-point integrations

Although B2C CRM Sync is not a productized solution, there are integrations between B2C Commerce and the Salesforce Platform that are provided natively and are supported features of the products. It's important to know what those are to avoid trying to rebuild something with custom code that is supported natively.

The first example of this is the synchronization of B2C Commerce order data in the Salesforce Platform. If a customer is using the Salesforce Order Management product, as we've decided will be the case for Packt Gear, orders placed in B2C Commerce are automatically copied to the Salesforce Platform as **Managed Orders** so that Order Management can leverage them for the rest of the fulfillment life cycle. For customers who don't have Order Management, it is still possible to leverage this productized integration to move orders between B2C Commerce and the Salesforce Platform using a capability called **Unmanaged Orders**. The primary difference between Managed Orders and Unmanaged Orders is that the latter are intended to be read-only.

The second example of a productized integration point between B2C Commerce and the Salesforce Platform is the **Omnichannel Inventory Service (OIS)**. Although the OIS is not in scope for this book, it is helpful to know that it provides a unified view of available product inventory across an organization to both B2C Commerce and Order Management. There is no need to develop custom integrations to support inventory synchronization with these products.

The final example of a productized integration is Marketing Cloud Connect, the primary integration point between Marketing Cloud and the Salesforce Platform. Marketing Cloud Connect will be covered separately in the *Marketing Cloud Connect* section later in this chapter.

Your focus, as a B2C solution architect, should always be to assess the current state of productized integrations and supplement with custom code or connectors only where required.

B2C CRM Sync

B2C CRM Sync is an open source enablement solution provided by the Salesforce Architect Success Team through GitHub. Importantly, this is *not* a supported Salesforce product. It's a reference implementation of an integration between B2C Commerce and the Salesforce Platform, including source code and tests supporting both sides of the integration. This solution is not supported by Salesforce, requires development expertise to integrate, and must be customized and extended for specific customer use cases. It is available free of charge and is constantly being improved by Salesforce and the community. Because B2C CRM Sync is an API-based integration, it counts toward normal Salesforce Platform governor limits.

B2C CRM Sync is available from GitHub at `https://bit.ly/3zryl13`.

> **Tip**
> Prior to the release of B2C CRM Sync in 2021, there was an older version of the Commerce and Service connector, also distributed by Salesforce through GitHub. While this is still in use by many customers, it does not follow best practices and is no longer the recommended solution for integration.

Since B2C CRM Sync is focused specifically on integrating B2C Commerce and the Salesforce Platform (CRM), it is useful for a variety of Salesforce Platform-based products, including Service Cloud, Health Cloud, Sales Cloud, Financial Services Cloud, and more. It is primarily focused on synchronizing the B2C Commerce Customer Profile record with the corresponding Salesforce Platform Account and Contact records.

B2C CRM Sync installation

B2C CRM Sync has detailed installation instructions in the GitHub repository's README linked to in the previous section. By default, it uses SFDX to deploy to a Scratch Org and can be configured to support either Person Accounts or Business Accounts. The installation process also deploys necessary code and data to a B2C Commerce Sandbox, but one must be pre-created and configured to accept the installation as described in the **README** before this can be executed.

The B2C Commerce instance integrated using B2C CRM Sync must be configured with certain OCAPI permissions as described in the **README**. This allows the B2C CRM Sync integration to access both the Shop and Data APIs using OCAPI as well as WebDAV to push both code and data. As part of documenting this integration, it will be necessary to review the detailed touchpoints available since this solution is constantly evolving.

Documentation for the B2C CRM Sync solution is available at `sfb2csa.link/sync/docs`.

The installation process and the **Node.js-based Command-Line Interface** (CLI)-driven cross-cloud test scripts both rely on a configurable `.env` text file with connection information and credentials for both the B2C Commerce Sandbox and SFDX Scratch Org. Deploying with the CLI to test environments can be accomplished in as little as 15 minutes by a developer with access to both environments and experience across both the Salesforce Platform and B2C Commerce.

After the initial integration, B2C CRM Sync can be moved to higher environments for both B2C Commerce and Service Cloud using normal application development life cycle processes. Review the *Cross-cloud application development life cycle* section for recommendations around coordinating test environments.

On the B2C Commerce side, B2C CRM Sync contains three cartridges with custom code:

- `int_b2ccrmsync`: Contains integration code and hooks to support OCAPI
- `plugin_b2ccrmsync`: Extends SFRA storefront controllers for Account and Order touchpoints
- `plugin_b2ccrmsync_oobo`: Extends SFRA storefront controllers for login to support CSR **Order On Behalf Of (OOBO)**

Most of the logic for the integration, however, resides in the Salesforce Platform and is supported by custom Apex classes, Triggers, Custom Objects, Flows, Lightning Web Components, and more. When implementing B2C CRM Sync in a real project, most of the development effort will be in the core Salesforce Platform.

B2C CRM Sync capabilities

Once installed, B2C CRM Sync supports configuring multiple B2C Commerce environments associated with the same Salesforce org. This can include multiple instances as well as multiple sites and customer lists within a given instance. The core capability for B2C CRM Sync is to keep the B2C Commerce customer records, which are stored in customer lists, in sync with the corresponding Salesforce Platform Account and Contact records.

For a detailed overview of integrating customer data between systems, see *Chapter 8, Creating a 360° View of the Customer*.

In addition, at the time of writing, B2C CRM Sync provides pre-built support for OOBO from Service Cloud into B2C Commerce. This allows **customer service representatives (CSRs)** working in Service Cloud to access the B2C Commerce storefront on behalf of a customer by clicking a button on the customer's Contact or Person Account record detail page in Service Cloud.

Since B2C CRM Sync is primarily built with Flow, it provides a natural extension point for integration with additional systems. Each time a Contact record is changed in the Salesforce Platform, a Flow activates to synchronize those changes to B2C Commerce. If changes also needed to be synchronized to an outside system, a customer **Data Warehouse** or **Master Data Management (MDM)** solution, for example, this could be added to the existing Flow for consistency.

In addition to customer data synchronization, B2C CRM Sync leverages Salesforce Platform **Matching Rules** and **Duplicate Rules** to provide a basic duplicate customer record detection capability. A more detailed discussion of customer data duplication will be provided in *Chapter 8, Creating a 360° View of the Customer*.

Finally, B2C CRM Sync leverages Salesforce Connect and External Objects to expose data from B2C Commerce in Service Cloud that doesn't need to be proactively synchronized between systems. Two examples of this include customer address data and customer wish list data, both of which are retrieved on demand from B2C Commerce rather than being proactively synchronized and stored in each system the way customer profile information is.

For use cases not supported by B2C CRM Sync natively, each customer can build upon the foundation provided to follow best practices and extend the integration.

B2C CRM Sync configuration

B2C CRM Sync uses **Custom Metadata Types** in the Salesforce Platform for configuration. This configuration stores the details of the associated B2C Commerce instance as well as the field mapping between B2C Commerce customer profile records and Salesforce Platform Account and Contact records. This allows declarative mapping of custom profile attributes in B2C Commerce to custom attributes in the Salesforce Platform where the data types are compatible.

B2C CRM Sync also uses Salesforce Platform Named Credentials to authenticate with B2C Commerce using a *Client ID* created in **Account Manager**. This allows server-to-server communication using the B2C Commerce **Open Commerce APIs (OCAPI)**. Details of authenticating with, and building upon, OCAPI can be found in *Chapter 3, Direct-to-Consumer Selling with Commerce Cloud B2C*.

On the B2C Commerce side, B2C CRM Sync leverages Service Credentials to store connection and authentication information required by the Service Cloud REST APIs. While most of this configuration is done for you in the initial deployment to a development environment, it must be understood and managed as the implementation moves into higher environments. In addition, it's important to understand that this solution is built entirely with APIs and capabilities that are available to anyone building on top of these platforms; there is no Salesforce magic here.

B2C CRM Sync data model

We've mentioned a couple of times so far how B2C CRM Sync moves data between B2C Commerce and the Salesforce Platform. The following diagram depicts this data integration in more detail:

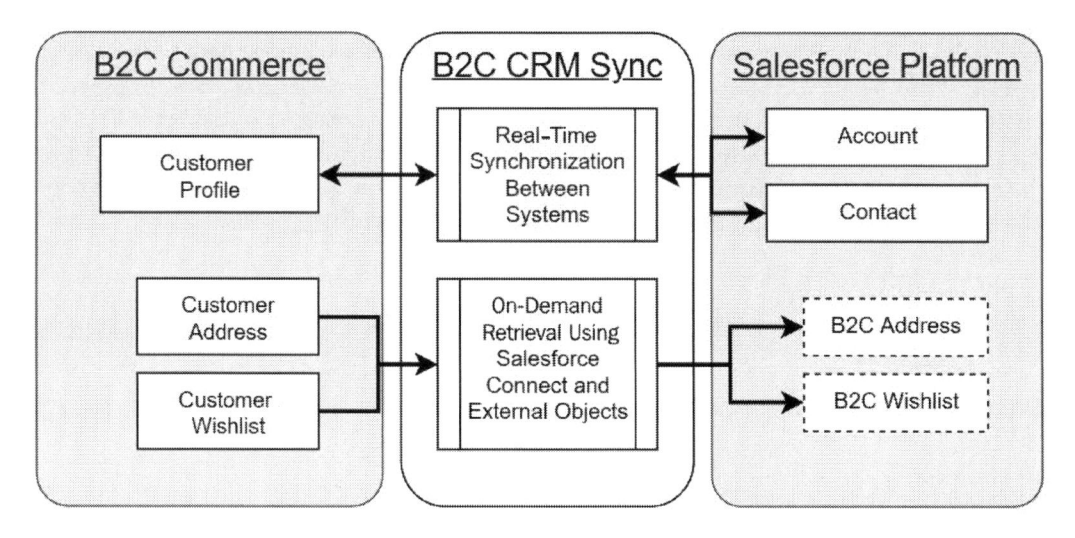

Figure 7.5 – B2C CRM Sync data model

This view shows that, depending on the use case, different methods of synchronizing or retrieving data may be appropriate. In the case of customer profile data, it is important that the information be readily available in both systems for foundational use cases. While it may not be necessary to synchronize every attribute, it is not sufficient to have customer data in only one system and retrieved on demand in another. Both B2C Commerce and Service Cloud have technical dependencies on their respective views of a customer, so the solution is to update one when the other changes.

In the case of a customer's wish list, however, Service Cloud and the underlying Salesforce Platform have no native understanding of that concept. There's no reason to proactively move that data into the Salesforce Platform (remember our discussion of platform data limits in *Chapter 2*, *Supporting Your Customers with Service Cloud*). Instead, the data is represented in the Salesforce Platform as an external object and Salesforce Connect is used to retrieve the data from the B2C Commerce instance using the OCAPI Data API on demand.

As you expand the baseline integration to support your specific use cases, consider both options before committing to an approach.

B2C CRM Sync limitations

Although B2C CRM Sync is a strong starting point for most B2C Commerce and Salesforce Platform integrations, there are a couple things it is not designed to handle. Most importantly, this solution is not designed to support bulk data loads or large-scale customer de-duplication efforts.

The B2C CRM Sync solution performs real-time synchronization of customer data between systems as that data changes. That means if hundreds of thousands or millions of records are loaded into one system or the other, that many flow interviews will be started in the Salesforce Platform and that many API calls will be made between systems to reconcile the data. For initial data loads, or bulk updates, it is preferable to exclude these from the B2C CRM Sync integration and push the data separately into both systems.

Customer data de-duplication is the process of attempting to consolidate duplicate or potentially duplicate representations of the same individual across multiple systems or within the same system. This process is complex and must be undertaken with care; it's not what B2C CRM Sync is intended to handle. We'll discuss handling customer data duplication in more detail in *Chapter 8, Creating a 360° View of the Customer*.

Marketing Cloud Connect

Marketing Cloud Connect, or **MC Connect** for short, is the point-to-point solution for integrating the Salesforce Platform with the core Marketing Cloud messaging and journeys platform (just called Marketing Cloud in this chapter for simplicity). While B2C CRM Sync is focused on creating a consistent view of the customer between B2C Commerce and the Salesforce Platform, MC Connect takes a much more holistic view of the integration space and strives to make Marketing Cloud and the Salesforce Platform behave like a unified solution. This includes synchronizing Account and Contact data with Marketing Cloud subscriber data, but that is just a component of the overall feature set.

> **Important note**
> Marketing Cloud Connect can occasionally encounter issues or conflicts synchronizing your Salesforce Platform and Marketing Cloud datasets. Carefully monitor the solution, especially immediately after implementation, until you're confident it's working as intended.

MC Connect is the only one of the three primary point-to-point connectors discussed in this section that is a supported product from Salesforce. This means that it is both more powerful and less flexible than the other connectors. It's more powerful because it has a robust feature set, no-code installation, is tested at scale for performance and reliability, and is eligible for Salesforce support. It's less flexible because it does not provide a reference code base that can be customized and extended for customer-specific use cases. Any use cases not supported by MC Connect must be implemented from scratch using the native platform integration options.

This lack of flexibility manifests with one specific constraint more than others. MC Connect requires the Marketing Cloud Subscriber Key to match the Salesforce Platform Contact, Lead, or User ID. This simple fact, which cannot be changed, often means that pre-work must be performed within Marketing Cloud to migrate the Subscriber Key to align with the Salesforce Platform expectations (when there is legacy data in an existing Marketing Cloud instance *before* the implementation of Marketing Cloud Connect).

> **Important note**
> Only Marketing Cloud Professional Services can execute a Subscriber Key Migration without losing all historical data related to Marketing Cloud contacts.

As we did with B2C CRM Sync, we'll cover the installation requirements, relevant capabilities, configuration options, data model, and limitations of the MC Connect product in the following sections.

MC Connect installation

MC Connect is installed as a managed package from AppExchange into a Salesforce org. It requires a dedicated MC Connect API user with access to the necessary business units to be created in Marketing Cloud and a corresponding CRM API User created in the Salesforce Platform to support the required connected app.

Once the managed package is installed in your Salesforce org, new components can be added to Page Layouts to support things such as displaying historical emails or triggering new emails for a Contact or Lead. Additional permissions and access are configured using **Permission Sets** in the Salesforce Platform before a similar setup is performed in Marketing Cloud.

The full MC Connect implementation guide is available at `https://sforce.co/3iKX0HX`.

MC Connect capabilities

Most importantly in a B2C solution architecture, MC Connect synchronizes Salesforce Platform Contacts with Marketing Cloud subscriber data. Adding this capability to the B2C CRM Sync provided integration between B2C Commerce customer profiles and Salesforce Platform Contacts, and you now have all three systems sharing the same view of the customer.

Building on the shared customer view it establishes, MC Connect also allows for direct email sends from the Salesforce Platform through Marketing Cloud. This keeps all brand communications centralized and trackable within the Marketing Cloud product without sacrificing the convenience for single-system communication for CSRs. Marketing Cloud sends can be individual emails to Leads or Contacts or broadcast emails to an entire Campaign or Report.

On the Marketing Cloud side, MC Connect enhances Journey Builder to allow for new Salesforce "Platform-based" journey entry sources and Salesforce Platform updates.

Because MC Connect is a Salesforce product, SOAP and REST API calls made to the Salesforce Platform by MC Connect do not count toward the rolling 24-hour API limits on the Salesforce Platform org.

The Bulk API, which is used primarily to push tracking data back to the Salesforce Platform based on Marketing Cloud activities, does still count against API request limits.

> **Further reading**
> For more information on troubleshooting MC Connect Bulk API usage, review the following article: `https://sforce.co/3BiFdOY`.

MC Connect configuration

Configuration for MC Connect in the Salesforce Platform relies on editing **Page Layouts**, **Permission Sets**, and **Triggers**. The Salesforce Platform is also the right place to configure any custom Reports and Dashboards based on Marketing Cloud subscribers or historical send data required for your unique solution.

On the Marketing Cloud side of the configuration, it is necessary to integrate the various features exposed through the Salesforce Platform. That means creating any emails you wish to make available through the Salesforce send capability, customizing Journeys to leverage Salesforce data, enhancing A/B tests in Marketing Cloud based on Salesforce data, and any Marketing Cloud Automations required.

> **Important note**
> MC Connect only supports the Salesforce classic UI. For organizations that have moved to Lightning, switching back to classic will be required to access certain features.

> **Further reading**
> The full Marketing Cloud Connect documentation, including configuration, is available at `https://sforce.co/2UieFwx`.

MC Connect data model

The core capability of MC Connect, as mentioned previously, is to extend the customer model through the Salesforce Platform into Marketing Cloud as follows:

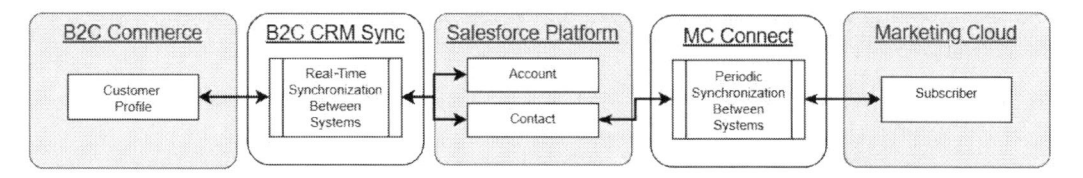

Figure 7.6 – MC Connect data model

This figure shows how a customer profile change in B2C Commerce could be *synchronized* through B2C CRM Sync to the Contact record in the Salesforce Platform, and then through MC Connect onto the Subscriber record in Marketing Cloud. This integration pattern works regardless of where the update is made, but it is not guaranteed to operate in real time.

Beyond the customer data use case, MC Connect synchronizes tracking and historical email data as well as preference and consent management, if the subscriber is synchronized. For use cases beyond this, it will be necessary to implement additional customization using the raw APIs and integration methods discussed in earlier chapters.

Email tracking data available in the Salesforce Platform includes the following:

- **Aggregate Level**: A comprehensive summary of email send behavior on email send record
- **Individual Level**: Email performance at the Contact or Lead level is available through the **Individual Email Result** (**IER**) record
- **Track Link Details**: Optional data stored both in aggregate and at the Contact/Lead level around links clicked and the total number of links
- **Track Sent Events**: Optional data stored for Contact/Lead for each email sent (not just opened/clicked)

In addition to Contact/Subscriber data, other Salesforce Standard or Custom Objects can be synchronized into Marketing Cloud using synchronized data sources in Contact Builder. This is a declarative one-way synchronization that stores Salesforce Platform data in the Marketing Cloud Contacts data model to enhance personalization and journey capabilities based on things such as case history in Service Cloud.

When leveraging Synchronized Data Sources to pull Salesforce Platform data into Marketing Cloud, be sure to only synchronize data that has a clear business value. Synchronize only the records needed by leveraging built-in synchronization filters for date range, email address included, or configurable Boolean test. For records that are synchronized, only include fields that are required for the initial use cases. Additional data can be added in the future, if needed.

When configuring MC Connect to support sensitive data, leverage **Encrypted Data Sending (EDS)** in Marketing Cloud to recognize any encrypted fields in the Salesforce Platform and ensure they are re-encrypted in Marketing Cloud after synchronization. This capability supports **Classic Encryption**, **Shield Platform Encryption**, and **Field-Level Encryption** from Salesforce.

You could also leverage Field-Level Encryption in Marketing Cloud, which allows data to be encrypted at rest. This capability supports compliance with data privacy regulations and corporate policies.

> **Important note**
>
> Leveraging Field-Level Encryption in Marketing Cloud imposes serious restrictions, including being unable to leverage this data for segmenting, filtering, or querying fields. Encrypted fields also can't be used in Mobile Studio message content and can't be used with the Transactional Messaging API.
>
> Since Field-Level Encryption cannot be turned off once it is enabled, be sure to fully understand the limitations before using.
>
> Read more about the limitations of Field-Level Encryption at `https://sforce.co/3etvJH6`.

> **Further reading**
>
> Learn more about Marketing Cloud Field-Level Encryption at `https://sforce.co/3rq80wz`.

MC Connect limitations

MC Connect is a no-cost product but has specific license requirements for both Marketing Cloud and the Salesforce Platform:

- **Marketing Cloud**: Requires Core Edition, Advanced Edition, Agency Edition, Enterprise 1.0 Lock and Publish, Enterprise 2.0 Edition, Reseller Edition, or a Marketing Cloud Sandbox.
- **Salesforce Platform**: Requires Unlimited, Enterprise, Performance, or Developer Edition.

As discussed earlier, it is not possible to access or modify the source code for MC Connect, so customization beyond what is available through configuration is not supported. Custom integrations can be built to supplement MC Connect, but they must start from the ground up.

While synchronization of Contacts, Users, or Leads via synchronized data extensions is an effective way of moving data from the Salesforce Platform to Marketing Cloud, there is no similar synchronization back to the Salesforce Platform from Marketing Cloud.

Leads and Contacts will also synchronize fields directly between All Subscribers and their associated Salesforce records, but only if the Contact in Marketing Cloud was created using a Salesforce Campaign, Report, or Triggered Send. When the contact was first added to All Subscribers via a Journey Send or Import, this feature is not supported.

> **Tip**
>
> To be safe, always add the Contact, User, or Lead to the Salesforce Platform first, then let it synchronize to Marketing Cloud, and then trigger interactions off the resulting Marketing Cloud record.

MC Connect is also not intended to drive personalized emails sent from the Salesforce Platform through Marketing Cloud. When sending an email from a Contact record in Service Cloud, for example, it is only possible to personalize the subject and sender information. Personalized email use cases require the Salesforce Distributed Marketing connector, which also integrates the Salesforce Platform and Marketing Cloud but for this more specific use case.

> **Tip**
>
> Distributed Marketing is more likely to be used to support Sales Cloud than Service Cloud and is rarely a component of B2C solution architectures and will not be covered in this book.

> **Further reading**
>
> You can read more about Distributed Marketing from Salesforce at `https://sforce.co/3xzt4ml`.

Commerce and Marketing Connector

The final point-to-point connector we'll cover in any detail is the Commerce and Marketing Connector. Like the B2C CRM Sync connector, this is an open source enablement solution provided by Salesforce. It is not a productized integration and is not eligible for support from Salesforce.

The Commerce and Marketing Cloud Connector is available from GitHub (access required) at `http://bit.ly/2qKQxDN`.

> **Important note**
> The Salesforce Commerce Cloud GitHub is private; instructions for gaining access are outlined in the following Trail: `http://bit.ly/SFCCGitHubAccess`.

This connector is primarily a B2C Commerce-based code solution consisting of several cartridges capable of supporting both modern SFRA-based storefronts and legacy SiteGenesis storefronts. Because all source code for the solution is provided as part of the GitHub repository, it is possible to extend, customize, and enhance any aspect of the integration by building upon the provided framework.

Just as we've done for the previous two point-to-point connector solutions, in this section, we'll cover the installation, capabilities, configuration, data model, and limitations of the Commerce and Marketing Connector.

Commerce and Marketing Connector installation

The installation of this solution happens within the B2C Commerce code base, where the provided cartridges must be installed and added to the site cartridge path(s).

For SFRA-based storefronts, the required cartridges are the following:

- `int_marketing_cloud`: This is the Marketing Cloud integration cartridge containing SOAP and REST API service implementations.
- `plugin_marketing_cloud`: This is the SFRA plugin cartridge, which overrides or supplements base site code for **My Account**, **Payment Instrument**, and **Address Handling**.
- `int_handlerframework`: This is a base cartridge to add flexible configurable event handling capability, which is a dependency for the Commerce and Marketing Connector.

Once the core cartridges are installed, a developer will have to import metadata definitions into B2C Commerce to support the configuration of required site preferences, service definitions, jobs, and custom Objects.

Within the integrated Marketing Cloud instance, a new installed package is required to support the B2C Commerce integration. The Installed Package credentials (Client ID, Client Secret, and Authentication Base URL) are required to configure the B2C Commerce Service Credentials.

Once this is done, the B2C Commerce site preferences can be configured with the Marketing Cloud **Member ID (MID)** corresponding to your Marketing Cloud instance.

Detailed installation and configuration instructions for the Commerce and Marketing Connector are available in GitHub (access required) at `https://bit.ly/3cPrhkQ`.

> **Tip**
> If you don't have access to the Salesforce Commerce Cloud GitHub repositories, follow the Trailhead Module Access GitHub repositories at `https://sforce.co/3gKwvzK`.

The final step in configuring the initial integration is setting up the B2C Commerce jobs used to send bulk data to Marketing Cloud on a recurring schedule. You'll first have to enable your Marketing Cloud SFTP server, if you haven't already done so, and then you can configure B2C Commerce to use it. Once files are posted to the Marketing Cloud SFTP Server, you can use Automation Studio to ingest them and store the information in Data Extensions.

For a refresher on how to configure the Marketing Cloud SFTP Server, set up Automations, or leverage Data Extensions, review *Chapter 4, Engaging Customers with Marketing Cloud*.

The B2C Commerce jobs will generally be configured to run nightly unless business needs require a different schedule.

Commerce and Marketing Connector capabilities

The Commerce and Marketing Connector, once installed, handles three primary aspects of the integration: **data sync**, **email management**, and **behavioral analytics**.

Data sync

The Commerce and Marketing Connector uses background jobs to push B2C Commerce data into Marketing Cloud via the Marketing Cloud SFTP server. The three use cases supported natively by the connector are **Product Data**, **Promotions**, **Pricebooks**, and **Orders**.

The Commerce and Marketing Connector in GitHub also supports synchronizing customer data into Marketing Cloud direct from B2C Commerce, but this approach is not recommended. Instead, it is preferable to synchronize all customer data through the Salesforce Platform and leverage MC Connect.

> **Important note**
>
> If you don't have any Salesforce Platform-based products (for example, Service Cloud) and are integrating B2C Commerce direct to Marketing Cloud, you may need to synchronize customer data. This will introduce significant rework and extra cost if you ever want to introduce a Salesforce Platform-based product and use MC Connect in the future. It is preferable to leverage a minimal license for the Salesforce Platform to serve as the customer data master if you're planning to add a product such as Service Cloud to the solution in the future.

As you may recall from the B2C Commerce unit, within a B2C Commerce realm, different data is mastered in different instances. The following diagram shows where each type of data will be sent from B2C Commerce to Marketing Cloud:

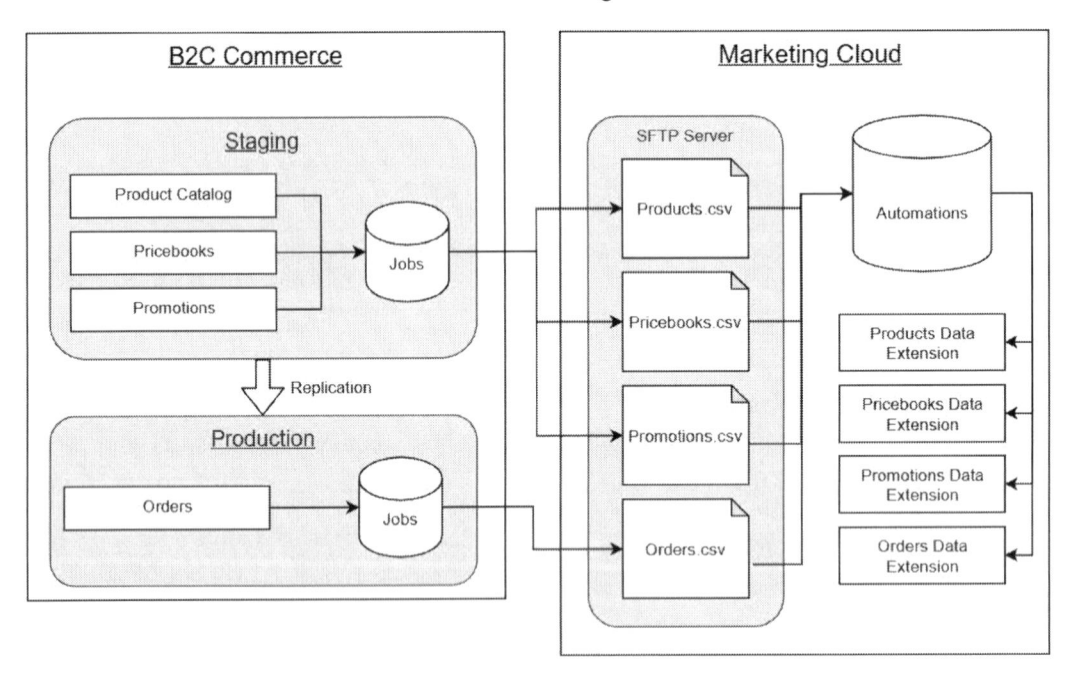

Figure 7.7 – Commerce and Marketing Connect data sync

This shows that Product, Pricebook, and Promotion data is pulled from Staging via a job that runs on that instance, transformed into a CSV file, and written to an SFTP server hosted by Marketing Cloud. From there, Marketing Cloud Automations created with Automation Studio pick up the CSV file and move the data into Data Extensions.

Email management

In a B2C solution, Marketing Cloud should be the email master system and all email-based communications should flow from that system regardless of whether they are triggered in B2C Commerce, Service Cloud, Order Management, or other systems.

The Commerce and Marketing Connector provides native support for using B2C Commerce to trigger emails sent by Marketing Cloud in the following use cases:

- Account Created
- Account Updated
- Password Changed
- Password Reset
- Account Locked Out
- Customer Service Contact Us
- Send Gift Certificate
- Order Confirmation

This functionality is built using transactional send classification emails in Marketing Cloud using triggered sends. Transactional Messaging API is not supported, but can be implemented if needed. It is possible to customize the data mapping from B2C Commerce into the triggered send definitions using the Custom Objects in B2C Commerce.

Sending additional emails for business specific use cases, such as signing up for a new guided hike in the Packt Gear use case, can be accomplished by copying the same pattern used above and repeating it for each new use case.

In addition to transactional email sends, new marketing email sign-ups as well as email preference control, including unsubscribe requests, should be passed from B2C Commerce into Marketing Cloud.

> **Important note**
> The Commerce and Marketing Connector uses email address as Contact and Subscriber Key as supplied by Salesforce. It must be customized to use the Salesforce Platform Contact ID in all multi-cloud use cases (see the *Commerce and Marketing Connector limitations* section for more information).

Behavioral analytics

The Commerce and Marketing Connector supports shopper behavior monitoring on the B2C Commerce storefront using `collect.js`, the Marketing Cloud tracking pixel. This JavaScript integration passes notifications from the user's browser to Marketing Cloud for the following shopper events:

- **Page view**
- **Search request**
- **Product view**
- **Category view**
- **Cart** (add/modify/remove)
- **Order placement**

Additional events can be added by following the provided implementation pattern. By including the Contact Key in the `collect.js notification` events for logged-in customers, this behavior can be used to drive shopper journeys configured in Marketing Cloud. This is the heart of the Abandoned Cart solution, which relies on knowing that a customer added a product to their cart but never purchased it.

Commerce and Marketing Connector configuration

Within Marketing Cloud, new or existing Transactional Send definitions will be required for the necessary B2C Commerce email sends. In addition, Data Extensions and Automations will be required to receive the data sent via the CSV file from the B2C Commerce jobs. Finally, any Journeys based on B2C Commerce behavioral data (such as Abandoned Cart) should be set up.

Details for configuring specific integration use cases such as Abandoned Cart are provided in *Chapter 9*, *Supporting Key Business Scenarios*.

Once the initial configuration is done on the Marketing Cloud side, B2C Commerce is configured to leverage those integration points. The Marketing Cloud Custom Object `MarketingCloudTriggers` is used to configure specific Marketing Cloud email triggers for various B2C Commerce use cases. The Custom Object `CommunicationHandlers` is used to enable or disable Marketing Cloud handling for specific storefront integration points.

Commerce and Marketing Connector data model

In large part, the data model that this connector supports is depicted in the *Data sync* section. The B2C Commerce business objects that the solution requires are exported from B2C Commerce, written as CSV files, posted to the Marketing Cloud SFTP server, and ingested as Data Extensions. Additional Data Extensions and Data Relationships can be configured to store additional data points and relate the existing data points together, as needed.

Keep in mind that the current guidance from Salesforce is *not* to rely on the Commerce and Marketing Connector to move customer data directly if any Salesforce Platform-based solution is available.

Commerce and Marketing Connector limitations

Because the Commerce and Marketing Connector is an open source solution and not a product from Salesforce, it is not possible to update the connector after it has been put in place except by manually applying updates to the code base. This model is common in the B2C Commerce space; however, since all cartridges from the marketplace and SFRA itself are distributed with the same model.

A more relevant concern, however, is that the Commerce and Marketing Connector itself hasn't been updated since November 2019. There are, in fact, several known issues filed against the GitHub repository that have not been addressed and will need to be considered for any new integration using this connector.

First, the connector uses an older *Triggered Send* method for activating emails from B2C Commerce through Marketing Cloud instead of the newer transactional messaging capability. Transactional Messaging is a dedicated API used for non-promotional emails that scales better and sends faster. Converting the connector to use Transactional Messaging takes a bit of work because the Triggered Send approach uses the *SOAP API* and the Transactional Messaging capability uses the *REST API*, so it essentially needs to be rebuilt.

The second important limitation is that the integration does not use the Salesforce Platform Contact ID as the Subscriber Key natively. This is a critical update that must be made for each implementation where a Salesforce Platform-based product is in use (for example, Service Cloud). If this isn't done properly, Marketing Cloud will store one subscriber keyed off the email address created by B2C Commerce and a second unrelated subscriber keyed off the Contact ID created by Marketing Cloud Connect.

Despite these limitations, the Commerce and Marketing Connector is still the best starting point for integrating these products at the time of writing. In the future, it is likely that additional productized integrations will be made available to support more native connection use cases. Always review the current state of products and connector options before moving forward with an implementation. Things change fast in the Salesforce space!

Now that we've reviewed the most important point-to-point connectors used to integrate B2C Commerce, Marketing Cloud, and the Salesforce Platform, we're going to review additional options for connecting products that may be appropriate in some circumstances, including integration middleware.

Integration middleware

When we talk about integration middleware in the Salesforce B2C solution architecture space, we're most commonly talking about MuleSoft. Most of the concepts outlined in this section will be applicable regardless of the specific technology chosen, but the accelerator solutions Salesforce has provided are only applicable to MuleSoft.

It is common to talk about point-to-point integrations and integration middleware solutions as being incompatible alternatives, but the reality is more nuanced. The point-to-point solutions outlined earlier perform some work that cannot be replaced by an integration-focused solution, but there are certainly advantages to using something such as MuleSoft to complement the point-to-point integrations.

The Salesforce Platform integration patterns are typically broken down by layer into the following general categories:

- User interface layer
- Business process layer
- Data layer

The following diagram illustrates this concept in a cross-cloud solution, including the integration-focused components of each product that sit in each layer:

	B2C Commerce	Salesforce Platform	Marketing Cloud	
User Interface Layer	iFrame, Client-Side Integration	Canvas App, Lighting Out, Mashups	-	
Business Process Layer	Server-Side Integrations, OCAPI Hooks, OCAPI Shop API, Commerce Shopper APIs	Platform Events, Flows, Outbound Messaging	Dynamic Content, SSJS or AMPScript	MuleSoft Anypoint Platform
Data Layer	Jobs and Feeds, Scheduled Backups, OCAPI Data API, Commerce APIs	Salesforce Connect, Apex, REST and SOAP APIs, Composite API, Bulk API	Automation Studio, SFTP Transfer, Data Extensions, REST and SOAP APIs	Heroku Connect

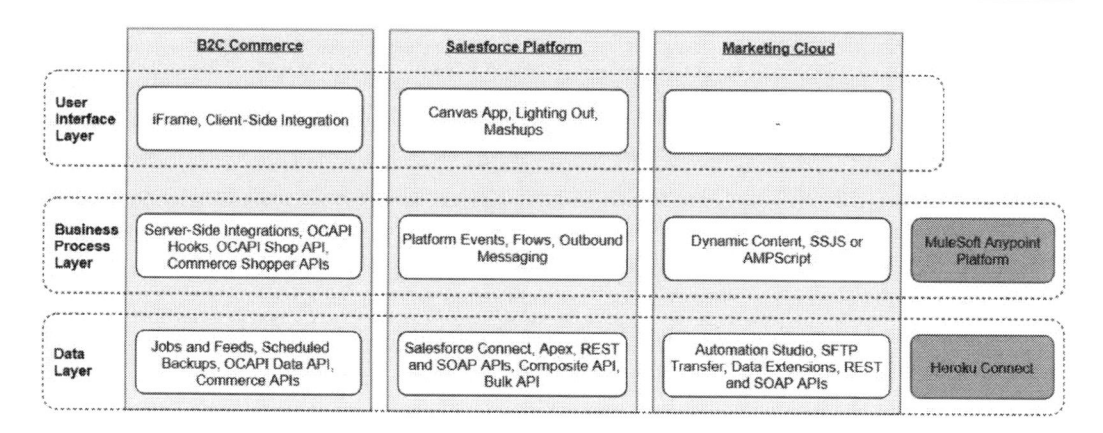

Figure 7.8 – Layered integration architecture

As the preceding diagram shows, there are different types of integrations to consider in a solution. The examples in each product column are not intended to be exhaustive, but to give examples of each type of integration as they apply in each product. On the right-hand side, you can see that an integration middleware solution such as MuleSoft Anypoint Platform can support business process layer integrations most appropriately. To be sure, an integration solution can also be used strictly to move data, but it adds value with its ability to apply business logic to that data, perform transformations, and aggregate information from multiple sources.

The **user interface layer** involves experiences that traverse multiple products or embedding one product in the user experience of another; for example, configuring Marketing Cloud to leverage Salesforce as an identity provider to support logging in to Marketing Cloud with Service Cloud credentials (SSO). With B2C CRM Sync, the best example is the capability for CSRs to place orders on behalf of customers by clicking a button on the Contact record detail page and navigating to the B2C Commerce storefront. A third example is creating a unified customer experience that involves components of both B2C Commerce and Experience Cloud blended. Integration middleware typically doesn't play a role in this type of experiential integration.

The second layer, the **business process layer**, involved orchestration of updates, changes, and logic between systems behind the scenes. In the case of the point-to-point connectors, this involves examples such as building Marketing Cloud journeys that account for open cases in Service Cloud for the same customer, which can be accomplished with MC Connect. This layer also includes the business logic that triggers updates to the data layer across systems.

The final layer, the **data layer**, is the underlying data storage and access mechanisms, including Objects in the Salesforce Platform, Business Objects in B2C Commerce, Data Extensions in Marketing Cloud, and the various APIs and integration mechanisms that can be used to operate against them.

> **Further reading**
>
> You can read more about the Salesforce layered approach to integration architecture at `https://sforce.co/3xEPsKS`.

In the following sections, we will cover when to explore integration middleware as an option, how using integration middleware interacts with the point-to-point connectors outlined earlier in this chapter, and the advantages of leveraging MuleSoft as your integration solution.

When to explore integration middleware

Introducing an integration middleware solution such as MuleSoft strictly to connect B2C Commerce and Marketing Cloud with the Salesforce Platform is unlikely to be justified. The advantages of a middleware solution manifest themselves when it is used as part of a broader enterprise integration strategy. In short, the more products integrated through MuleSoft, the greater the value of MuleSoft.

When designing a B2C solution, the key factors that should cause you to think about introducing a dedicated integration middleware solution such as MuleSoft are the following:

- MuleSoft is already being used in the client ecosystem.
- There are plans for multiple integration points beyond the core three Salesforce platforms.
- Point-to-point connector integration patterns are not appropriate for the specific customer scenario and a more complex integration is required.
- There's a strong preference for minimizing product customization and keeping integration in a dedicated solution.

In any of the aforementioned cases, it's worth exploring a product such as MuleSoft.

When you're leveraging integration middleware, several of the integration patterns covered in the *Point-to-point integrations* section should be reviewed and revised. The general rule should be to leverage the integration solution wherever possible and only incorporate point-to-point connectors for scenarios where they are required, such as unified authentication on the storefront.

Integration middleware and the point-to-point connectors

The primary function of integration middleware is to serve as the single interface point for integrations, regardless of source system. When combining that expectation with the capabilities of the point-to-point connectors, there are quite a few areas where leveraging a middleware solution would replace the functionality of the connectors. In this case, we're going to talk about the B2C Commerce-related connectors to the Salesforce Platform and to Marketing Cloud. The MC Connect solution between the Salesforce Platform and Marketing Cloud is a productized solution and, in most cases, should not be replaced with middleware.

> **Tip**
> Prefer to use productized integrations that work natively over middleware, when available.

Leveraging the layered integration architecture approach from Salesforce, we can map the functionality of the two connectors we're discussing into the appropriate layers, as shown in the following diagram:

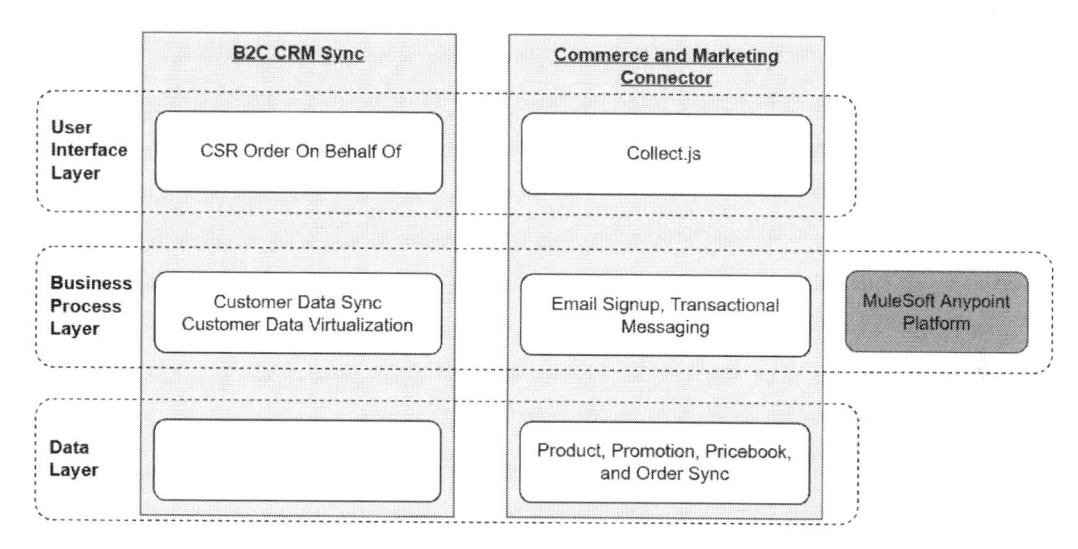

	B2C CRM Sync	Commerce and Marketing Connector	
User Interface Layer	CSR Order On Behalf Of	Collect.js	
Business Process Layer	Customer Data Sync / Customer Data Virtualization	Email Signup, Transactional Messaging	MuleSoft Anypoint Platform
Data Layer		Product, Promotion, Pricebook, and Order Sync	

Figure 7.9 – Connector layered integration

As this view makes clear, the **User Interface Layer** features such as **OOBO** and **Collect.js** are not appropriate to leverage the integration middleware layer. Both require direct interaction with the user in the browser between systems. Collect.js, for example, sends data directly from the customer's browser to Marketing Cloud based on their browsing activities on the storefront. It doesn't depend on the B2C Commerce data model or APIs.

At the **Business Process Layer**, we're talking about real-time calls between systems to synchronize data under specific conditions or trigger emails. Running this through a system such as MuleSoft could have several advantages. For customer data synchronization, it would provide a single point of contact where customer data updates could be syndicated to any additional systems that needed to be updated without having to rebuild those integrations from each triggering system. For email management, it would support loose coupling better, allowing systems to be interchanged in the future, if needed.

> **Tip**
> Why is customer data synchronization often at the Business Process Layer rather than the Data Layer? Because additional logic is injected to synchronize only records that meet specific criteria, only configured fields on those records, and to map fields between systems.
>
> The Data Layer synchronization of information such as product records from B2C Commerce to Marketing Cloud is just a bulk transfer of information without additional business logic.

> **Further reading**
> Read more about the Salesforce layered approach to integration architecture at `https://sforce.co/3xEPsKS`.

Depending on the integration middleware solution, it may also be possible or even preferable to replace direct data integrations such as product feeds with a middleware integration. This can be especially helpful when the data needs to be moved to more than one system.

In general, when using integration middleware, you should prefer to leverage it whenever possible if there's no native integration that supports your use case.

Advantages of MuleSoft

Salesforce has made significant investments in MuleSoft as the integration middleware layer of choice for the Salesforce ecosystem. There are hundreds of pre-built connectors from MuleSoft and the open source community in the Anypoint Exchange covering all the core Salesforce products discussed here as well as popular third-party systems such as Amazon S3, SAP, Workday, Slack, Concur, PIM solutions, payment solutions, OMS solutions, and a great deal more.

> **Further reading**
> You can explore the MuleSoft Anypoint Exchange at `https://bit.ly/3d6pDLN`.

By leveraging these connectors, it's possible to save significant development effort and time through re-use.

The specific MuleSoft connectors to be aware of in a B2C solution architecture include the Salesforce Connector, B2C Commerce Cloud Data Connector, B2C Commerce Cloud Shop Connector, and the Marketing Cloud Connector.

In the following sections, we'll provide a high-level overview of the use cases for each of these connectors before bringing it all together with an example solution.

Salesforce Connector

The Salesforce Connector is a MuleSoft solution to accelerate any integration with the Salesforce Platform, including Service Cloud. This pre-built solution supports the standard Salesforce API authentication mechanisms described in *Chapter 2, Supporting Your Customers with Service Cloud*.

This connector also supports the following Salesforce APIs:

- SOAP API
- Bulk API
- Streaming API
- Metadata API
- Apex SOAP Web Services
- Apex REST Web Services

By leveraging the connector, you can focus on any business logic or aggregation needed to support your integration use case without having to rebuild these standard APIs in each system that needs to interact with Salesforce.

> **Further reading**
> Learn more about the MuleSoft Salesforce Connector at `https://bit.ly/3db7D2X`.

B2C Commerce Cloud Shop and Data Connectors

These two connector solutions together support the Salesforce OCAPI Shop and Data APIs natively. For more information on these two APIs, review *Chapter 3, Direct-to-Consumer Selling with Commerce Cloud B2C*. In short, the Shop API supports all storefront use cases that mirror the behavior a customer would see when interacting with a commerce web store. The Data API is for data integration, merchandising, and administrative use cases.

The Shop API supports standard Shopper JWT authentication for B2C Commerce as well as OAuth2 authentication. The Data API supports OAuth2 flows only.

Leveraging the B2C Commerce connector solutions in a MuleSoft implementation will greatly reduce the need to develop custom integrations with B2C Commerce, again allowing you to focus on the business logic needed to support integration use cases.

You can read more about the B2C Commerce Shop and Data API connectors here:

- **Salesforce B2C Commerce Shop Connector**: `https://bit.ly/3vR0nQw`
- **Salesforce B2C Commerce Data Connector**: `https://bit.ly/35Vx5Fz`

MC Connector

The MC Connector leverages the Marketing Cloud SOAP API to streamline integration use cases with the core Marketing Cloud messaging and Journeys platform. The supported use cases include scheduling email sends, importing subscribers, and retrieving tracking information.

The MC Connector also supports **create, update, and delete (CRUD)** operations against Marketing Cloud Data Extensions. This capability can be used to implement custom integration logic. For example, the aforementioned B2C Commerce Cloud Data Connector could be used to retrieve product data from a B2C Commerce instance, and then the Marketing Cloud Connector's CRUD capability could be used to push that product data into a Marketing Cloud Data Extension without having to write the integration from scratch.

> **Important note**
> MC Connector does not support the REST API and, therefore, does not support Journeys and Transactional Messaging without additional customization.

> **Further reading**
> Read more about the Salesforce Marketing Cloud Connector at `https://bit.ly/3xURjLR`.

MuleSoft Accelerator for B2C Commerce

These connectors provide the raw integration points supporting the underlying product APIs to provide a layer of abstraction. Putting these together into a solution can be further expedited by using an accelerator solution from MuleSoft such as the **MuleSoft Accelerator for Salesforce B2C Commerce Cloud**.

Integration middleware 217

This solution leverages integrations with the APIs described previously, but adds additional logic to support specific business use cases. The solution also adds support for integration with other systems such as an ERP, OMS, and PIM solution.

To understand how those things come together, it's helpful to review the MuleSoft layered approach to integration architecture. In short, MuleSoft organizes APIs into three categories: **experience layer**, **process layer**, and **system layer,** as shown in the following diagram:

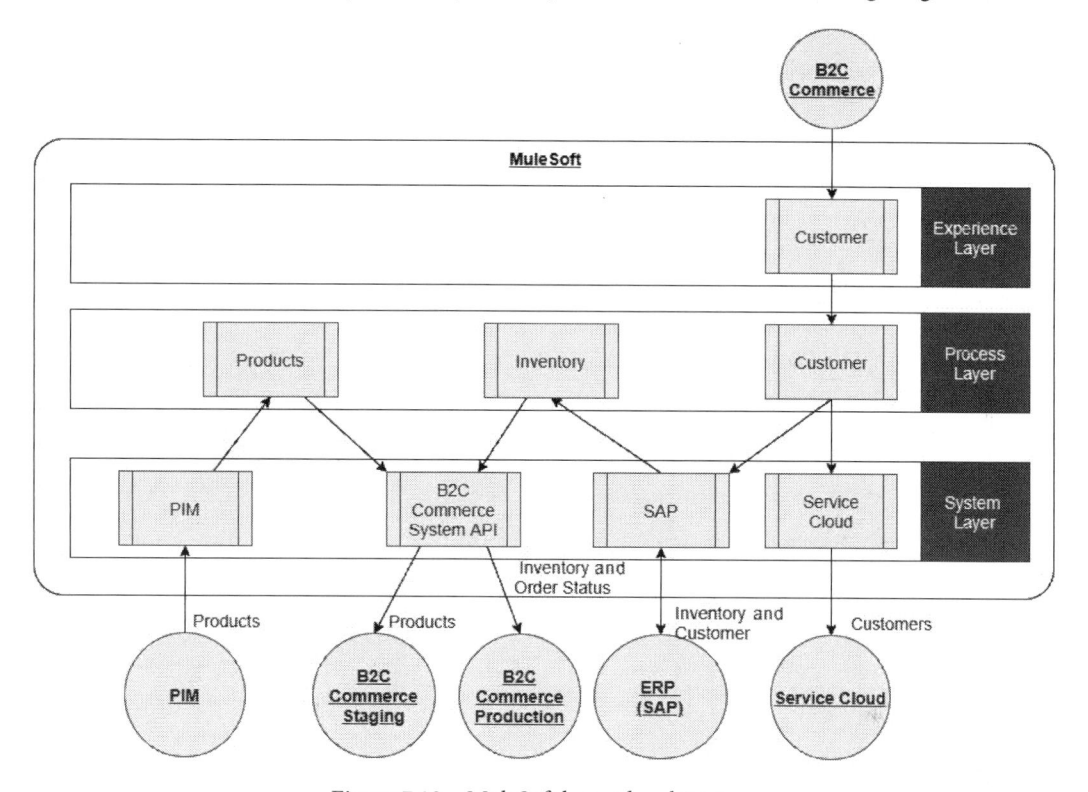

Figure 7.10 – MuleSoft layered architecture

The preceding diagram is a simplified version of the full solution overview diagram provided for the MuleSoft Accelerator for B2C Commerce at `https://bit.ly/3jkZlt9`.

In MuleSoft terms, the system layer handles the raw integration with the component products of the overall solution. This is where the connectors described in the previous sections are helpful. The process layer adds any business logic needed to operate the system layers. In the examples depicted in the preceding diagram, the system layer receives a product data update from PIM, which triggers the process layer to handle that data. In the process layer component for Products, the solution provides logic to push that update to the B2C Commerce Staging instance, which uses the system layer component for B2C Commerce. The process layer orchestrates interactions between the various system layer components.

Finally, the experience layer is responsible for interacting with user experiences. In this case, that means taking updates made on the B2C Commerce storefront by the customer, such as registration or updating data in the **My Account** section. The experience layer pushes that customer data update to the process layer, which knows to update both Service Cloud and the ERP. In this case, the ERP is SAP, but the componentized structure would allow any system API connector component supporting a different ERP to be integrated.

If the update also needed to be pushed to a loyalty system, for example, an off-the-shelf or custom connector for that loyalty system could be added to the solution and triggered from the customer process layer component without having to integrate directly with each source system.

The full set of use cases supported natively by the MuleSoft Accelerator for B2C Commerce includes the following:

- Orders flowing from B2C Commerce Production to an OMS
- Order status updates flowing from the OMS back to B2C Commerce Production
- Product data flow from a PIM system to B2C Commerce Staging (as well as B2B Commerce)
- Inventory data flowing from an ERP to B2C Commerce Production
- Customer data flowing from B2C Commerce to both an ERP and the Salesforce Platform

MuleSoft Accelerator for Retail

The MuleSoft Accelerator for B2C Commerce described in the previous section supports common B2C Commerce integration use cases for various data types.

The **MuleSoft Accelerator for Retail** is focused on customer data synchronization.

The MuleSoft Accelerator for Retail is also a full accelerator solution that leverages multiple API connectors and includes custom components to support B2C Commerce and the Salesforce Platform. Out of the box, it supports synchronizing customer data between B2C Commerce, the Salesforce Platform, Marketing Cloud, SAP, and a potential **Master Data Management** (**MDM**) solution.

> **Further reading**
>
> You can find the MuleSoft Accelerator for Retail at `https://bit.ly/3h8MgRf`.

Leveraging MuleSoft in a B2C solution

To summarize, whether you use the MuleSoft Accelerator for Retail to support customer profile synchronization or the MuleSoft Accelerator for B2C Commerce to support product and inventory data synchronization, using MuleSoft as an integration solution can streamline and centralize your integration effort between products.

If MuleSoft is an option for your unique case, you should leverage it for as much of the integration solution as possible. There will still be some use cases where the point-to-point connectors are required, but that should not be the default solution.

Despite its advantages, the extra cost and complexity of having MuleSoft in a B2C solution architecture won't always be justified. In those cases, the point-to-point connectors are more than capable of solving the integration needs within the B2C solution architecture ecosystem.

In addition to using the point-to-point connectors or integration middleware to support data synchronization between systems, there is a third option. Some organizations may opt to take a **Golden Record** or single source of truth approach to architecture, as discussed in the following section.

Single source of truth

Architecting for a single source of truth means designing a system where each component pulls from a single authoritative location for data and all updates flow back to that central system. This practice is typically referred to as **master data management** (**MDM**). Although it is helpful to be familiar with this concept when designing a B2C solution architecture, this approach alone cannot create an integrated B2C solution on Salesforce.

The primary reason why we need to integrate products together rather than leverage a single source of truth is that each component product in the Salesforce B2C solution architecture ecosystem is designed to rely only on its own internal representation of data. Because these are SaaS solutions, there's no way to change the underlying data model. By building custom components using tools such as Salesforce Platform Lightning Web Components (LWC) or B2C Commerce SFRA changes, the user experience can be decoupled from the platform data model, but this introduces significant complexity and maintenance concerns.

To provide some specific examples, B2C Commerce must have a customer record in its own data model to support login. That customer could be externally authenticated, but the record needs to exist in B2C Commerce. Similarly, Marketing Cloud cannot be customized to use an external data source directly for subscriber information and Service Cloud requires its Account and Contact records.

In many cases, it is possible to *update* those records on the fly, or to override some default behavior and use custom code to fetch data from an external system, but it requires customization and does not remove the need for these data objects entirely.

Incorporating a single source of truth

Ultimately, the best approach is to design an architecture where each of these component products is kept synchronized where data is shared, especially customer data. If an organization also has a data warehouse or MDM solution that should always be up to date, those updates can still flow to that system and then be pushed out to each component product of the B2C solution architecture.

When leveraging the direct integration approach described in the *Point-to-point integrations* section earlier in this chapter, the Salesforce Platform serves as the central repository for customer data. This then becomes the natural point of integration to support a data warehouse or MDM solution. The flows used for the B2C CRM Sync product can be revised to also update the data warehouse and any updates pushed into the Salesforce Platform from the data warehouse will automatically be synchronized to B2C Commerce and Marketing Cloud.

When leveraging the *integration middleware* approach described in the previous section, the integration middleware will be responsible for orchestrating sending updates to, and receiving updates from, the data warehouse.

In either case, a single source of truth approach should be used to supplement the B2C solution architecture, not as a replacement for integrating the component products together.

Leveraging Heroku

The high-speed Heroku Connect integration between the Salesforce Platform and a Heroku Postgres relational database supports a couple of compelling use cases. Heroku Connect allows for the configuration-driven, no-code, bi-directional synchronization of Salesforce Platform data into a Heroku PostgreSQL database at enterprise scale.

First, if a custom **Data Lake** or **Data Warehouse** is needed, Heroku could be evaluated as a comparatively simple solution. Using Heroku Connect, data can be synchronized into a PostgreSQL database as part of a larger data strategy.

The design of a complete master data solution is not in the scope of a B2C solution architecture, or of this book, but if you'd like to learn more about leveraging Heroku within a Salesforce solution, the following Trail is a good place to start: `https://sforce.co/3h01A3H`.

Single source of truth 221

The second use case for Heroku is to provide a high-scale API wrapper over the Salesforce Platform APIs, which are governed by strict limits. The example depicted in the following diagram is an example of this type of solution:

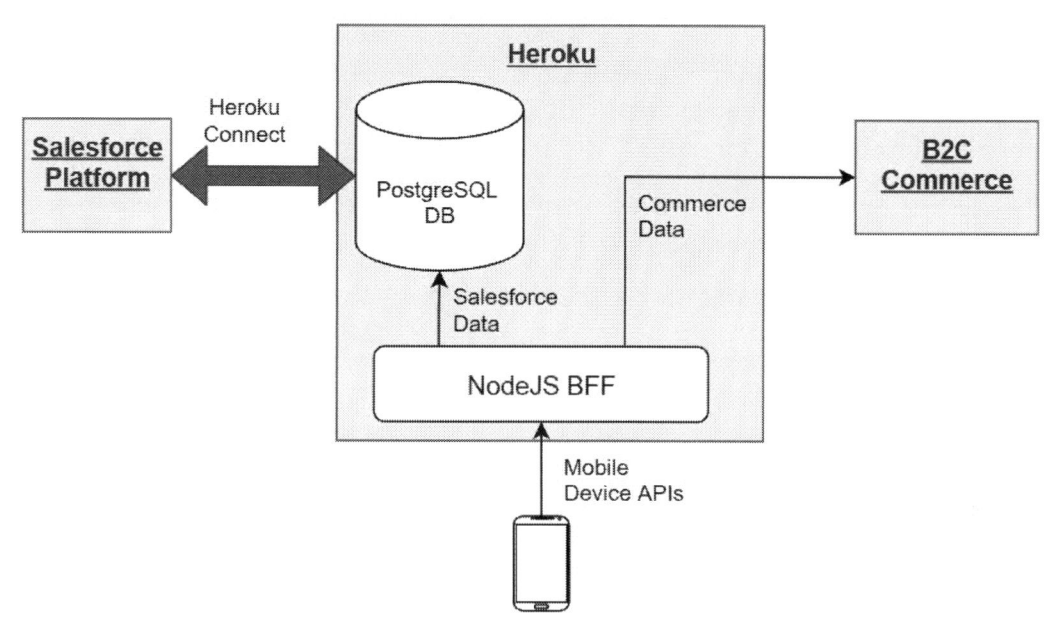

Figure 7.11 – Heroku-based backend for the frontend

In this example, a mobile app requires high-performance and high-scale API access to a build experiences that require data from both the Salesforce Platform and B2C Commerce. To avoid requiring the mobile device to make multiple different requests to different systems, and to avoid running into API limits on the Salesforce Platform, a custom **Backend for Frontend (BFF)** solution is leveraged.

Heroku Connect synchronizes Salesforce Platform data into a Heroku PostgreSQL database, which is leveraged by the NodeJS BFF. The BFF is also responsible for orchestrating potentially multiple queries for Salesforce data and B2C Commerce API calls using OCAPI to create a single mobile device API page response.

> **Further reading**
> The following article is a great place to learn more about the BFF integration pattern: `https://bit.ly/3BgY6C8`.

The Packt Gear approach

To recap our solution so far for Packt Gear, we've decided they need Service Cloud, Order Management, B2C Commerce, and Marketing Cloud to form their basic B2C solution architecture.

Based on the information learned in this chapter, we'll need to decide whether they should be leveraging the point-to-point integration approach, integration middleware, or a single source of truth architecture.

Let's start by reviewing the key reasons why adding an integration middleware solution such as MuleSoft would be the right choice for a solution:

- MuleSoft is already being used in the client ecosystem.
- There are plans for multiple integration points beyond the core three Salesforce platforms.
- Point-to-point connector integration patterns are not appropriate for the specific customer scenario and a more complex integration is required.
- There's a strong preference for minimizing product customization and keeping integration in a dedicated solution.

In the Packt Gear case, we're focused on creating an integrated solution within the Salesforce ecosystem. They aren't currently using MuleSoft and don't have a larger integration strategy or digital transformation effort that this initiative fits into. They also don't have internal integration developers who would be able to focus on learning MuleSoft. The foundational use cases are primarily those supported by the point-to-point solutions natively.

Based on this, adding an integration middleware solution for Packt Gear would not be justified. We also know that a single source of truth approach is a supplement to, not a replacement for, an integrated approach to B2C solution architecture.

For Packt Gear, we'll use the point-to-point connectors for the initial implementation.

If the organization evolves and a more robust integration middleware solution becomes necessary, some of the use cases of the point-to-point connectors could be phased out, but others would still be required.

Summary

In this chapter, you learned about how to support a cross-cloud application development life cycle and how to do cross-cloud environment planning not just for production but at each stage of the life cycle.

Building on this, you learned how point-to-point connectors play a key role in B2C solution architecture and what the three Salesforce provided connectors support natively. Specifically, you should now be able to describe the capabilities of B2C CRM Sync, Marketing Cloud Connect, and the Commerce and Marketing Connector. You should know that Marketing Cloud Connect is the only one of the three that is a productized solution and that the other two are development frameworks that will need to be integrated and customized by a developer. The Salesforce Order Management and B2C Commerce integration is another example of a productized connector between platforms.

After reading this chapter, you should also be able to assess when MuleSoft or another integration middleware solution would be a good fit for a B2C solution and what accelerators Salesforce provides from the MuleSoft Anypoint Exchange to streamline B2C solution architecture.

Finally, you should understand how a B2C solution would integrate with a single source of truth organizational approach and how that would combine with both point-to-point and integration middleware techniques.

In the next chapter, we'll focus specifically on synchronizing data between systems to create a unified and consistent understanding of the customer.

Questions

1. In a cross-cloud application development life cycle, why is it important to discuss environment mapping between systems at each stage of the development life cycle?
2. Of the three Salesforce point-to-point connectors discussed in this chapter, which is a supported Salesforce product? Is the Order Management and B2C Commerce integration a productized integration or custom code?
3. In an integrated B2C solution, which of the following products should serve as the central repository for customer data: B2C Commerce, Marketing Cloud, or the Salesforce Platform?
4. Which of the following is the primary use case for B2C CRM Sync: creating cases in Service Cloud from the B2C Commerce storefront, synchronizing orders from B2C Commerce into Service Cloud, or synchronizing customer data between B2C Commerce and Service Cloud?

5. True or false? MC Connect can be configured to use any system attribute on the Contact record as the Subscriber Key in Marketing Cloud.

6. Name one B2C use case where point-to-point integrations are still required when using a product such as MuleSoft as an integration middleware solution.

7. Why is leveraging an external system as the only source of customer data within a B2C solution not a viable option?

Further reading

- *Salesforce Solution Architecture for Retail*: https://sforce.co/2SWrkVf
- *Salesforce Connector*: https://bit.ly/3db7D2X
- *Salesforce B2C Commerce Data Connector*: https://bit.ly/35Vx5Fz
- *Salesforce B2C Commerce Shop Connector*: https://bit.ly/3vR0nQw
- *Salesforce Marketing Cloud Connector*: https://bit.ly/3xURjLR
- *Get Started with Salesforce and Heroku*: https://sforce.co/3h01A3H

8
Creating a 360° View of the Customer

The term **Customer 360** describes the idea of Salesforce products working together in a customer-centric way. It's a suite of interconnected tools and applications that operate as a single unified platform. Although there are many aspects of integration that must be considered as part of a B2C solution architecture, none are more important than the goal of creating a single view of the customer.

This chapter builds upon *Chapter 7, Integration Architecture Options*, and will focus specifically on customer data representation in each component product and how to keep it synchronized. Regardless of the integration approach you've chosen for your architecture, you'll eventually need to address customer data within the component products.

This chapter will focus specifically on B2C Commerce, Service Cloud, and the core Marketing Cloud messaging and journeys platform (just called Marketing Cloud here for convenience). Despite that, the same concepts should be applied to any other component products in your solution, Salesforce or otherwise. First, you must understand the data model as it relates to customers, then understand the integration options (APIs and feeds), and then understand the data events that will be used to drive that integration.

Similarly, although this chapter is focused on customer data, the same concepts and patterns could be applied to any other data that needs to be integrated, such as product data, order data, or marketing interaction history.

In this chapter, we're going to cover the following main topics:

- Identifying the customer
- Mastering customer data
- 360° view of the customer
- Seamless identity

By the end of this chapter, you'll be able to explain how a customer is represented internally within each system. You'll be able to draw a cross-cloud customer data model and explain the purpose of each identifier required. Expanding on that, you'll be able to plan a new implementation with customer data, as well as a legacy data migration. Finally, you'll understand what seamless identity means for the customer on the storefront and how to implement it!

Identifying the customer

Identifying customers, just like any other data record, requires understanding two important concepts. The first is the **unique identifiers (IDs)** that point to that record and the second is the scope in which that identifier is unique.

Some IDs, most notably **Universally Unique Identifiers (UUIDs)**, are unique across all systems for all time. Statistically speaking, the same ID will never be generated twice. Other IDs, such as an order number that increments each time an order is placed, are unique within the scope of a particular commerce site or organization.

These IDs are particularly important because the integration options for each product require internal IDs. That means each system must know the appropriate ID for the systems it needs to update or retrieve a record from to do so efficiently.

The following table shows the required customer identifiers for each of the three-component systems we've discussed so far:

System	Identifier	Key	Scope
Marketing Cloud	Subscriber Key	X	
	Contact Key	X	
Salesforce Platform	Account ID		X
	Contact ID	X	
B2C Commerce	Customer List ID		X
	Site ID		X
	Customer ID	X	
	Customer No	X	

Figure 8.1 – Customer identifiers and scopes

As we can see, the Marketing Cloud key is the Subscriber Key, which should be equal to the Contact ID from the Salesforce Platform. This key is unique within the scope of the entire Marketing Cloud instance. Within the Salesforce Platform, the Account ID is both a key identifying the Account record and scope for the Contact ID. Although both are unique within the Salesforce Platform, since only the Contact record is synchronized to Marketing Cloud through Marketing Cloud Connect, the Contact ID and associated Contact record is the most important record in the Salesforce Platform customer data model.

> **Important note**
>
> You will sometimes see both Subscriber Key and Contact Key referring the Marketing Cloud data model. While some would argue there are subtle differences between the two, they are generally used interchangeably, and the differences are not relevant when designing B2C solution architectures. In this book, we've used both in different contexts, so you need to know that they are essentially the same thing.
>
> See *Set the Subscriber Key or Contact Key* at `https://sforce.co/3iME0IM` for more information.

Finally, B2C Commerce has four identifiers that need to be tracked. The Customer ID is unique within an instance and needs to be paired with the Site ID when using the B2C Commerce APIs. The Customer Number is unique within a given Customer List and must be paired with the Customer List ID when using the B2C Commerce APIs.

For each of the component products, we're going to cover the identifiers that they use and the scope in which they are unique. After that, we'll look at a cross-cloud data model that can be used to tie these records together across systems.

Service Cloud customer identifiers

For Service Cloud and the Salesforce Platform in general, two different data models can be used to represent customers. The data model that will be used depends on the Salesforce org being used to host Service Cloud.

These two models are Person Accounts and Business Accounts, each of which will be covered here. Person Accounts and Business Accounts were also covered in more detail in *Chapter 1, Demystifying Salesforce, Customer 360, and Digital 360*.

In both cases, the underlying data structures are the Account and Contact Objects. The primary difference is that, for Person Accounts, the fields of the Account and Contact record are rolled up onto a single Person Account record.

Because they are used to model data for individuals rather than organizations, the Person Account style is generally more appropriate for B2C solution architectures and other direct-to-consumer selling scenarios. Accounts and Contacts can be helpful in direct-to-consumer scenarios, however, when modeling households and individuals. Turning on Person Accounts in an org impacts the entire org and cannot be undone. When Person Accounts are enabled, they are still not required, but it adds some complexity to the data model and should be coordinated with other users of the org in advance.

> **Further reading**
> For more about the implications of enabling Person Accounts, review the following article: `https://sforce.co/3xkzHI1`.

Within the Salesforce Platform, to properly plan for customer data, you'll need to understand the data events that trigger changes, the underlying customer data model, and the mechanisms for accessing customer data.

Salesforce Platform data events

Within the Salesforce Platform, or Service Cloud, in particular, the most common data event is the Contact or Person Account record being manually edited by a Customer Service representative.

> **Tip**
> By data event, we just mean any change to customer data that needs to be reflected in the other component products within the B2C solution architecture.

Since the Salesforce Platform can activate a variety of automation options in response to record changes, it is not necessary to include code to update outside systems in response to user interface actions directly. Instead, the approach taken by B2C CRM Sync is to leverage a Record Triggered Flow to call B2C Commerce and push updates from Contact record changes, regardless of how those changes occur.

This means that regardless of whether changes happen because of CSR interaction through the Service Console, DML events in Apex, external API calls, or any other use case, the appropriate flow will trigger and update B2C Commerce.

As we discussed in *Chapter 7, Integration Architecture Options*, it is not necessary to write custom code to update Marketing Cloud when using Marketing Cloud Connect for most use cases.

Salesforce Platform customer data model

Regardless of whether your org is using Person Accounts or Business Accounts, behind the scenes, the data is stored in Account and Contact records. Going back to our idea of IDs and scopes, in the Salesforce Platform, a Contact is a child record of exactly one Account, and both IDs are only guaranteed to be unique within the context of a given org. It is possible to re-parent a Contact under a new Account or leverage the Contacts for the Multiple Accounts setting in Salesforce to create associations between Contacts and Accounts, other than the primary account.

> **Further reading**
> You can learn more about Contacts to Multiple Accounts in Salesforce here: https://sforce.co/2V0ti8t.

The following diagram shows the relationship between Account and Contact within an org:

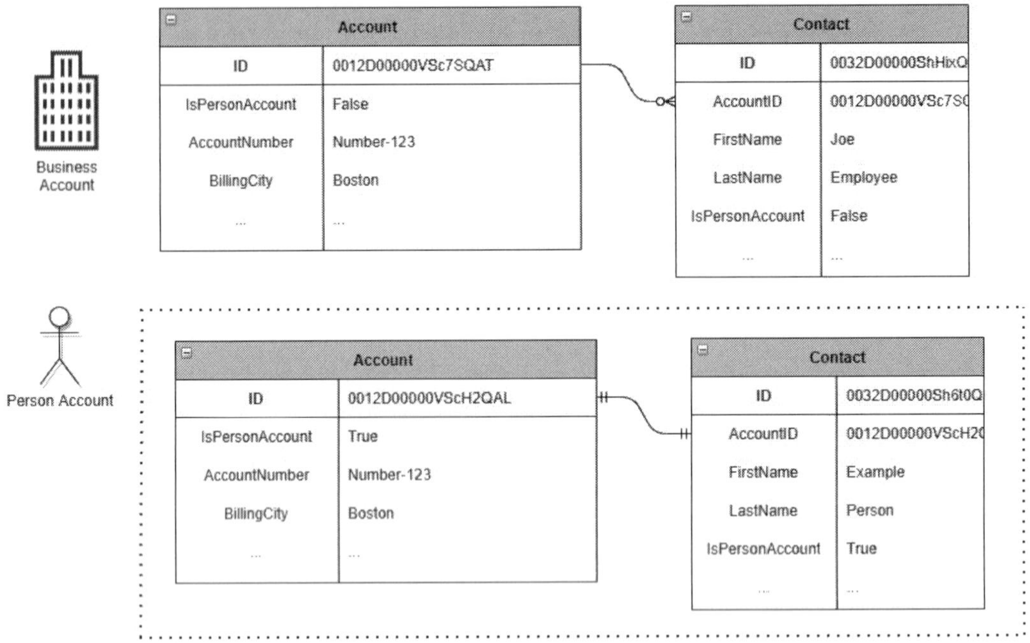

Account	
ID	0012D00000VSc7SQAT
IsPersonAccount	False
AccountNumber	Number-123
BillingCity	Boston
...	...

Business Account

Contact	
ID	0032D00000ShHixQ
AccountID	0012D00000VSc7SQ
FirstName	Joe
LastName	Employee
IsPersonAccount	False
...	...

Person Account

Account	
ID	0012D00000VScH2QAL
IsPersonAccount	True
AccountNumber	Number-123
BillingCity	Boston
...	...

Contact	
ID	0032D00000Sh6t0Q
AccountID	0012D00000VScH2Q
FirstName	Example
LastName	Person
IsPersonAccount	True
...	...

Figure 8.2 – Account and Contact relationships

As you can see, knowing the **Contact ID** within a given org is sufficient to uniquely identify a given customer record.

Other data related to a customer, such as their case history, live chats, and email engagement data from Marketing Cloud, are all related to their Contact record, so this is the key to accessing all Salesforce Platform data for that customer.

Salesforce Platform customer data access

Accessing customer data in the Salesforce Platform relies on the Contact ID, but the methods that are used to retrieve and update those records vary based on the use case.

For fewer than 50k records, the REST API and SOAP API are reasonable choices. Both APIs support real-time record CRUD access at scale. When you need a response immediately, the REST API and SOAP API are good choices. The Composite API can be used to bundle multiple related REST API requests in the same overall package.

With the REST API, resource URLs are constructed like so:

```
https://{instance}.salesforce.com/services/data/v52.0/sobjects/{Object}/{RecordID}
```

In this example, {instance} would be replaced with the domain name for your Salesforce Org, {Object} would be replaced with the sObject property you were trying to access (Account or Contact), and {RecordID} would be replaced with the specific record you were trying to retrieve or update.

If you wish to update more than 50k records, you should use the Bulk API, which also supports CRUD access but at a significantly higher volume and with asynchronous processing. The Bulk API is based on the REST API but operates at a higher scale.

For more information on the Salesforce API options, including the REST, SOAP, and Bulk APIs, please review *Chapter 2, Supporting Your Customers with Service Cloud*.

> **Further reading**
>
> Some example code for the REST API is available here: `https://sforce.co/3ji5oip`.
>
> Some example code for the SOAP API is available here: `https://sforce.co/3qu3OeK`.

By leveraging B2C CRM Sync, as outlined in *Chapter 7, Integration Architecture Options*, you can provide pre-built integration with the Salesforce Platform that covers the most important customer data use cases.

B2C Commerce customer identifiers

Within the B2C Commerce platform, the representation of a customer is known as a **Profile**. A Profile record is required for every authenticated customer in B2C Commerce and is created automatically when a customer registers on the storefront. Your responsibility, as a B2C solution architect, is to ensure that the B2C Commerce customer profile record is related to a corresponding Salesforce Platform Contact record in all cases.

Just as we did with the Salesforce Platform, we'll now review the B2C Commerce data events, customer data model, and customer data access mechanisms that are used in an integrated solution.

B2C Commerce data events

B2C Commerce, unlike the Salesforce Platform, cannot trigger code or automation in response to data changes directly. Instead, hooks must be added to all places where data changes could occur to trigger updates to Service Cloud.

The minimum integration points that should be considered in a typical B2C Commerce implementation include the following:

- Customer registration
- Customer login
- My Account page updates
- Guest checkout
- Marketing communication signup
- Marketing consent management/unsubscribe

For each of those integration points, consider both the storefront integration (typically, SFRA) and any API-based integrations (typically, OCAPI). The same hooks can be used in both scenarios to minimize code duplication.

The other ways the customer profile could change in B2C Commerce are via direct edits in Business Manager or via the Commerce APIs. Neither of these options provides a way to directly trigger code in response, so these changes *cannot* be synchronized to external systems in real time.

An approach to address this, if it's needed, would be to build a backend job that synchronizes any customer profile changes that have a last modified date that is more recent than the last synchronized date, as tracked in a custom attribute, to the Salesforce Platform.

> **Important note**
> In this scenario, be sure to update the last synchronized date any time the data is pushed to Service Cloud or updated from Service Cloud. Otherwise, you'll end up triggering a loop of updates where Service Cloud updates B2C Commerce, which changes the last modified date and triggers an update to Service Cloud.

It is not necessary to send customer data updates from B2C Commerce directly to Marketing Cloud if the Salesforce Platform is also being used. Updating the Salesforce Platform Contact record will be sufficient since Marketing Cloud Connect will then synchronize that change to Marketing Cloud for you.

B2C Commerce customer data model

The B2C Commerce customer profile is stored within a B2C Commerce **Customer List**. Each B2C Commerce instance can have any number of Customer Lists, which are then assigned to Sites. This allows multiple B2C Commerce sites within the same realm to potentially share customers.

The following diagram shows an example of mapping Customer Lists to Sites within B2C Commerce:

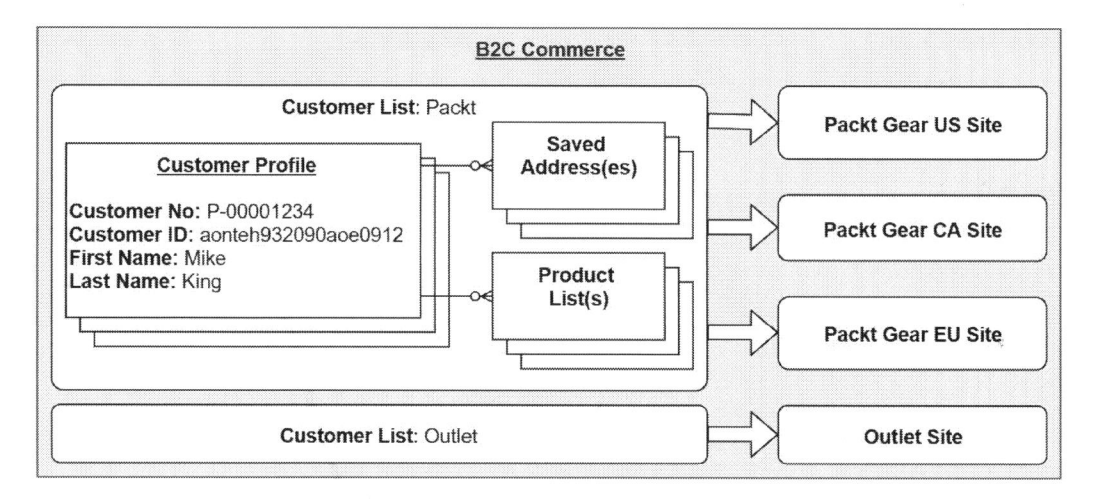

Figure 8.3 – B2C Commerce customer lists and sites

As the preceding diagram shows, a B2C Commerce customer profile is the key to accessing not just information stored directly on the profile, such as their first name and last name, but related records such as the customer's saved addresses and product lists.

Two identifiers are used within the B2C Commerce product for customers, depending on the context: **Customer Number** and **Customer ID**.

The B2C Commerce customer number is a sequence number that's generated following a pattern that can be controlled by the merchant at the Customer List level. The customer number is only guaranteed to be unique within the context of the Customer List it's associated with. The Customer ID, however, is a system-generated identifier that is unique within the entire instance across all Sites and Customer Lists.

B2C Commerce customer data access

Now that you understand the data model *within* B2C Commerce, you'll need to understand how to access and modify customer data from outside systems. The primary mechanism that's used here is the B2C Commerce REST APIs.

The following table shows the two different B2C Commerce APIs (OCAPI and Commerce APIs), each of which has a customer API for use in storefront use cases and a customer API for use in backend data use cases:

API Category	API Resource	Scope Required	Identifier Required
OCAPI Shop API	/customers	Site ID	Customer ID
OCAPI Data API	/customer_lists	Customer List ID	Customer Number
Commerce API	Shopper Customers	Site ID	Customer ID
Commerce API	Customers	Customer List ID	Customer Number

Figure 8.4 – B2C Commerce APIs and customer identifiers

As we can see, the **Customer Number** must always be used in conjunction with the **Customer List ID**. The **Customer ID** is always used in conjunction with a specific **Site ID**.

The following request path is an example of retrieving a single customer record using the OCAPI Data API. Note the `list_id` and `customer_no` components of the path:

```
/customer_lists/{list_id}/customers/{customer_no}
```

Here's the corresponding request path for the Commerce API's Customers API, including the same components:

```
/customer-lists/{listId}/customers/{customerNo}
```

The following request path is an example of retrieving a single customer record using the OCAPI Shop API. Note the `customer_id` parameter used:

```
/customers/{customer_id}
```

Since the Shop API is authenticated with a single storefront for a particular Site, the Site ID has already been supplied.

Finally, here's the corresponding request path for the Commerce API's Shopper Customers API:

```
/customers/{customerId}
```

The B2C Commerce data model and APIs were reviewed in more detail in *Chapter 3, Direct-to-Consumer Selling with Commerce Cloud B2C*.

Marketing Cloud customer identifiers

For the most part, Marketing Cloud will *receive* customer data updates from other systems. Marketing Cloud does not provide an interactive user experience in the same way that B2C Commerce does, and it is not intended for data manipulation the same way the Salesforce Platform is.

Instead, Marketing Cloud will be used to drive customer touchpoints such as email, SMS, social media, advertisements, and push notifications based on the data supplied by other systems and by **engagement data** collected by Marketing Cloud. Engagement data is information about how a customer interacts with the brand rather than information about the individual.

The number of emails a customer opened and how frequently they clicked links in communications is an example of customer engagement data that can be tracked by Marketing Cloud and associated with a customer's profile. Additional engagement data can be collected from the B2C Commerce storefront and fed directly into Marketing Cloud using `collect.js`. Examples of this type of engagement data include which products a customer viewed and how many they added to their cart.

Engagement data is made available in the Salesforce Platform automatically with Marketing Cloud Connect but generally, this does not need to be synchronized to other systems – it's used in Marketing Cloud.

In Marketing Cloud, you'll need to understand the customer data model and the data access mechanisms that are available. These are covered in the following sections.

Marketing Cloud customer data model

Marketing Cloud tracks customer data in multiple ways behind the scenes, but the record you'll be integrating with as a B2C solution architect is the **Contact** or **Subscriber**. These terms are often used interchangeably. Generally, it's called a Contact in the context of Contact Builder or Mobile Studio and a Subscriber in the context of Email Studio. There are subtle differences between the two that are not relevant to the solution architecture.

For clarity, within a project, pick one and be consistent. If your organization or client is primarily using the Email Studio functionality of Marketing Cloud, it may be easier to standardize on Subscriber. Otherwise, standardize on Contact.

The Contact Key and Subscriber Key are the same and should always match the Contact ID from the Salesforce Platform.

> **Tip**
> The Contact record is the representation of a customer for Marketing Cloud that will be related to the Contact record in the Salesforce Platform and the customer profile record in B2C Commerce.

Marketing Cloud always maintains a master list of All Contacts for a given instance, which includes all Contacts that have ever received communication, as well as all Contact records that have been synchronized from the Salesforce Platform via Marketing Cloud Connect.

The Contact record tracks engagement data for the corresponding individual, subscription channels, related data stored in **Data Extensions** (**DE**), and contact information.

Identifying a Contact record in Marketing Cloud is primarily accomplished with a Contact Key. The Contact Key is a cross-channel identifier that's used to ensure that all touchpoints can recognize an individual as belonging to a single record, without relying on channel-specific identifiers such as an email address or mobile phone number.

This same identifier is used to relate this Contact to other Marketing Cloud DE that track data related to this individual, such as B2C Commerce product back-in-stock notifications, wish lists, or anything else that's been loaded into Marketing Cloud DE using the *Subscriber Key*.

> **Important note**
> Marketing Cloud Connect can only use the Salesforce Platform Contact, User, or Lead ID as the Subscriber Key, so this should always be preferred as part of the initial setup.

Marketing Cloud customer data access

We covered the various Marketing Cloud integration options in detail in *Chapter 4, Engaging Customers with Marketing Cloud*, and these will be your primary means of accessing and updating customer data in Marketing Cloud.

Specifically, the Marketing Cloud REST API is the best choice for real-time access to Marketing Cloud Contact data, which is where information about customer consent and preferences will be tracked. The Marketing Cloud SOAP API is the best choice for email-specific Subscriber data related to the same customer.

CSV files transferred through the Marketing Cloud's integrated SFTP server, which are then ingested with Automation Studio, can also be used for bulk data transfer.

> **Tip**
> With a B2C solution architecture customer, data should always be inserted and updated in the Salesforce Platform first, then synchronized to Marketing Cloud using Marketing Cloud Connect.

If you need to access contact data with the REST API, the base URL is formed as follows:

`https://{subdomain}.rest.marketingcloudapis.com{path}`

Here, `{subdomain}` is replaced with your Marketing Cloud instance-specific subdomain, while `{path}` is replaced with the specific resource you're trying to access.

Here's a complete example path for deleting a Marketing Cloud contact by Contact Key:

```
POST https://{subdomain}.rest.marketingcloudapis.com/contacts/v1/contacts/actions/delete?type=keys
{
    "Values": ["Key1", "Key2"],
    "DeleteOperationType": "ContactAndAttributes"
}
```

The preceding example, when made with valid Contact Keys and carrying a valid access token, will delete the contact records and all associated attributes from the Marketing Cloud account.

> **Further reading**
> To learn more about Marketing Cloud APIs, please review *Chapter 4, Engaging Customers with Marketing Cloud*, or review the Rest API reference here: `https://sforce.co/3xjckiD`.

Cross-cloud customer identification

Now, we'll take the customer identification concepts we outlined in the previous sections and bring them together. The concept of cross-cloud customer identification means recognizing and relating records that correspond to a single individual in different systems or different data stores within the same system.

Within the basic B2C solution architecture, that means recognizing a B2C Commerce customer profile as corresponding to the same individual as a Salesforce Platform Contact record and a Marketing Cloud Contact record.

The following diagram represents a complete customer dataset across these three-component systems, fully annotated with cross-cloud identifiers:

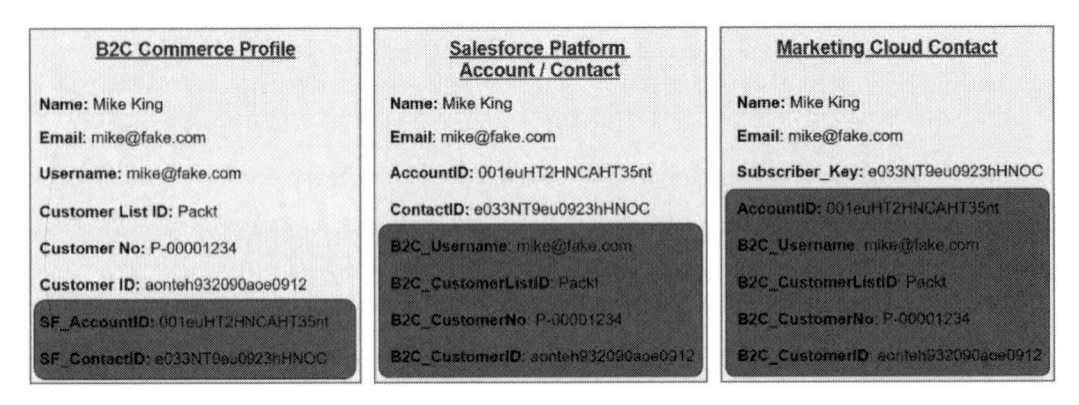

B2C Commerce Profile	Salesforce Platform Account / Contact	Marketing Cloud Contact
Name: Mike King	**Name:** Mike King	**Name:** Mike King
Email: mike@fake.com	**Email:** mike@fake.com	**Email:** mike@fake.com
Username: mike@fake.com	**AccountID:** 001euHT2HNCAHT35nt	**Subscriber_Key:** e033NT9eu0923hHNOC
Customer List ID: Packt	**ContactID:** e033NT9eu0923hHNOC	**AccountID:** 001euHT2HNCAHT35nt
Customer No: P-00001234	**B2C_Username:** mike@fake.com	**B2C_Username:** mike@fake.com
Customer ID: aonteh932090aoe0912	**B2C_CustomerListID:** Packt	**B2C_CustomerListID:** Packt
SF_AccountID: 001euHT2HNCAHT35nt	**B2C_CustomerNo:** P-00001234	**B2C_CustomerNo:** P-00001234
SF_ContactID: e033NT9eu0923hHNOC	**B2C_CustomerID:** aonteh932090aoe0912	**B2C_CustomerID:** aonteh932090aoe0912

Figure 8.5 – Cross-cloud identifiers

The preceding diagram shows each customer record with system-specific identifiers, as well as the required identifiers from the related systems. As you'll recall from the previous sections on the system-specific customer identifiers, API access for retrieving and updating customer data can only be accomplished with the relevant system-specific identifiers, such as **ContactID** in the Salesforce Platform or **Customer No** and **Customer List ID** in B2C Commerce. Because of this, it's necessary to keep these values in sync across systems using one of the integration patterns we covered in *Chapter 7, Integration Architecture Options*.

The following sections cover progressive identity resolution, which is the process of gradually improving our understanding of a customer, and additional systems beyond Salesforce that may contain customer data we need to incorporate.

Progressive identity resolution

In many cases, the full view of the customer won't be available immediately in all systems. For a customer that has signed up for marketing emails but never registered on the B2C Commerce storefront, for example, we won't have a B2C Commerce customer profile. This gradual expansion of customer data across systems is known as **progressive identity resolution**.

Let's take a specific use case for Packt Gear and explore the steps of progressive identity resolution. As we've determined in the chapters leading up to this one, Packt Gear is using B2C Commerce, Service Cloud, Order Management, and Marketing Cloud. They're also using the Salesforce-supplied point-to-point connectors in a typical retail solution architecture, as discussed in *Chapter 7*, *Integration Architecture Options*.

Now, let's go through a typical customer journey with the brand and ensure we have a plan for cross-cloud data updates. First, the customer signs up for marketing emails on the B2C Commerce storefront, as shown in the following diagram:

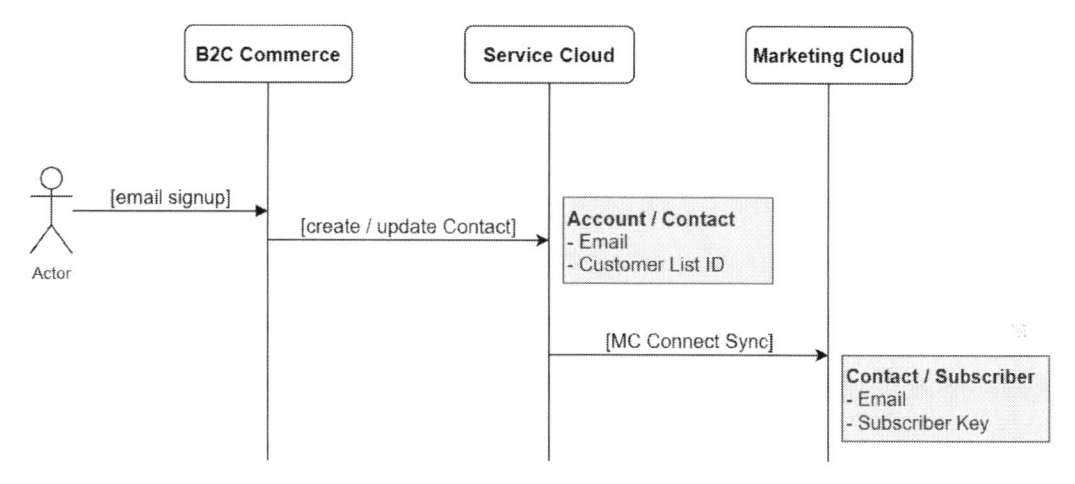

Figure 8.6 – Marketing email signup

Note that in this case, the customer has not created an account in **B2C Commerce**, so they have no customer profile, no Customer ID, and no Customer Number to synchronize. All we know about them is the **Customer List ID** that's assigned to the B2C Commerce site and the **email** they've supplied. With that information, we'll leverage B2C CRM Sync to create or update the Contact record in the Salesforce Platform (home of **Service Cloud**) using the email and the Customer List ID.

From there, Marketing Cloud Connect will automatically synchronize that information to Marketing Cloud by creating or updating the Contact record and Subscriber record based on the new channel-specific subscription preference (email).

If the customer then places an order in B2C Commerce that gets sent to Order Management, creates a case in Service Cloud, or generates engagement data in Marketing Cloud by clicking on marketing email links, it can all be traced back to the same individual.

If the same customer creates an account on the B2C Commerce storefront, the cross-cloud identity picture expands, as shown in the following diagram:

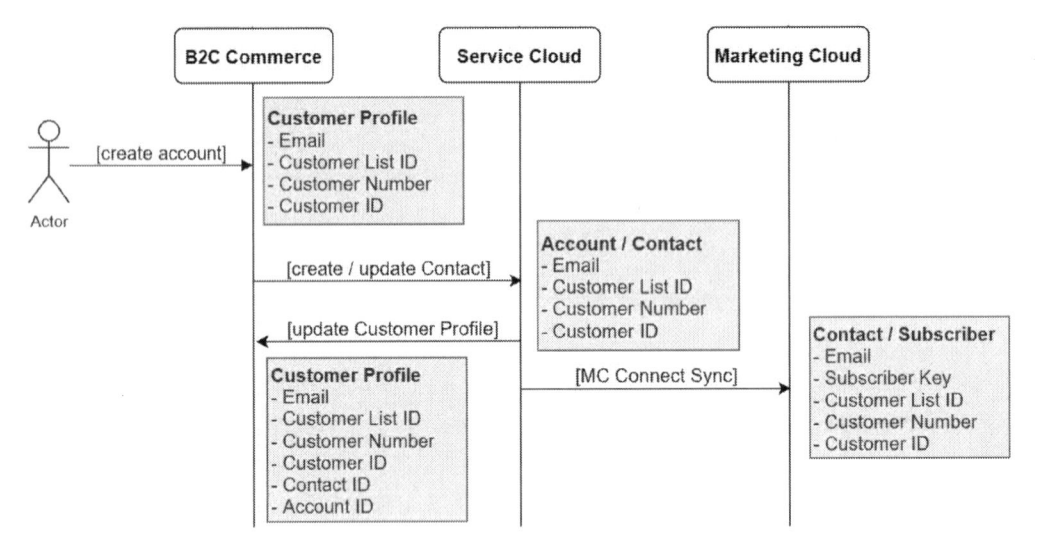

Figure 8.7 – B2C Commerce customer registration

The preceding diagram shows how additional data is captured and added to the cross-cloud identity picture when the customer registers on the B2C Commerce storefront. By the end of this sequence, the full set of cross-cloud identifiers is known and tracked.

> **Tip**
> Note that at no point does B2C Commerce update customer data directly in Marketing Cloud; it always goes through the Salesforce Platform and leverages Marketing Cloud Connect.

While working through the Packt Gear use case, or any other B2C solution architecture use case, be sure to think through how customer data can be introduced and updated in various systems. How will changes made by a customer in My Account through the storefront be updated? If you introduce a mobile app using OCAPI, how would that integration interact with the solution architecture that's been outlined so far? Would it be different using the Commerce APIs for B2C Commerce?

At this point, with the knowledge you've gained in the preceding chapters and this one, you should have the tools to think through and create cross-cloud solutions like the one outline previously for each of these use cases within the Salesforce ecosystem.

Now, let's talk briefly about how to handle customer data outside of the Salesforce ecosystem.

Customer data in additional systems

The basic approach we've outlined so far can be extended for any system, Salesforce or otherwise. Follow these steps for each additional system you're looking to introduce to the system:

1. Identify how customer data is represented in the target system.
2. Document the required customer identifiers and scopes needed to recognize an individual record.
3. Determine the available integration options for data retrieval and updating it.
4. Evaluate the business needs and journeys that impact customer data to orchestrate necessary cross-cloud updates.

Your integration architecture is going to drive the mechanics of how updates are passed between systems (integration middleware or point-to-point), but the overall approach is the same regardless. The important thing is to know how customer data can be introduced to or updated within your organization and have a plan for passing those updates to the systems that need them.

In the Packt Gear scenario, and in many B2C solution architectures, the point-to-point connectors are leveraged, and the Salesforce Platform is the system of record for customer data. This means that an additional system being introduced only needs to integrate with the Salesforce Platform to implement bi-directional synchronization of customer data. This centralized approach simplifies architectures and allows the Salesforce ecosystem to be treated as a unit in many enterprise architecture strategies.

Now that we've reviewed cross-cloud customer representations and identifiers, we'll extend our perspective so that it includes customer data in general and how it is represented in our architecture.

Mastering customer data

In the first four chapters of this book, we covered the capabilities, data model, and constraints of each of the major components of a Salesforce B2C solution architecture. This information is relevant when designing solutions that require additional customer data beyond the native attributes available in the component systems.

Synchronizing a customer's first name or email address is straightforward since there's an attribute for exactly that in each of the component systems. Information such as a customer's saved shipping address from B2C Commerce or their associated cases from Service Cloud is a bit more complex, though, as they may not be needed in other systems, depending on the business needs.

Finally, information that is introduced to meet the unique needs of a given customer must be stored and either exposed or systematically synchronized to other systems.

This process of mastering customer data involves three primary stages: evaluating business needs, cross-cloud customer data mapping, and data privacy and consent management. We'll discuss each of these stages in the following sections and then conclude with a brief section on handling legacy data.

Evaluating business needs

Evaluating business needs means assessing what you're trying to accomplish with a particular category of data. From there, you'll be able to make informed decisions about where to store it and whether/how to synchronize it.

Let's take the Packt Gear example we introduced in *Chapter 1, Demystifying Salesforce, Customer 360, and Digital 360*. To recap, we've determined that Packt Gear's business need is to be able to schedule a guided hike associated with one of their physical store locations. Customers should be able to sign up for these guided hikes through the website and CSRs should be able to view, create, modify, and delete signups on behalf of customers. Packt Gear employees should also be able to generate reports based on guided hike signups to see how customers are responding.

We also learned that Packt Gear wants to be able to send updates and build marketing journeys based on guided hike signups using Marketing Cloud.

The only people who can create or modify the hikes themselves are the guides, who will be set up as users in Service Cloud.

In this section, we're going to build upon the data model we established for the Salesforce Platform to incorporate B2C Commerce and Marketing Cloud.

> **Tip**
> To review the Guided Hike data model for the Salesforce Platform, see *Chapter 1, Demystifying Salesforce, Customer 360, and Digital 360*.

Based on what we know so far, the requirements we've heard for B2C Commerce are as follows:

- Display available guided hikes by store location
- Allow registered users to sign up for a hike
- Allow registered users to view/cancel their hike signups

Given these requirements and knowing the limitations of the B2C Commerce data model, which we covered in *Chapter 3, Direct-to-Consumer Selling with Commerce Cloud B2C*, the best approach would be to perform a real-time API integration to the Salesforce Platform for each use case leveraging the REST API.

An alternative approach would be to store the data in B2C Commerce using Custom Objects, but B2C Commerce Custom Objects have strict quota limits and have performance limitations that make this a poor fit. We also know that most of the updates, editing, and reporting for hikes will be done in Service Cloud, so that's where the data belongs.

To meet the Marketing Cloud requirement to be able to build customer journeys around hike signups, we can set up a **Salesforce Data Event** in Marketing Cloud based on the `HikerSignup__c` Custom Object. When a new record is created, it will place the associated Contact in a journey, which can be used to help the hiker plan for their hike, including purchasing all the right gear!

Since Salesforce Data Events are part of Marketing Cloud Connect, no custom integration work is required to support this use case.

In this case, the best solution for Packt Gear's business need is to store the data in the Salesforce Platform, expose it to B2C Commerce using the REST API, and leverage Marketing Cloud Connect to trigger marketing journeys based on signups.

This process should be repeated for any additional cross-cloud business that needs to ensure the right data is stored in the right systems and available when and where it's needed.

For some data, especially a customer's identity data, the best solution is to synchronize the data between systems. In these cases, cross-cloud customer data mapping is the right tool to use.

Cross-cloud customer data mapping

Cross-cloud customer data mapping is the process of identifying how each piece of customer data will be stored in each component system. We can also use this process to note what data should be synchronized and what data is only required in specific systems.

In the following table, we've mapped the basic customer data between B2C Commerce, Marketing Cloud, and Service Cloud:

Sync?	B2C Commerce Profile	Salesforce Platform Contact	Marketing Cloud Contact
X	firstName	FirstName	FirstName
X	lastName	LastName	LastName
X	birthday	Birthdate	Date of Birth
	preferredLocale	-	-
X	phoneMobile	Mobile	PhoneNumber

Figure 8.8 – Cross-cloud customer data mapping

This example should be extended to include all customer attributes, both standard and custom, that are required by each of the component products (including the non-Salesforce products included in the solution). During the requirements gathering phase, also note whether each attribute currently exists in the system or whether it will be created as new. It's also a good idea to document the data type and any size constraints in each system.

Data type compatibility can be particularly important in the following scenarios:

- Localizable data
- Data represented as a picklist in the Salesforce Org (such as State and Country codes)
- Text fields with a length constraint

Once these have been documented thoroughly, it will become clear if any changes are needed to receive the data in a compatible fashion for each system.

This concept can also be extended for data beyond the basic profile data that is associated with the customer. Common examples in the B2C solution architecture space include their saved addresses or wish lists in B2C Commerce or their case history in Service Cloud. Leverage a table like the one shown in the preceding table for each data type to describe how it maps between systems if it's synchronized.

Data privacy and consent management

Data privacy and consent management topics are complex and require support from a company's legal team. From a technical perspective, it's important to document and track where data lives and how you'll comply with common data laws or industry standards, including but not limited to the following:

- **Payment Card Industry (PCI)**
- **Health Insurance Portability and Accountability Act (HIPAA)**
- **General Data Protection Regulation (GDPR)**
- **California Consumer Privacy Act (CPA)**

Each of these standards has nuances that are outside the scope of this book, but being aware of a few guiding principles can help you establish a firm foundation and steer clear of problem areas.

The guiding principle of data privacy and consent management, as covered in the following section, is to minimize access to sensitive data. We'll also provide a very high-level overview of tools for complying with GDPR and related regulations.

Minimizing movement and access to sensitive data

To support PCI compliance, ensure that credit card data is never synchronized to systems that don't require it and always store encrypted at a minimum, preferably tokenized. The ideal payment integration tokenizes the customer's credit card in the browser directly with the payment gateway and then sends the token to B2C Commerce, which includes it in the order data so that the order management system can capture funds. This ensures that raw credit card data never passes through any merchant-controlled system.

For HIPAA compliance, be careful to evaluate HIPAA compliance for each component product separately as this is not a guarantee, even within the Salesforce ecosystem. Even if products are HIPAA compliant, customizations built on top of those products will have their own requirements and, in many cases, a tokenized solution for customer data may be the best approach to avoid storing any patient data in any merchant-controlled system.

GDPR and its related data privacy legislation

For the various **Personally Identifiable Information (PII)** regulation categories, be sure to flag PII data during the customer data mapping exercise and do not synchronize data to systems that do not require it. GDPR also covers sensitive information such as health, gender, and race, which may or may not constitute PII.

Three of the core rights that are allowed by recent PII regulations, including GDPR and CCPA, include the following:

- The right to be forgotten
- The right to stop processing
- The right to data portability

To support these and other requirements, each system within the B2C solution architecture has different capabilities that need to be considered and coordinated.

As with most customer data that is relevant for multiple products within the solution, overall customer consent management should be stored and tracked within the Salesforce Platform and synchronized to other systems. This includes consent for specific communications channels, such as email, as well as consent for tracking and privacy.

Right to be forgotten

The right to be forgotten, sometimes called the right to data erasure, allows individuals to request that companies delete any information they have about that individual. In an integrated solution, where customer data is being synchronized across systems, this can be a technical challenge.

Review the solution overview diagram artifact discussed in *Figure 6.7* in *Chapter 6, Role of a Solution Architect*. For each component system, note which stores customer data. This is also a good time to document where this information is stored to document data residency requirements. Work with your Salesforce Account Executive to gather this information as the available locations for B2C Commerce realms, Salesforce Platform org hosting, and Marketing Cloud instance hosting are always changing.

Knowing which systems are impacted, you can document which systems could *initiate* an erasure request. Most commonly, this will include a CSR in Service Cloud for handling a customer request or, if enabled, a self-service request via the B2C Commerce storefront. From there, document a process that satisfies those requests that are consistent and considers the technical capabilities of each platform.

In the Salesforce Platform, for example, it is not possible to delete a User record – it can only be anonymized by clearing fields. In B2C Commerce, there is no API to delete orders; this requires manual intervention or a similar anonymization approach.

> **Tip**
> A combination of documented business processes and technical capabilities may be required to ensure compliance with the relevant legislation.

Right to stop processing

There is no simple way to meet this requirement in a SaaS platform such as Salesforce. For B2C Commerce, the recommended approach is to export all customer data and delete it from the system. If a customer allows the organization to resume processing later, the data can be re-imported. If a customer requests their data be deleted, the export can be purged.

This requires customization or manual intervention in either case.

Marketing Cloud allows a contact to be restricted, which stops all communication with that individual while they're still collecting unsubscribe requests as needed.

Right to data portability

Data portability is the right for customers to receive a copy of their data. B2C Commerce provides this capability through the SFRA storefront natively and via APIs to support customer data extract in JSON format. This extract will include all the customer's profiles and order data from B2C Commerce and can be further enhanced with custom code.

The simplest way to comply with self-service data portability requests is to ensure that all customer PIIs have synchronized to the B2C Commerce customer profile and leverage this feature.

The B2C Commerce storefront provides capabilities to allow customers to opt in or opt out to cookie tracking. This should be synchronized to the Salesforce Platform Contact record if it's relevant for any other customer touchpoints. B2C Commerce also provides the ability for customers to submit data portability requests, which will generate a JSON extract of all B2C Commerce resident customer data.

> **Further reading**
>
> You can learn more about the privacy law by looking at the following Trail: https://sforce.co/3xp9oBU.

See the *Further reading* section at the end of this chapter for additional links related to data privacy and consent management within a B2C solution architecture.

Handling legacy data

Our hypothetical Salesforce customer, Packt Gear, has the advantage of starting from scratch. They're building from the ground up and can get their customer data and cross-cloud integration right the first time. In the real world, that's not always the case, and there are a couple of legacy data issues you'll have to know how to handle.

The first issue is data duplication, which is where multiple records are representing the same individual. We'll cover that in the next section, *360° view of the customer*.

The second issue, and perhaps the biggest thing to ask about when implementing a B2C solution architecture approach in a live environment, is the Marketing Cloud Contact Key. In many environments where Marketing Cloud Connect is not being used, the email address or another identifier is used as the Marketing Cloud Contact Key. We've already discussed that Marketing Cloud Connect can only use the Salesforce Platform Contact ID as the Contact Key, so how can we handle this?

The answer is a process called **Subscriber Key migration**.

> **Important note**
> A Subscriber Key migration is a paid service that can only be executed by Marketing Cloud professional services, and it requires a complete shutdown of all Marketing Cloud activities for a certain period. This process is used to update both the Contact Key and the Subscriber Key so that they're identical and align with the Salesforce Platform's Contact, User, or Lead ID (generally, this is the Contact ID in a B2C solution architecture).

If you, or a customer you're working with, has an existing Marketing Cloud implementation with real data in place that needs to be integrated with the Salesforce Platform, the first step is to engage Marketing Cloud professional services. They can help you plan for a Subscriber Key migration that aligns your existing Marketing Cloud data with your Salesforce Platform Contacts before the integration is enabled.

> **Further reading**
> You can learn more about Subscriber Key migration here: `https://sforce.co/3qYClSK`.

Now that we understand how to map and relate customer data across records within the Salesforce ecosystem, we need to cover how to handle potential duplicate records and conflicting data sources to create a 360° view of the customer.

360° view of the customer

So far in this chapter, we've focused primarily on how to link individual records together to create a consistent view of a customer across systems. To understand your customer as an individual, however, a more holistic approach is required.

You must recognize that customers can and often do possess multiple profiles in various systems that represent them and that sometimes, they use inconsistent data points and that sometimes, customers share the same identifiers. One person can place an order as a guest user on the storefront, initiate a live chat with a service agent, create an account with their work email, and sign up for marketing communications with their email.

This progression from linking individual records together across systems to recognizing an individual supports experience delivery maturity. To get there, you'll have to start recognizing customers as humans, which we'll cover in the following sections.

Experience delivery maturity

Salesforce talks about experience delivery maturity at the beginning and advanced stages. In the beginning stages, capabilities such as individual channel optimization and best practices for user experience are a priority.

In the intermediate stages, connected capabilities begin to take shape, as we've discussed so far in this chapter. We can pull a customer's order history, but only if it's explicitly tied to the logged-in account. We can generate reports and the estimated total lifetime value, but individuals may be double-counted or appear fragmented across multiple records.

The advanced stages of experience delivery maturity attempt to recognize customers as humans and supporting them accordingly.

The following table shows examples of intermediate experience delivery on the left and advanced experience delivery on the right:

Identify Customers via Individual Profiles	Identify Customers as Human Beings
Order on Behalf Of	Complete Order and Case History
Abandoned Cart	Full Engagement History
Journey Abandonment	Business Analytics
Service Chat (Agent and Bot)	Journey Suppression
Single Channel Personalization	Cross-Channel Personalization
Basic Consent and Privacy	Advanced Consent and Privacy

Figure 8.9 – Intermediate and advanced experience delivery

By evolving from associating individual record association to treating multiple records across systems as representing a single person, it's possible to move up the experience delivery curve to more advanced use cases.

Recognizing customers as humans

To recognize customers as human beings, we must go beyond individual profiles and records. By doing so, we'll start to unlock business intelligence and capabilities that truly deliver on the connected Customer 360 experience.

First, we'll talk about what exactly this means before talking about the capabilities that can be unlocked by having an overlay view of individuals across records. Then, we'll cover some of the ways this can be achieved.

To explain this concept, let's take the example we used earlier in this chapter of a cross-cloud customer identification model (repeated here for clarity):

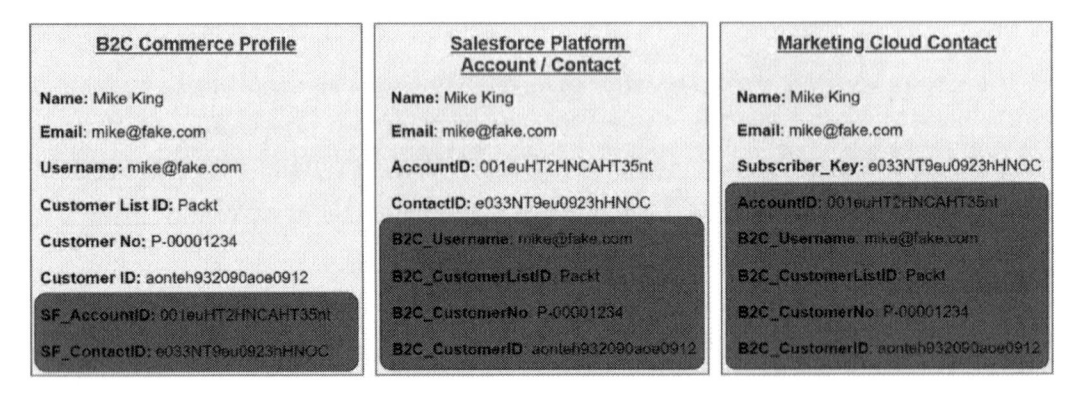

B2C Commerce Profile	Salesforce Platform Account / Contact	Marketing Cloud Contact
Name: Mike King	**Name:** Mike King	**Name:** Mike King
Email: mike@fake.com	**Email:** mike@fake.com	**Email:** mike@fake.com
Username: mike@fake.com	**AccountID:** 001euHT2HNCAHT35nt	**Subscriber_Key:** e033NT9eu0923hHNOC
Customer List ID: Packt	**ContactID:** e033NT9eu0923hHNOC	**AccountID:** 001euHT2HNCAHT35nt
Customer No: P-00001234	**B2C_Username:** mike@fake.com	**B2C_Username:** mike@fake.com
Customer ID: aonteh932090aoe0912	**B2C_CustomerListID:** Packt	**B2C_CustomerListID:** Packt
SF_AccountID: 001euHT2HNCAHT35nt	**B2C_CustomerNo:** P-00001234	**B2C_CustomerNo:** P-00001234
SF_ContactID: e033NT9eu0923hHNOC	**B2C_CustomerID:** aonteh932090aoe0912	**B2C_CustomerID:** aonteh932090aoe0912

Figure 8.10 – Cross-cloud identifiers

In this example, the customer has exactly one record in each system, and they all relate to each other. This is the foundational use case but this is not always what happens in the real world, especially if the place where this integration is happening is a messy environment with live data already in place.

The following table depicts a realistic scenario where an individual has multiple records in each system with different components of the overall picture:

B2C Commerce	Customer No	Customer ID	Email Address	Phone
	2011933	Net39ont3	testuser@gmail.com	555-123-1234
Salesforce Platform	Contact ID	First Name	Email Address	Phone
	X1234	Test	t.user@gmail.com	555-123-1234
	B3920	Testeroo	testuser@yahoo.com	+44 555-123-1234
Marketing Cloud	User ID	First Name	Email Address	Phone
	200	Test	T.USER@gmail.com	555-512-1234
	300	Testfriend	testuser@yahoo.com	5551231234

Figure 8.11 – Multiple records for the same purpose

In this example, we need to introduce an additional layer of identification that encapsulates the component profiles and contact records. By assigning a common unique ID to the component records, we can begin to recognize them as relating to a single human.

Recognizing duplicate records

Before we can assign an identifier to these records, we need to be able to recognize that they exist and that they describe one individual. This can be accomplished in a variety of ways but the simplest way, without introducing additional software solutions, is to leverage the Salesforce Platform's **matching rules** and **duplicate rules**.

If you're following the best practices outlined so far, you're going to be using the Salesforce Platform as the system of record for customer data, so it makes sense to use the capability of that platform to recognize duplicates. Matching rules in Salesforce allow you to configure rules that are used to decide if two different records of the same object are equivalent. Duplicate rules leverage matching rules to determine what to do when a match is detected.

Matching rules can be configured to evaluate a variety of different data points related to the record in question, typically a Contact record in this case, including identifiers such as the first name, last name, email address, and phone number. When configuring match rules, also remember the concept of *scopes*, as discussed earlier regarding customer identifiers.

Essentially, just because two records represent the same individual doesn't *necessarily* mean they should be combined or related.

To help explain this concept, let's take the example of Packt Gear's US and Canadian sites. Since both sites are for Packt Gear, it would be helpful to ensure that a customer is only represented once across both so that we know their full history and engagement behavior.

If Packt Gear's parent company, Packt Enterprises, adds additional brands to their Salesforce ecosystem, however, those brands don't want their customer data consolidated with Packt Gear customer data. Being able to assess a customer's total lifetime value to a brand is important and it would be lost if it were merged across all brands.

We'll explore Packt Enterprises and their larger operations in *Chapter 10, Enterprise Integration Strategies*.

The B2C CRM Sync solution, as discussed in detail in *Chapter 7, Integration Architecture Options*, leverages match rules and duplicate rules in this way. The match rules provided for B2C CRM Sync can be customized. However, they leverage the B2C Commerce Customer List to partition data so that customers associated with different Customer Lists are not detected as duplicates.

Matching rules and duplicate rules can be leveraged from Apex and embedded in Flows to cross-reference data as it is introduced to the system. This helps prevent duplicates or ensure that they're attributed with a common identifier representing an individual.

> **Further reading**
> You can read more about matching rules and duplicate rules in the Salesforce documentation here: `https://sforce.co/2SVC3PQt`.

Adding global identifiers

A common global identifier, if leveraged, should be added as a custom attribute to the B2C Commerce Profile, the Salesforce Platform Person Account or Contact record, and the Marketing Cloud Contact record.

> **Tip**
> Even if a global identifier is added to records, the native identifiers still need to be synchronized between systems because they are leveraged by the platform APIs to support external access.

Leveraging a global identifier

Because each component system in the B2C solution architecture leverages native identifiers to provide access to records related to a customer, the global identifier alone is not sufficient to enable data access. Fortunately, if the Salesforce Platform is being used as the system of record for customer data and to represent customers in various systems, even if duplicated, it should be synchronized to a corresponding Contact in the Salesforce Platform.

The simplest solution for creating a holistic view of the customer based on a common global identifier is to leverage the Salesforce Platform's native reporting for Accounts and Contacts. This will allow you to retrieve all related records for an individual grouped by their global identifier. This will aggregate different records that describe the same individual. Additionally, using custom report types, related objects, including the cases and orders for that individual, can be included, despite being associated with separate records.

In this way, metrics such as the total lifetime value for an individual can be generated across records and used to drive marketing efforts or inform customer support.

For more information on Salesforce Platform reports, review *Chapter 1, Demystifying Salesforce, Customer 360, and Digital 360*.

The final step in creating a 360° view of the customer is to ensure that the customer experience has the same consistency as the backend data through seamless identity.

Seamless identity

The topics we've covered in this chapter have described how to relate customer data records across systems so that a complete and connected picture emerges and new capabilities are unlocked. These capabilities, however, are primarily on the backend data side or to support the organization.

Creating a 360° view of the customer should also benefit the customer, however, and this can break down when the user experience crosses system boundaries.

The most common example of this is creating a hybrid experience for the customer that is partially hosted in B2C Commerce and partially hosted in **Experience Cloud** (formerly known as Community Cloud). In these cases, we can do a lot to make the two frontend experiences *look* similar, but customers who create an account in either system are interacting with two different backends.

In B2C Commerce, creating an account or logging in creates a B2C Commerce customer profile record, which handles authentication. On the Experience Cloud frontend, creating an account or logging in relies on a Salesforce Platform User record.

If we're leveraging B2C CRM Sync between B2C Commerce and the Salesforce Platform, as described earlier in this chapter, the B2C Commerce customer registration on the storefront will automatically create an Account and a Contact in the Salesforce Platform, but not a User record.

The solution here is to leverage one set of credentials to authenticate across both portions of the solution. Fortunately, B2C Commerce supports using external **OAuth2** providers for authentication and the Salesforce Platform, through Salesforce Identity, can serve as an OAuth2 authentication server. Together, this allows B2C Commerce to delegate customer registration and log into the Salesforce org.

In this scenario, a customer logging into B2C Commerce is redirected to Experience Cloud to log in and then back to B2C Commerce after authentication, at which point they are logged in for both.

> **Further reading**
> Salesforce provides a detailed explanation of this seamless identity capability in the associated solution kit here: `https://sforce.co/3yDuBYN`.

Now that we've covered the full Customer 360 approach, including identifying the customer, mastering customer data, building a 360° view of the customer, and seamless identity, we'll bring it all together for Packt Gear.

The Packt Gear approach

In the first part of this book, we explored the capabilities of the Salesforce products that could potentially complement a B2C solution architecture for Packt Gear. We settled on B2C Commerce, Service Cloud, Order Management, and Marketing Cloud for the initial release. In *Chapter 7, Integration Architecture Options*, we explored various ways of connecting these products and settled on point-to-point connectors for this phase.

Now, it's time to bring the customer data together. Packt Gear has the distinct advantage of letting you start from a new implementation, so we don't have to address concerns about Subscriber Key migration or potential data duplication. We'll focus on getting the customer data picture right from the start and avoiding future duplicates using matching rules and duplicate rules in the Salesforce Platform.

The B2C Commerce customer profile will synchronize the Customer ID, Customer Number, Customer List ID, and Site ID to the Salesforce Platform Contact record. The Salesforce Platform will store the account and Contact IDs on the B2C Commerce customer profile. Marketing Cloud Connect will then create a contact in Marketing Cloud for leveraging the Contact ID as the Contact Key.

With this in place, Salesforce Platform Reports and Dashboards can be leveraged for customer insight across all systems.

Summary

After completing this chapter, you should be able to document a cross-cloud customer data strategy for a new or existing Salesforce customer. You should also be able to specify which identifiers from each system need to be synchronized and why.

When creating a full picture of customer data, you can work with legal experts to document a plan for compliance with relevant privacy laws and standards.

For customers that have existing live data that pre-dates the integration effort, you should be able to describe the additional challenges they may face with data duplication and Subscriber Keys, as well as how to address them.

Finally, if Experience Cloud is part of the B2C solution architecture, you should have a high-level understanding of how to integrate the Experience Cloud's public-facing site with a B2C Commerce storefront seamlessly.

In the next chapter, we'll move on from fundamentals such as the integration architecture and the customer data strategy and discuss a few common examples of business capabilities that are built on top of this architecture.

Questions

1. What are the required customer identifiers from the Salesforce Platform to support a Service Cloud integration?
2. What are the required customer identifiers from the B2C Commerce platform and what are the associated scopes that are required with them?
3. Why do we need to synchronize platform-specific customer identifiers, even if we're leveraging a global ID that is used across customer data records?
4. What is the primary concern when implementing a cross-cloud data integration on a live Marketing Cloud instance and how should it be addressed?
5. When would a seamless identity integration be recommended as part of a B2C solution architecture?

Further reading

To learn more about the topics that were covered in this chapter, take a look at the following resources:

- *European Data Privacy Laws Basics (Trailhead)*: `https://sforce.co/3xp9oBU`
- *B2C Commerce Data Protection and Privacy*: `https://sforce.co/3dTBGN1`
- *Salesforce Platform GDPR FAQ*: `https://sforce.co/3xpa8aa`
- *Salesforce Platform Store Customers Data Privacy Preferences*: `https://sforce.co/2TALkNR`
- *Marketing Cloud GDPR Compliance*: `https://sforce.co/3xnDm97`

9
Supporting Key Business Scenarios

By this point, you should be comfortable recognizing and describing the capabilities of the various Salesforce products that make up a typical B2C solution architecture, especially the core B2C Commerce, Service Cloud, and Marketing Cloud components. Building on that baseline product knowledge, you've created a team that can support you by providing in-depth product knowledge and an understanding of the larger enterprise architecture context.

Finally, you know the most common options used in a Salesforce B2C solution architecture to integrate the component products and create a complete picture of customer data.

In this chapter, we'll move on to example business scenarios that span multiple products. We'll start by reviewing some of the resources from Salesforce that can streamline multi-cloud integration efforts aimed at specific business cases. Then, we'll use a couple of example scenarios to practice recognizing use cases that require functionality from more than one component product, orchestrating supporting data and user flows, and creating the necessary integrations.

These use cases will be based on the business cases we've specifically identified for our fictional organization, Packt Gear, and will help set the stage for whatever business cases a real organization requires.

In this chapter, we're going to cover the following main topics:

- Multi-cloud use case solution kits
- Integrating chat bots and agent-supported chat
- Capturing revenue with abandonment journeys

By the end of this chapter, you'll have learned how to review and interpret the resources available from Salesforce for the B2C solution architecture. You'll have also learned how to expand upon the available solutions to improve the level of detail, adjust products in scope, and add implementation-specific use cases.

Multi-cloud use case solution kits

As part of their B2C solution architecture approach, Salesforce provides sample multi-cloud solution kits to support common business and integration needs. These solution kits are part of a larger Customer 360 Guide for Retail and focus on the architectural and implementation details of specific use cases.

In this section, we'll review what the Customer 360 Guide for Retail supplies, how to assess business needs using this framework, and the overall structure of a solution kit.

Customer 360 Guide for Retail

The Customer 360 Guide for Retail from Salesforce is a set of guides, targeted training, business insights, and solutions aimed primarily at retail and B2C customers using the Salesforce Customer 360 suite of products. This is an important resource for a B2C solution architect to be familiar with since it provides an all-purpose starting point for best practices and discussions around Customer 360 in retail.

You can find and review the Customer 360 Guide for Retail here: `https://bit.ly/3e80lxo`.

The guide itself is broken down into the following four sections: *Get Started*, *Assess Your Needs*, *Map Your Goals*, *and Deliver Solutions*. Let's look at these in more detail.

Get Started

The starting resources are primarily focused on high-level guidance and best practices in the retail industry. While many of the concepts could apply to any B2C company, retail is the focus. The topics we've covered so far in this book are significantly more technically detailed than this section, which is targeted at a business audience.

Assess Your Needs

In this section, you can assess your needs. This is where topics such as understanding industries and requirements are covered. Review *Chapter 6, Role of a Solution Architect*, for in-depth coverage of conducting stakeholder interviews and mapping business requirements to technical solutions.

Map Your Goals

Once a directional understanding of an organization's business needs has been established, the next step is to establish clear and specific capabilities required to support those needs. Examples here include discussing how to support data-driven advertising using information from various customer touchpoints, as well as how to drive conversational commerce using Service Cloud chat, which will be covered later in this chapter.

At this point, the B2C solution architect should be using their understanding of the capabilities of the various component products to recognize business needs that require cross-cloud solutions and thinking about how to meet them. Being familiar with the available Salesforce solution kits will help you recognize opportunities to streamline a capability using established practices, as well as where a more custom solution will be required.

Deliver Solutions

Finally, the Customer 360 Guide for Retail concludes with resources related to building cross-cloud solutions. In the *Deliver Solutions* portion of the Customer 360 Guide for Retail, topics such as the solution architecture for retail from *Chapter 7, Integration Architecture Options*, are covered.

This section also covers solution kits, which are an important resource of the solution architect's toolbelt. We'll review how to interpret and update solution kits next.

Solution kits

Each solution kit describes a specific capability that is commonly required in a B2C solution architecture. Each of these capabilities requires more than one Salesforce product to fulfill, so it requires some type of integration. In almost all cases, the fundamental integrations and cross-cloud data modeling we've covered so far in this book provide the baseline understanding required to leverage this approach.

To streamline the implementation of the target capability, each solution kit provides a solution architecture, workflow, design considerations, and other materials such as the configuration details that are required to support the integrated capability.

Each solution kit has been reviewed by Salesforce product and solution architecture experts to ensure they follow best practices, making them a good starting point for most customization on top of a B2C solution architecture.

> **Important note**
> Solution kits are not part of the product documentation and may not always reference the most current product names or technical capabilities. The B2C solution architect should always review the product documentation and verify the approach outlined in a solution kit before leveraging it.

In the following sections, we'll quickly cover the most important sections of a solution kit and how to leverage them. Later in this chapter, we'll use several real solution kits as examples to demonstrate how to use the content of the solution kit, as well as developing it to the point where it's ready for use in a real-world project.

You can find and review the full library of solution kits here: https://sforce.co/3hVyIsL.

Solution architecture

The solution architecture documentation for each solution kit shows the integration points between systems and how the data flows between them. Most commonly, this is a more specific version of the point-to-point connector-based retail solution architecture that we covered in *Chapter 7, Integration Architecture Options*.

> **Tip**
> If you're leveraging an integration middleware approach to cross-cloud architecture, most of the solution kits will need to be adapted to suit that approach.

The following diagram shows a simple example of a solution architecture from the *Engage Customers with Conversational Commerce* solution kit:

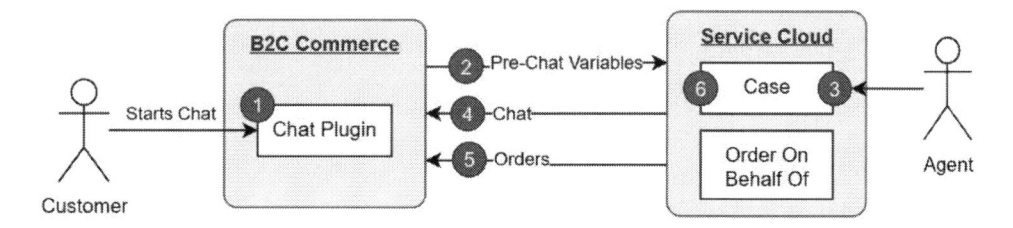

Figure 9.1 – Live chat solution architecture

The preceding diagram shows the two component systems in the example solution; that is, **B2C Commerce** and the **Service Cloud**. We'll expand on this specific diagram later in this chapter when we cover *Integrating chat bots and agent-supported chats*. At this stage, just know that the solution architecture diagram in any solution kit depicts the component systems, data flows, and interactions covered by that solution kit.

In this case, the interaction begins when the **customer** interacts with the **chat plugin** in the B2C Commerce storefront experience (**1**). The chat plugin is a JavaScript component provided by Service Cloud that is customized and delivered by B2C Commerce to the customer.

The customer then fills in some **pre-chat variables** such as the email address, name, order number, and the nature of their case. Other pre-chat variables will be embedded into the chat plugin as hidden form fields capturing B2C Commerce-specific data points including the Site ID, Customer Number, Customer ID, and Customer List ID (if known). This information is sent to Service Cloud and used to create a **case** (**3**).

Once the case has been created in Service Cloud, Omni-Channel routing is used to guide that case to an available **agent** that has the right skill set to meet the customer's needs (**3**). This connects the agent with the customer via a chat window embedded in the B2C Commerce storefront (**4**), where they can interact.

If necessary, the agent can use the **Order on Behalf Of (OOBO)** capability provided by the B2C CRM Sync enablement solution to create an order for that customer (**5**). At that point, the Service Cloud case is closed and resolved (**6**).

For a review of Service Cloud's chat capabilities, including Omni-Channel routing, see *Chapter 2, Supporting Your Customers with Service Cloud*.

Workflow

The solution kit workflow depictions go a level deeper than the solution architecture diagram and show systems and users interacting in sequence. Let's use the following example from the *View Order History and Cancel Orders* solution kit as a reference:

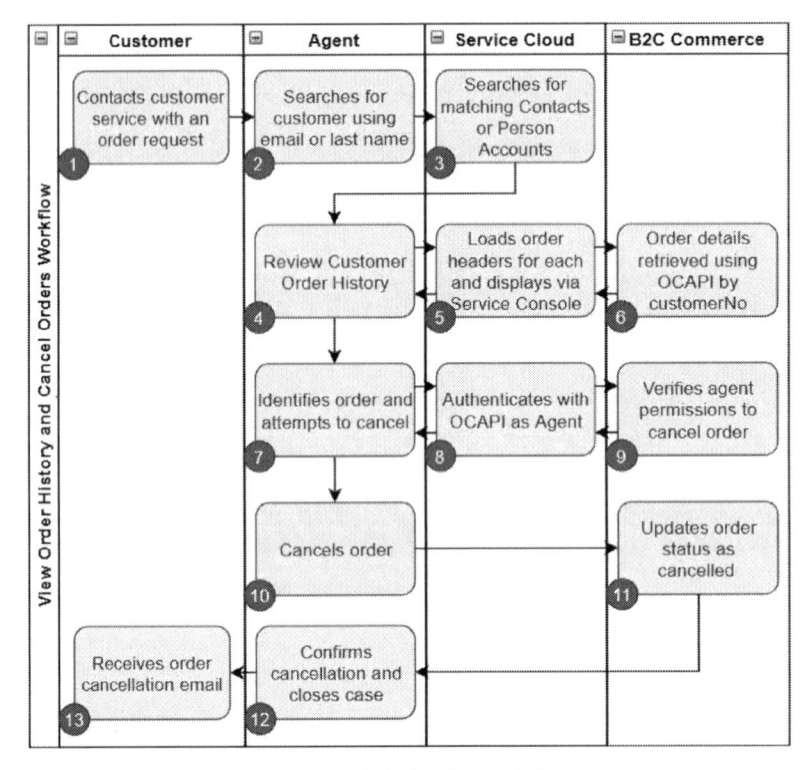

Figure 9.2 – Solution kit workflow

In this example, you can see that the participants in the workflow are **Customer**, **Service Agent**, **Service Cloud**, and **B2C Commerce**. The first two are individuals, while the next two are systems. In a workflow, we're not focusing on the data flow and integration mechanisms that are covered in the solution architecture section. Here, we are documenting the sequencing of interactions, including possible variations.

When reviewing workflows from the solution kits, look for business-specific variations that require further elaboration in your situation.

> **Tip**
> Solution kits are not intended to be implemented exactly as written in all cases. You should use your judgment, knowledge of the products, and business requirements to drive the final solution.

Multi-cloud use case solution kits   263

Reviewing this workflow example, with the knowledge we've gained so far in this book, what must change to fit the Packt Gear example? Develop the habit of looking for any requirements that would need to change from the solution kit-provided workflow in a particular implementation.

Starting with step **6**, the solution kit notes that the order header and details are pulled from B2C Commerce using OCAPI so that they can be displayed within the Service Console. Since we know Packt Gear will be leveraging Salesforce Order Management, however, this is not the right approach.

The following workflow presents a revised version that's more appropriate for Packt Gear:

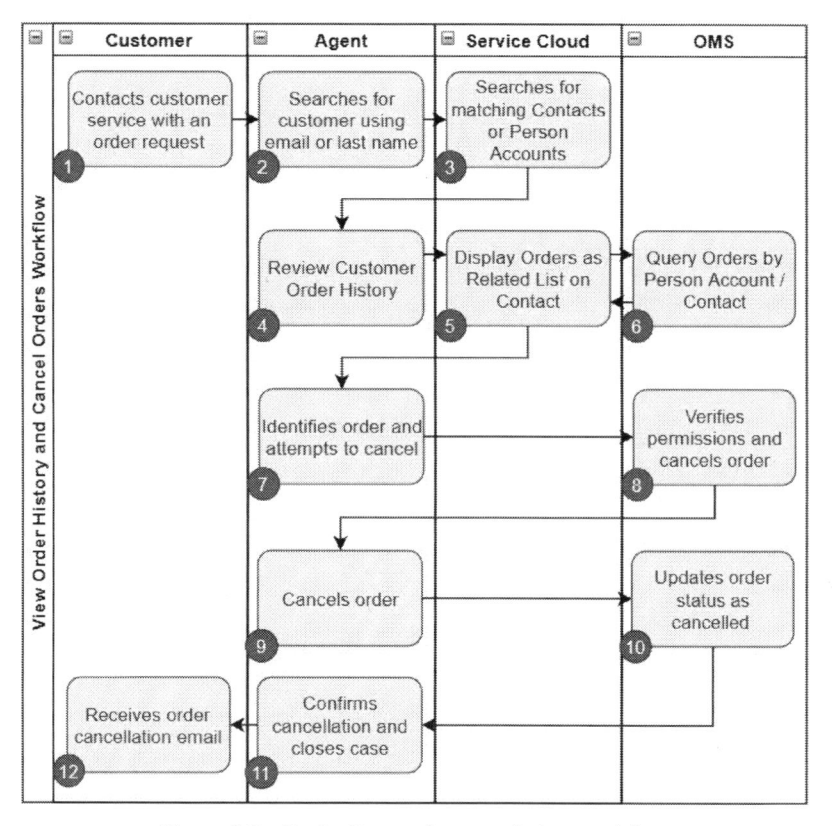

Figure 9.3 – Packt Gear order cancelation workflow

For Packt Gear, the interaction is between **Service Cloud** and **Order Management**. Since Order Management resides within the Salesforce Platform along with Service Cloud, no integration is required. The overall workflow follows a similar pattern but is simplified.

Design considerations

The design considerations section of a solution kit provides guidance on areas of the solution where additional solutions will be required or where things could deviate from the expectations of the kit.

The *Seamless Cross-Cloud Identity* solution kit, for example, notes the following design consideration: *To minimize synchronization and migration of customer profile data, set up the primary profile in Communities.*

As we did with the preceding workflow example, let's interpret that guidance through the lens of Packt Gear's solution. The guidance here is to set up the primary profile in communities, but what does that mean? As we noted earlier in this chapter, the solution kits are not part of the product documentation and can sometimes get a bit out of date. In this case, communities is a reference to Community Cloud, which is the former name of Experience Cloud.

Since we know that Experience Cloud is part of the Salesforce Platform, we can fall back on the customer data strategy we outlined in *Chapter 8, Creating a 360° View of the Customer*, where we established that the Salesforce Platform should be the source of truth for cross-cloud integration, which aligns with this guidance.

As you work through each of the design considerations outlined in a solution kit, evaluate it against the integration and customer data strategy you're using in each situation and adjust it as necessary.

Configurations

The final section that you'll commonly encounter in the solution kits covers the configuration required to support the target use case. The Salesforce Platform makes extensive use of configuration over custom code, so this can be a significant part of the solution.

The following are examples of configuration requirements:

- Creating OAuth2 providers within B2C Commerce
- Mapping customer attributes to Marketing Cloud via Marketing Cloud Connect
- Leveraging Salesforce Platform custom metadata to configure settings
- Setting up service credentials in B2C Commerce to support an API integration
- Applying permission sets to users in the Salesforce Platform

Leveraging these solution kits to streamline configuration can save significant time.

In the next section, we'll review and expand on the *Engage Customers with Conversational Commerce* solution kit by adding additional details and Packt Gear-specific use cases. This will provide a realistic view of how these kits can be leveraged for your projects.

Integrating chat bots and agent-supported chats

The Service Cloud chat-focused solution kit is called *Engage Customers with Conversational Commerce* and it's available here: `https://sforce.co/36Is97L`.

We're not going to try and recreate the existing solution kit as it's available from Salesforce already. Instead, we're going to use it with the Packt Gear example to review how we would apply this to a specific implementation. During the review, we'll dive a bit deeper into technical details and provide commentary on specific sections.

As a B2C solution architect, reviewing and understanding these solution kits and related documentation is an important part of the job. At this point, you should know enough about the products and integration options to follow along, so feel free to review the solution kit before proceeding further.

To review the capabilities of Service Cloud chat, see *Chapter 2, Supporting Your Customers with Service Cloud*.

As we walk through this solution kit, we're going to start by reviewing and revising the supported use cases, then cover how to extend the solution architecture by adding additional chat workflows, relevant design considerations, configuration, and the modifications required for B2C CRM Sync.

Supported use cases

This solution kit includes documentation to support exposing Service Cloud through the B2C Commerce storefront. On the B2C Commerce storefront, this includes both customer-initiated and pro-active chats triggered by criteria such as basket total value, time on site, or invalid promotional code use.

Once the chat session has been initiated, the solution kit provides documentation around both bot-supported (automated) and live agent-supported chats. In either case, the customer can leverage the chat session to get help with a coupon code, check on their order status, cancel an order, or change an order.

Let's review what Packt Gear needs in particular and then cover how we can extend the supported use cases to account for that.

Packt Gear chat support needs

These are common use cases for customers using B2C Commerce and Service Cloud, but each customer has their own unique business. To support Packt Gear, where we know guided hikes are a big part of how the customer connects with the business, let's add a couple of additional use cases:

- Inquire about hikes
- Sign up for a hike
- Cancel a hike registration

This will interact with the custom data model we set up for Packt Gear back in *Chapter 1, Demystifying Salesforce, Customer 360, and Digital 360*, to support guided hike signup and management.

We'll follow along with the solution kit and make updates to the approach that's recommended based on what we know about Packt Gear and these additional use cases we want to support.

Extending the chat-supported use cases

Let's start by updating the *Live Agent versus Chatbot* section of the *Supported Use Case* documentation from the solution kit, which has been reproduced here for convenience:

Action	With Live Agent Chat	With Chatbots
Required Setup	Send Pre-Chat Variables	Send Pre-Chat Variables
Before Placing Order		
Add Discount to Basket (Coupon, Order Discount, Shipping Discount)	Via Order on Behalf (OOBO)	Via APIs
After Placing Order		
View Latest Order Status	Via Order Object in Core	Query Order Object in Core
Cancel Order Within Forgiveness Window	Via SFCC	Via APIs
Change the Order	Via OMS	Transfer to Agent
Answer Common Questions	Via Knowledge	Query Knowledge

Table 9.1 – Live chat versus chatbots

In this table, Salesforce has provided a simple framework for documenting how we'll accomplish each of these use cases in both the live agent scenario and the chat bot scenario.

For convenience, the data model from *Figure 1.3* has been provided here as well:

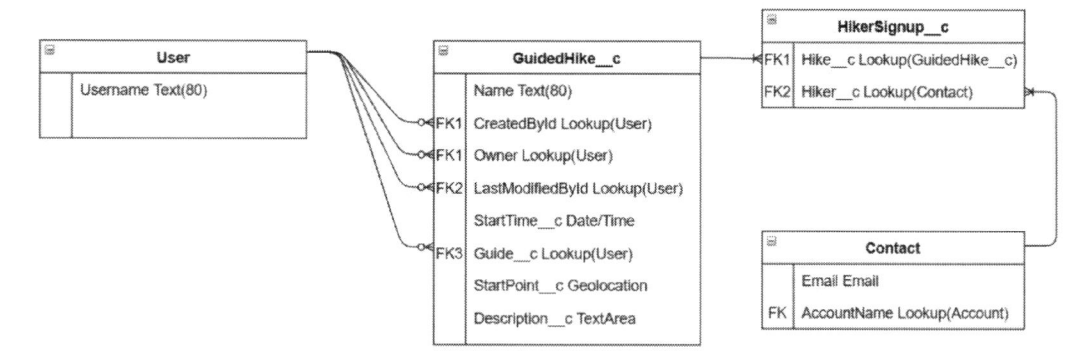

User		GuidedHike__c			HikerSignup__c	
Username Text(80)		Name Text(80)		FK1	Hike__c Lookup(GuidedHike__c)	
	FK1	CreatedById Lookup(User)		FK2	Hiker__c Lookup(Contact)	
	FK1	Owner Lookup(User)				
	FK2	LastModifiedById Lookup(User)				
		StartTime__c Date/Time			Contact	
	FK3	Guide__c Lookup(User)			Email Email	
		StartPoint__c Geolocation		FK	AccountName Lookup(Account)	
		Description__c TextArea				

Figure 9.4 – Entity relationship diagram (ERD) of GuidedHike__c signups

Now, let's figure out how to leverage this data model to support chat use cases. We're going to leverage the `GuidedHike__c` and `HikerSignup__c` objects in the Salesforce Platform to query which hikes are available, register a `Contact` (customer) for a hike, or cancel an existing registration.

For agent chat, the native search capabilities of the Service Console can be used to search for available hikes. The `GuidedHike__c` record detail page with its `HikerSignup__c`-related list can also be used to register a new `Contact` for a hike or cancel an existing signup.

To automate this process with chat bots, we'll use SOQL queries to retrieve the available hikes based on proximity or host store. We can also use SOQL queries for filtering the `HikerSignup__c` records on the `Hiker__c` attribute to retrieve existing registered hikes for a given contact.

Finally, a chat bot could use DML to create or delete `HikerSignup__c` records to support signup and cancelation use cases without ever involving an agent!

Let's use this approach to add a few additional rows to the live agent versus chatbot table while incorporating our new Packt Gear use cases:

Action	With Live Agent Chat	With Chatbots
Guided Hike Support		
Inquire about Hikes	Search for Store Record and view the Guided Hikes related list on the Store record detail page	SOQL query on the Store__c Object by Name and Join with the GuidedHike__c Object to display Hikes
Sign up for a Hike	Search for the customer Contact record and use the Guided Hike Signups-related list to sign up	Use DML to insert the HikerSignup__c record joining the selected GuidedHike__c and Contact
Cancel a Hike registration	Search for the customer Contact record and use the Guided Hike Signups-related list to cancel a signup	Use DML to delete the HikerSignup__c record joining the selected GuidedHike__c and Contact

Table 9.2 – Packt Gear live chat versus chatbot use cases

By keeping the approach consistent with the solution kit, we can ensure that the extended functionality required by this implementation covers the same requirements that the integration from Salesforce does.

Extending the chat solution architecture

Building on the new use cases we're looking to add to the solution kit, we need to revise the solution architecture shown in *Figure 9.1*.

We need to update the solution architecture diagram to document the requirements and data sources related to our guided hike use cases. We're also going to go a level deeper and incorporate the Packt Gear Salesforce Order Management requirements.

Integrating chat bots and agent-supported chats 269

The following diagram shows a revised and expanded solution architecture specific to the Packt Gear use case:

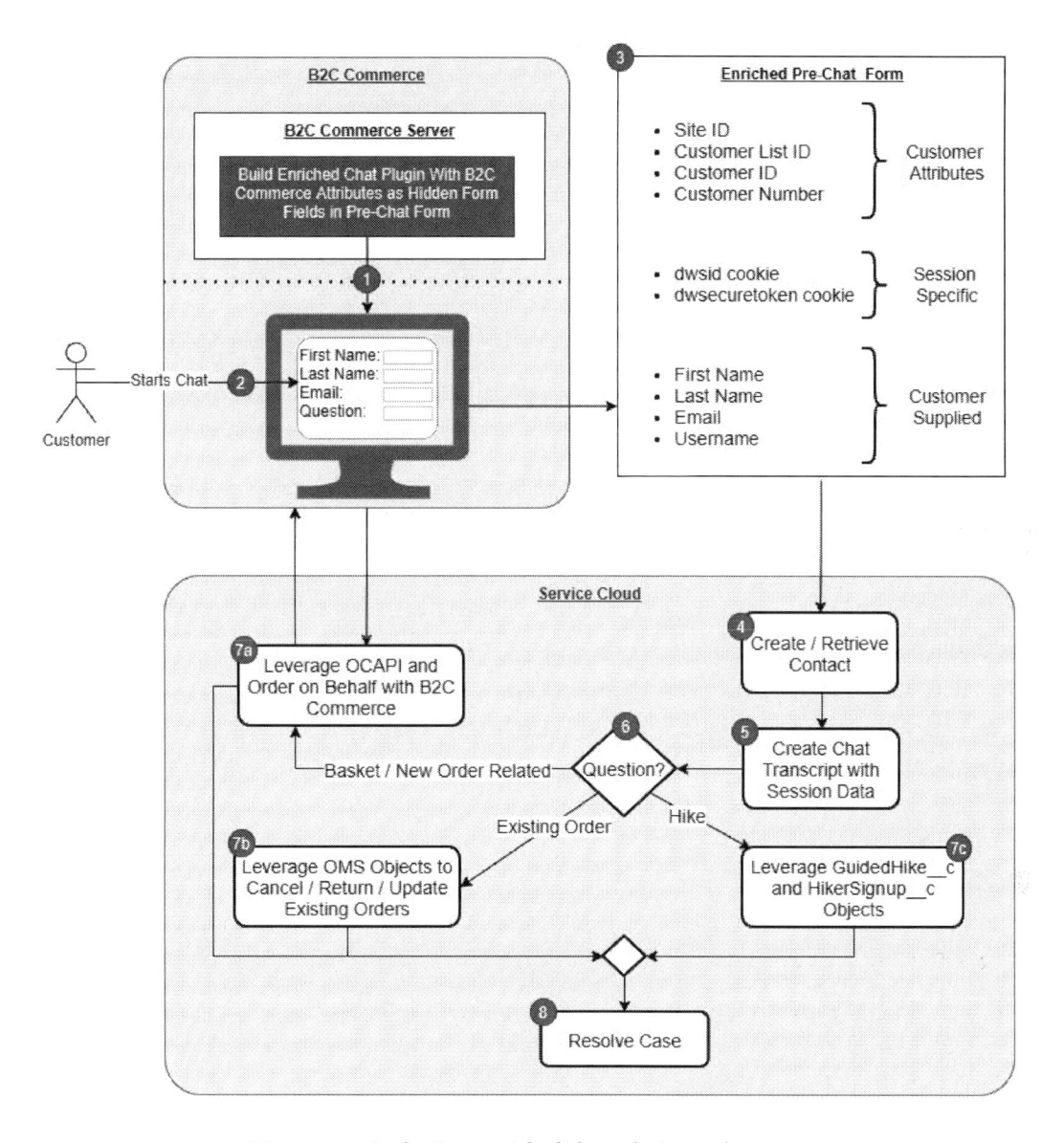

Figure 9.5 – Packt Gear enriched chat solution architecture

This diagram presents a deeper look at the chat solution architecture diagram that has been tailored to Packt Gear's requirements and solution. We still have the chat plugin rendered by the **B2C Commerce** server displayed in the customer's browser (**1**), where the customer can initiate the chat session (**2**).

The **pre-chat form** has been expanded to include the four required B2C Commerce customer identifiers that were covered in *Chapter 8, Creating a 360° View of the Customer* (**Site ID**, **Customer List ID**, **Customer ID**, and **Customer Number**). In addition, we've incorporated the session-specific cookie values required to initiate a session transfer using OCAPI, which facilitates OOBO and other B2C Commerce use cases. Review *Chapter 3, Direct-to-Consumer Selling with Commerce Cloud B2C*, for additional details on how these attributes are used with the B2C Commerce APIs.

The **Service Cloud** portion of the solution is also expanded to represent the creation/retrieval of a **Contact** record (**4**), the creation and annotation of the **chat transcript** with the session-specific variables (**5**), and a decision point supporting multiple different paths, depending on the customer's specific question (**6**).

Here, we can see the three categories of support needs that were discussed in the previous section on extending the chat-supported use cases: **Basket / New Order Related** (**7a**), **Existing Order Related** (**7b**), and **Guided Hike Related** (**7c**). From here, we can refer to the table in the previous section, which describes how each of these use cases will be supported before ultimately leading to a successful case resolution (**8**).

This exercise of taking the reference solution kit provided by Salesforce, expanding upon it, and adapting it for your use cases is a great way to design effective solutions quickly without starting from scratch every time.

Extending the chat workflow

In the following workflow diagram, which follows the format of the existing solution kit workflows, we're documenting one possible customer interaction with the chat process related to guided hike management:

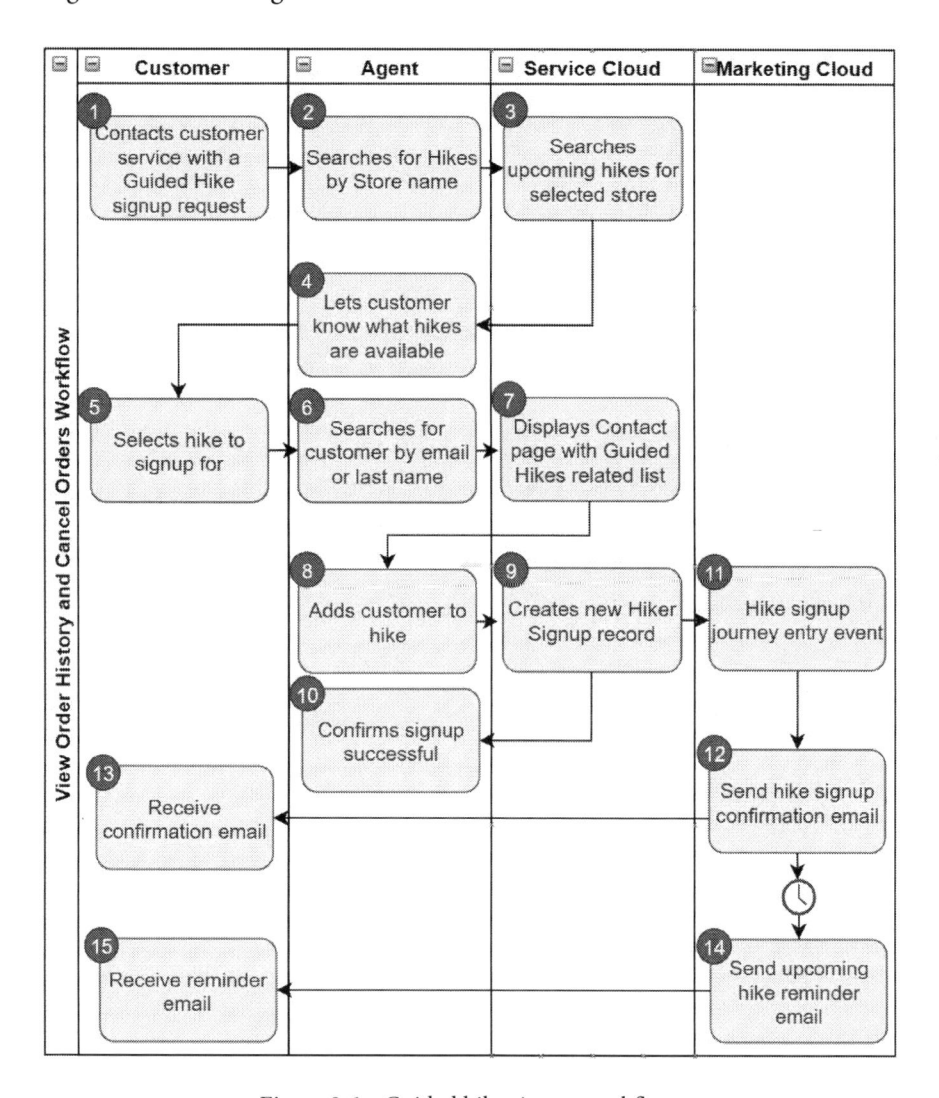

Figure 9.6 – Guided hike signup workflow

In the supported use case, we documented the business requirement that customers will be able to manage their guided hike signups through chats. In the solution architecture, we determined that that would require interacting with the `GuidedHike__c` and `HikerSignup__c` objects. Now, in the workflow, we're being more specific about how this works.

Here, we're showing that a customer should, at a minimum, be able to search for guided hikes related to a given store (**2**) and sign up for one of the upcoming hikes (**9**). A logged-in customer will be signed up with their previously stored email, while a new customer will have a contact created for them and will be signed up based on the data provided during the hike signup process.

At the end of the workflow, the customer is placed into a guided hike signup journey in **Marketing Cloud** (**11**). This journey manages customer communication first, sending a confirmation email letting them know their signup was successful (**12**), including details about their hike, as well as links to the recommended gear available for purchase through the Packt Gear web store.

When the scheduled date of the hike is getting close to the typical shipping time for online store purchases, a *last chance* email is sent (**14**). This email reminds the customer of their upcoming hike with information about the meeting place, the guide, and hike details, and adjusts the recommended gear based on the anticipated weather with links and a reminder that they must order now to receive their gear in time for the hike!

Additional chat design considerations

The existing solution kit does an excellent job of documenting the discussion points and caveats for a chat. Let's extend that to support the Packt Gear use cases.

> **Tip**
> As you're reading through the examples provided here for Packt Gear, try making the extensions and additions to the solution kit to support a use case that's specific to your organization!

For design considerations, the documentation covers several areas and gets more granular about the APIs to use in support of specific integration points. For the Packt Gear solution, there are a few considerations that should be added:

- Collect sufficient information when registering a guest user for a hike to create a person account for that user or encourage the user to sign up on the storefront first.
- Extend the Service Cloud chat flow to accept variables related to store name or postcode to facilitate store search.

- Extend the proactive chat scenarios to include indicators that a customer is interested in hike signup, such as browsing available hikes by store.

- For hikes with gear recommendations, leverage the OOBO capabilities documented in the existing solution kit to allow the customer to add that gear to their cart directly from the chat flow.

By expanding these design considerations, you can start thinking about the edge cases that are likely to be encountered when implementing or using the solution.

In addition, the design considerations section of the solution kit refers to a **Postman collection** and **environment template** that can be used to test cart interactions that are used in the solution kit.

The Postman collection is available here: `https://bit.ly/3wFoylc`.

The environment template is available here: `https://bit.ly/3kadry4`.

Chat configuration extensions

The final section to cover for extending the *Engage Customers with Conversational Commerce* solution kit is configuration.

To support the agent use case, you'll need to ensure that the CSR profile or permission set grants access to the `GuidedHike__c` and `HikerSignup__c` custom objects. We'll also need to make sure that they have permission to read from the `GuidedHike__c` object and create, read, or delete `HikerSignup__c` records. We should also make sure that the `HikerSignup__c`-related list has been added to the `GuidedHike__c` record detail page and the `Contact` record detail page. All of this will allow a CSR to meet the customer's needs through the Service Console.

For the bot use case, once the initial bot has been configured, there should be minimal configuration required. Setting up the initial bot requires documenting the data entities and variables used by the bot. Data entities are types or categories of data that's collected from the customer, while variables are locations where that data is stored. In this case, data entities are things such as store names or customer email addresses.

Custom dialogs and menus can be created to integrate with the chat bot; these make the underlying SOQL queries or DML updates we discussed earlier to support this use case.

To learn more about building Einstein chat bots with Service Cloud, review the following Trailhead project: `https://sforce.co/3ebwGDF`.

Now that we've extended the *Engage Customers with Conversational Commerce* solution kit to support Packt Gear, let's cover some specific changes that need to happen to support the latest tool for connecting B2C Commerce and Service Cloud: B2C CRM Sync.

Chat modifications for B2C CRM Sync

If you want to review the capabilities of B2C CRM Sync in general, revisit *Chapter 7, Integration Architecture Options*. This enablement solution from Salesforce provides a pre-built example integration covering both the B2C Commerce and the Salesforce Platform sides of a customer data-focused synchronization solution.

If you're leveraging this option for integration of the Salesforce Platform and B2C Commerce point to point, there are a few things that should be revised in the existing solution kit.

For convenience, B2C CRM Sync is available on GitHub at `https://bit.ly/3zryl13`.

> **Tip**
> The goal here is to practice reviewing and adapting solution kits to your unique situation and requirements. If you're using MuleSoft or another integration layer approach, there may be other adaptations you'd wish to make for this or any other solution kit.

In the *Design Considerations* section of the solution kit, there is guidance around leveraging the *Service Cloud Chat Developer Guide* to support automated record creation in Service Cloud for person accounts or contacts representing the customer. B2C CRM Sync provides a `B2CContactResolve` flow that is adapted specifically for the B2C Commerce integration to support this use case. By leveraging that flow in your chat implementation rather than building something custom, you can create a more consistent result.

When building your OCAPI-based integrations between the Salesforce Platform and B2C Commerce, as described in the *Design Considerations* section of the solution kit, you should also account for the B2C CRM Sync data model. This integration solution leverages Salesforce custom objects to represent a B2C Commerce instance (`B2C_Instance__c`), site (`B2C_Site__c`), and customer list (`B2C_CustomerList__c`).

This model supplies most of the needed connection information for OCAPI-based connections to B2C Commerce and, combined with the customer identifiers stored on the Contact record, will support the required use cases.

Finally, there is a section in the *Engage Customers with Conversational Commerce* solution kit that deals entirely with the connector. This is a reference to the legacy Service Cloud connector for B2C Commerce that has been replaced with B2C CRM Sync, which we covered in *Chapter 7, Integration Architecture Options*, so you should be comfortable with that component of the solution already.

In the next section, we'll provide a final example of integration between B2C Commerce and Marketing Cloud while using the *Turn Abandoned Carts into Complete Sales* solution kit as an example.

Capturing revenue with abandonment journeys

Abandonment journeys, such as an abandoned cart, aim to reengage a customer who initiated some action on the storefront but didn't complete the process.

The example provided in the solution kit is for an abandoned cart, which aims to re-capture potentially lost revenue by targeting customers who have populated a basket on your site with relevant reminders and incentives to complete their transactions. This might be something simple such as an email with a coupon code for free shipping, incentivizing a customer to return. It could also be a bit more elaborate with multiple email touchpoints, social ads, and AI-powered product recommendations to get the customer to return.

As we begin to map these business requirements to a technical solution, we know that there are components of this that require B2C Commerce and parts that require Marketing Cloud. Without a shopping cart and a product browse experience, there's no cart to abandon, and without a marketing engine to orchestrate and coordinate the communications, there's no way to retarget that customer.

This example is going to draw heavily from the existing Salesforce solution kit, *Turn Abandoned Carts into Completed Sales*, available here: `https://sforce.co/3kgHhkI`.

Just as in the previous example, we're not going to recreate the existing solution kit. Instead, we're going to expand upon it and explain it in the context of the B2C solution architecture we've been evolving throughout this book for Packt Gear. Feel free to review the solution kit ahead of time or in parallel.

To start, the solution kit provides the stated goals, which are as follows:

- Increase completed purchases.
- Drive **gross merchandise volume** (**GMV**).
- Give your shoppers a personalized experience when you connect Commerce Cloud and Marketing Cloud.
- Gain insights into what your shoppers want.
- Increase shopper engagement.

For Packt Gear, continuing with the previous example, we're going to build an abandonment journey around our guided hike experiences. If a customer who has opted in for marketing communications browses hikes on the B2C Commerce storefront but doesn't sign up, we'll send them a reminder email with a link back in case they want to complete the registration process.

> **Important note**
>
> Sending your customer a confirmation email because they've subscribed for a hike is a transactional email; sending your customer an email because you'd like them to sign up for a hike is a marketing communication. Always be mindful of and respect your customer's consent for communication!

In the following sections, we'll discuss the workflow, data model, integration methodology, and additional customizations we may need to consider.

Abandoned cart workflow

An effective cart campaign relies on understanding three things: **customer behavior**, **available products**, and **effective communication**. The following workflow provides a high-level overview of an abandoned cart approach:

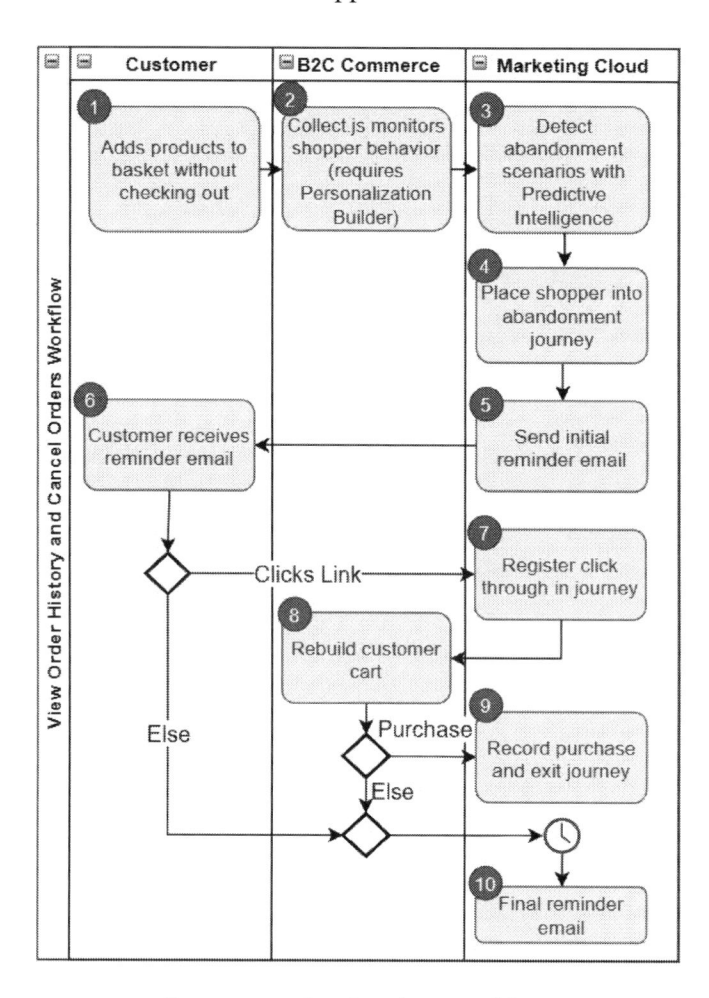

Figure 9.7 – Abandoned cart workflow

In this example, **B2C Commerce** uses **collect.js** to notify **Marketing Cloud** of shopper behavior events such as adding a product to the cart and checking out. In short, any customer who adds products to their cart but doesn't proceed through checkout is a candidate for an abandoned cart campaign, and they could be placed into a journey in Marketing Cloud.

From the Marketing Cloud journey, various communication mechanisms, including email and social, could be used to entice the customer to return and finish their purchase. If they click through on the provided link, their cart is rebuilt in B2C Commerce, allowing them to complete their purchase.

Let's review the data model that is used to support this, the details of collect.js for behavioral monitoring, and the required additions for Packt Gear.

Abandoned cart data model

To support the workflow discussed in the previous section, we need several data points across systems. We reviewed the B2C Commerce and Marketing Cloud integration accelerator solution in *Chapter 7, Integration Architecture Options*. This will be the basis of the data synchronization to support abandoned carts.

We'll rely on B2C Commerce sending order data from the production instance and product and catalog data from the staging instance to the Marketing Cloud SFTP server, as shown in the following diagram:

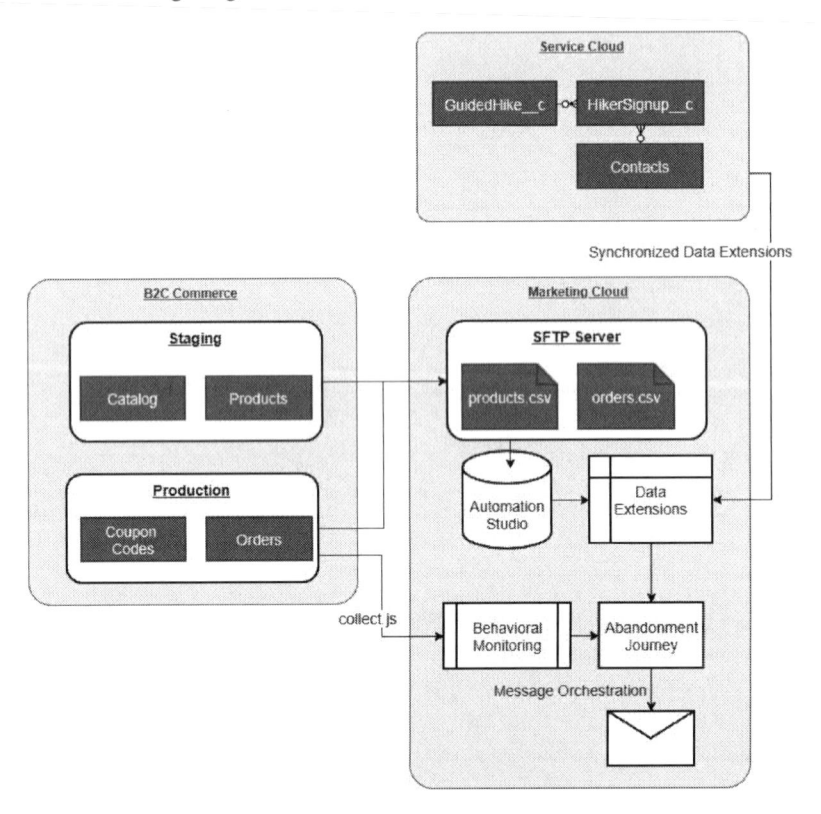

Figure 9.8 – Packt Gear abandonment journeys data flow

Once the CSV files generated by the jobs in the integration accelerator are sent from **B2C Commerce** to **Marketing Cloud**, they can be ingested via **Automation Studio** into **Data Extensions** for this purpose. This workflow makes the B2C Commerce data available to Marketing Cloud to support **Journey Builder**, which can leverage communication channels such as Email Studio for message orchestration based on customer consent and preferences.

As shown in the preceding diagram, data regarding **catalogs** and **products** are sent from **B2C Commerce staging**, because they've mastered and replicated them to the production instance, where they are essentially read-only. Other data, such as order information, is sent from **B2C Commerce production** because that's the only place real customer information exists. Review *Chapter 3, Direct-to-Consumer Selling with Commerce Cloud B2C*, for a refresher on B2C Commerce instances and replication.

For Packt Gear, we've extended the reference data model to use **Synchronized Data Extensions**, a feature of Marketing Cloud Connect, to make guided hike and hiker signup data available in Marketing Cloud from **Service Cloud**. This will be essential to support our custom abandonment journey around guided hikes. With this information, we can build reminder emails that include details of hikes (from the guided hike data extension) and remove customers from the journey if they sign up (based on the hiker signup data extension).

Collect.js for abandonment scenarios

The **collect.js** integration, which is a client-side integration between the B2C Commerce storefront and Marketing Cloud, leverages three data events to support an abandoned cart journey: `setUserInfo`, `trackCart`, and `trackConversion`.

Collect.js setUserInfo

The collect.js `setUserInfo` call is used to establish the current customer's identity with Marketing Cloud from the B2C Commerce storefront. It should be called in client-side JavaScript anywhere the customer signs in or enters their email address and you're able to retrieve a contact ID on their behalf, including the following:

- Login/registration pages
- Checkout billing pages
- Marketing email signup

> **Important note**
> In an integrated B2C solution architecture, the email address should never be used with Marketing Cloud directly. Always retrieve a contact ID from the Salesforce Platform to use as the contact key first!

In an integrated B2C solution, the user's information should include their email address as well as contact key, which is the contact ID from Service Cloud. See *Chapter 8, Creating a 360° View of the Customer*, for additional details on cross-cloud customer identity.

The following code snippet is an example of a `setUserInfo` call that includes cross-cloud identity information:

```
<script type="text/javascript">
    _etmc.push(["setOrgId", "MID"]);
    _etmc.push(["setUserInfo", {
        "email": "customer@email.com",
        "Subscriber Key": "0129be9134boe09e92"
    }]);
</script>
```

In this snippet, the contact key will be a value associated with the logged-in customer's profile matching the contact ID from the Salesforce Platform. Alternatively, it will be retrieved directly from the Salesforce Platform based on the email address and the customer list ID associated with the current B2C Commerce site.

Collect.js trackCart

The `trackCart` call is used to update the Marketing Cloud tracking based on changes in the customer's current cart state. It should be used in the same session as a `setUserInfo` call to ensure that the customer's identity is known and available.

Call `trackCart` any time the contents of the customer's shopping cart changes in B2C Commerce, including the following:

- Add to cart from the product detail page, product list page, or wish list
- Remove item from cart or category
- Clear cart on the cart page
- Move to wish list on the cart page

Making a call to `trackCart` to refresh the tracked cart with the current state looks like this:

```
<script type="text/javascrip">
    _etmc.push(["trackCart", {
        "cart": [{
            "item": "Fancy Hat",
            "quantity": "1",
            "price": "$25.99",
            "unique_id": " PID1234"
        }]}]);
</script>
```

In this example, exactly one product is in the cart, with a quantity of one (1) and a price of $25.99.

> **Tip**
> Always pass the full current cart state with `trackCart`, not just changes.

To clear the cart, use a call to `trackCart` with `clear_cart` set to `true`, as shown in the following snippet:

```
<script type="text/javascript">
    _etmc.push(["trackCart", {"clear_cart": true}]);
</script>
```

With these two snippets in play, Marketing Cloud will always know what's in the basket for the current customer. The final piece of the behavioral tracking puzzle is matching that to transactions if the customer completes the checkout.

Collect.js trackConversion

The final tracking component required for an abandoned cart journey specifically is tracking completed purchases on the B2C Commerce storefront. A complete purchase, somewhat obviously, does not require an abandonment reminder.

To support this, use the `trackConversion` JavaScript event provided by collect.js, as shown here:

```
<script type="text/javascript">
    _etmc.push(["trackConversion", {
        "cart": [{
```

```
                "item": "Fancy Hat",
                "quantity": "1",
                "price": "$25.99",
                "unique_id": " PID1234"
            },
            "order_number": "OL-1209403"}]);
</script>
```

These three events provide enough context to trigger abandonment journeys built in Marketing Cloud.

To learn more about collect.js tracking code, review the Salesforce documentation here: `https://sforce.co/3iQczfR`.

Guided hike abandonment tracking

In the data model section earlier, we covered how to get the required data for guided hikes from Service Cloud into Marketing Cloud using synchronized data extensions.

To trigger an abandonment journey for this use case, however, we need to expand on the behavioral tracking using collect.js so that we can build a Marketing Cloud behavioral trigger based on viewing a hike but not signing up.

To do this, you can use two additional collect.js functions: `trackPageView` and `trackEvent`.

Collect.js trackPageView

The `trackPageView` event passes information to Marketing Cloud about the page currently being viewed on the B2C Commerce storefront. By including a category representing the guided hike section and the ID of a hike, we can inform Marketing Cloud about the specific hike the user showed interest in.

Collect.js trackEvent

The generic collect.js `trackEvent` method can be used to register custom events with Marketing Cloud. In this case, a custom event for guided hike registration can be leveraged. This event would be fired anytime a customer completes registration for a custom hike in B2C Commerce, and it would serve the same purposes as `trackConversion` in the abandoned cart journey.

Customers that view a guided hike but don't register would be added to the marketing journey to try and entice them to return and register.

> **Important note**
> An engagement with Marketing Cloud professional services is required to enable custom behavioral triggers with Marketing Cloud for use in Journey Builder.

Rebuilding the customer's cart

The final step in setting up an abandoned cart journey is to ensure that a customer can return to the B2C Commerce storefront on any device and see their original cart rebuilt. This is not native functionality for B2C Commerce and it's not provided by Marketing Cloud, but we know enough about these two products to map out a solution.

First, we need to know what products the customer was looking at. We've tracked that information with `trackCart` events from collect.js in Marketing Cloud. We've also synchronized product data from B2C Commerce to Marketing Cloud data extensions, so we have the full product details, including images. This allows us to build an email that reproduces the cart within the email, including a complete checkout button.

The complete checkout button should be set up to target a new B2C Commerce page that accepts query string parameters with the desired product names, like so:

```
/rebuildCart?pids=PId123,PID456,PID789
```

From there, B2C Commerce can add the passed products by ID to the current basket and redirect the customer to the cart page. Additional storefront customization within B2C Commerce can be used to control whether an existing basket is replaced or the new products are added to it.

With these updates, we now have a solution kit that has been revised to provide additional implementation detail and cover use cases that are specific to our fictional organization, Packt Gear, in the same way that you could in a real-world B2C solution architecture.

Summary

Throughout this chapter, you've acquired a few new skills that should add to your understanding of the component products, integration methodologies, and customer data model we've established so far in the book.

You should now understand the resources that are available from Salesforce in the form of multi-cloud solution kits that cover core business use cases. You now know how to interpret them, including understanding the overall solution architecture, workflow, and design.

Using Packt Gear, you've also seen how to take a provided solution kit and adapt it for a real organization's needs. When it comes to *integrating chat bots and agent-supported chats*, this means understanding how to expand on the capabilities of live agents and chat bots when Salesforce Order Management is being used or when custom objects in the Salesforce Platform are part of the solution.

With *Capturing revenue with abandonment journeys*, you learned how to drill down deeper in the solution by building out additional data models across all three clouds and expanding on behavioral monitoring with collect.js. We also covered how to enhance B2C Commerce to support rebuilding a customer's cart based on a URL in the Marketing Cloud reminder email.

In the next chapter, we're going to cover how the solution designs we've established so far change in a larger enterprise.

Questions

1. True or false: As an official part of the Salesforce product documentation, you can count on the solution kits to be the most up-to-date reference on cross-cloud integration best practices.
2. Which section of a solution kit provides an overview diagram showing the component systems of an overall solution and how they interact for a particular use case?
3. Why is it necessary to interpret and revise the provided solution kits in specific situations?
4. When revising the live chat solution kit for Packt Gear, why did we move away from using OCAPI to query and modify existing orders in B2C Commerce?
5. In the abandoned cart solution kit, why do we send the products and catalog information from staging but customer information from production?
6. In the abandoned cart solution kit, what client-side integration component is used to track customer behavioral data on the B2C Commerce storefront in Marketing Cloud?

10
Enterprise Integration Strategies

By this point in the book, you've learned a lot about the Salesforce B2C solution architecture. You know what the most important component products are, what their capabilities are, and how to integrate them to create a holistic view of the customer.

In most of our examples so far, we've only looked at one B2C Commerce realm, one Salesforce Platform org, and one Marketing Cloud instance. In larger enterprises, the Salesforce picture is often more complex. Multiple B2C Commerce realms could exist in different parts of the world, Salesforce Platform orgs could be set up by different corporate entities at different times, and your Marketing Cloud instance could be subdivided into numerous **Business Units (BUs)**.

This chapter covers some of the complexities involved in implementing a B2C solution architecture in these scenarios. In addition, we'll look at some of the considerations for incorporating additional integration points beyond the Salesforce ecosystem and monitoring the overall solution.

In this chapter, we're going to cover the following main topics:

- Multi-org, realm, and BU scenarios
- Point-to-point integration impacts
- Enterprise integration using middleware
- Integrations beyond Salesforce
- Monitoring the solution

By the end of this chapter, you should understand the implications and options when implementing a B2C solution architecture in a larger organization with multiple orgs, realms, or BUs. You should also understand how to integrate external applications that rely on or influence the Salesforce ecosystem and how to think about monitoring in this context.

Multi-org, realm, and BU scenarios

Each of the three primary products in your Salesforce B2C solution architecture partitions data in different ways and has a different structure for an instance. This section covers the reasons organizations end up with multiple orgs, realms, and BUs in the first place and why you may or may not want to consolidate that data into a single viewpoint.

Throughout this chapter, we'll use the example of a fictitious organization that has multiple brands and geographies. We'll call this company Packt Enterprises, the parent company of Packt Gear. They also own Packt Sport, an athletics and leisurewear brand.

Each brand has operations in multiple parts of the world, as shown in the following org chart:

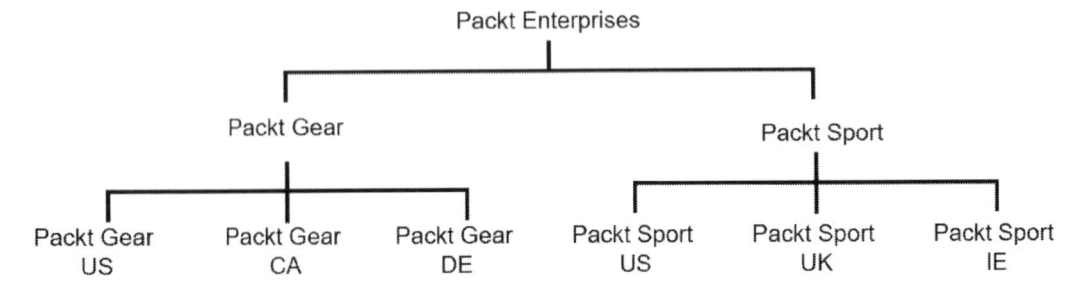

```
                        Packt Enterprises
                       /                 \
                  Packt Gear          Packt Sport
                /     |     \        /     |      \
         Packt Gear Packt Gear Packt Gear Packt Sport Packt Sport Packt Sport
            US        CA        DE          US          UK          IE
```

Figure 10.1 – Packt Enterprises org chart

This view is focused on the structure of the organization, not the technology they use—we'll evolve that viewpoint as we work through the example in this chapter.

We're also going to cover a few different techniques for creating a more cohesive view of data within an enterprise B2C solution architecture, including the implications for the point-to-point integration options we've discussed so far.

Finally, we'll review some options for extending the Salesforce customer data model beyond the Salesforce ecosystem.

Component product scopes and structures

In this section, we'll continue to evolve the Packt Enterprises example to show why one organization might have multiple orgs, realms, and BUs and how that could be structured across the enterprise.

> **Tip**
> There are a lot of implications for everything from business processes to DevOps workflows when designing your org, realm, and BU structure that aren't in scope for this book. Always work with your platform-specific technical architects to ensure that the solution you're designing works at both the macro-level (solution architecture) and the platform level (technical architecture).

To explore this approach, we'll take each of the three component products in sequence and break down the Packt Enterprises approach. We'll start with the Salesforce Platform, then cover B2C Commerce, and finally Marketing Cloud.

Salesforce Platform multi-org structure

In the Salesforce Platform, an org is a single instance that could serve a variety of purposes, such as development, testing, integration, staging, or production. In this chapter, we're specifically covering organizations that have multiple Salesforce Platform *production* orgs.

There are a variety of reasons why an organization might have multiple production orgs. The following are some common possibilities:

- Mergers and acquisitions
- Separate BUs
- Data residency requirements
- Geographical proximity
- Minimizing complex customization

In our example, Packt Enterprises uses one org for its direct-to-consumer (B2C) BU, which is set up to use person accounts to model the organization's customers. This org uses Salesforce Service Cloud and Order Management.

They also have a separate org that is used primarily to support their wholesale business (B2B) with B2B Commerce, Sales Cloud, and CPQ. The following figure shows the Salesforce orgs used by Packt Enterprises:

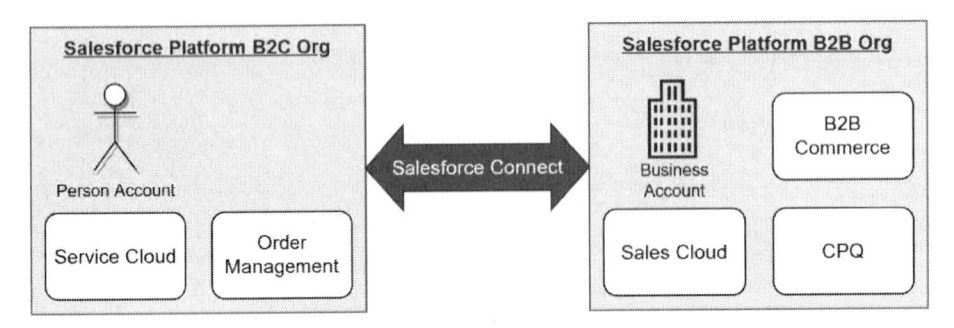

Figure 10.2 – Packt Enterprises Salesforce orgs

Although not required, this configuration allows Packt Enterprises to keep their business processes, customizations, and customer data models distinct from their BUs. Within each org, however, both brands are represented (Packt Gear and Packt Sport).

> **Tip**
> The preceding figure also shows using Salesforce Connect between two Salesforce Platform orgs. This tool, while not in scope for this book, can be used to synchronize some standard and custom objects between orgs within an enterprise. You can learn more about Salesforce Connect here: `https://sforce.co/3ixWsEQ`.

For a review of Salesforce Platform org concepts, see *Chapter 1, Demystifying Salesforce, Customer 360, and Digital 360*.

B2C Commerce multi-realm structure

A B2C Commerce realm is different in that a single realm includes a staging, development, and production instance as well as multiple sandbox instances. In this chapter, we're focused on the production instance, and the architectural considerations when an organization has multiple realms and, therefore, multiple production instances.

The reasons for having multiple realms in B2C Commerce mostly mirror the reasons for having multiple orgs, although geographical proximity plays a bigger role.

For Packt Enterprises, the performance of their online stores is critical to their direct-to-consumer business, so they have a dedicated B2C Commerce realm in **North America (NA)** and a second in the UK. This allows them to have separate sites for Packt Gear and Packt Sport in each region of the world that are geographically close to the customers they serve.

The following figure shows the Packt Enterprises B2C Commerce realm model:

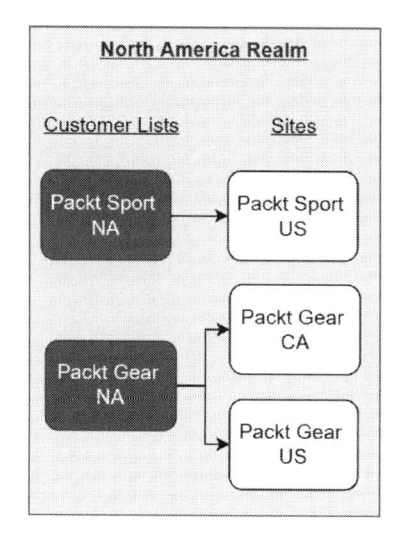

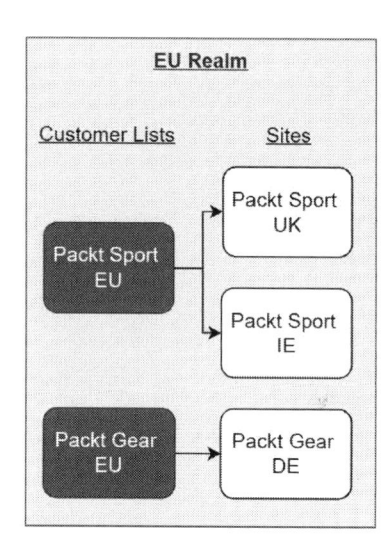

Figure 10.3 – Packt Enterprises realms

In this case, rather than dividing based on business function as we did with the Salesforce org approach, we're dividing based on geography. Since B2C Commerce is focused only on direct-to-consumer selling, we aren't worried about the wholesale business here, but we do need to keep the Packt Gear and Packt Sport customer lists separate.

This is another important difference with B2C Commerce. An instance can have multiple copies of similar data structures, such as separate customer lists, product catalogs, inventory lists, or price books, in the same instance. These constructs further partition the relevant data within a given instance.

> **Important note**
> Some B2C Commerce customers have a dedicated realm specifically for testing. Although this realm includes a production instance, it's not used for real customers, so it should be treated as a test environment in this discussion.

For a review of B2C Commerce realm concepts, see *Chapter 3, Direct-to-Consumer Selling with Commerce Cloud B2C*.

Marketing Cloud BU structure

In Marketing Cloud, the third pillar of our foundational B2C solution architecture, most customers have only one instance. Marketing Cloud does not have a concept of staging versus production instances, and it's generally cost-prohibitive and excessively complex to have a dedicated non-production instance.

The construct within a Marketing Cloud instance that's used to offer some limited data partitioning to support larger enterprises is the Marketing Cloud BU. In this chapter, we're going to look at considerations for organizations with multiple BUs in Marketing Cloud that are supporting real customers.

> **Important note**
> While Marketing Cloud BUs allow some conceptual separation of data and customization, ultimately all contacts in a Marketing Cloud instance are added to the All Contacts list, which is shared across all BUs. There are additional areas where data segregation is not guaranteed, which should be reviewed with your Marketing Cloud technical architect peer if data segregation is a priority.

Packt Enterprises use their Marketing Cloud instance for both their wholesale and direct-to-consumer businesses for both brands. To keep things organized, they've licensed multiple BUs within their Marketing Cloud Enterprise instance.

The following figure shows the structure of the Packt Enterprise BUs:

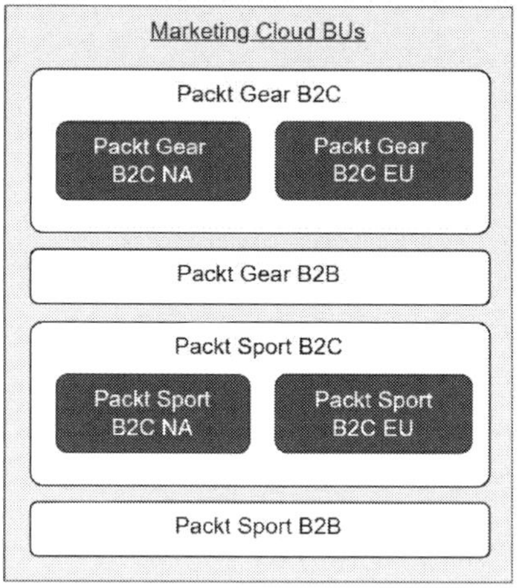

```
┌─────────────────────────────────────────┐
│  Marketing Cloud BUs                    │
│  ┌───────────────────────────────────┐  │
│  │  Packt Gear B2C                   │  │
│  │  ┌──────────────┐ ┌──────────────┐│  │
│  │  │ Packt Gear   │ │ Packt Gear   ││  │
│  │  │ B2C NA       │ │ B2C EU       ││  │
│  │  └──────────────┘ └──────────────┘│  │
│  └───────────────────────────────────┘  │
│  ┌───────────────────────────────────┐  │
│  │         Packt Gear B2B            │  │
│  └───────────────────────────────────┘  │
│  ┌───────────────────────────────────┐  │
│  │  Packt Sport B2C                  │  │
│  │  ┌──────────────┐ ┌──────────────┐│  │
│  │  │ Packt Sport  │ │ Packt Sport  ││  │
│  │  │ B2C NA       │ │ B2C EU       ││  │
│  │  └──────────────┘ └──────────────┘│  │
│  └───────────────────────────────────┘  │
│  ┌───────────────────────────────────┐  │
│  │         Packt Sport B2B           │  │
│  └───────────────────────────────────┘  │
└─────────────────────────────────────────┘
```

Figure 10.4 – Packt Enterprises Marketing Cloud BUs

Since all the contacts for B2C and B2B across Packt Gear and Packt Sport will be represented in the shared All Contacts list, this doesn't guarantee data isolation, but it does allow us to logically separate these contacts and subscribers. Also notice that we're subdividing the brand-specific B2C BUs based on NA and the **European Union** (**EU**). This aligns with best practices regarding Marketing Cloud BU and B2C Commerce customer list mapping, which we'll discuss later in this chapter.

For a review of Marketing Cloud BU concepts, see *Chapter 4, Engaging Customers with Marketing Cloud*.

In the next section, we'll discuss some of the considerations that will ultimately drive your architecture when incorporating instances from the various component products.

Solution design considerations

Regardless of the business reason for having multiple orgs, the question that will drive your multi-org cross-cloud architecture is whether these orgs should *share* data or *partition* data. If the goal is to share data to understand concepts such as the total lifetime value of a customer within the larger organization, the solutions in this chapter will help.

If the goal is to fully partition data, perhaps to maintain separation for legally distinct corporate entities, parallel B2C architectures would be required. The following figure shows a fully partitioned B2C solution architecture where all customer data remains in brand-specific systems:

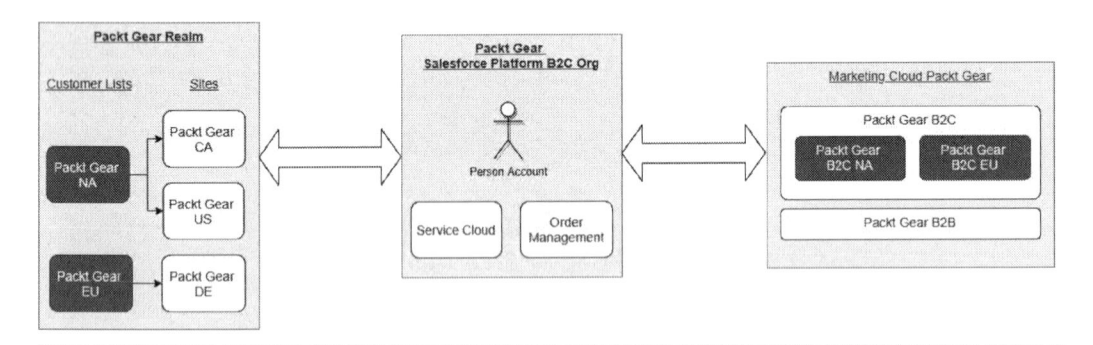

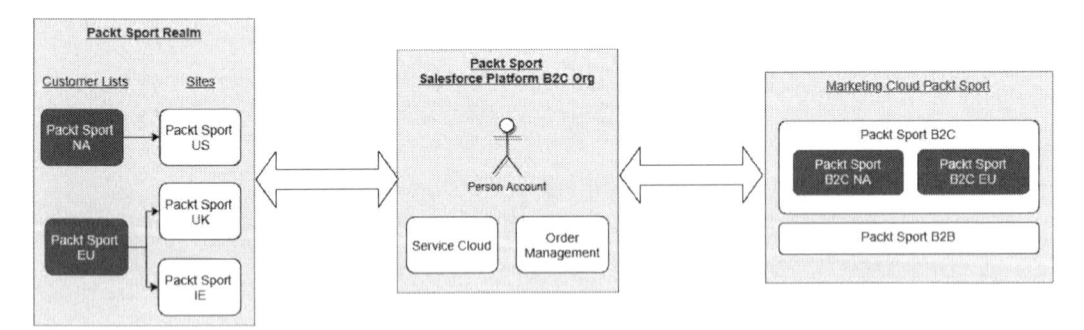

Figure 10.5 – Parallel solution architectures

As this figure shows, if fully partitioned data is required across your organization, you'll need to have a separate org, realm, and Marketing Cloud instance (not BU) for each corporate entity. This is effectively the single org, realm, and instance configuration we've been discussing throughout this book multiple times. Since we've already covered this configuration in earlier chapters, let's assume Packt Enterprises *does* need to share some data across brands.

For organizations that are looking to share data in some capacity, there's a lot more complexity to manage. Use the following questions to help guide the solution:

- Should data be *synchronized* between instances or *read-only*?
- What data specifically needs to be related between instances (for example, customer data only, products, inventory, content, or analytics)?
- Which instances will be related to each other, and which will remain independent?
- Do local regulations require you to keep data resident in a particular country?

Using these example questions, and a landscape of existing or planned environments, you can start to think about how they'll relate to each other.

Returning to Packt Enterprises, we've established the target architecture for each component product in isolation, but how should they relate to each other?

We'll cover the technical details of how to connect these products later in the chapter, so let's just focus on the enterprise data model for now. Specifically, let's talk about customers. This is typically the most complex topic and addresses all the considerations you'll need when performing the same exercise for other data types.

The following table shows the outcome when using the scoping questions with Packt Enterprises; the responses are in the voice of the client and will need to be interpreted and applied:

Question	Response
Should data be *synchronized* between instances or *read only*?	Customer data specifically should be synchronized (bi-directional) between B2C Commerce realms and the Salesforce org but should only be visible (not editable) in Marketing Cloud. The exception to this rule is customer consent, which is managed through the Marketing Cloud preference center.
What data specifically needs to be related between instances (for example customer data only, products, inventory, content, or analytics)?	Let's focus on customer data for now. Products will be synchronized from PIM, inventory updates will come from the warehouse, content we'll need to figure out because we don't really have a dedicated DAM or CMS at the moment.
Which instances will be related to each other, and which will remain independent?	We need both of our B2C Commerce realms to integrate with our direct-to-consumer Salesforce org so our customer service agents can support them. We also need some data shared between our two orgs, specifically knowledge articles, and everything needs to be integrated with Marketing Cloud.
Do local regulations require you to keep data resident in a particular country?	We're governed by GDPR regulations regarding data residency in our European markets. Our legal team has reviewed the Salesforce Binding Corporate Rules (BCRs) and determined we are complying if EU customer data is used within the Salesforce ecosystem.

Table 10.1 – Enterprise scoping questions

As you can see, there's a lot of information here from just four questions that will need to be digested and used to inform the solution. Specifically, we now know that the B2C Commerce realms need to bi-directionally synchronize customer data with the direct-to-consumer Salesforce Platform org, that the two orgs need to share some data, and that everything needs to connect to Marketing Cloud.

Regarding data residency requirements, this is a complex topic that will require legal guidance this book cannot provide.

> **Further reading**
>
> To learn more about the Salesforce perspective on EU resident personal data, review the *June 2021 FAQ on International Transfers of EU Personal Data to Salesforce's Services* here: `https://sforce.co/3l3cjwy`.

Based on what we've learned so far, the following figure represents an appropriate architecture Packt Enterprises Salesforce ecosystem:

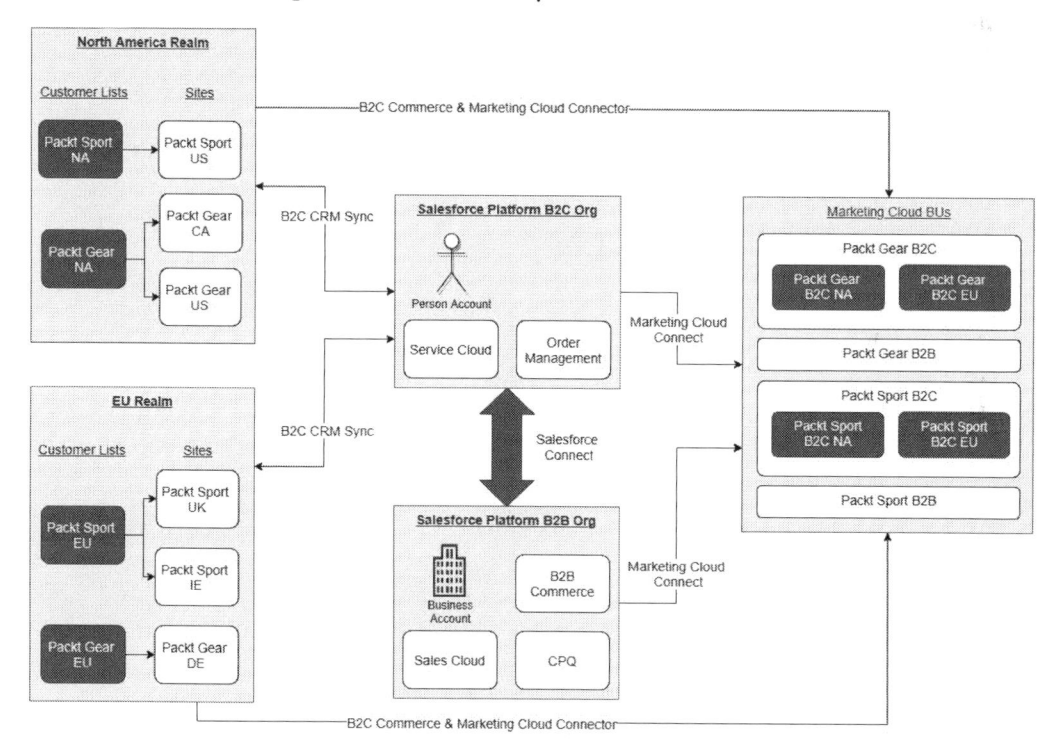

Figure 10.6 – Packt Enterprises Salesforce ecosystem

This represents an ecosystem where the two B2C Commerce realms, one in the EU and one in NA, each hosts sites for the two brands. Both realms are integrated with the Packt Gear B2C org, the direct-to-consumer org, where Service Cloud and Order Management are enabled. Both realms are also integrated with Marketing Cloud, and the two orgs are integrated with each other using **Salesforce Connect**. Finally, both orgs are integrated with Marketing Cloud using Marketing Cloud Connect in a multi-org configuration, which we'll discuss later in this chapter.

> **Important note**
> If you are using the Salesforce **Omnichannel Inventory (OCI)** service, the mapping of B2C Commerce instances to Salesforce Order Management orgs must be 1:1.

By this point, we've taken the three different platform configurations and related them to each other, but there's another level to this.

In the next section, we'll explore how to map data within each system and across the solution.

Enterprise data management

There are many different types of data used in a B2C solution architecture. Customer data is perhaps the most important, but we also have order data, product data, content, inventory, analytics data, and much more.

Regardless of the type of data, there are two concepts that you'll need to keep in mind when integrating that data between systems: scopes and identifiers.

We've covered this topic a bit in previous chapters, but the fundamental idea is that *scope* is the context in which a given *identifier* is unique. In B2C Commerce, a customer is unique in a customer list, so the customer list is the scope of the customer. Since multiple sites can share the same customer list, and therefore the same set of customers, a site is *not* an appropriate scope for a customer.

This concept is important because when data is synchronized between systems, especially in a larger enterprise, you'll need to ensure that data integrity is maintained within these boundaries.

In the following sections, we'll focus on customer data as an example starting with the considerations for identifiers and scopes, then moving on to what makes a representation of a customer unique within a given system, taking each system one at a time to build the cross-cloud data model.

Enterprise customer data

Considering what we know of scopes and identifiers, in this section, we'll cover the concept of customer identity and how/why it's partitioned in various systems (customer lists versus BUs). We'll also cover how this impacts matching rules and duplicate rules associated with B2C CRM sync.

The guideline in a Salesforce B2C solution architecture, when it comes to customer data, is that the Salesforce Platform representation of the customer is the key. Each unique representation of a B2C Commerce customer must relate to exactly one contact in the Salesforce Platform, which will be represented as one unique contact in Marketing Cloud.

B2C Commerce customer uniqueness

Following this guideline, we need to start from what makes a customer unique within B2C Commerce. If we have the B2C Commerce customer ID, that's a unique identifier within a given B2C Commerce instance. If we have a customer number, that's unique within a given customer list. If we have neither of those things, we can fall back on the email address, which we can also treat as unique within a given customer list.

The following table shows the B2C Commerce customer identifiers and their associated scopes:

B2C Commerce Identifier	Scope
Customer ID	Instance
Customer Number	Customer List
Email	Customer List

Table 10.2 – B2C Commerce customer identifiers and scopes

As this figure shows, we need both the **customer list** and the instance to be able to recognize customers consistently. We also know that **email** alone is not sufficient, since we could have the same email in different customer lists for the same instance.

Since multiple different sites in B2C Commerce can share a customer list, the site identifier doesn't add much value in disambiguating customers.

Salesforce Platform customer uniqueness

To ensure that these unique B2C Commerce customers are mapped one to one into the Salesforce Platform, we use matching rules and duplicate rules configured as shown in the following figure:

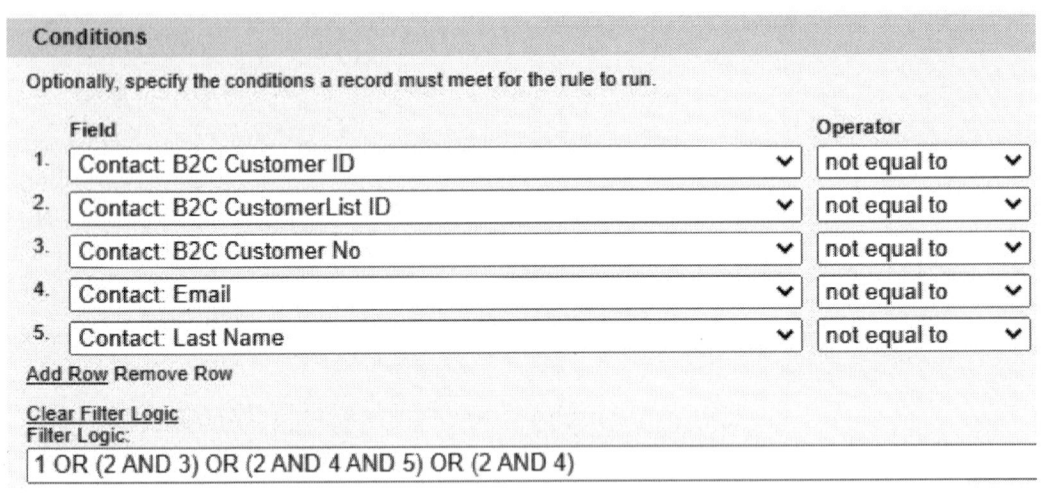

Conditions

Optionally, specify the conditions a record must meet for the rule to run.

#	Field	Operator
1.	Contact: B2C Customer ID	not equal to
2.	Contact: B2C CustomerList ID	not equal to
3.	Contact: B2C Customer No	not equal to
4.	Contact: Email	not equal to
5.	Contact: Last Name	not equal to

Add Row Remove Row

Clear Filter Logic
Filter Logic:
1 OR (2 AND 3) OR (2 AND 4 AND 5) OR (2 AND 4)

Figure 10.7 – B2C CRM sync duplicate rules

This sample duplicate rule looks at five fields related to the Contact record to check for potential duplication. The **Filter Logic** section describes how those fields are combined.

In this example, the duplicate rule is configured to treat a customer ID as unique by itself, **1**, the customer list ID and customer number as unique together, **(2 AND 3)**, the customer list ID, email, and last name as unique combined, **(2 AND 4 AND 5)**, and finally, the customer list ID and email together as unique, **(2 AND 4)**.

Anything that doesn't match one of these rules is considered a unique record, and the B2C CRM sync integration will create a new contact (or person account) to represent that record, which will be connected to the B2C Commerce customer record.

> **Important note**
> This configuration, and B2C CRM sync in general, does not account for different B2C Commerce instances using the same customer list IDs.

For Packt Gear, to ensure that their EU customers and their NA customers are kept separate within their shared Salesforce org, we've used unique customer list IDs in each: Packt Sport NA, Packt Gear NA, Packt Sport EU, and Packt Gear EU.

With this configuration, we've successfully connected two B2C Commerce realms to one Salesforce Platform org. Now we need to configure the next leg, which is connecting that org to Marketing Cloud via Marketing Cloud Connect.

Marketing Cloud customer uniqueness

To maintain this separation in Marketing Cloud, and to ensure that Marketing Cloud users have a clear picture of which customers they're communicating with at any given time, we need to set up Marketing Cloud BUs that align to B2C Commerce customer lists.

To accomplish this, each Marketing Cloud BU should be set up to filter the All Subscribers list on the B2C Commerce customer list ID from the Contact record, as shown in the following figure:

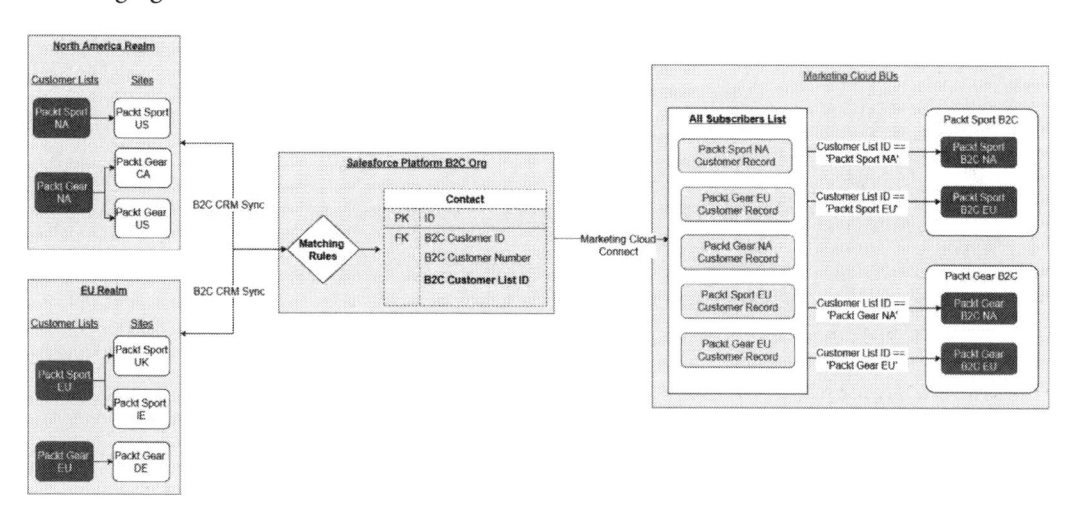

Figure 10.8 – Packt Enterprises customer mapping

Now we've successfully mapped customer data from multiple realms through your shared org into the single Marketing Cloud instance without unintentional mingling.

> **Tip**
> If you're using Einstein Product Recommendations or behavioral monitoring in Marketing Cloud, the Marketing Cloud BU should be mapped to the B2C Commerce site to avoid having behavior or recommendations from one site exposed on another site sharing the same customer list.

This is our final viewpoint on multi-realm, multi-site, multi-customer list customer data mapping across environments.

This data model provides an overview of how the data should be mapped between systems, but we also need to consider the details of how that will be implemented with the available point-to-point connectors discussed in *Chapter 7, Integration Architecture Options*.

Point-to-point integration impacts

When integrating two systems point to point, the connection is necessarily one to one. In a larger enterprise, however, you may be making multiple connections between instances in this fashion.

Continuing to build on the Packt Enterprises example, we'll have two different Salesforce Platform orgs connected to a single Marketing Cloud instance. We'll also have two different B2C Commerce realms connected to a single Salesforce Platform org and Marketing Cloud instance. This overall view is shown in *Figure 10.7* in the previous section.

In the following sections, we'll examine the implications of this configuration for Marketing Cloud Connect, B2C CRM sync, and the Commerce and Marketing connector.

Multi-org with Marketing Cloud Connect

Marketing Cloud Connect supports a native multi-org configuration with Enterprise 2.0 accounts. When this configuration is enabled, Marketing Cloud BUs can be associated with individual Salesforce Platform orgs.

This configuration synchronizes each org's contacts, leads, or users into the associated BU in Marketing Cloud. You must contact Salesforce support to enable multi-org for your Marketing Cloud instance.

> **Important note**
> The Marketing Cloud All Contacts list will contain subscribers from all BUs, regardless of the org they originated from. Restrict access to All Contacts and use subscriber BU filters to ensure Marketing Cloud users can only see subscribers in their associated BU.

When using Marketing Cloud Connect in a multi-org configuration, the native Marketing Cloud Profile Center is unable to properly track and update customer preferences. In this case, you must implement a custom Profile Center to allow customers to view and edit profile attributes as well as subscription preferences.

> **Important note**
> Honoring unsubscribe requests is required both by law and by the terms of your Marketing Cloud contract with Salesforce.

Your custom preference center is responsible for updating the custom fields on the Contact, Lead, or User record in the Salesforce Platform in the associated org for the subscriber. This preference will then be synchronized to Marketing Cloud via Marketing Cloud Connect synchronized data extensions.

> **Further reading**
> Learn more about Profile Center and Marketing Cloud Connect here: `https://sforce.co/3AjJhxp`.

Multi-org configurations for Marketing Cloud Connect cannot be disabled once they're turned on by Salesforce support, but orgs can be disconnected from individual BUs.

In addition, Marketing Cloud Connect supports integrating many Salesforce Platform orgs into one Marketing Cloud instance by mapping them to specific BUs. It does *not* support mapping one Salesforce Platform org to multiple Marketing Cloud instances. This configuration, while much less likely, would require a custom solution.

> **Further reading**
> To review the full details or multi-org account configuration in Marketing Cloud Connect, see the following Salesforce help article: `https://sforce.co/3inlUNf`.

Implications for B2C CRM sync

B2C CRM sync is the enablement solution provided by Salesforce for integrating customer data between B2C Commerce and the Salesforce Platform. We covered B2C CRM sync extensively in *Chapter 7*, *Integration Architecture Options*, so in this section, we'll just focus on the changes when you have multiple realms or orgs in your environment.

Unlike Marketing Cloud Connect, B2C CRM sync could potentially be leveraged with either multiple Salesforce Platform orgs connected to a single B2C Commerce instance or with one B2C Commerce instance integrated with multiple Salesforce Platform orgs.

Each configuration has implications for how the connector is installed, configured, and potentially customized. We'll cover these implications in the following sections, first on the B2C Commerce side and then on the Salesforce Platform side.

B2C CRM sync B2C Commerce implications

The following figure shows one potential configuration where a single B2C Commerce instance is integrated with multiple Salesforce Platform orgs:

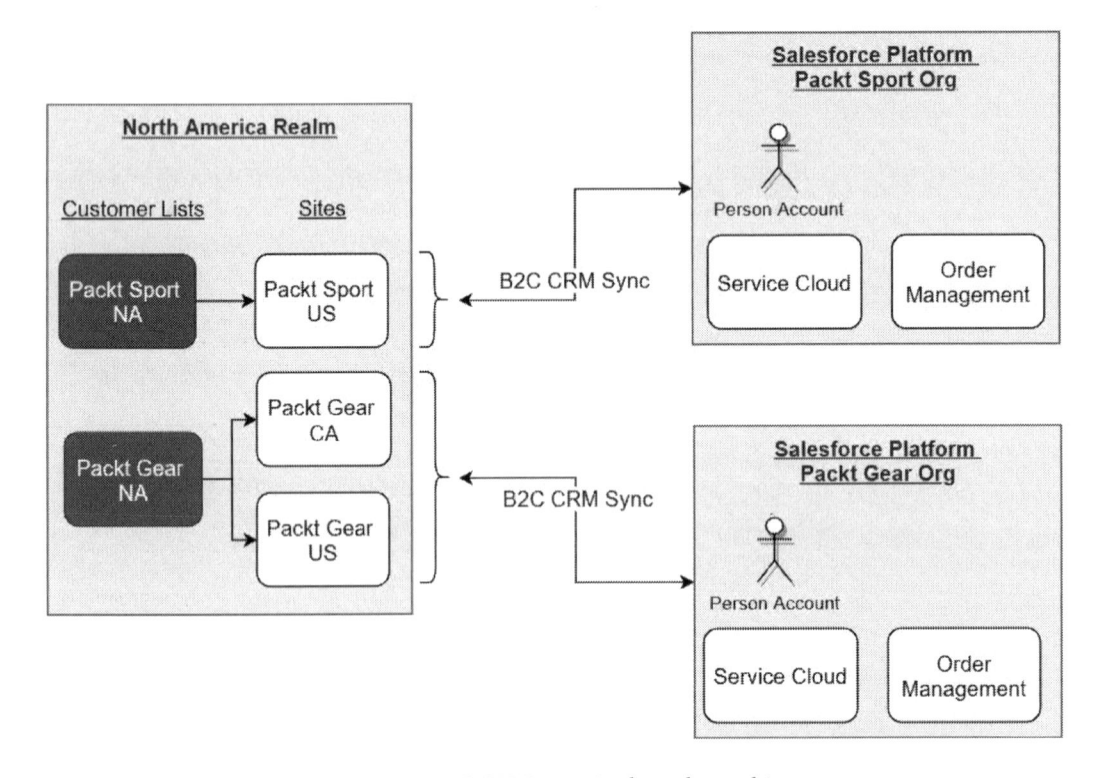

Figure 10.9 – B2C CRM sync single-realm multi-org

As this figure shows, the recommended mapping in this configuration is to ensure that each customer list is synchronized with one Salesforce Platform org. If multiple B2C Commerce sites share that customer list, they should all be synchronized with the same Salesforce Platform org.

> **Important note**
> If you try to map separate B2C Commerce sites that share a customer list to different Salesforce Platform orgs, the results will be inconsistent customer data in all three systems because updates will not be made consistently.

To support this configuration, all sites should share the same B2C CRM sync code base, which is accomplished using B2C Commerce cartridges added to each site's cartridge path. From there, the only change required is to update the site-specific service credentials for all sites sharing the same customer list to reference the Salesforce Platform org associated with that customer list.

Configuring service credentials in B2C Commerce involves entering the service user from the Salesforce Platform org and the connected app credentials setup in the org.

The Salesforce Platform org accepting the integration then needs to be configured to call back to the appropriate B2C Commerce instance, as described in the next section.

B2C CRM sync Salesforce Platform implications

Within the Salesforce Platform, integrating to multiple B2C Commerce instances using B2C CRM sync is supported natively, with one important caveat.

> **Tip**
> Separate B2C Commerce realms integrated with the same Salesforce Platform org *cannot* have customer lists with the same ID.

This is the configuration required by the Packt Enterprises use case. Here, the Salesforce Platform side of the B2C CRM sync integration already tracks the customer list ID as a scope for the B2C Commerce customer record. If the customer list IDs are unique, and each is assigned to the appropriate B2C Commerce instance, the integration will make updates in the right system at the right time.

The final piece of the point-to-point connector picture is the integration between B2C Commerce and Marketing Cloud.

B2C Commerce and Marketing Cloud connector

Since the B2C Commerce and Marketing Cloud integration accelerator should not be moving customer data, the implications here are for other data points. Specifically, this integration will likely be sending the following data feeds to the Marketing Cloud SFTP server, which will then be imported into data extensions:

- Product catalog
- Content catalog
- Orders
- Campaigns and promotions

Using the product catalog example for Packt Enterprises, we need to know how the B2C Commerce instance links product data with sites. For customer data, we know that all sites for the same brand share the same customer list. With product catalog data, we have a similar option because product catalogs can be assigned to one or more sites in B2C Commerce.

Since our different sites in B2C Commerce are supporting different parts of the world, however, we can't assume that they'll all share the same product assortment. We certainly don't want to send a customer a promotional email recommending a product that's not available in their area!

> **Tip**
> B2C Commerce storefront catalogs should map 1:1 with Marketing Cloud BU catalogs.

The following figure shows a data mapping between B2C Commerce and Marketing Cloud that builds on the Packt Gear example we've been using so far:

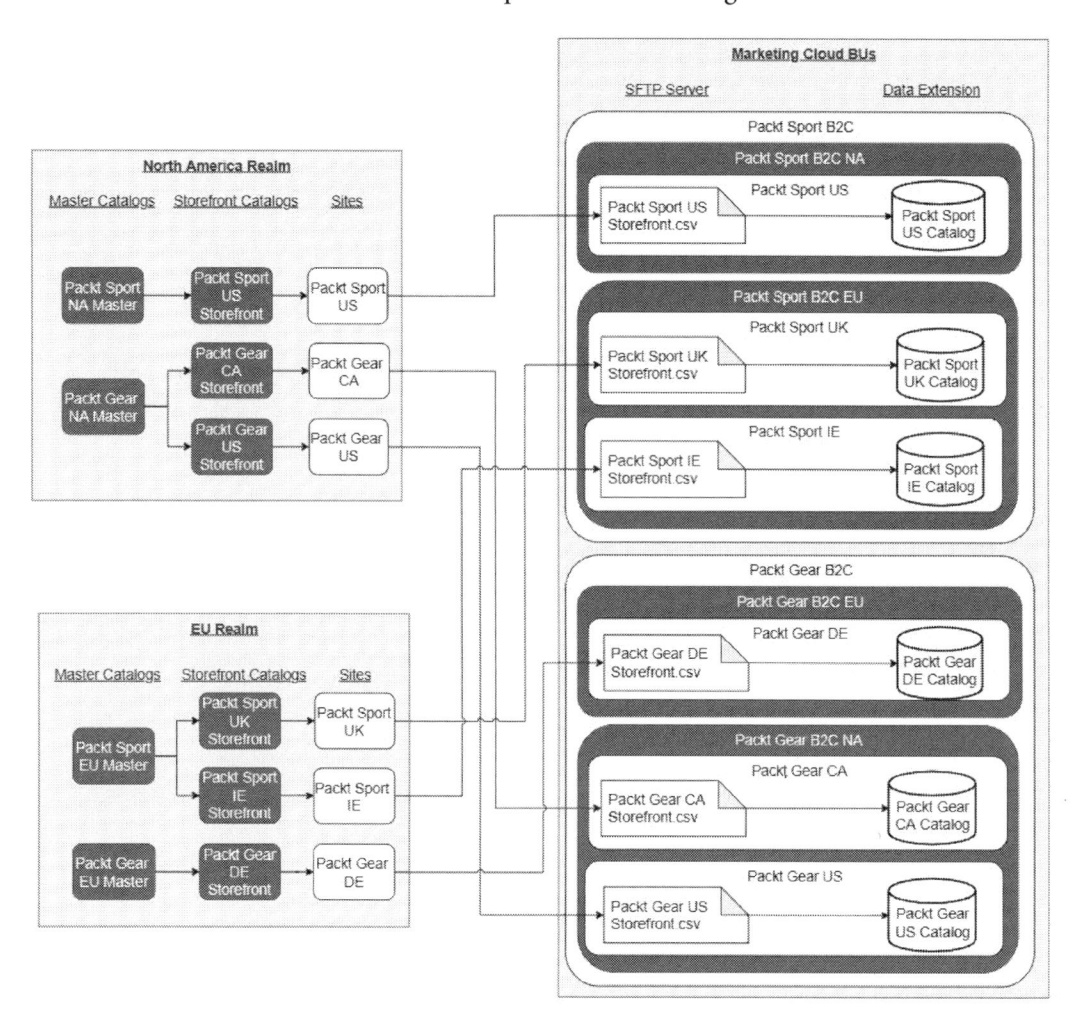

Figure 10.10 – Multi-realm catalog mapping

In the preceding figure, we can see that the storefront catalogs are being sent separately to the Marketing Cloud SFTP server from the NA realm and the EU realm. From there, they're picked up by Automation Studio and ingested into Marketing Cloud data extensions per catalog. Each data extension is used by a site-specific BU on the right to fuel their marketing efforts.

> **Tip**
> If all sites for the same brand share the same product assortment, a significantly simpler approach leveraging one catalog and one BU for that brand is recommended.

The architecture shown in *Figure 10.12* also supports behavioral tracking using `collect.js` at a per-site level, which is required for campaigns such as abandoned cart recapture, which need to know what site the customer was using when they abandoned their cart.

This pattern should be repeated for each data type fed from B2C Commerce to Marketing Cloud using the integration accelerator.

In the next section, we'll review options for designing a scalable solution using tools such as Heroku or MuleSoft.

Enterprise integration using middleware

While the architectural options described previously may be appropriate if you have 1 or 2 instances in each system, they'll quickly become unmanageable if you have 10, 20, or more. Even in smaller ecosystems, there are significant benefits to taking a more rigorous approach to integration both within the Salesforce ecosystem and across the enterprise.

Using an integration middleware tool such as MuleSoft, it is possible to both simplify and scale the integration architecture described previously. In *Chapter 7*, *Integration Architecture Options*, we started by discussing point-to-point integration options and then covered options using integration middleware. Here, we'll do the same.

> **Tip**
> We're primarily using MuleSoft and Heroku here as our integration middleware choices. They have significant advantages, especially in the Salesforce ecosystem, but the same concepts apply with any integration tool like MuleSoft or a **Platform as a Service** (**PaaS**) tool like Heroku.

We'll start by covering options for centralizing and scaling data access across Salesforce Platform orgs using Heroku and then extend that concept to cover Marketing Cloud and B2C Commerce using MuleSoft.

Virtualizing data access at scale

As we've discussed throughout this book, one of the constraints of the Salesforce Platform is API limits determined by your org license model. Based on these constraints, it may be prohibitive to provide real-time access to data aggregated from multiple orgs behind a service.

A natural solution to this would be to wrap your Salesforce Platform orgs with Heroku, as shown in the following figure:

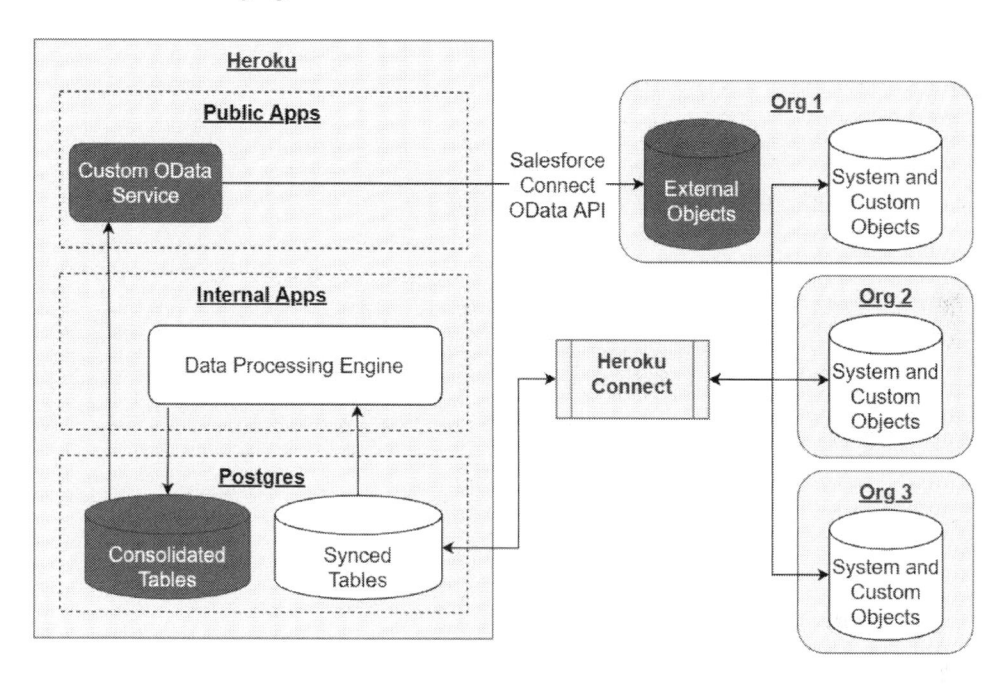

Figure 10.11 – Heroku Connect org consolidation

With this approach, multiple Salesforce Platform orgs are synchronized using Heroku Connect into a Heroku Postgres database. From there, Heroku custom code is used to consolidate and apply business logic to the various data sources before writing it to a consolidated table. A custom OData service layer deployed to Heroku is used to expose the consolidated multi-org view of the data source. Finally, Salesforce Connect using the OData adapter is used to expose the consolidated data view from all orgs in a primary org (**Org 1** in the preceding figure).

This architecture is representing Heroku in a layered architecture where custom public, internet-facing apps are deployed to host a custom service layer and compute dynos are deployed with internal routing to protect them from external access. These internal apps are used to process and consolidate data, which is then exposed via the public-facing web service app.

This approach ensures that the Salesforce Platform APIs are only used for synchronizing data once, not for every query, and it centralizes business logic related to data consolidation within Heroku. The Heroku-based OData service can also be used to expose the Salesforce Platform data to other systems both within the Salesforce ecosystem and beyond.

> **Further reading**
> Learn more about archiving and consolidating Salesforce Platform data using Heroku in Trailhead here: `https://sforce.co/2VSySda`.

While this pattern works well with Salesforce Platform orgs, primarily due to the power of Heroku Connect, it's more challenging when incorporating B2C Commerce and Marketing. Custom code would have to be written in each system to synchronize data into the Heroku databases. In addition, these systems don't have the same API volume constraints that the Salesforce Platform does.

To scale this pattern, we should look at a dedicated integration middleware layer such as MuleSoft.

Aggregating data through services

Using an integration-focused tool such as MuleSoft, you can design highly scalable architectures that support many systems across different technologies.

To review the capabilities and advantages of MuleSoft in general, return to *Chapter 5, Salesforce Ecosystem – Building a Complete Solution*. In this section, we're going to focus on using MuleSoft to create a data federation service.

> **Tip**
> A data federation service is a service exposing a virtual database aggregating information from multiple component data sources, in this case, multiple Salesforce Platform orgs, B2C Commerce instances, and Marketing Cloud BUs.

Using a data federation service approach requires consideration of two important concepts: the service framework architecture and the data routing rules.

Data framework architecture

The following diagram depicts a potential architecture incorporating multiple Salesforce Platform orgs, B2C Commerce realms, and Marketing Cloud instances:

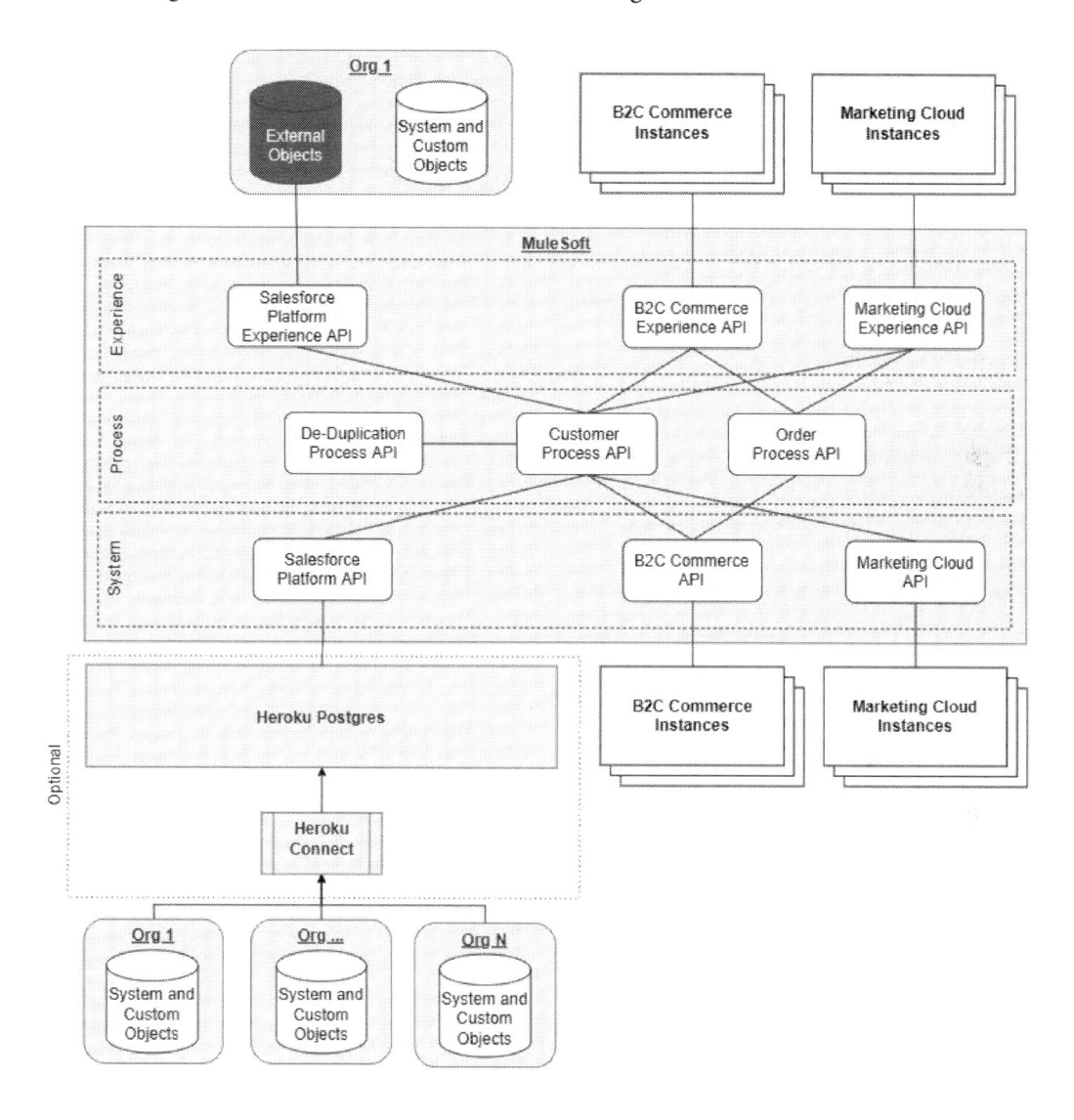

Figure 10.12 – MuleSoft data federation

In this architecture, the number of Salesforce Platform orgs, B2C Commerce instances, and Marketing Cloud instances or BUs is irrelevant. Each source system leverages a system-specific **Experience API**, which is responsible for presenting the data in a way that is appropriate for the calling system. That might be an OData-compliant service to support Salesforce Connect for the Salesforce Platform, or a real-time REST API for B2C Commerce or pushing data to Marketing Cloud data extensions.

Regardless of the source system, all requests for customer data go through the **Customer Process API**, and this API handles orchestrating the request to the relevant **System APIs**.

Depending on the systems in play and the needs of the organization, there are many ways this could be designed. Be sure to work with a MuleSoft technical architect to design that portion of the solution as it fits into the overall B2C solution architecture.

Data routing rules

Once the overall architecture is established, start thinking about how data will be routed within the system.

How will data be queried? What identifiers will be used? Email? Contact ID? First name + last name? Order number?

Reflecting on our rules for identifiers and scopes, we also need to consider any rules for scopes and system boundaries. If a **Customer Service Representative** (**CSR**) in the Service Console searches the consolidated customer external object, which is driven by the Salesforce Platform Experience API via Salesforce Connect, how will the Customer Process API know which systems to query?

There's no single right answer to these questions; it depends on what you're trying to achieve. If the goal is to return a unified view of that customer across all systems, route the request to all component systems and return a consolidated result. If the goal is to return that customer's profile data related to a single brand within an enterprise, restrict the request by brand and map that to a customer list or other scope that is system-specific.

The example shown in the following figure depicts an **Enterprise Data & Analytics** user querying for a customer's total lifetime value and propensity to buy based on engagement data from Marketing Cloud, purchase history from B2C Commerce, and demographics from the Salesforce Platform person account records:

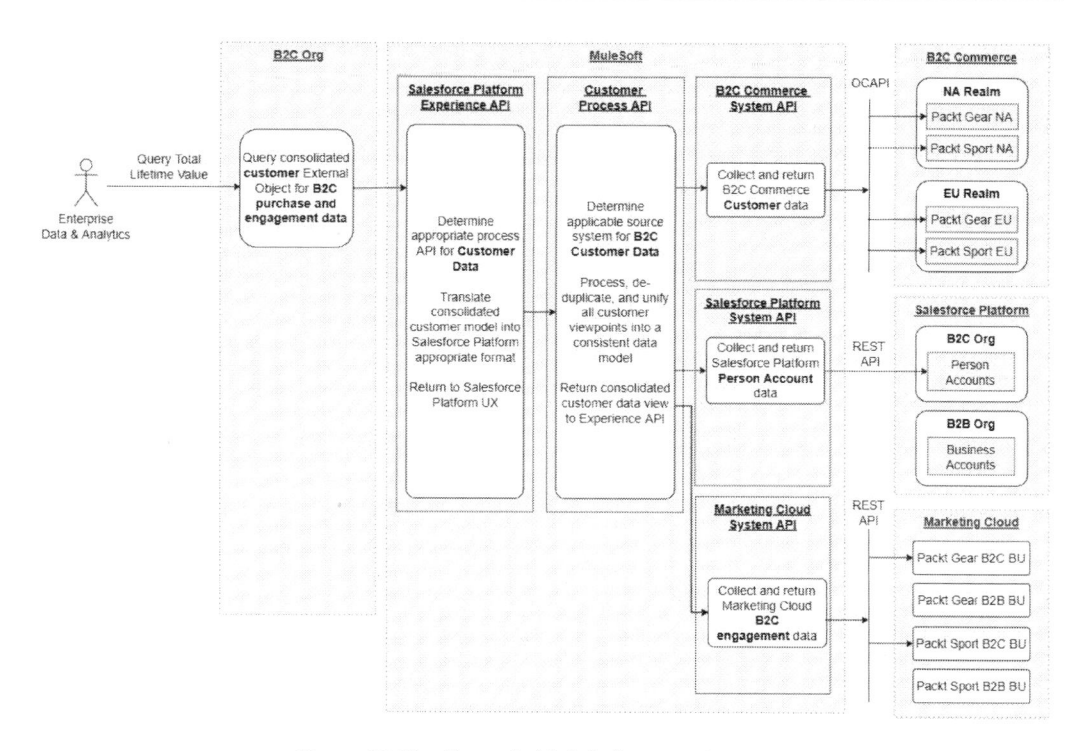

Figure 10.13 – Example MuleSoft enterprise query

Working through this example from left to right, the query originates in the UX layer of the Salesforce Platform B2C org, where an **Enterprise Data & Analytics** user is making the query. Based on this, the query should include all customer data regardless of affiliated brand or geography. Since the request is coming from the Salesforce Platform, it first hits the MuleSoft Salesforce Platform Experience API.

The Experience API is responsible for presenting and returning data in a format the Salesforce Platform can understand. It's also responsible for orchestrating the request across the relevant Process APIs. In this case, since the request is for customer data, the query is passed through to the Customer Process API.

The Customer Process API is responsible for presenting and returning data in a consistent and platform-agnostic data model that can include and represent data from all component systems. It's also responsible for orchestrating the request to the appropriate System APIs. Since we're querying for customer engagement, purchase history, and profile data, the Customer Process API queries the Marketing Cloud System API, B2C Commerce System API, and Salesforce Platform System API, respectively.

The System APIs are responsible for communicating with the systems they represent in the relevant formats (**OCAPI** or Commerce APIs for B2C Commerce, SOAP or **REST APIs** for the Salesforce Platform and Marketing Cloud). They are also responsible for determining how to format the query and return it to the Process API in a platform-agnostic way.

In this case, we're querying for B2C customer data. Since the request is not brand- or geography-specific, all B2C Commerce customer lists across all instances are included. Since we only want B2C customer data, only the B2C Salesforce Platform org has been included, so we query person account records for demographic data. For Marketing Cloud, we include engagement data for contacts in the two brand-specific B2C BUs.

This data, pulled from the component instances, is consolidated and de-duplicated, and business rules are applied at the Process API layer before it's translated into a Salesforce Platform appropriate format back at the Experience API layer and the result is returned.

If the query were instead performed by a brand-specific CSR, the request would only be routed to customer lists and BUs for that brand. If it were performed for an enterprise marketing user responsible for the EU territory, it would be forwarded to all B2C Commerce instances and Marketing Cloud BUs associated with the EU, regardless of brand.

This pattern is also more scalable as additional realms, orgs, Marketing Cloud instances or BUs, or systems beyond Salesforce are incorporated.

Integrations beyond Salesforce

With enterprise integration scenarios in the Salesforce ecosystem, we explored two complementary areas.

First, we explored the data *scopes* and *identifiers* used across different systems and how they map to each other based on business requirements.

Second, we explored the implications for integration points needed to preserve these relationships and mappings as data moves between systems.

In this section, we extend exactly this concept to integrations beyond the Salesforce ecosystem. We'll start by examining identifiers and scopes from beyond Salesforce and how they can be incorporated into the Salesforce data model. Then, we'll look at how best to incorporate external systems into the Salesforce ecosystem data flows.

External customer data sources

For customer data, within the Salesforce ecosystem, we leverage the Salesforce Platform contact ID as the primary identifier for a customer. The B2C Commerce customer identifiers are carried into the other systems to facilitate integration with B2C Commerce.

Complimentary Salesforce products, such as MuleSoft and Tableau, can use the collection of customer identifiers from B2C Commerce, the Salesforce Platform, and Marketing Cloud to create a holistic viewpoint.

> **Tip**
> Although we're continuing to use the customer data example in this section, the same concept of scopes and identifiers extends to any data type in Salesforce.

To extend the customer data model into external systems such as a **Master Data Management** (**MDM**) or **Enterprise Resource Planning** (**ERP**) system, the customer data should be synchronized from Salesforce to these systems. Equally importantly, the corresponding customer identifiers from these systems should be synchronized back to Salesforce, as shown in the following figure:

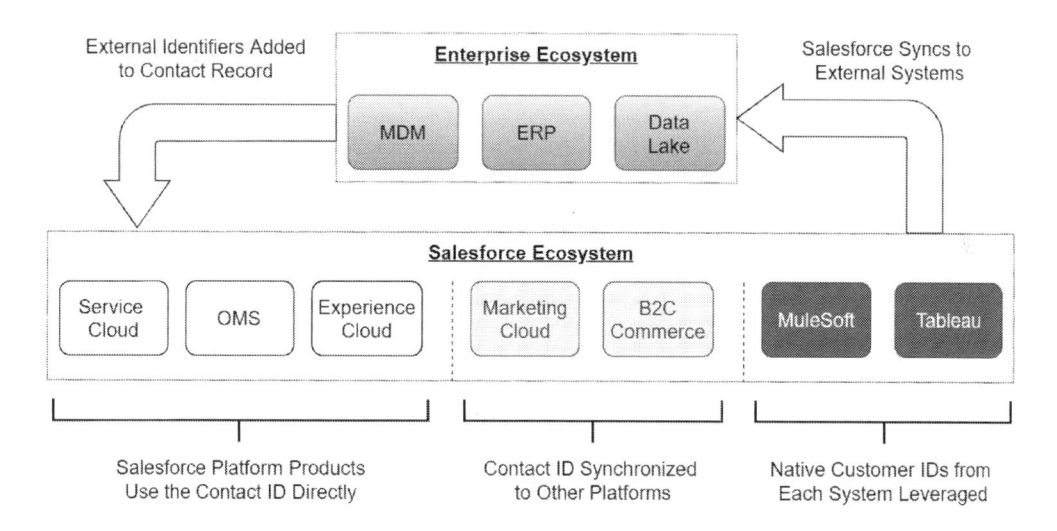

Figure 10.14 – External customer identifiers

In the model shown here, the Salesforce view of the customer contributes to the overall enterprise view of the customer. In addition, the enterprise customer records are attributed to the Salesforce Platform view of the customer, so this relationship is maintained.

> **Tip**
> The fundamental premise within the Salesforce ecosystem is that the CRM view of the customer, the Salesforce Platform contact or person account record, is the data master. *This means the only record that needs to be synchronized to external systems to provide a full picture is the contact or person account from the Salesforce Platform.*

A cross-cloud customer data model incorporating an external MDM system would look something as in the following figure:

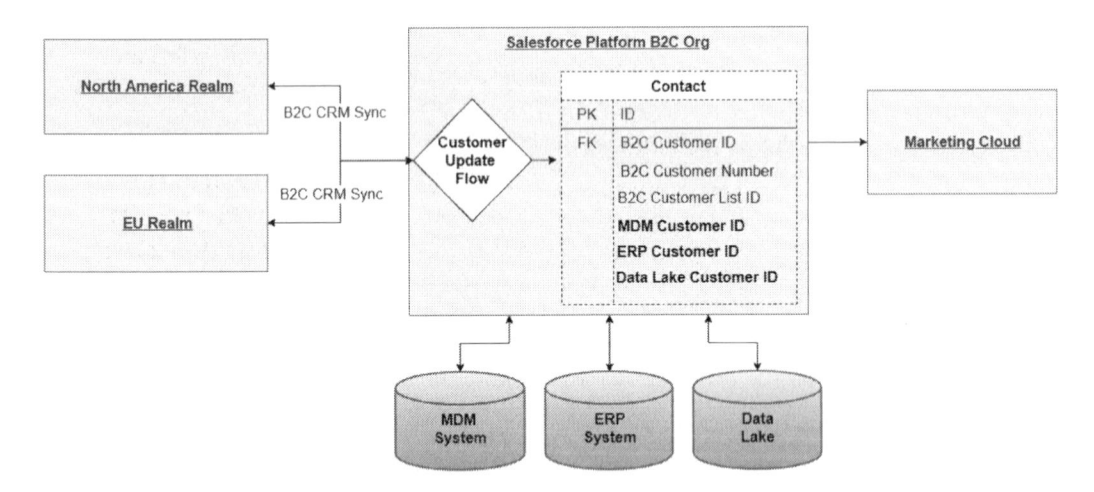

Figure 10.15 – Extended customer data model

In this example, you can see we've extended the Salesforce Platform Contact record to incorporate the additional external identifiers as well as pushing the Contact data to the **MDM**, **ERP**, and **Data Lake** systems. By incorporating the external identifiers into the Salesforce Platform data model, you can leverage Salesforce Connect to expose external data from external systems. This is accomplished by creating an indirect lookup relationship between the external object representing the corresponding ERP record and the Contact record in Salesforce.

> **Tip**
> To review Salesforce Connect and related topics, see *Chapter 1, Demystifying Salesforce, Customer 360, and Digital 360*, or read more here: `https://sforce.co/3ixWsEQ`.

Importantly, note that these external systems are not integrated with either the B2C Commerce realm or with Marketing Cloud directly, at least not for anything related to customer data. All customer data within the Salesforce ecosystem is synced to the Contact record in the Salesforce Platform, which is then integrated with external systems.

In the next section, we'll touch on some options for integrating with external systems.

External system integration points

The Salesforce Platform provides many options for integrating with external data. The Salesforce Certified Integration Architecture Designer certification, one of the prerequisite certifications for B2C Solution Architect, covers these options in far more detail than is possible in this book. Review *Chapter 12, Prerequisite Certifications*, for a high-level overview of the important topics on this exam.

To continue developing our Packt Enterprises example, where we are now focused on integrating their Salesforce Platform B2C org with their MDM, ERP, and data lake systems, let's review some options for how that can be accomplished within the existing framework.

Outbound data options

There are many options in the Salesforce Platform for updating external systems when data changes. The following list includes some of the most common options you'll want to consider:

- **Platform events**: Used to publish events in real time that can be consumed by Salesforce or external systems, which must support the CometD protocol.
- **Outbound messages**: Used to send a SOAP message to an external endpoint from a workflow, approval process, or entitlement process, allows the external service to call back using the provided session ID without reauthenticating.
- **Change Data Capture**: Used to update an external data store anytime a Salesforce record is created, updated, or deleted in near-real time from Salesforce or an external system, which must support the CometD protocol. Change Data Capture is a type of platform event triggered automatically by Salesforce.

- **Apex triggers**: Custom code implemented to call an external service when a Salesforce Platform record is created, updated, or deleted.

- **External services**: Low - or no-code solution for integrating with external services providing an OpenAPI definition, which can be called directly from flows.

- **Pub/Sub API**: Modern API built using the **Google Remote Procedure Call** (**gRPC**) specification, which provides a streamlined way of both subscribing to and publishing platform events without the need for a CometD-compliant client.

> **Tip**
> The Pub/Sub API is in pilot for customers as of fall 2021. Review the Salesforce Developer blog post on the topic here: `https://sforce.co/3u3NnHN`.

For Packt Enterprises, which needs a solution to update their external customer data sources with changes to Salesforce records, two candidates are outbound messages and external services. Outbound messages would allow the recipient to call back using the provided session ID updating the Salesforce Platform record with the external identifier, but *outbound messages can only be triggered from workflows, approval processes, or entitlement processes. The solution we've evolved so far doesn't use any of these.*

> **Tip**
> The number of integration options available on the Salesforce Platform can be overwhelming. Always focus on choosing the simplest option that meets your needs, preferring low- or no-code options over custom development.

External services is another candidate. The B2C CRM sync toolset we've already put in place supports the matching rules and update flows across B2C Commerce and the Salesforce Platform. The gap we need to fill is now to connect the Salesforce Platform to an external-to-Salesforce system such as an MDM or ERP.

By declaratively configuring external services for third-party systems that support this feature, we can incorporate them into our existing flows and use the returned identifiers to update the Contact record. This would be an ideal solution if the external system supports OpenAPI, which is a requirement for external services.

If OpenAPI is not supported, and outbound messages aren't a good fit due to their restriction to workflows and outbound SOAP messages, we could evaluate Change Data Capture, which would be appropriate if the target system supports CometD. Failing that, the best option is an Apex trigger calling the external system directly and receiving back the external ID to update the Salesforce record. This would require custom development in Salesforce and would be more complex to implement and maintain, but it's the most robust option.

Inbound data options

We already established that the preceding integration process would allow the external system data to be exposed in Salesforce using Salesforce Connect. This is driven by the external system's customer identifier being added to the Contact record, which can then be used to power lookup relationships using external objects mapped to records in the third-party system.

What if we need data to *originate* in external systems, however?

Packt Gear has a robust in-store loyalty program, and they want to make sure that their customer service agents are aware of their loyal customers whether they signed up in store or online.

To support this, let's focus on two possible options, based on data volume.

The simplest option is to have your third-party system, in this case, the Packt Gear loyalty vendor, make REST API calls into Salesforce to trigger flows based on the B2C CRM sync pattern ingesting customers and returning a matching contact ID. This ensures that we don't introduce duplicates, because we can leverage the same matching rules we would use if the customer originated in the Salesforce ecosystem.

For larger data volumes, such as bulk loading the initial customer dataset, you'll need to review the Salesforce Platform Bulk API. This API supports hundreds of thousands or millions of records in a batch. The Bulk API has substantially higher overhead than other APIs, so it will take longer to update a small number of records than leveraging those APIs directly.

Review the Salesforce Platform API options in *Chapter 2, Supporting Your Customers with Service Cloud*.

When integrating external systems with Salesforce in an enterprise, you'll face the same challenges of data routing and consolidation faced within Salesforce but magnified. Here again, leveraging specialized integration middleware can help.

In the next section, we'll focus on incorporating external systems into the Packt Enterprises MuleSoft-driven approach developed earlier in the chapter.

External integrations through middleware

Adding non-Salesforce systems to the MuleSoft-based layered integration architecture described earlier in the chapter is fundamentally no different from how we incorporated the Salesforce Platform, Marketing Cloud, and B2C Commerce. We need to create a System API for each new system incorporated, which will be responsible for communicating with that system in a format and method it understands. We also need to review and agree upon routing rules for data requests moving through the Process API layer so that they can reach the appropriate systems.

The following figure extends the MuleSoft viewpoint to incorporate an MDM and ERP external system, without changing the integration approach:

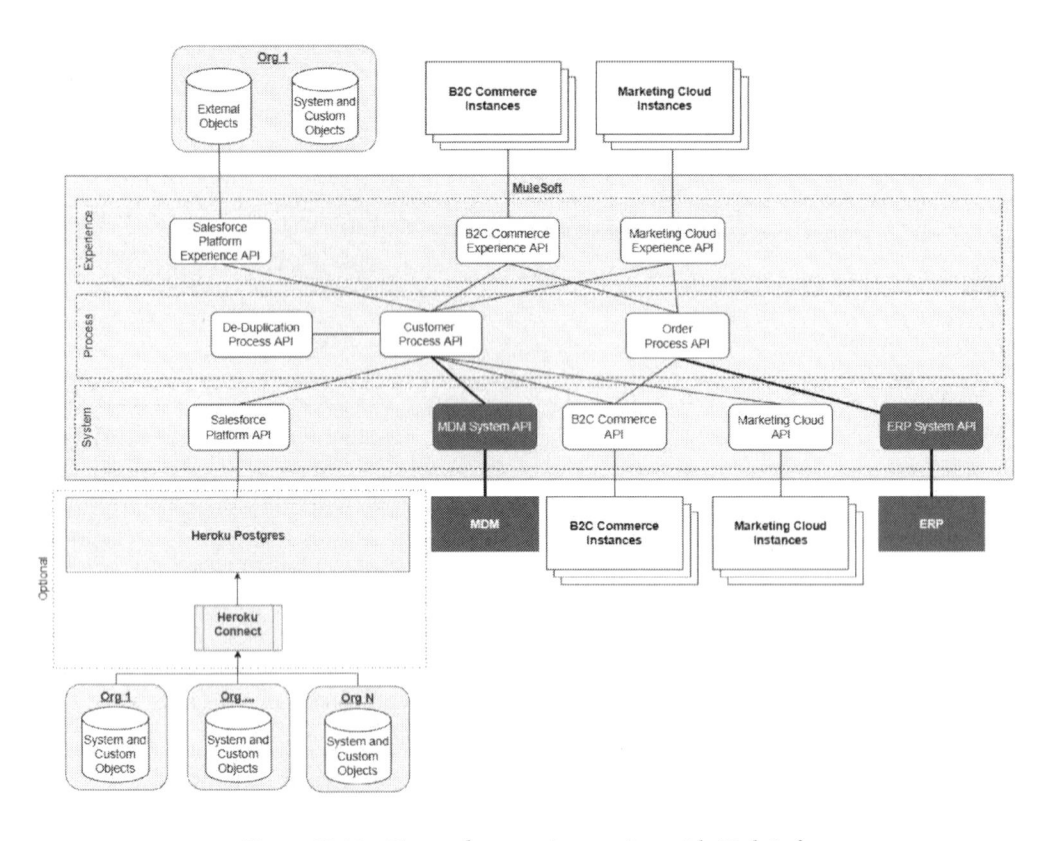

Figure 10.16 – External system integration with MuleSoft

In this example, the MDM system is connected to the Customer Process API. This allows it to both participate in retrieving customer data and to receive updates to customer data triggered by other systems. The ERP System API is also introduced and connected to the Order Process API to ensure that the ERP can receive orders placed and return order statuses.

In a real organization, there would be many more systems that participate in this type of integration layering architecture. Working through the use cases and participating systems is just a question of following the same process we outlined earlier with the customer data query example for each use case.

Now that we've covered implications for point-to-point and middleware approaches to integration in a larger enterprise, we're going to conclude this chapter by reviewing some options for monitoring your Salesforce B2C solution architecture as a whole.

Monitoring the solution

Each component product in a B2C solution architecture provides dedicated tools for monitoring performance, integrations, errors, and other aspects of the implementation.

In the Salesforce Platform, there are dedicated tools such as **Setup Audit Trail**, **Apex Exception Email**, **API Usage Notifications**, and **Lightning Usage App** reports available to monitor your solution. In B2C Commerce, there are dedicated log files for a variety of use cases, including error handling, integration monitoring, and platform usage concerns. You can also configure B2C Commerce to automatically notify an email address for job failures, quota violations, and replication issues. Marketing Cloud provides **Alert Manager**, which can be configured to alert users of errors or critical events in your marketing automation.

> **Important note**
> This is not intended to be an exhaustive list of monitoring and alert capabilities for all products. Please refer to product-specific documentation for additional information.

As a B2C solution architect, you don't need to design all aspects of platform-specific monitoring, but some consideration should be made of the overall monitoring solution.

If you find that new customers registering on the B2C Commerce storefront aren't showing up in Marketing Cloud as expected, how will you troubleshoot?

- B2C Commerce isn't notifying the Salesforce Platform.
- The Salesforce Platform service or flow is failing to receive the update.
- The Salesforce Platform customer record isn't created properly.
- Marketing Cloud Connect integration isn't synchronizing.

As you can see, there are many places where things could go wrong, and potentially multiple teams involved.

At a high level, there are a few options to consider for monitoring your overall solution: log aggregation, integration middleware, manual approaches, and custom solutions.

Log file aggregation

For B2C Commerce and the Salesforce Platform, log files can be a rich source of data. They can be mined and aggregated using tools such as Splunk, which provides a Salesforce-specific add-on, pulling all the data into a central location for easier review. This can help to identify service errors in B2C Commerce that may point to credentials issues or API limits in the Salesforce Platform that could be preventing calls.

Salesforce Marketing Cloud, however, doesn't provide comprehensive error log support so another solution is required there.

Integration middleware

Leveraging tools such as MuleSoft can provide significant benefits for monitoring an integrated solution. Having a consistent framework and dashboard for the health of the integration layer can quickly identify the component system for problems that appear to span multiple systems.

In the example we provided previously around customer data, if these integrations flowed through middleware, it would be trivial to see where the integration was breaking down and isolate the system that needs additional attention.

Manual approaches

For simpler solutions, a run-book approach with documented steps for researching cross-platform issues may be sufficient. Following the example provided earlier, documenting in one place where to check for issues with Marketing Cloud Connect, the Salesforce Platform flow, the connected app used by B2C Commerce, and the B2C Commerce service status dashboard would help determine the issue quickly.

With this approach, your support team needs to be familiar with and have access to the required components of each system in your B2C solution architecture. In the log file aggregation or integration middleware approaches, your monitoring team doesn't necessarily need to know the details of each component system. They can help to identify which system is the culprit and what's going wrong, then alert the relevant technical experts.

Custom solution

The final option for monitoring the health of your integrated B2C solution architecture is to build something custom. The Salesforce Platform provides many capabilities to monitor data events, security events, logs, and other capabilities. Issues with flows and Apex can trigger notifications to email addresses or calls to custom monitoring API endpoints. B2C Commerce service failures and other issues can also be integrated with custom code to dedicated monitoring services.

Marketing Cloud may require an engagement with Proactive Services, a paid service from Salesforce, to leverage Smart Alerts.

> **Further reading**
> Learn more about Proactive Services for Marketing Cloud here: `https://sforce.co/3CZ4zT6`.

With a custom solution, even one built using an industry-standard monitoring toolset, there will be custom code and configuration required in each component system. As with all customizations, you'll have to weigh the benefit of centralization and consistency against the implementation and long-term maintenance costs. There's no one right answer here.

Summary

In this chapter, we've taken the knowledge we learned so far in this book and extended it to enterprise use cases incorporating multiple realms, orgs, and BUs. These scenarios are complex and each one is unique. Use the approach outlined in this chapter, with the example of Packt Enterprises, to guide the overall architecture used in your own enterprise.

When working in larger enterprises, it is also more important than ever to coordinate closely with your enterprise and technical architect peers. The enterprise architect will have a bigger - picture view of the overall technology landscape and where your Salesforce ecosystem fits in. The technical architects will help guide the approach and options within each of the component systems, especially the complex integration options available within the Salesforce Platform.

At this point, you should understand the reasons an organization might have multiple instances in component systems and the decisions that drive how data is shared between them. You should also understand the implications of point-to-point connectors when they are used in an enterprise environment. Finally, you should have an approach in mind for integrating customer data into the larger enterprise ecosystem beyond Salesforce.

In the next chapter, we're going to move on to looking at the B2C Solution Architect certification exam specifically.

Questions

1. Why might you choose to have one Marketing Cloud BU for each B2C Commerce site or customer list?
2. What is the best integration point within the Salesforce ecosystem for external customer data systems?
3. True or false: leveraging separate BUs in Marketing Cloud securely separates data within a given Marketing Cloud instance ensuring separate organizational units in the same enterprise never mingle data.
4. When integrating multiple B2C Commerce instances with the same Salesforce Platform org, which data structure in B2C Commerce must have a unique ID to support B2C CRM sync?
5. What is one advantage of decorating the Salesforce Platform Contact record with unique identifiers for that customer used in external systems?

Further reading

- **Marketing Cloud Profile Center**: https://sforce.co/3ylP7O9
- **Marketing Cloud Connect Multi-Org FAQs**: https://sforce.co/3lnwFks
- **Platform Events Developer Guide**: https://sforce.co/3jIfast
- **Outbound Messaging Developer Guide**: https://sforce.co/3yDcH91
- **Change Data Capture Developer Guide**: https://sforce.co/3CysI2y
- **Apex Tigger Developer Guide**: https://sforce.co/37A9vPL
- **MuleSoft Accelerator for Retail**: https://bit.ly/3h8MgRf
- **Marketing Cloud Alert Manager**: https://sforce.co/2VYIwv9

Section 3 Salesforce-Certified B2C Solution Architect

This final section reviews the main topics of this book in the context of the Salesforce B2C Solution Architect certification, its prerequisite certifications, and optional supplemental commerce certifications. For each, we'll dissect the Salesforce exam guide, providing additional context around specific topics and references within this book and beyond to learn more. This section will help guide you through the process of using the information from the rest of this book to become a Salesforce-certified B2C solution architect.

Chapter 13, Commerce and Integration, provides additional information about B2C Commerce technical architecture beyond the scope of the B2C Solution Architect exam. If you're interested in going deeper on that platform or becoming a certified *B2C Commerce* architect, this chapter will help. We conclude by reviewing four realistic scenarios to demonstrate how to process requirements, evaluate potential solutions, and arrive at a design outcome in a way that serves both in the real world and in the context of certifications.

This section comprises the following chapters:

- *Chapter 11, Exam Preparation Tools and Techniques*
- *Chapter 12, Prerequisite Certifications*
- *Chapter 13, Commerce and Integration*
- *Chapter 14, Certification Scenarios*

11
Exam Preparation Tools and Techniques

The first 10 chapters of this book have been preparing you for this exam by covering the relevant subject matter as it relates to the topic areas. In this chapter, we're focusing less on the materials and more on the certification exam.

By this point, you should understand the capabilities, data model, and integration options of the Salesforce Platform and Service Cloud, B2C Commerce, and Marketing Cloud. You should also understand the capabilities and use cases for complementary products such as Order Management, Heroku, MuleSoft, Tableau, and Salesforce CDP.

Building on the understanding of each product, you should understand and be able to make informed decisions about the cross-cloud data model and integration architecture options between systems. You should also have a clear perspective regarding the target state customer data architecture and best practices.

Preparing for any certification exam requires carefully reviewing the relevant subject matter, an understanding of the composition of the exam, and the relevant professional experience. This chapter reviews the structure of the exam, the available resources for preparation, and provides recommendations for gaining hands-on experience where possible.

In this chapter, we're going to cover the following main topics:

- Exam structure
- Study materials
- Hands-on experience

By the end of this chapter, you should feel confident in your knowledge of the structure and weighting of the exam components. You should also know where to look, aside from this book, for additional study and preparation materials leading up to the exam. Finally, you should be able to start expanding your current work experience to include additional components.

Exam structure

As with any Salesforce certification exam, the first place you should stop in your preparation path should be the exam guide. This Salesforce resource is your roadmap to the certification and highlights the most important topics and their weighting in the exam, as well as their overall structure.

> **Further reading**
> You can find the *B2C Solution Architect Exam Guide* here: https://sforce.co/3xEgrFS.

In this section, we'll cover the essential components of the exam guide for completeness and provide additional commentary. When preparing for your certification, it's best to consult the exam guide directly since the contents will change over time.

The exam guide covers the following topics:

- About the Salesforce B2C Solution Architect Credential
- Audience Description: Salesforce Certified B2C Solution Architect
- Purpose of this Exam Guide
- About the Exam

- Recommended Training and References
- Exam Outline
- Exam Candidate Code of Conduct
- Maintaining Your Certification

In the following sections, we'll review the credential and target audience and then outline the most important topics. We will provide references to the relevant sections of this book that cover them.

Later, in the *Study materials* section, we'll provide a more comprehensive set of training and references.

Credential and target audience

Becoming a Salesforce-certified B2C solution architect is an impressive achievement that will require significant preparation. If you've read and understood the first 10 chapters in this book, then you're well on your way!

This certification is more than just a feather in your cap, however. A B2C solution architect is expected to play a leadership role by driving business value by articulating cross-cloud use cases, providing delivery leadership across different workstreams and processes, and owning the overall technical solution.

We'll break down the qualifications into non-technical skills and prerequisite certifications here. After that, we'll talk a little about the related certifications in the ecosystem.

Required non-technical skills

In *Chapter 6, Role of a Solution Architect*, we covered many non-technical skills that are needed to help you form and lead a delivery team, ask questions to shape business value, and drive the overall vision before moving into technology.

To practice these skills, you should look for opportunities for the following real-world experiences:

- Participate in or lead pre-sales conversations focused on business needs and the technical requirements to support them, especially across multiple Salesforce products.

- Create cross-cloud architecture artifacts such as system overview diagrams, integration architecture diagrams, data mapping documents, and process diagrams.

- Shape the cross-cloud delivery methodology by working closely with platform technical leadership, including DevOps, environment mapping, testing, and release planning.

Prerequisite certifications

To qualify for the B2C Solution Architect certification exam, you'll need the following prerequisite certifications:

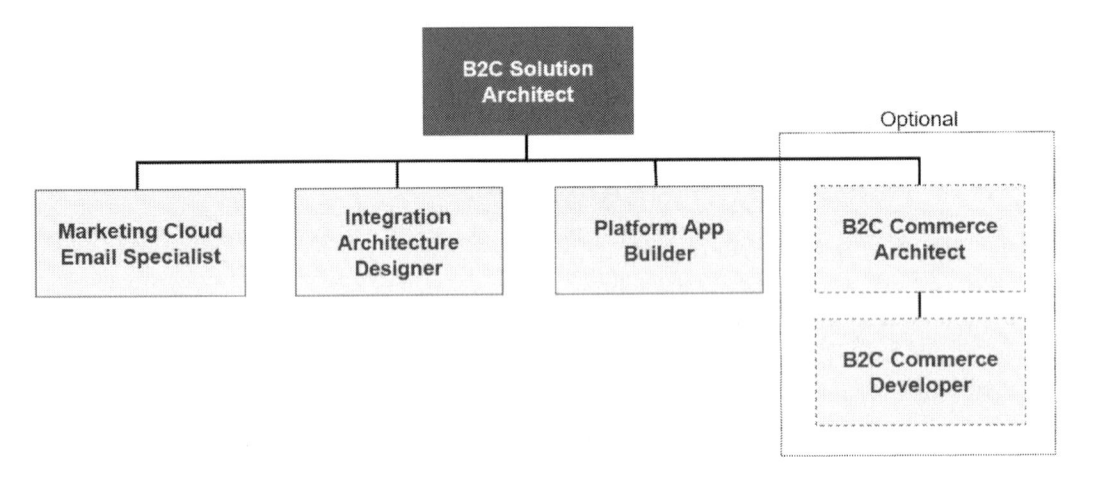

Figure 11.1 – Prerequisite certifications

As you can see, just qualifying for the B2C Solution Architect certification exam can be a substantial undertaking! The only three true prerequisite certifications currently are **Marketing Cloud Email Specialist**, **Integration Architecture Designer**, and **Platform App Builder**. We're going to cover each of these in *Chapter 12, Prerequisite Certifications*.

In this set, there are two certifications focused on the core Salesforce Platform and one focused on Marketing Cloud, but there are no B2C Commerce-related certifications. To fill this gap in your preparation, you may wish to look at the **B2C Commerce Architect** certification. The **B2C Commerce Developer** certification is a prerequisite for the B2C Commerce Architect certification, but it's probably more than you'll need as a solution architect. We'll spend some time on the B2C Commerce Architect topics in *Chapter 13, Commerce and Integration*.

Related certifications

Salesforce offers several different certifications targeted to the architect role. The architect certifications from Salesforce are detailed here: https://sforce.co/3CWoqSV.

In addition to the B2C Solution Architect, there is also a **B2B Solution Architect** certification. Although this certification is outside the scope of this book, it's helpful to be aware of it. The B2B Solution Architect certification serves a similar role around designing solutions that meet the needs of business-to-business-focused organizations on Salesforce. Often, but not always, these solutions will include the B2B Commerce product.

The prerequisite certifications for the B2B Solution Architect certification are as follows:

- Data Architecture and Management Designer
- Sharing and Visibility Designer
- Platform Developer 1
- Platform App Builder

Each of these certifications is a respectable undertaking on its own!

If you're familiar with these certifications, one thing you may notice is that these are all Salesforce Platform-related certifications. Where the B2C Solution Architect certification is focused primarily on designing integrated solutions across B2C Commerce, Marketing Cloud, and the Salesforce Platform, the B2B Solution Architect certification is primarily focused on the Salesforce Platform.

Finally, I need to mention the pinnacle certification in the Salesforce ecosystem, the mighty **Certified Technical Architect (CTA)**.

Few people in the world qualify for, let alone achieve, this certification. It is the result of years of study and hands-on experience. It also requires two prerequisite architecture certifications, **Application Architect** and **System Architect**, each of which has four prerequisite certifications.

While the CTA certification unquestionably represents the peak of Salesforce Platform expertise, it is not focused on any of the other Salesforce products outside of the core platform. This means that Marketing Cloud and B2C Commerce are not in the scope of this achievement, so the B2C Solution Architect certification, as well as **B2C Commerce Architect**, is very much complementary.

Now that you know a bit more about the landscape, let's talk about the exam topics and how they're weighted.

Topic outline and weighting

Part of preparing for any Salesforce certification is reviewing the exam topics and evaluating your knowledge and experience against them. The exam has 60 scored questions and 4 unscored questions, which are not differentiated during the exam. You need to score at least 63% to pass (at the time of writing, see the exam guide the most current passing score).

According to the exam guide, the topics and their weights are as follows:

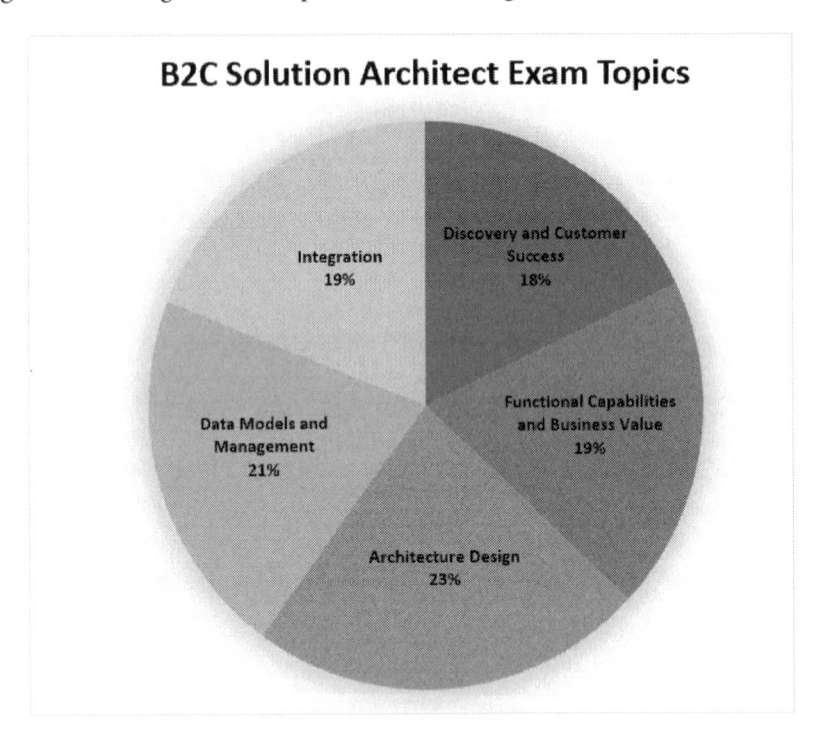

Figure 11.2 – Exam topic weighting

In many cases, you'll find that Salesforce certification exams place unequal weight on various topics, but that's not the case here. Each of the five component topics is of roughly equal weight in the exam.

What's more, *none of the topics are technology- or product-specific.*

Each section requires having an understanding of each of the core technologies and how they interact in areas such as integration, data models and management, architectural design, functional capabilities and business value, and discovery and customer success. This means that the first five chapters of this book are important as they establish the product-level understanding of the technology landscape.

The **Discovery and Customer Success** and **Functional Capabilities and Business Value** topics were primarily addressed in *Chapter 6, Role of Solution Architect*, and *Chapter 9, Supporting Key Business Scenarios*.

These topic areas focus on facilitating successful discovery conversations, asking the right questions, documenting requirements, and creating technical designs.

These chapters, in conjunction with the first five product chapters, also cover how to evaluate business requirements against the technical capabilities of Salesforce products to help shape a cross-cloud solution. Given a set of requirements, you should be able to ask questions to help anchor the solution, determine the required component products and systems of record for critical cross-cloud data models, and articulate the benefits of an approach.

Based on the solution outline, you'll also need to be able to produce the relevant documentation for describing the overall solution, including a system overview diagram, integration specification, data mapping diagrams, and sequence diagrams.

Being able to identify and articulate the capabilities that are unlocked by the solution is also expected. What can an organization do with a unified B2C solution architecture that is not possible with the component products working in isolation?

Chapter 9, Supporting Key Business Scenarios, covered the Salesforce B2C solution kits for various common integration scenarios, as well as how to tailor them for unique scenarios. This is an excellent starting point for building on the foundation of the core product capabilities.

The **Integration** and **Architecture Design** topics were primarily addressed in *Chapter 7, Integration Architecture Options*. Here, we will expand upon the business processes, use case-driven design, and data modeling concepts. Data security and residency requirements are addressed in these chapters as are customer identity concerns throughout the product set and the customer journey.

Strategies for incorporating external customer data sources and third-party systems were outlined in *Chapter 10, Enterprise Integration Strategies*.

The **Data Models and Management** topics were primarily addressed in *Chapter 8, Creating a 360° View of the Customer*. This section is primarily concerned with understanding the data models in each component system and how they can be extended. This also includes understanding how each system's data objects relate to the data objects in other systems, especially as it relates to customer data.

Chapter 10, *Enterprise Integration Strategies*, added additional context appropriate for larger enterprises to all topics, especially **Integration**, **Data Models and Management**, and **Architecture Design**.

If there's an area you feel you need to pay more attention to, review that chapter and the links for further reading within. After you've taken the B2C Solution Architect certification exam, you'll be given a section-by-section breakdown of how you did.

If you don't pass on the first try, don't despair! Identify the sections you had a hard time with and review the relevant material again, focusing on any areas that weren't clear the first time.

Beyond this book, there is a wealth of resources available for further study. We'll cover the primary ones in the next section.

Study materials

In such a quickly evolving space, it can be difficult to know where to start.

The Salesforce materials are mostly divided into three categories: guidebooks, Trailhead, and **Partner Learning Camp** (**PLC**). We'll provide some examples of each in the following sections.

Solution architecture guidebooks

The *Solution Architect Pocket Guide* is a great resource for both the B2C Solution Architect and B2B Solution Architect certifications. This ever-evolving Quip document contains an overview of each certification, how they fit into the Salesforce ecosystem, and where to find the most up-to-date training materials from Salesforce.

> **Further reading**
>
> You can review the *Solution Architect Pocket Guide* here: `https://bit.ly/3jU3yCL`.
>
> In a similar vein, *B2C Solution Architect Resources* is a more focused and comprehensive Quip document covering the core resources available regarding the B2C Solution Architect certification: `https://bit.ly/3xTALUd`.

Finally, *Customer 360 Guide for Retail* provides a roadmap of how to design and deliver comprehensive solutions across the Salesforce Customer 360 ecosystem, including the B2C Solution Architect certification. In this guide, the most relevant section for the B2C Solution Architect certification is the section called *Deliver Solutions*.

> **Further reading**
> You can find *Customer 360 Guide for Retail* here: `https://bit.ly/3e80lxo`.

Trailhead resources

In addition to the exam guide, the following Trailmixes provide a wealth of materials for reviewing and focusing on topics that need more attention:

- *Prepare for the Salesforce B2C Solution Architect Credential*: `https://sforce.co/2UjJlOg`
- *Study for the B2C Solution Architect Certification*: `https://sforce.co/3xKIIdY`

> **Further reading**
> In addition, for those who don't have access to PLC, there is an index of freely available courses on the B2C Solution Architect certification provided in Trailhead here: `https://sforce.co/3g18F2X`.

> **Tip**
> If you are a Salesforce partner, you should take the courses through PLC to ensure you and your organization receive credit for the training. Using the links from Trailhead exposes the same material but does not track your learning. These courses also do not provide Trailhead points or badges.

For the employees of a Salesforce partner organization, PLC provides the most structured training for the B2C Solution Architect exam.

Partner Learning Camp

Salesforce's **PLC** includes a full curriculum dedicated to the B2C Solution Architect exam. At the time of writing, this includes 26 courses across a variety of topic areas, but this is an ever-evolving resource.

This book covers most of the topics in the PLC curriculum, so this is a great way to reinforce learning and review. As new materials are released, PLC will also provide a helpful resource for what's new in the B2C solution architecture space.

> **Important note**
> Some of the content in this book presents a more current viewpoint than the subject matter in PLC, which has become a bit out of date. Over time, this situation is likely to reverse since PLC will continue to be updated after this book is published. When you find discrepancies, take the time to review the relevant product documentation to determine which is the most current resource.

> **Further reading**
> If you're an employee of a Salesforce partner organization, you can find the B2C solution architecture curriculum here: `https://sforce.co/31XIJcj`.
>
> If you don't have access to PLC, you can review most of the same courses in Trailhead here: `https://sforce.co/3g18F2X`.

Despite the wealth of training materials, there's no substitute for hands-on experience with these topics. In the next section, we'll provide some tips for broadening your viewpoint on your projects.

Hands-on experience

If you're looking to move into the B2C solution architecture space, there's a good chance you're already operating as a platform technical architect in either Salesforce Platform/Service Cloud, B2C Commerce, or Marketing Cloud. If that's you, you know a lot about one product, maybe a little about others, and you're looking to expand that perspective. This is essentially a bottom-up approach to the B2C solution architecture.

Another possibility, the top-down approach, is that you're more of an enterprise architect looking to learn more about the Salesforce ecosystem in general and the B2C solution architecture space specifically.

The following diagram, originally shown in *Chapter 6, Role of a Solution Architect*, represents these two approaches to the B2C solution architecture:

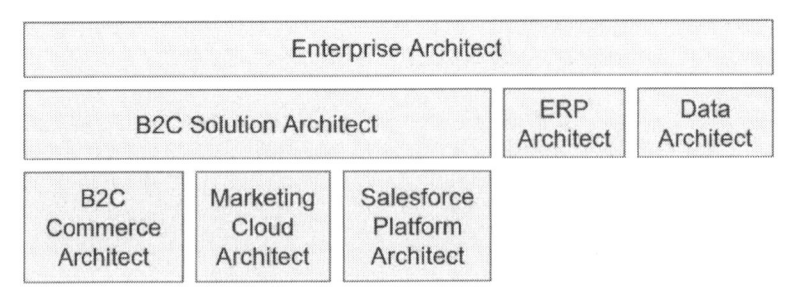

Figure 11.3 – Types of architects

Although it's certainly possible for other types of architects, such as **ERP** or **Data Architects** in this diagram, to move into the B2C solution architecture, you will need to learn more.

In the following sections, we'll focus on guidance for either broadening your perspective as a platform technical architect or going deeper as an enterprise architect, followed by some general recommendations for moving into the space from another area altogether.

Broadening your perspective

As a platform-specific technical architect, you're accustomed to knowing everything there is to know about a particular piece of a solution. You've designed integrations, but only from one perspective. You've also designed complex customizations that sit entirely within one product.

In the following diagram, you can see the areas of responsibility for each type of architect in an integrated solution:

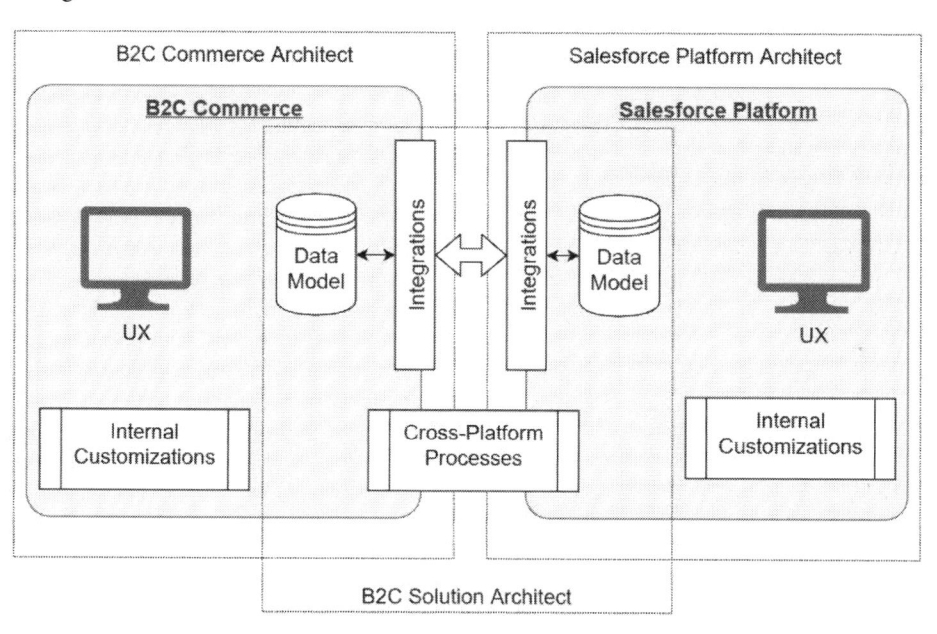

Figure 11.4 – Technical and solution architect overlap

As you can see, there are lots of overlapping areas where the solution and technical architects must collaborate on a solution. If you're working as a platform-specific technical architect, this is a great opportunity to gain broader experience!

Instead of focusing solely on the data modeling needs of a single product, look at how that data model translates into an integration (file-based or API), and how those integrations feed into the data model that's used by another platform. Take some time to research and understand the way data is stored, volume constraints, options for extending the data model, the available data types, and the available validation rules.

By starting from a place of familiarity and comfort, you can continue to add value to your projects while starting to learn more about related areas. You won't be an expert, and you don't need to be, but you can start by reviewing the documentation that's been created by other architects and then volunteer to work on data mapping or integration specifications yourself.

For examples of the types of documentation that fall into the solution architecture space, review *Chapter 6, Role of a Solution Architect*.

Reviewing the product-specific chapters in the first part of this book is a great way to learn more about the features and functionality that are the most relevant for a solution architecture. Gradually, as you become more comfortable working across product boundaries and collaborating with others, you can start to create specs for review and oversee aspects of a project until you're ready to fly solo!

Gaining product-specific knowledge

If your background is in the enterprise architecture space, you must be familiar with many of the important concepts of solution architecture. Designing integrations, data models, system overview diagrams, and dependency mapping will all feel like second nature. That's a great start!

The area of focus for an enterprise architect looking to learn more about B2C solution architecture in the Salesforce space will be product-specific knowledge. Specifically, you'll want to review the reference materials Salesforce provides and the contents of this book, related to how to integrate Salesforce products to create a complete view of the customer. Salesforce has done a lot of work to ensure there's a clear and consistent viewpoint on this topic, so understanding and following that beats reinventing the wheel every time!

To learn about product knowledge, the hub of the B2C solution architecture is the Salesforce Platform, and that's where you should focus the lion's share of your time and attention. Most of Salesforce's products are built on top of the Salesforce Platform, including the flagship Sales Cloud and Service Cloud products. Learning enough about B2C Commerce and Marketing Cloud to understand how they all tie together should also be a priority.

Getting started with Salesforce

If you're new to Salesforce *and* architecture, make no mistake, there's a lot to learn!

You essentially have two options: top-down or bottom-up. You can start from the overall architecture perspective, essentially learning enough about the enterprise architecture and integration to understand how it all comes together, or you can start by learning about one product at a time. I'd recommend the second option.

Most consulting firms, project teams, and internal capabilities are organized around product boundaries. You're going to have an easier time learning enough about Marketing Cloud, B2C Commerce, or Service Cloud to be valuable on a project. Then, you can grow your role from there rather than trying to gain real-world experience as an architect without that background.

If your goal is the B2C solution architecture, start with the Salesforce Platform and Service Cloud. This is the hub of the customer data model and the most complex space for integrations and capabilities. From there, layering in B2C Commerce knowledge and Marketing Cloud will be comparatively easy, and you can rely on platform-specific technical architects for the details of each.

Regardless of your approach, Trailhead is going to be your best resource. There are countless modules and trails available in Trailhead on each of the topics covered in this book. When you've gotten the basics down, return to this book and review the solution architecture details, as well as the study materials referenced earlier in this chapter and the *Further reading* notes.

There's so much to learn that it can be overwhelming. Create a cadence of learning or make a game of it. One new Trailhead badge a day, a chapter a week, two PLC courses each weekend, whatever works for you.

Personally, my goal is to attain three new certifications per year. For me, that's a sustainable pace that allows me time to live my life and meet the expectations of my day job. Whatever goal and cadence work for you, don't be discouraged – continue to reassess your timeline and move forward!

Summary

In this chapter, we covered the content and structure of the B2C Solution Architect exam, as well as the target audience. We also reviewed where you can find further study materials beyond this book to improve your knowledge of the B2C solution architecture space.

At this point, you should know what to expect when you sit the B2C Solution Architect exam. For each of the topic areas, you know which chapters of this book provide additional information and where to look for the latest documentation and Salesforce training materials beyond this book.

You should also know how to begin broadening or deepening your perspective as an architect coming from either a technical architecture or enterprise architecture background. With all of this, you can round out your preparation for the exam or just grow your capabilities within your organization or team.

In the next chapter, we'll focus on the three prerequisite certifications for any B2C solution architect.

Questions

1. What should be your first step when preparing for any Salesforce credential so that you can understand the overall structure of the exam?
2. What are the three prerequisite certifications for any B2C solution architect?
3. Where should you continue your B2C solution architect learning journey after reading this book?
4. How might you expand your perspective as a platform-specific technical architect looking to gain hands-on experience as a solution architect?

12
Prerequisite Certifications

The Salesforce Certified B2C Solution Architect exam has three prerequisite certifications: **Marketing Cloud Email Specialist**, **Platform App Builder**, and **Integration Architecture Designer**.

These certifications are related to Salesforce Platform and Marketing Cloud. As we know from this book, B2C Commerce is also a major component of the B2C Solution Architect exam but is not represented in the prerequisite certifications. *Chapter 13, Commerce and Integration*, will provide some recommendations and tips for addressing the B2C Commerce portion of your exam preparation.

In this chapter, we'll take a high-level look at each of the three prerequisite certifications, their subject matter, and where to learn more about them to help you qualify for the B2C Solution Architect exam. Although preparation for these three independent exams is outside the scope of this book, it's important to understand the context they set for the B2C Solution Architect exam.

As we discussed in *Chapter 11, Exam Preparation Tools and Techniques*, preparing for any Salesforce certification requires reviewing the exam guide and the topic weighting, creating a study plan, and focusing on gaps. We'll use this same approach when reviewing the prerequisite certifications in this chapter.

None of the prerequisite exams for B2C Solution Architect have other prerequisites, and none are dependent on each other. Because of that, you can take them in any order, but I'd recommend the order in which they're presented in this chapter. This allows you to focus on Marketing Cloud initially and get one of the more straightforward certifications completed early, before moving on to the two Salesforce Platform-focused certifications.

Between Platform App Builder and Integration Architecture Designer, the former is focused primarily on declarative customization and automation where the latter is focused on integration capabilities. For most audiences, the context provided by Platform App Builder will be helpful in Integration Architecture Designer, which might otherwise feel overly technical and difficult to grasp.

In this chapter, we're going to cover the following main topics:

- Marketing Cloud Email Specialist exam overview
- Platform App Builder exam overview
- Integration Architecture Designer exam overview

By the end of this chapter, you should understand the subject matter of the prerequisite certifications, their role in your preparation for the B2C Solution Architect exam, and where you can continue your journey.

Marketing Cloud Email Specialist exam overview

The **Marketing Cloud Email Specialist** certification is focused primarily on the Marketing Cloud Email Studio, Content Builder, and Journey Builder components of the core messaging and journeys product. Contextual knowledge of other Marketing Cloud components is also helpful. This certification is particularly helpful in understanding the role of Marketing Cloud email-based communications in the overall B2C Solution Architecture.

> **Further reading**
>
> The Marketing Cloud Email Specialist Exam Guide is here: `https://sforce.co/3jcA5VA`.

In the following sections, we'll cover the exam outline topics and study materials.

Marketing Cloud Email Specialist topic overview

This section reviews the topics currently included in the Marketing Cloud Email Specialist exam with recommendations for further learning about each. As always, you should review the exam guide for the latest version of this information, as it is subject to change.

The current topics and their weighting according to the exam guide are shown in the following figure:

Marketing Cloud Email Specialist Exam Topics

- Email Marketing Best Practices 16%
- Email Message Design 14%
- Content Creation and Delivery 19%
- Marketing Automations 21%
- Subscriber and Data Management 30%

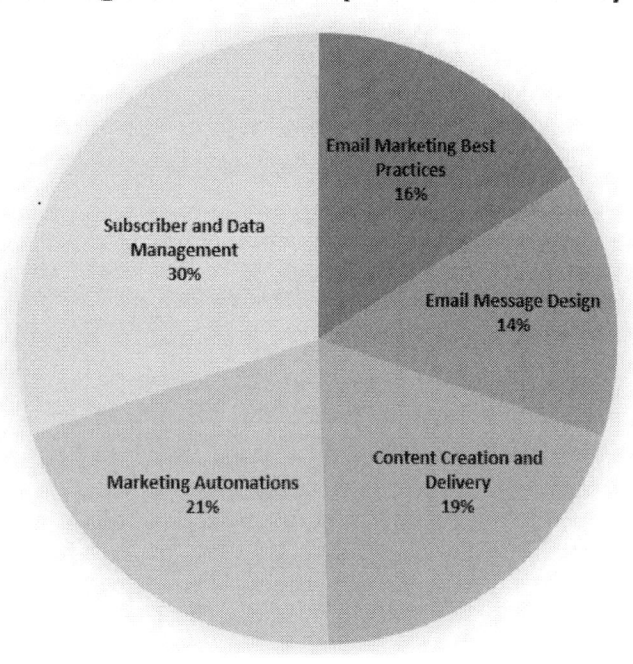

Figure 12.1 – Marketing Cloud Email Specialist exam topics

Clearly, some topics, such as **subscriber and data management (30%)**, are given much more weight than others, such as **email message design (14%)**. Review the current weightings and topics when deciding where to focus your study time, especially if you have noticeable gaps. If you take a Salesforce practice test or take and fail an exam, you'll receive your score *per section*, which can be deceptive, as not all sections are equally weighted.

Many, but not all, of the topics in this certification are covered in *Chapter 4, Engaging Customers with Marketing Cloud*. Use the topic outline and study materials to build upon the knowledge gained in this book and focus on Marketing Cloud in particular.

For each of these topic areas in the exam, the following sections provide additional details.

Email marketing best practices

This section is focused primarily on creating effective and legally compliant email message campaigns that maintain deliverability and efficacy. It also covers the basics of Marketing Cloud messaging and journeys and Email Studio. A significant amount of the focus is on compliance with legislation such as **CAN-SPAM**, **GDPR**, and **CCPA** within Marketing Cloud.

> **Tip**
> Although this certification is only focused on Marketing Cloud, many of the compliance topics are applicable more broadly in a B2C solution architecture. As you're preparing, think about how this would impact an integrated B2C solution.

Deliverability, as covered in this section of the exam, focuses on aspects of email sends that may trigger recipient spam detection flags. This also covers the difference between email hard bounces, which occur when the recipient address doesn't exist, and soft bounces, which can occur based on transient states, such as a full email box.

Email message design

Email message design focuses specifically on the design of email communications rather than on the larger concepts around campaigns and subscriber growth strategies. To be successful in this section, you'll need to understand the tools that are available in Marketing Cloud for designing emails and their contents.

Marketing Cloud emails are intended to be responsive, displaying appropriately on a variety of devices. For this section, also be sure you understand which aspects of an email can be A/B tested as well as techniques for using **A/B testing** to improve email open rates and click-through rates.

> **Tip**
> A/B testing is a technique for testing multiple versions of an email subject line or content area from the name, send time, or preheader to optimize the open rate or click-through rate.

You should also review topics related to Distributed Marketing, a way of powering customizable branded emails from Sales Cloud using Marketing Cloud, and with overall Marketing Cloud administrative tasks.

Content creation and delivery

Creating reusable email content components and ensuring that content included in emails is relevant for the recipient is the primary focus of this section. Be familiar with Marketing Cloud Content Builder and how that can be used to prepare assets for use within Email Studio.

Understanding the declarative and programmatic ways that email can be personalized for the recipient at send time is also important. This section is also a good opportunity to reflect on how an integrated B2C solution would impact the types of emails you're sending and the sources of content you're providing. Leveraging product and content data feeds from B2C Commerce in your marketing and transactional emails can be a great way to reinforce a consistent brand experience across touchpoints.

Marketing automation

The most important tool in the marketing automation toolbox is **Journey Builder**. Spend some time in your preparation getting familiar with Journey Builder and its capabilities. How do customers enter journeys, how do they move through journeys that include decision splits, and how and when do they exit journeys? You should also be aware of audience segmentation capabilities that are native to Marketing Cloud (additional tools such as Salesforce CDP are not within the scope of this certification).

As you think about automation in the marketing space, again reflect on the way that this will change with the introduction of something like Marketing Cloud Connect integrating the user, lead, or contact records from Salesforce Platform. How might customer service touchpoints, such as open cases, impact the way you move customers through a post-purchase journey and the types of content you choose to share with them?

Subscriber and data management

Marketing Cloud has several different ways of storing structured data, all of which you should be familiar with for the Marketing Cloud Email Specialist certification. Most importantly, learn the difference between lists and data extensions, as well as the different types of data extensions used in Marketing Cloud.

This section is also where you'll want to review topics related to **Automation Studio** and how that can be leveraged to trigger imports based on files delivered to Marketing Cloud's integrated SFTP server or to schedule data exports. Automation Studio can also be used to schedule queries using *SQL* to create snapshot views of contacts or subscribers that meet a particular query for automation purposes.

Other tools for subscriber and data management you can expect questions around include exclusion lists, suppression lists, and publication lists. Each of these tools is used to manage who receives what communications and how your customers can choose to opt out of communications, but they all serve different purposes.

> **Further reading**
>
> Read more about exclusion lists here: `https://sforce.co/3gDYSA1`.
>
> Read more about suppression lists here: `https://sforce.co/3kuhvrE`.
>
> Read more about publication lists here: `https://sforce.co/3sUTgGA`.

Using these tools together to get data in and out of Marketing Cloud, store it appropriately, and leverage it for your marketing strategies is a major component of this certification.

Tracking and reporting

Finally, a Marketing Cloud Email Specialist should understand how to measure the efficacy of an email send, journey, or overall campaign. This means knowing the available metrics in Marketing Cloud, such as deliverability, open rates, and click-through rates. You should know where to find this information and how to review the results.

For journeys, you should understand how to optimize and analyze active journeys based on customer behavior. For reports, understand how to create custom reports and what data is available to include. You should also know how permissions are managed on reports and how reports can be generated and retrieved from Marketing Cloud using automation and SFTP capabilities.

> **Further reading**
>
> Learn more about reporting in Marketing Cloud in the Salesforce *Get Started with Reports* document here: `https://sforce.co/2WoufYV`.

Based on your comfort level in each of these areas, review the study materials referenced in the following section of this book to focus on areas where you need improvement.

Marketing Cloud Email Specialist study materials

Within this book, the bulk of the Marketing Cloud topics are covered in *Chapter 4, Engaging Customers with Marketing Cloud*. This chapter covers much of what you'll need to know in terms of integrations, data models, and automation. Where this chapter falls short in terms of the Marketing Cloud Email Specialist exam is primarily around the Marketing Cloud content, best practices, and email creation capabilities.

> **Further reading**
>
> The most comprehensive preparation guide focused on this exam is the Trailhead *Prepare for your Marketing Cloud Email Specialist Credential* trailmix here: `https://sforce.co/3jlbjCT`.

This includes much of what you'll need to review as part of your preparation, and it's organized to follow the exam guide topics outline in the previous section of this book. You can use this structure to further focus on topic areas.

> **Tip**
>
> Go through everything in the trailmix, and then return and review the further reading provided in any sections where you need additional detail.

If you have access to Partner Learning Camp, the *Get Started on the Marketing Cloud Email Specialist Fast Path to Certification* curriculum includes great resources focused on this certification as well: `https://sforce.co/3DCPdnF`.

Unfortunately, unlike with Salesforce Platform, it is not possible to get access to a live Marketing Cloud environment to learn on as an individual. If you're a member of a Salesforce partner organization or a current Marketing Cloud customer, you may have access to an instance, but it's likely to be a shared production instance used by others.

The lack of test environments in Marketing Cloud requires particular care during training. Be aware of conventions that your organization has around the naming of test data extensions, journeys, triggers, and other created artifacts. If you're training without access to an environment, some Salesforce Trails provide access to a simulated environment that can help give you a sense of the look and feel of a real Marketing Cloud environment.

In the next section, we'll move on to the first Salesforce Platform-focused prerequisite certification: **Platform App Builder**.

Platform App Builder exam overview

The **Platform App Builder** certification covers the declarative customization capabilities of the Salesforce Platform as well as the fundamentals of Salesforce. This certification is geared toward candidates who have some experience or familiarity with Salesforce Platform and understand basics such as license types, data storage fundamentals, and platform capabilities.

The Platform App Builder certification overlaps with the **Salesforce Certified Administrator** and **Platform Developer I** certifications. If you have experience with either or both, it will certainly help with the concepts covered by Platform App Builder (although neither is required). The administrator certification focuses more on topics related to user management, operations, and the day-to-day support of a Salesforce org. The Platform Developer I certification covers programmatic customization, which is not within the scope of the Platform App Builder certification.

> **Further reading**
> The Platform App Builder Exam Guide is here: `https://sforce.co/3DmlVtj`.

In the following sections, we'll cover the exam outline topics and study materials.

Platform App Builder topic overview

This section reviews the Platform App Builder exam topics, providing context and recommendations for further reading on each. As always, you should review the exam guide for the most current version of this information, as it is subject to change.

The current topics and their weighting according to the exam guide are shown in the following figure:

Platform App Builder Exam Topics

- App Deployment 10%
- Salesforce Fundamentals 23%
- Data Modeling and Management 22%
- Business Logic and Process Automation 28%
- User Interface 17%

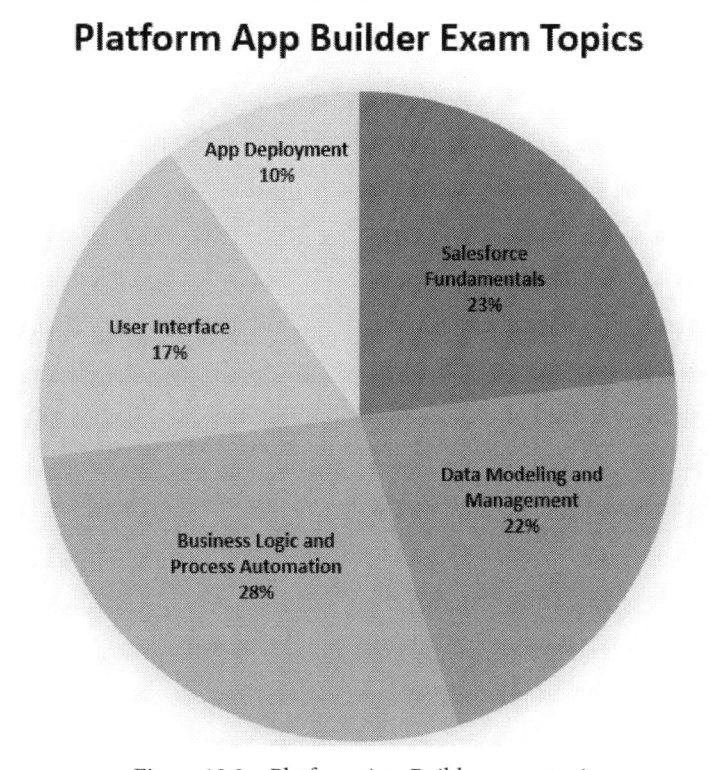

Figure 12.2 – Platform App Builder exam topics

The most important topics on this exam, together constituting almost half of the overall content, are **business logic and process automation** as well as **data modeling and management**. Be sure you're rock solid on these two before attempting this certification. After that, review the current weightings and topics when deciding where to focus your study time, especially if you have noticeable gaps. If you take a Salesforce practice test or take and fail an exam, you'll receive your score *per section*. Use that to guide your study approach as you prepare for the next attempt!

Most of the topics from this certification are covered in *Chapter 1*, *Demystifying Salesforce, Customer 360, and Digital 360*. Many of the topics on the exam, however, are not in the scope of this book and will require additional study and focused preparation to master.

> **Tip**
> Leverage the resources in the *Platform App Builder study materials* section later in this chapter to learn more about topics not covered in this book.

For each of these topic areas on the exam, the following sections provide additional details.

Salesforce fundamentals

The Salesforce fundamentals topics are likely not new if you have some experience already with Salesforce. These cover core topics required for a variety of roles, including developers, administrators, and architects. You should know what can be accomplished in Salesforce using declarative customization and when you'll need to turn to programmatic customization (which is not within the scope of this book).

This section also covers core concepts around security, related to object, record, and field access. You'll also need to understand how to securely share access to records within an organization, using hierarchies, sharing rules, and manual sharing. Capabilities of Salesforce Platform related to identity management, including SSO, where Salesforce is either the identity provider or where Salesforce is using an external identity provider, are also relevant here.

Other topics in the general category of Salesforce fundamentals include the different types of applications available through AppExchange to enhance your Salesforce org, basics around reports, report types, and dashboards, as well as the use cases and customization capabilities of Chatter.

The Salesforce mobile app is also an important topic. This covers the native behavior of the mobile app for various concepts, such as quick actions, the mobile app home page, and page layouts. It also covers customization specific to the mobile app, although only declarative customization.

Data modeling and management

Data modeling and management is one of the two anchor topics for this exam, along with business logic and process automation. Review any topics related to standard and custom objects, the various types of relationships you can create between objects, and the creation and administration of picklists, including dependent picklists.

Although this certification is not specific to Sales Cloud or Service Cloud, you should understand the common Salesforce objects and how they relate to each other. This includes Accounts, Contacts, Leads, Opportunities, Users, Cases, Campaigns, Activities, and Orders.

> **Important note**
> There are far more standard objects in Salesforce Platform than those listed previously; these are just some of the core objects that have special relationships with each other, and which are leveraged in just about every Salesforce Platform-based product.

In addition to considerations around designing a new data model based on requirements, be sure to understand the implications of making changes to an existing model. This includes things such as adding or removing picklist values or changing field types for existing datasets.

Business logic and process automation

Business logic and process automation is the second anchor topic of the exam. Salesforce provides a wealth of methods for automating business processes. At the most basic level, using formula fields and roll-up summary fields allows you to avoid manual calculations when representing data available on the same or related records. Knowing how formula and roll-up summary fields can traverse object relationships, including master-detail or lookup relationships, is important when evaluating these tools as solutions for a given use case.

Data quality can be maintained with validation rules on objects and by using required fields or external IDs to require values or uniqueness on record fields. To incorporate human validation into business workflows, review how to leverage approval processes, which objects they are supported for, and the different approval options available.

More complex declarative automation is accomplished primarily with workflows, Flow Builder, and Process Builder. Knowing the capabilities of each of these tools and the appropriate use cases for each is a significant component of the Platform App Builder certification. As a rule, always choose the simplest tool for the job. With Flow Builder in particular, make sure you know the different types of flows that can be created, including screen flows and auto-launched flows.

User interface

Salesforce Platform supports user interface customization through the creation and customization of apps, tabs within those apps, and the page layouts used to render those tabs. Knowing how to create and customize each and control who has access to them will help you succeed in the user interface portion of the exam.

In addition to these elements, know how to create and manage custom buttons, links, and actions, as well as the capabilities and use cases for each. Given a requirement, determine how it can most efficiently be accomplished with minimal complexity and maintenance cost. This includes knowing how to add buttons, links, and actions to record pages and global quick actions to trigger automation, such as screen flows.

While programmatic customization is not in the scope of this exam, being able to recognize when a situation requires programmatic customization is. You should know the capabilities of declarative user interface customization and automation, and you should be able to identify situations that call for more complex solutions.

App deployment

The final section of the Platform App Builder exam is the **app deployment** section, which covers all aspects of the development lifecycle in Salesforce and a variety of options for moving changes through to production. You should be able to sketch out an application development lifecycle in Salesforce using *sandboxes* for development, integration, and testing before moving to production.

For Salesforce environments, you should also be familiar with the different Salesforce sandboxes, including Developer sandboxes, Developer Pro sandboxes, Partial Copy sandboxes, and Full Copy sandboxes. Each instance supports progressively more system resources and a larger copy of the production dataset, building up to a full copy of production in the Full Copy sandbox. Salesforce application development lifecycles typically have designated roles for each.

When deploying changes with Salesforce, there are a few different models, including the use of change sets and package deployment using *managed and unmanaged packages*. For this exam, you should know the use cases, capabilities, limitations, and best practices of each. You don't need to know the details of the Salesforce CLI, commonly called **SFDX**, nor do you need to understand code-level details.

After reviewing each of these sections, hopefully you'll have a good idea of where you are most confident and where you might need to spend a bit more time preparing. The next section provides resources for further preparing for the Platform App Builder certification.

Platform App Builder study materials

The bulk of the content that's relevant for this certification is covered in *Chapter 1, Demystifying Salesforce, Customer 360, and Digital 360*. This chapter is primarily written with the B2C Solution Architecture point of view, so it goes a bit deeper on some topics, such as other Salesforce ecosystem products, than you'll need for the Platform App Builder certification. For additional information on the Salesforce data model, which will also apply to the Platform App Builder certification, review *Chapter 2, Supporting Your Customers with Service Cloud*.

> **Further reading**
>
> For topics not covered in this book, the most comprehensive preparation guide focused on this exam is the Trailhead *Prepare for Your Salesforce Platform App Builder Credential* trailmix here: `https://sforce.co/3gIKOFJ`.

This includes much of what you'll need to review as part of your preparation, and it's organized to follow the exam guide topics outline in the previous section of this book. You can use this structure to further focus on topic areas. Be sure to take advantage of the free Trailhead instances or create a developer instance to further explore these topics in a live Salesforce org that's just for your use.

> **Tip**
>
> Go through everything in the trailmix, and then return and review the *Further reading* provided in any sections where you need additional detail.

One note, from personal experience – **Trailhead superbadges** are a great way to develop experience solving problems in a real organization without step-by-step instructions. They encourage you to play and explore, which can help reinforce learning. Unfortunately, the solutions often require very specific approaches that aren't always obvious. Very often, you can solve problems in multiple ways in Salesforce. Don't be discouraged if you're not getting the *right* answer on a superbadge. Focus on the experience and learning, not the outcome.

> **Further reading**
>
> If you have access to Partner Learning Camp, the *Prepare for Your Salesforce Platform App Builder Credential* curriculum is also a great way to reinforce learning from Trailhead: `https://sforce.co/3mJNAy8`.

In the next section, we'll continue our focus on Salesforce Platform by moving on to the Integration Architecture Designer certification.

Integration Architecture Designer exam overview

The **Integration Architecture Designer** certification is focused on the integration capabilities of Salesforce Platform, with a particular emphasis on choosing the optimum integration approach for a given situation. To prepare for this exam, you should have some experience with integration design patterns and integration documentation methodology. You should also understand the basics of data modeling and governance on Salesforce Platform.

Although the Platform App Builder certification is not a prerequisite for the Integration Architecture Designer certification, it's helpful to take them in this order. The fundamentals of Salesforce Platform covered in the Platform App Builder topics are an essential backdrop and lend context to the integration-focused topics of the Integration Architecture Designer exam.

> **Further reading**
> The Integration Architecture Designer Exam Guide is here: `https://sforce.co/3t0ogW2`.

In the following sections, we'll cover the exam outline topics and study materials.

Integration Architecture Designer topic overview

This section reviews each section in the Integration Architecture Designer exam and provides additional context around each. As always, you should review the exam guide for the most current version of this information, as it is subject to change.

The current topics and their weighting according to the exam guide are shown in the following figure:

Integration Architecture Designer Exam Topics

- Evaluating the Current System Landscape 9%
- Evaluate Business Needs 12%
- Translate Needs into Integration Requirements 24%
- Design Integration Solutions 30%
- Build Solution 25%

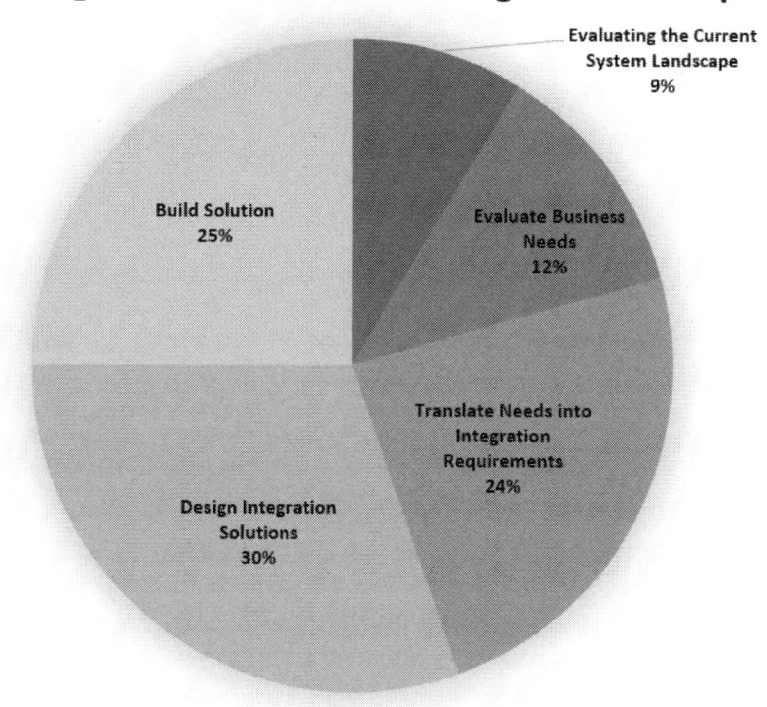

Figure 12.3 – Integration Architecture Designer exam topics

This exam is particularly strongly weighted toward three subjects: **build solution (25%)**, **design integration solutions (30%)**, and **translate needs into integration requirements (24%)**. These three sections together constitute 79% of the total value of the exam, which requires 67% to pass, so they are well worth the time and attention. The other two topics are good ways to pad your score if they're areas of comfort for you, but they are not as heavily represented in the exam space.

Also note the required score to pass this exam, 67%. Compare this to the 63% for Platform App Builder and 65% for Marketing Cloud Email Specialist and it's clear this certification is not to be taken lightly. You truly need a solid understanding of the topics to succeed on this exam.

> **Tip**
> Of the three prerequisites, the Integration Architecture Designer topics are also among the most relevant for the B2C Solution Architect practitioner, as they focus predominantly on integration. This is another reason to take this certification last if you're working through prerequisites; it keeps the material fresh in your mind.

Most of the topics from this certification are covered in *Chapter 2*, *Supporting Your Customers with Service Cloud*. Review this chapter and the study materials provided later in this chapter to prepare yourself for this certification.

For each of these topic areas on the exam, the following sections provide additional details.

Evaluating the current system landscape

As architects, we don't always have the luxury of starting from a clean slate when designing a solution. This section covers the tools available in Salesforce Platform for evaluating an existing Salesforce org and determining the overall health, performance characteristics, and potential pain points.

Make sure you're familiar with Salesforce Optimizer, license limitations and platform governance, and overall best practices. You should also know how to evaluate performance using tools such as **Experience Page Time** (**EPT**) and the **Lightning Performance Dashboard**. These tools can help when reviewing a set of requirements to determine the optimum Salesforce solution.

Evaluating business needs

In this book, we covered some of the topics related to evaluating business needs in *Chapter 6*, *Role of a Solution Architect*. This includes concepts such as functional and non-functional requirements, capturing requirements through stakeholder interviews, and understanding which requirements impact integration and data model requirements.

Be familiar with the Salesforce frameworks and processes used to guide the blueprint or discovery phase of a project, including the **Lean Governance Framework**, the Salesforce **Software Development Lifecycle (SDLC)**, and strategies to drive communication and adoption. You should also be familiar with various org operating models, including centralized, decentralized, and hybrid, which trade common processes and solutions for autonomy across business units.

Translating needs into integration requirements

Translating needs into integration requirements, along with designing integrated solutions, are core capabilities, not just for the Integration Architecture Designer certification but for the B2C Solution Architect role. There are many capabilities in Salesforce Platform related to integrating with outside systems. You should know the strengths and weaknesses of each, security considerations, and overall capabilities.

This includes understanding the use of certificates and keys for integration security, how and when to configure **remote site settings** or **CSP trusted sites**, as well as the use of **connected apps** and **named credentials**. One of the central capabilities for secure integration is the design of OAuth flows supporting various use cases, such as **IoT**, **web server flow**, **user-agent flow**, and **server-to-server flows**. Another example of non-functional requirements you'll need to understand and design for is data volume, response times, and license constraints on Salesforce Platform.

Now you understand these topics related to securing your integrations, we can move on to the next section, which focuses on the integrations and data flows between systems.

Design integration solutions

The design of integration solutions is, justifiably, the most heavily weighted section of this exam. This section focuses predominantly on the various integration patterns and capabilities of Salesforce Platform. There is also an emphasis on the Salesforce Platform APIs and the use cases for each. You should understand the integration patterns commonly used in Salesforce, including **Remote Process Invocation – Request and Reply**, **Remote Process Invocation – Fire and Forget**, **UI Update Based on Data Changes**, **Data Virtualization**, **Remote Call-In**, and **Batch Data Synchronization**.

The Salesforce integration capabilities you should familiarize yourself with include **Outbound Messaging**, **Canvas**, **External Services**, and **Apex Callouts**. Each of these has specific use cases it's best suited to, capabilities it supports, and design considerations you'll need to be familiar with. Be particularly mindful of where declarative (no-code) solutions offer an alternative to custom development, as this should always be preferred.

Build solutions

There is a lot of overlap between this section and the prior two sections, but here there is a clear emphasis on creating secure, scalable, and resilient integrations through good design. You'll need to understand best practices for API planning, but there are also additional topics related to integration capabilities, such as **platform events**, **Salesforce Connect**, and **Apex Integration Services**.

Another significant component of building scalable solutions is understanding the implications of large data volumes on solution design. This includes considerations and best practices around account data skew, ownership skew, and lookup skew, all of which can negatively impact the performance and stability of a Salesforce solution if they aren't considered. Large data volume topics also include the use of **bulk queries** and **batch Apex** as well as **skinny tables** to work with very large datasets.

Maintain integration

Maintaining the integration focuses on maintenance, error handling, and reporting requirements for an integrated solution using Salesforce Platform. There are topics related to **event monitoring**, which is used to track user behavior and activity in an org, as well as the use of third-party tools for monitoring, such as **Splunk for Salesforce**. Focus on proactive monitoring as well as forensic research techniques for addressing problems.

For the topics where you need some additional focus, leverage the study materials referenced in the next section to improve your comfort level and comprehension.

Integration Architecture Designer study materials

Of the three prerequisite certifications, Integration Architecture Designer has the most coverage in this book. The Salesforce Platform-specific topics are primarily covered between *Chapter 1, Demystifying Salesforce, Customer 360, and Digital 360*, and *Chapter 2, Supporting Your Customers with Service Cloud*. Many of the business requirements definition and documentation topics are covered in *Chapter 6, Role of a Solution Architect*. Finally, integration best practices are covered in *Chapter 7, Integration Architecture Options*.

> **Further reading**
>
> Beyond this book, the trailmix *Architect Journey: Integration Architecture* provides the most comprehensive overview of the topics on this exam: `https://sforce.co/3zETWm0`.
>
> You may also find the *Integration Patterns and Practices* documentation from Salesforce useful, as it provides a central list of many different patterns and capabilities: `https://sforce.co/3kylnYG`.

After reviewing the trailmix and the relevant topics in this book, the *Further reading* section in each Trailhead module can be a great way to go a level deeper on topics you're struggling with. Be sure to practice in a developer org or Trailhead org as much as possible to lock in what you've learned.

Summary

In this chapter, we've reviewed the three prerequisite certifications for the B2C Solution Architect certification at a very high level. We've also provided a recommended sequence in which to tackle these prerequisites to streamline your own learning and to maximize transference to the B2C Solution Architect certification itself. For each exam, we've also provided a list of topics and a description of what you should know to be successful in each.

At this point, you should know what to expect from each of these three certifications. You should also be able to assess your own comfort level based on the topic outline and description, and know where to look for additional training resources so you can address any weaknesses. This approach of reviewing the exam topics and weighting, understanding the composition of each section, self-assessing, and then diving deeper into training is a repeatable pattern you can apply to any Salesforce certification.

In the next chapter, we'll focus specifically on B2C Commerce topics that aren't covered by the three prerequisite certifications, but which can help to round out your understanding of the overall solution space.

Questions

1. Of the three primary B2C Solution Architecture products we've discussed in this book, which is not covered by the prerequisite certifications?
2. Why might you choose to take the Marketing Cloud Email Specialist exam first and then move on to the Salesforce Platform exams?
3. True or false – all Salesforce certification exams have 60 questions and require a minimum of 65% to pass?
4. Across all three certifications, what's the best resource for preparing for your certification?

13
Commerce and Integration

The three prerequisite certifications for the B2C Solution Architect certification covered in the previous chapter focused entirely on the Salesforce Platform and Marketing Cloud. However, there's much more to preparing for this capstone certification than only knowing those two products. In this chapter, we'll focus predominantly on B2C Commerce exam preparation topics that will help round out your core knowledge.

In *Chapter 3*, *Direct-to-Consumer Selling with Commerce Cloud B2C*, we covered the most important B2C Commerce capabilities that are relevant for the B2C Solution Architect exam. In this chapter, we'll highlight several of those areas that are worth revisiting and complete the picture by covering some of the preparation topics that are required for the **B2C Technical Architect** certification. While this certification isn't necessary for a B2C Solution Architect, it provides an excellent complement to the Salesforce Platform and Marketing Cloud-focused prerequisites.

In addition to the three primary B2C Solution Architecture component products, that is, the Salesforce Platform, Marketing Cloud, and B2C Commerce, there are numerous other products that you'll have to be aware of to round out your solutions in the real world and to be successful with this certification. These include products such as Order Management, Experience Cloud, MuleSoft, and Salesforce CDP. These topics are primarily covered in *Chapter 5*, *Salesforce Ecosystem – Building a Complete Solution*. So, here, we'll again focus on highlighting specific areas where you'll want to spend additional time and attention as part of your focused exam preparation.

In this chapter, we're going to cover the following main topics:

- B2C Commerce exam preparation topics
- Complementary component topics
- Overall solution design topics

By the end of this chapter, you should have a more complete picture of B2C Commerce, specifically, within the context of the B2C Solution Architect exam. You should also know what the key points are regarding complementary products beyond B2C Commerce, Marketing Cloud, and the Salesforce Platform, along with which design topics you should focus on.

B2C Commerce Architect exam preparation topics

Preparing for the B2C Solution Architect certification requires an understanding of the B2C Commerce product and its related architecture topics. If your background isn't in B2C Commerce, there are a couple of ways to grow this skill set. The first and most comprehensive way is to obtain your **B2C Commerce Architect** certification.

> **Important note**
> Specifically, the B2C Commerce Architect certification is focused on the Salesforce B2C Commerce product. It's not the same as B2C Solution Architect, which is the overall focus of this book. B2C Solution Architect is a much broader certification that covers the design of solutions spanning multiple Salesforce products, including B2C Commerce.

In this chapter, we are referring to a platform-specific technical architect when we're talking about an architect who specializes in one product, such as B2C Commerce. We say solution architect or B2C Solution Architect when we're talking about an architect who is responsible for the overall integrated solution across multiple component products in the B2C space.

The following diagram, which also appeared in *Chapter 11, Exam Preparation Tools and Techniques*, depicts the role of the B2C Commerce-specific certifications in supporting the B2C Solution Architecture certification:

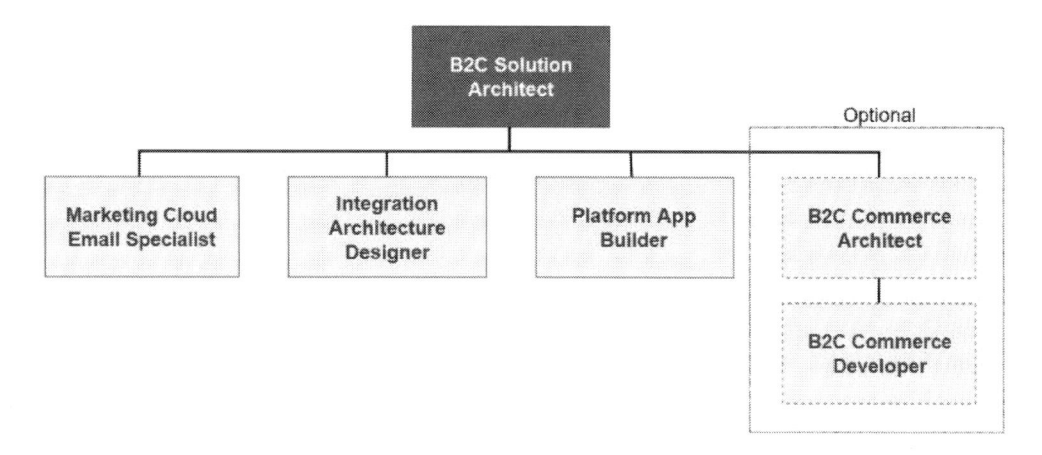

Figure 13.1 – The B2C Solution Architect certification path

In the next section, we'll cover the B2C Commerce Architect certification along with its prerequisites, topics, and study materials. After that, we'll cover some specific B2C Commerce topics that were not discussed in *Chapter 3, Direct-to-Consumer Selling with Commerce Cloud B2C*.

The B2C Commerce Architect certification

If you read *Chapter 12, Prerequisite Certifications*, you'll also be familiar with the formula that we're going to take here. The goal of this section is not to teach you everything you need to know in order to pass the B2C Commerce Architect certification, it's to help you become familiar with the content and composition of the exam so that you can accurately assess your own preparedness and focus your study efforts on areas where they are needed.

The B2C Commerce Architect certification is for technical architects who are specifically focused on the design of B2C Commerce solutions. This includes some areas that overlap with the B2C Solution Architect areas of responsibility, including integrations and data modeling, along with many areas that are specifically the domain of a B2C Commerce Architect. This certification is aimed at individuals who already have some experience in designing solutions for B2C Commerce.

To prepare for this exam, you should have a good understanding of the architectural concepts around the **Storefront Reference Architecture** (**SFRA**), the B2C Commerce platform, REST APIs including OCAPI and Commerce APIs, the B2C Commerce data model, batch file, and real-time integrations to external systems, the role of the B2C Commerce marketplace, and other related topics.

> **Further reading**
> As always, the official B2C Commerce Architect exam guide is the best source for an up-to-date overview of the certification. You can locate it at `https://sforce.co/38TNbBr`.

In the following subsections, we'll cover the prerequisites, topics, and study materials that you need to help you prepare for your B2C Commerce Architect certification.

The B2C Commerce Developer certification

Before you can qualify for the B2C Commerce Architect certification, you'll need to take and pass the prerequisite B2C Commerce Developer certification. This certification is focused on code-level details, developer tools, best practices, platform capabilities, and more.

> **Tip**
> Because of the B2C Commerce Developer prerequisite, adding B2C Commerce Architect to your list of qualifications actually adds two additional certifications, which is a significant investment of your time and effort. If you don't have a background in B2C Commerce, it might be worthwhile. However, you can also simply use the topics and study guide without ever going for the actual certification.

The topics listed in the B2C Commerce Developer certification breakdown are as follows:

- B2C Commerce setup (11%)
- Work with a B2C site (12%)
- Data management using Business Manager usage (24%)
- Application development (53%)

As you can see, more than half of the exam is focused on application development with another quarter focused on data and the backend administrator tool, Business Manager. If you are knowledgeable in these two areas, the required 65% correct to pass should be straightforward.

> **Further reading**
>
> You can review the full B2C Commerce Developer exam guide at https://sforce.co/3tgnF2h.

B2C Commerce Architect topic overview

This area covers each topic of the exam with additional context and further reading, where relevant. As always, please review the exam guide referenced earlier for the most current version of this information.

The current topics and their weighting, according to the exam guide, are shown in the following diagram:

B2C Commerce Architect Exam Topics

- Launch 16%
- Design/Discovery 29%
- Build 19%
- Monitoring/Troubleshooting 14%
- Integrations and Customizations 22%

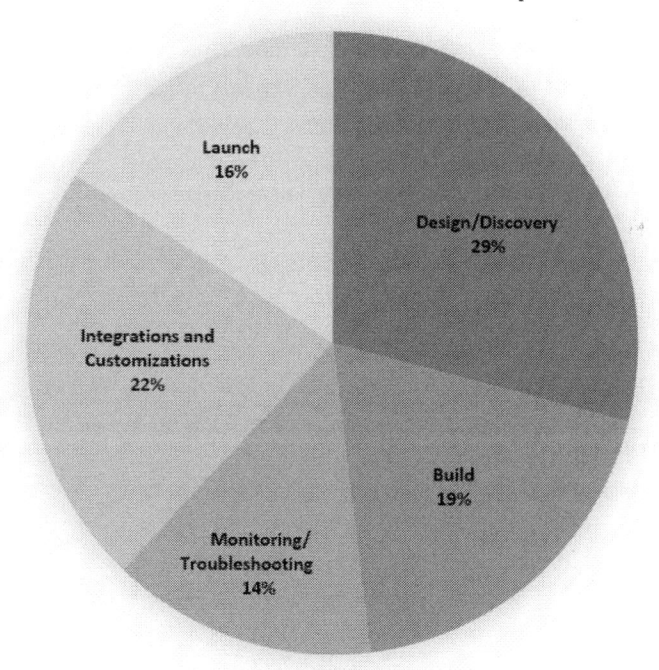

Figure 13.2 – B2C Commerce Architect Exam Topics

In this exam, no topic is trivial, although evidently, **Design/Discovery** and **Integrations and Customizations** are the most significant. The good news is those two sections have the greatest overlap with the topics that are relevant to the B2C Solution Architect exam, which we have already covered in this book. We'll provide additional information that is relevant to the remaining topics in this chapter.

> **Important note**
> The different topic areas on the exam are not separated or otherwise identified; you won't know what topic a given question relates to, so just use this as a guideline to focus your preparation.

In the following sections, we'll break down what you can expect in each topic area as you work through your preparation for the exam.

Discovery/design overview

In *Chapter 6, Role of a Solution Architect*, we covered some of the technical design documents expected of a B2C Solution Architect. This included a system overview diagram, an integration diagram, and a data mapping diagram. This section of the B2C Commerce Architect exam includes similar concepts that focus on the design of B2C Commerce solutions.

You should understand how to create standard technical documentation that accurately captures business requirements, how to structure a discovery conversation to address the necessary topics, how to design for long-term stability and growth, and the role of the LINK partner marketplace in selecting third-party integrations. When focused on B2C Commerce, the technical documentation becomes more in-depth and product-specific.

> **Further reading**
> Review the project documentation for the Salesforce B2C Commerce Technical Architects Trailhead module for additional information on this topic. You can find this at `https://sforce.co/3DLWuBu`.

The discovery/design topics for B2C Commerce also include knowing the difference between functional and technical topics and documenting each appropriately. For every third-party integration, you will also need to be able to map out the integration methodology, document the direction and volume of data flow, account for any data migration requirements, and align the design with platform constraints and governance.

Build overview

The build topic is focused on leveraging technical documentation to create a fully realized solution that follows the best practices for performance, scalability, and future maintenance. This includes things such as code management using cartridges, build and integration processes, and troubleshooting implementation work.

Typically, this is a shared responsibility between a platform technical architect and a senior developer. Since it's rarely the role of a solution architect, unless they're doubling as a platform technical architect in a workstream, most of these topics haven't been covered in this book. The *B2C Commerce supplemental topics* section of this chapter provides some additional information, but the *study materials* are the best way to get the depth of expertise that is needed for this certification.

Monitoring/troubleshooting overview

Effective monitoring and troubleshooting in B2C Commerce rely on several tools, including the log center, technical reports, pipeline and script profilers, cache utilization, deprecated API usage, and quota violation dashboards. You should be familiar with these tools and understand how to use them to research and provide recommendations to mitigate performance issues, including loading testing results, along with functional or technical issues.

We covered some monitoring topics as they relate to the overall solution architecture in *Chapter 10, Enterprise Integration Strategies*. However, you'll need far more B2C Commerce-specific knowledge to function as a platform technical architect or become certified as a B2C Commerce Architect.

Integrations and customizations overview

Designing integrations is a core responsibility of a B2C Solution Architect across every component product, including B2C Commerce, so this area is of particular importance. As it's relevant for the B2C Solution Architect space, it was covered in depth in *Chapter 3, Direct-to-Consumer Selling with Commerce Cloud B2C*. Please review that chapter for a refresher on the core concepts.

For the B2C Commerce Architect certification, you'll also need to research the older SiteGenesis storefront architecture that preceded the Salesforce Reference Architecture. This older architecture is still in use for many live customers and comes in two flavors: pipelines and controllers. Pipelines are the original XML-based visual modeling language used by Salesforce B2C Commerce, which has since been replaced with JavaScript controllers. The B2C Commerce Architect certification expects you to understand how to convert and upgrade older implementations into newer implementations and how this impacts the use of LINK cartridges from the B2C Commerce partner marketplace.

Launch overview

The launch section of the B2C Commerce Architect exam covers platform-specific configuration around the use of aliases for storefront URL configuration and SEO. Additionally, it includes the appropriate configuration and use of locales and currencies on global sites. Finally, you'll need to be familiar with the production migration and launch process.

In B2C Commerce, every first-time customer launch to production requires a review and sign-off from Salesforce through a process called a **Site Readiness Assessment** (**SRA**). Understanding how to guide your customers through the SRA process and ensuring that all necessary data is migrated to production, the configuration of jobs and replications is complete, and any errors are cleaned up in the logs are critical for a successful launch.

In the following section, we'll provide some resources in which you can learn more on your own as part of preparing for the B2C Commerce Architect certification or to improve your knowledge of the platform in preparation for the B2C Solution Architect certification.

Study materials

Aside from the relevant sections of this book referenced in the previous sections, there are a few resources that you can use to learn more about B2C Commerce on your own. Bear in mind as you study that, unlike with the Salesforce Platform, it is not possible to create your own B2C Commerce sandbox for experimentation unless you're a B2C Commerce customer or partner organization.

> **Further reading**
> Start by working through the B2C Commerce Architect Certification preparation trailmix at `https://sforce.co/3kQMRJ4`.

This trailmix covers many of the topics that are relevant for the exam. If you have access to Partner Learning Camp, you can deep dive into specific topics there. Navigate to the **Browse Catalog** section and select **B2C Commerce** from the product filters on the left-hand side.

> **Further reading**
> The *Get Started on the B2C Commerce Fast Path to Certification: Foundations* curriculum is a great place to start. You can locate it at `https://sforce.co/3DLZvSi`.
>
> *Note that access to Partner Learning Camp is required to access this resource.*

In addition to these resources, in the next section of this chapter, we will provide additional B2C Commerce-specific information to supplement the content in *Chapter 3, Direct-to-Consumer Selling with Commerce Cloud B2C*.

B2C Commerce supplemental topics

This section covers specific B2C Commerce topics that are more likely to be handled by the platform-specific B2C Technical Architect than the B2C Solution Architect. For that reason, they weren't covered in the earlier chapter on B2C Commerce, but they are important topics for the B2C Commerce Architect certification and can provide helpful context and an improved depth of understanding for B2C Solution Architects where B2C Commerce is an important part of the solution.

The following sections follow the exam topic areas, including discovery/design, build, monitoring/troubleshooting, integration, customization, and finally, launch.

Discovery/design topics

Structuring a discovery process for B2C Commerce means understanding the questions that you need to ask early on that drive foundational architecture decisions. Decisions around realm structure and site structure, data architecture, identity management, and integrations will drive the rest of the solution. Generally, storefront customizations can be layered on top of a solid foundation in an agile manner after it's established.

Many of the topics required to drive a successful discovery have already been covered in this book, especially where B2C Commerce is part of a larger B2C Solution Architecture. In the next two sections, we'll fill in a couple of gaps around site architecture followed by job and replication schedules.

Site architecture

One of the most important architectural decisions you'll make during a discovery process in B2C Commerce is how to structure sites and share data. We've already covered the B2C Commerce capabilities around data sharing and the architecture of sites and realms, but we haven't spent much time discovering how to select the right option.

There are three potential options regarding how to set up sites in B2C Commerce:

- A single shared site for all brands and geographies
- Sites grouped by brand and/or geography
- Unique sites for brands and geographies

The following diagram shows each of these options:

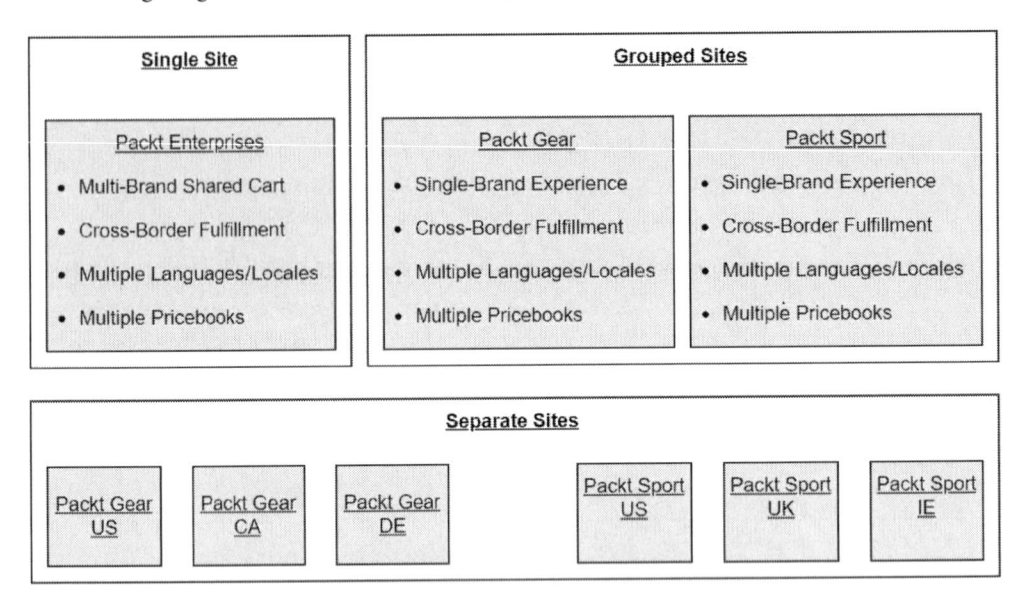

```
┌─────────────────────────────┐  ┌───────────────────────────────────────────────────────────────┐
│         Single Site         │  │                         Grouped Sites                          │
│  ┌───────────────────────┐  │  │  ┌───────────────────────┐    ┌───────────────────────┐       │
│  │   Packt Enterprises   │  │  │  │      Packt Gear       │    │      Packt Sport      │       │
│  │ • Multi-Brand Shared  │  │  │  │ • Single-Brand        │    │ • Single-Brand        │       │
│  │   Cart                │  │  │  │   Experience          │    │   Experience          │       │
│  │ • Cross-Border        │  │  │  │ • Cross-Border        │    │ • Cross-Border        │       │
│  │   Fulfillment         │  │  │  │   Fulfillment         │    │   Fulfillment         │       │
│  │ • Multiple            │  │  │  │ • Multiple            │    │ • Multiple            │       │
│  │   Languages/Locales   │  │  │  │   Languages/Locales   │    │   Languages/Locales   │       │
│  │ • Multiple Pricebooks │  │  │  │ • Multiple Pricebooks │    │ • Multiple Pricebooks │       │
│  └───────────────────────┘  │  │  └───────────────────────┘    └───────────────────────┘       │
└─────────────────────────────┘  └───────────────────────────────────────────────────────────────┘

┌──────────────────────────────────────────────────────────────────────────────────────────────────┐
│                                         Separate Sites                                            │
│   ┌──────────┐   ┌──────────┐   ┌──────────┐     ┌──────────┐   ┌──────────┐   ┌──────────┐       │
│   │Packt Gear│   │Packt Gear│   │Packt Gear│     │Packt Sport│  │Packt Sport│  │Packt Sport│     │
│   │    US    │   │    CA    │   │    DE    │     │    US    │   │    UK    │   │    IE    │     │
│   └──────────┘   └──────────┘   └──────────┘     └──────────┘   └──────────┘   └──────────┘       │
└──────────────────────────────────────────────────────────────────────────────────────────────────┘
```

Figure 13.3 – B2C Commerce site models

For Packt Enterprises, as discussed in *Chapter 10, Enterprise Integration Strategies*, we've taken the approach of separate sites. The preceding diagram shows how a different architectural decision around sites would have impacted the B2C Commerce portion of the solution. A single-site approach would have allowed us to have a shared shopping cart between brands. But this would have required both brands to have all of their products in the same storefront catalog, inventory list, and price book. Additionally, this would have required a shared customer list for both brands across all geographies.

A hybrid approach, in this case, grouping sites by brand or by geography, allows for distinct brand experiences. In this example, we're still combining the geographies for a single brand under one site, which requires multiple languages, locales, and price books by currency. It also requires cross-border fulfillment capabilities for each site to support the various parts of the world that products are shipped to. Here, an alternative would have been to create regionally shared sites maintaining the shared cart approach across brands but having distinct sites per region.

The decision of which model to use comes down to several factors, not the least of which is how your organization is structured. When using a single or grouped site, replications to production at the site level must be coordinated for all the brand teams or geographies using that site. This can be challenging in organizations where different teams operate independently. The decision can also be driven by fulfillment requirements, integrations, data sharing, or requirements around data residency.

Exploring all of these topics, knowing which data can be shared between sites and which can't, and how to align the architecture to the needs of an organization are all vital topics in the discovery/design phase of a project and the relevant section of the exam. Finally, if your implementation has multiple B2C Commerce realms in different parts of the world, this will, at the very least, necessitate separate sites per realm. B2C Commerce has no native capabilities in which to share data between realms.

Job and replication scheduling

B2C Commerce jobs are backend scheduled processes that can be used for either batch processing data or for integrating with external systems. They are commonly used for processing import and export files, but they can also support batch API integrations or on-platform data transformations.

The most important design considerations for jobs and replications are as follows:

- B2C Commerce instances
- Inter-dependencies
- Server load
- Storefront impact
- Merchandising and marketing

Together, these factors combine to form a picture of data coming into and out of the overall system, the instances involved, and the impact they'll have.

Start by simply listing each job that was uncovered during discovery, as shown in the following table:

Job	Instance	Dependency	Frequency
Import inventory (full)	Prod, Stg, Dev	-	Daily
Import inventory (delta)	Prod	-	Hourly
Catalog import	Stg	-	Daily
Price book import	Stg	-	Daily
Auto-merchandising job	Stg	Catalog and price book Import	Daily
Order export	Prod	-	15-minute

Figure 13.4 – Job schedules

Following this, identify a time to replicate data to production daily where storefront traffic is low. Typically, this is early in the morning, between 3 a.m. and 5 a.m., local time, to avoid impacting shoppers. For Packt Sport US, we'll say their daily replication will happen at 4:15 a.m., Eastern time.

> **Important note**
> Replicating to production is non-disruptive but forces a cache clear in production, which can have a noticeable impact on performance under load. Avoid replications during high-traffic times.

Working backward from that replication time, schedule each of your jobs with time between for the jobs to complete; this will be based on typical data volume. In the preceding example, this might mean scheduling your auto-merchandising job for 3:27 a.m., your price book import for 2:12 a.m., your catalog import for 1:03 a.m., and your full inventory job for 11:18 p.m.

> **Tip**
> Try to avoid scheduling your jobs and replications at common times such as on the hour, quarter after, half past, or in five-minute intervals. This type of scheduling makes it more likely that you'll have job runs chunking up over time, increasing your server load.

Although it is possible to adjust job and replication schedules at any time in Business Manager, it's a good idea to take the time to plan it out in this way to minimize the risk of issues in advance. Take the time to monitor your job runs, especially early on, to ensure runtimes don't overlap for interdependent jobs. Additionally, you should also set up job alert emails in Business Manager in the case of long-running or failed jobs that require manual intervention.

Build topics

The most important topics regarding the B2C Commerce build section of the exam are those concerning the design of B2C Commerce cartridge structures and the support of various types of testing. Within B2C Commerce, cartridges are the primary unit of modularity for code. We discussed LINK cartridges in *Chapter 3*, *Direct-to-Consumer Selling with Commerce Cloud B2C*, but there's more to this topic than just leveraging pre-built integrations from the marketplace.

On the topic of testing, the B2C Commerce Architect exam expects you to know the platform capabilities around unit testing, integration testing, functional testing, performance testing, and load testing. Some of these testing topics, especially unit testing and integration testing, are more relevant to B2C Commerce developers than architects, but you'll need to be familiar with all of them to some extent.

In the next two sections, we'll provide a high-level overview of important cartridges and testing considerations.

The B2C Commerce cartridge structure

At the most basic level, a B2C Commerce cartridge is just a folder full of code with a known structure. Organizing code into cartridges ensures logical partitioning and a clear code structure; it is the fundamental way code-based capabilities are enabled for B2C Commerce sites.

You can create separate cartridges for each of the following reasons:

- Third-party integrations
- Complex customizations
- Brand-specific styling or capabilities
- Regional forms, localizations, or customizations

Although all sites in a B2C Commerce realm share a common code base, the cartridges that are *active* for a specific site are controlled by that site's cartridge path. This allows each site to be configured to only leverage the code that is relevant for that site.

The following table shows a simple cartridge configuration that might be leveraged for Packt Enterprises:

Cartridge	Packt Gear US	Packt Gear CA	Packt Gear DE	Packt Sport US	Packt Sport UK	Packt Sport IE
app_packtgear_style	X	X	X			
app_packtsport_style				X	X	X
app_eu_localization			X		X	X
app_na_localization	X	X		X		
int_na_oms	X	X		X		
int_eu_oms			X			X
int_uk_oms					X	
int_worldpay	X	X	X	X	X	X
int_avatax	X	X		X		
plugin_applepay	X	X	X	X	X	X
plugin_comparison	X	X	X	X	X	X
app_storefront_base	X	X	X	X	X	X

Figure 13.5 – The cartridge structure

In this example, a mix of brand-specific styling cartridges, regional localization cartridges, regional and shared integrations, and common plugins are leveraged across brands. Although all of the cartridges listed are in the shared code base, each site is configured to only use the ones that are relevant to its brand and geography.

The cartridge path for the Packt Gear DE site would look like this: `app_packtgear_style:app_eu_localization:int_eu_oms:int_worldpay:plugin_applepay:plugin_comparison:app_storefront_base`

The cartridge path is always evaluated from left to right, top to bottom in the preceding table. This allows more specific code to override any shared, general-purpose code. This allows brand-specific styling to override the base styling provided by SFRA in `app_storefront_base`, which should never be modified directly to preserve future upgrade paths.

You can learn more about this important concept, in B2C Commerce, from the product documentation at `https://sforce.co/3toT1ns`.

B2C Commerce testing

B2C Commerce provides some native capabilities for testing and test automation, some testing that should be done manually by the implementor or users, and some testing that should be done by dedicated third parties.

At a high level, B2C Commerce testing is divided up into automated testing, manual testing, and load and performance testing, as shown in the following diagram:

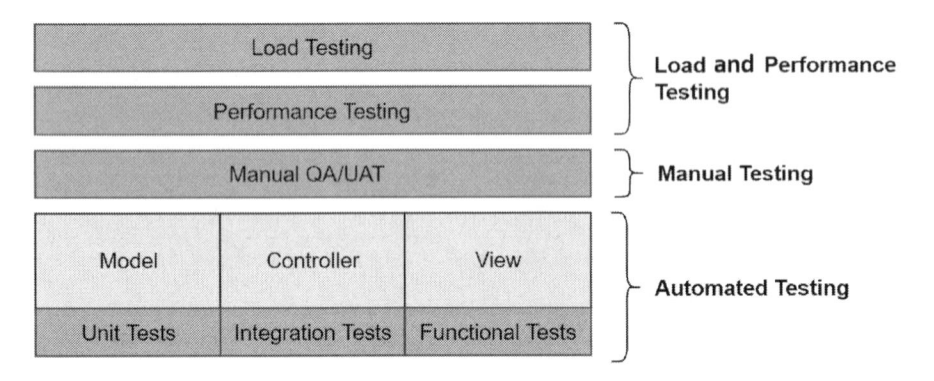

Figure 13.6 – B2C Commerce testing

Because SFRA uses a **Model-View-Controller** (**MVC**) architecture, it lends itself particularly well to a three-part approach to **automated testing**, which focuses on each component of the architecture separately.

The first component of testing in B2C Commerce SFRA is unit testing, which uses mock objects to test the models in the SFRA code base. This can and should be automated as part of a build process to leverage the `dw-api-mock` library, which can be found in the community GitHub at `https://bit.ly/3l1A2Md`.

The second component of testing is integration testing, which is typically performed using **mocha**, **chai**, and **request-promise** in SFRA. Typically, this is performed as part of a CI/CD workflow on a dedicated instance where work from multiple developers is combined into one build. Integration testing focuses on the controllers of the MVC architecture.

The final component of testing is functional testing on the views of the MVC architecture, which leverages **webdriver.io**. Functional testing can also be automated as part of the build or integration process in a CI/CD pipeline.

You can learn more about SFRA testing technologies in the product documentation at `https://sforce.co/2WXSvRW`.

With basic automated testing in place to help avoid regressions, manual QA and UAT are still needed to validate the overall code base against requirements, including functional, technical, and creative. This step is performed at the level of a user story, feature, or page rather than focusing on code components.

Performance testing is used to review and, ultimately, optimize the customer experience using an SFRA storefront on B2C Commerce. This includes client-side components such as the JavaScript load time, render time, cumulative layout shift, and other related concepts. Performance testing includes both server-side performance and client-side performance, as they impact an individual using the site.

In contrast, load testing is concerned with the ability of a B2C Commerce site to scale under load. Typically, establishing a target load that is 20%–50% higher than recorded maximums from previous years is a good goal. This type of testing requires a third party that is capable of creating and executing test scripts that mimic real user behavior at scale.

> **Important note**
> Load testing must be coordinated with Salesforce support and any involved third parties to avoid impacting the production infrastructure or triggering bot attack defense measures.

For a B2C Solution Architect, these topics of B2C Commerce should be considered in the larger context of the overall solution. If B2C Commerce relies on the Salesforce Platform for login and authentication or makes real-time calls to Marketing Cloud for transactional email sends, these systems will need to be included in load testing or the services will need to be mocked.

In the next section, we'll review several additional integration topics that are specific to B2C Commerce and have not been covered elsewhere in this book.

Integration topics

In *Chapter 3, Direct-to-Consumer Selling with B2C Commerce Cloud*, we covered *B2C Commerce APIs and integrations* in some detail. By now, you should understand the B2C Commerce capabilities for outbound and inbound integrations, which is the most important factor for a B2C Solution Architect. However, a B2C Commerce platform technical architect should also understand the way that outbound integrations are configured and managed in B2C Commerce.

All outbound integrations originating in B2C Commerce, whether FTP, SFTP, WebDAV, REST, SOAP, or a custom HTTP service, should leverage the B2C Commerce **Service Framework**. The Service Framework is a methodology used to implement external integrations in code that supports the monitoring of both performance and error rates. Service Framework-based integrations also support securely managing credentials in Business Manager and configuration related to scalability, rate limiters, and circuit breaker patters.

The Service Framework consists of three separate components, as depicted in the following diagram:

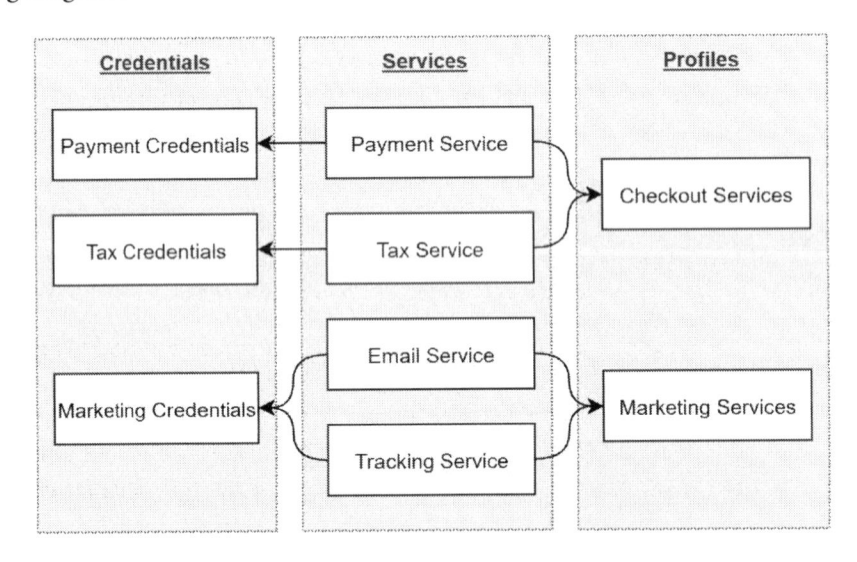

Figure 13.7 – Services, Credentials, and Profiles

Services define specific integrations and profiles define the characteristics of that integration, including timeouts, rate limits, mocked responses, and circuit breakers. Credentials define the authentication mechanism, such as the username and the password, that is used to securely connect to the service. As the preceding diagram shows, credentials and profiles can be shared between services.

Timeouts should be set to the highest response time seen for successful calls to the external service under a realistic load. This prevents long-running failures from tying up storefront threads without impacting successful responses.

You can learn more about service configuration in B2C Commerce from the product documentation at `https://sforce.co/3l1P5Wd`.

Monitoring/troubleshooting topics

We covered monitoring for overall B2C solutions in *Chapter 10, Enterprise Integration Strategies*, but there are a couple of additional topics, specific to B2C Commerce, that you'll need for the B2C Commerce Architect certification and for serving as a platform technical architect. In the next two sections, we'll cover B2C Commerce logging and provide an overview of the B2C Commerce infrastructure.

B2C Commerce logging

The most important topic related to monitoring and troubleshooting in B2C Commerce is the proper use of B2C Commerce logs. Detailed and well-structured logs are a vital tool for conducting a root-cause analysis of potential issues in test environments and production. Additionally, reviewing log files regularly is the best way to ensure your implementation does not run afoul of quotas, deprecated APIs, or system errors.

At a high level, log files are divided into system logs and custom logs. System logs are controlled by Salesforce and can only be modified by Salesforce support. However, custom logs allow granular control of log details, categories, and filenames.

Custom logging is configured in Business Manager under **Administration | Operations | Custom Log Settings**. For each log category defined in code, specify what level of detail to include in logs. The possible levels, from most to least granular, are `debug`, `info`, `warn`, `error`, and `fatal`. Debug logging should only be used in limited situations since it impacts performance; also, debug logging is not available on production instances.

In addition to managing log categories and log levels to track, Business Manager also allows declarative control over which log levels are written to files. Logs in B2C Commerce are accessible in three ways: WebDAV files, a request log that is accessible from the storefront toolkit, and in Log Center. Accessing log files from WebDAV gives you the raw log form and is only available for log levels that are configured to write to files. The storefront toolkit viewer, which is not available in development or production, can be used to view transient log messages that are enabled by category but not written to disk.

The B2C Commerce Log Center is the primary tool for log searching, reviewing, and monitoring. It supports querying across logs, the tracking of request IDs, and reviewing logs across multiple instances simultaneously. Within Log Center, it is also possible to filter by log category to refine your results further. In particular, for production, Log Center is the best option in which to review logs. This is because it does not require you to download multiple large text files and search them separately.

Keeping logs, especially error logs, to the minimum useful size is important because log files will be suspended when they reach 10 MB per day. Logs are also retained for a maximum of 30 days after creation; they should be retrieved and archived off-instance before that point if they are required.

> **Further reading**
>
> You can learn more about B2C Commerce log files in the Salesforce documentation at `https://sforce.co/3l7un7q`.

B2C Commerce instance infrastructure

When troubleshooting in B2C Commerce, it's helpful to understand the architecture of an instance so that you can isolate the component where the problem might be arising. By working through each component and evaluating the function against the symptom, often, you can narrow down the problem substantially.

The following diagram depicts the documented components supporting a B2C Commerce instance, in order of evaluation:

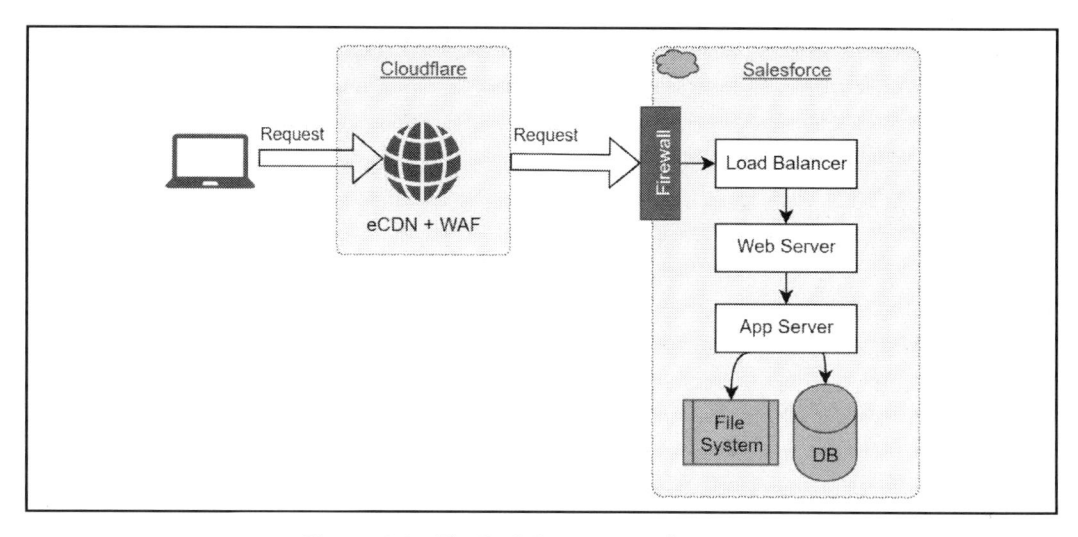

Figure 13.8 – The B2C Commerce infrastructure

As this diagram shows, a single incoming request for a B2C Commerce storefront page passes through many steps of processing before returning a result to the user. The first step, and the one geographically closest to the user, is the **Embedded CDN (eCDN)** and **Web Application Firewall** (**WAF**). These components serve two important roles: performance and security. The eCDN supports caching static content in servers that are close to the user. Additionally, it supports dynamic image optimization, compression, and other configuration-driven performance tools. The WAF offers bot protection and defense against common **Open Web Application Security Project (OWASP)** vulnerabilities.

> **Further reading**
>
> You can learn more about the eCDN and WAF at `https://sforce.co/3DVXAuq`.

After a request passes through the eCDN, it reaches the **firewall** and **load balancer**. This networking tool is responsible for **Distributed Denial-of-Service (DDoS)** protection and load balancing within the B2C Commerce infrastructure. The load balancer routes incoming requests to web server instances, which host the B2C Commerce **Web Adapter**.

The Web Adapter renders storefront templates and manages page-level caching on the server instance. For uncached pages, a call is made to the **application server**, which handles all business logic and processing, including caching database objects. Finally, the application server instances are responsible for controlling access to the shared database and the underlying filesystem.

> **Further reading**
> The B2C Commerce infrastructure components and their functions are documented at https://sforce.co/3jXPnOx.

The final topic area that we'll cover in this book to help you prepare for your B2C Commerce Architect certification is how to launch a B2C Commerce site.

Launch topics

The most important part of launching a new site that you'll need to understand as a B2C Commerce Architect is the Salesforce SRA process. The SRA process is a multistep process coordinated between the customer, Salesforce professional services, and the implementation partner (if applicable). The goal of the SRA process is to help ensure a smooth and successful launch with long-term stability and a customer who is prepared to operate their site in the long term.

The stages of the SRA process are depicted in the following diagram:

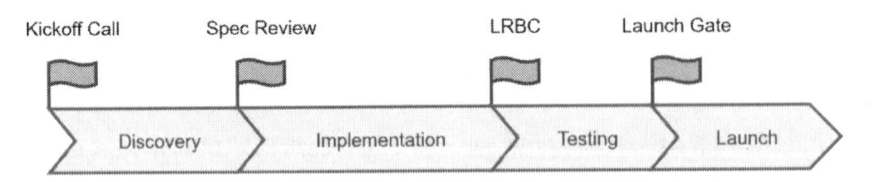

Figure 13.9 – The SRA timeline

Throughout the process, it's important to maintain accurate and comprehensive technical and functional documentation for the new site, as we discussed in the *Discovery/design topics* section. As the preceding diagram shows, the process begins with a kickoff call, which should be scheduled during the discovery phase of the project.

As the requirements are finalized, a spec review phase begins where Salesforce reviews the site documentation along with the implementation to date. Results from this review are tracked in a common spreadsheet against a set of standard review questions with any discrepancies or gaps being discussed and addressed.

A Salesforce lead training session, called a **Launch Readiness Bootcamp (LRBC)**, is conducted with new clients to ensure they're prepared to own and manage their new site when it goes live. Finally, a launch gate step provides a final review to ensure that everything is prepared for go-live including job configuration, data migration, alias setup, error notifications, fallback handling, log files are cleaned up, replications are scheduled, and custom error pages are created.

> **Further reading**
>
> To learn more about this vital step in the launch of a new B2C Commerce experience, please review the *Salesforce B2C Commerce Site Readiness Assessment Trailhead* module at `https://sforce.co/3jYn2aF`.

Complementary component topics

No topics factor as heavily into the B2C Solution Architect certification or on-the-job responsibilities as the three primary products, that is, Salesforce Platform, Marketing Cloud, and B2C Commerce, and how to integrate them. The other products you should be familiar with to be fully prepared are those that complement the core B2C Solution Architecture.

For the most part, these products have been covered in sufficient detail in *Chapter 5, Salesforce Ecosystem – Building a Complete Solution*. Additional products in the Commerce Cloud space were covered in *Chapter 3, Direct-to-Consumer Selling with Commerce Cloud B2C*. The goal of these chapters and the goal of a B2C Solution Architect should be to recognize when another Salesforce product might meet the needs of a solution, its overall role in the solution, and how it would integrate.

If you're looking to focus on any of these components in more detail, your best resources are going to be Trailhead and Partner Learning Camp. You can search for the products that you're interested in there. You can look for certifications on Trailhead, but with a few exceptions, the Salesforce Platform-based products don't have their own certifications. Most of the certification ecosystem is focused on the capabilities of the platform, which are shared by the products that are built on top of it.

To develop your expertise and gain credentials around specific products, you should look at *accreditations* through Partner Learning Camp instead. This partner-only option provides low-cost options in which to gain product-specific credentials in areas such as Einstein, industry clouds, Pardot, Headless Commerce APIs, Order Management, B2B Commerce, and Salesforce CDP. Accreditations are less expensive and generally require less preparation than certifications.

The following table compares traditional certifications with partner accreditations:

	Certification	Accreditation
Cost (USD)	$200 – $400	$150
Training Through	Trailhead	Partner Learning Camp
Exam Through	Webassessor	Examity
Exam Duration	105 – 120 minutes	30 – 120 minutes
Counts for Partner Credit	Yes	Yes

Figure 13.10 – Certification versus Accreditation

For MuleSoft and Heroku, which can be used as tools for integrating other components, please refer to *Chapter 7, Integration Architecture Options*, and *Chapter 10, Enterprise Integration Strategies*. Together, these chapters cover the high-level knowledge that you'll need to speak intelligently about the role of MuleSoft and Heroku and to know when to engage with a platform technical architect who has deeper expertise.

> **Further reading**
>
> If you'd like to dive deeper into MuleSoft in particular, the MuleSoft Certified Integration Architect certification and associated training would be a great place to start. You can find more information at `https://bit.ly/3BMbWvM`.
>
> To learn how to fully design solutions leveraging Heroku, consider pursuing the Salesforce Certified Heroku Architecture Designer certification. More information can be found at `https://sforce.co/3BLkSkK`.

In the next section, we'll conclude this chapter by explaining some non-product-specific solution design topics that should be reviewed or studied in preparation for your B2C Solution Architect certification.

Overall solution design topics

Even after you have mastered the relevant topics for each of the component products in the landscape, you'll need to understand some of the overlay topics that are critical for success as a B2C Solution Architect. Topics such as how to structure a discovery conversation, align stakeholders for a common outcome, guide a development team, produce architecture documentation, and provide technical leadership are all equally important to product knowledge.

We covered many of these topics in *Chapter 6, Role of a Solution Architect*, and *Chapter 9, Supporting Key Business Scenarios*. I suggest you review these topics, especially if the role of a solution architect is new for you.

> **Further reading**
>
> To learn more about Salesforce Architecture in general, and to leverage pre-built templates and approaches, you can leverage the Salesforce Architects portal at https://sforce.co/2X1aw1B.
>
> As you establish yourself in Salesforce, you'll also want to join some of the Trailblazer communities, including the *Customer Architect Community*. This can be found at https://sforce.co/3zQFibw.

The Salesforce Trailblazer communities are an excellent place in which to learn from other working professionals, ask questions, and get updates from the Salesforce team as solutions evolve. Additionally, you can look for other product-specific communities to join to stay up to date and interact on topics across the Salesforce ecosystem.

> **Further reading**
>
> Finally, the *Build Your Architect Career on Salesforce* trailmix offers an in-depth tour of both existing architecture resources and dedicated Trailhead modules. They can help you to build your architecture capabilities on the Salesforce Platform and beyond. Please refer to https://sforce.co/3l1gNlI.

Summary

In this chapter, we covered the B2C Commerce Architect certification, which is an optional additional step in your preparation journey to become a B2C Solution Architect. To help prepare you for the B2C Commerce Architect certification, we covered the various exam topics and what to expect from each.

Additionally, we covered some supplemental B2C Commerce topics that are more relevant for the B2C Commerce Architect certification than for the B2C Solution Architect certification. Finally, we reviewed some further study topics around additional components beyond B2C Commerce, Salesforce Platform, and Marketing Cloud, along with which sections of this book to review regarding integration.

At this point, you should know the difference between the B2C Commerce Architect and B2C Solution Architect certifications. You should understand the content of the B2C Commerce Architect certification and how to prepare for it beyond this book. If you're planning to focus on B2C Commerce Architecture, you should know where to start with the B2C Commerce Developer certification as you work your way up to B2C Commerce Architect and, ultimately, B2C Solution Architect. If you're primarily interested in solution or enterprise architecture, it's not necessary to obtain your B2C Commerce-specific certifications, but the background knowledge is helpful.

In the next chapter, we'll conclude this book by reviewing a selection of realistic scenarios a B2C Solution Architect would encounter in the real world or on the certification exam and explain the best approaches to take to address them.

Questions

1. True or false, the B2C Commerce Architect certification is a prerequisite for the B2C Solution Architect certification?
2. What is the difference between a B2C Commerce Architect and B2C Solution Architect?
3. Explain the role of the SRA process in a new B2C Commerce launch?
4. What are the driving factors when designing a job and replication schedule for B2C Commerce?
5. What are some of the reasons for creating separate sites in B2C Commerce versus using one site for multiple brands/geographies?
6. What are some of the ways B2C Commerce logging can be configured in Business Manager?
7. What is the primary Salesforce product targeted at solving integration problems?

14
Certification Scenarios

By this point, you've had a chance to learn, in depth, about the core products in a Salesforce B2C solution. Additionally, you've learned about many of the potential complementary component products at a higher level. In the middle chapters of this book, we covered the responsibilities, outputs, and role of a solution architect within a delivery team before going deeper into how to choose the right integration option for solving business needs.

If your goal is to get certified, you know exactly what the process is and how to prepare for not just the B2C Solution Architect exam but also the required and optional prerequisite certifications. The goal of this chapter is to help you exercise those new architecture skills!

We're going to return to the Packt Gear sample company. Throughout this book, we've discussed Packt Gear in a variety of contexts. We know they're a direct-to-consumer company, and we know they use Service Cloud, Order Management, B2C Commerce, and Marketing Cloud. For the most part, they leverage the point-to-point integrations between Salesforce clouds, but that approach could change depending on the scenario.

In the four sections of this chapter, we're going to present a new business requirement for Packt Gear. We'll start by deconstructing the requirement looking for business needs that indicate what products are required. Then, we'll check for any governor limits, constraints, quotas, or best practices that would potentially impact the solution. Following this, we'll evaluate integration options that look for the simplest solution that meets the customer's needs and ultimately settle on a recommended approach.

This is the fundamental process used when evaluating business requirements and mapping to technology in real-world projects as well as during the certification exam. During the certification exam, you won't have access to this book or any other references. You'll also have to work efficiently to get through all 60+ questions in 105 minutes.

> **Important note**
> This chapter is *not* a practice exam or question bank; it's a chance to practice your solutioning skills as an architect. Don't attempt to memorize these scenarios; instead, focus on the process and consider other scenarios that might apply in your business.

In this chapter, we're going to cover the following main topics:

- Authentication and customer identity scenarios
- Customer service scenarios
- Marketing-focused scenarios
- Data integration scenarios

By the end of this chapter, you should be comfortable leveraging the knowledge and skills developed throughout this book to solve real-world business requirements in the same way you'll need to when taking the B2C Solution Architect certification exam.

Authentication and customer identity scenarios

Authentication and customer identity are the heart of a B2C solution. The goal of the Salesforce Customer 360 concept is to structure your products, services, and organization around the central idea of a customer. However, that doesn't happen automatically, as it requires careful planning and execution. Most of the information you'll need for these scenarios, aside from the raw product knowledge, is covered in *Chapter 8, Creating a 360° View of the Customer*.

When reviewing these scenarios, consider the following:

- How will the customer enter the ecosystem (for example, via registration, email signup, customer service touchpoint, in-store purchase, or loyalty program)?
- Which system will be the core golden representation of the customer (generally the Salesforce Platform as the CRM)?
- How are customers represented in each component system, and how will we keep these records synchronized?

In the following sections, we're going to start by presenting a realistic scenario that focuses on keywords or clues that should help guide the solution. We'll work through some options to ultimately land on a potential solution based on the requirement provided. We'll conclude by considering any licensing limits, quota limits, governor limits, or other constraints that could impact the design.

An example authentication and customer identity scenario

For our Packt Gear example, we'll use the following new requirement:

Packt Gear needs a forum for outdoor enthusiasts looking to discuss their favorite hiking spots and build a community. Packt Gear employees should be able to log in using their enterprise SSO credentials through Active Directory, so they can help customers and recommend products. The entire experience should be seamless with the existing commerce storefront.

There's a lot to unpack in these three sentences. At this point, in your B2C solution architect journey, there are a few keywords that should jump out at you. In the first sentence, there's a mention of a *forum for outdoor enthusiasts* and a desire to *build a community*. These aren't features of B2C Commerce, Service Cloud, Order Management, or Marketing Cloud, so another product will be required to meet these needs.

In the second sentence, we can see *Packt Gear employees* and *enterprise SSO credentials through Active Directory* standing out. These aren't capabilities that native B2C Commerce storefront login can support. So, we're going to have to leverage something else for employee login. However, as we can gather from the final sentence, it needs to *be seamless with the existing commerce storefront.*

Based on this requirement, we have the following gaps that need to be addressed:

- A new product where a community of customers and employees can interact
- A new login and registration mechanism for employees that supports Active Directory
- Support for seamless login across the new community and the existing commerce storefront for customers and employees

Based on this, we can start to evaluate potential solutions.

Scenario solution development

Within the Salesforce ecosystem, the terms *community* and *forum* should immediately make you think of Experience Cloud. As we already have a core Salesforce Platform org hosting Service Cloud and Order Management, also leveraging Experience Cloud is a natural fit. That solves the capabilities in this new portal, but how will we integrate it?

Thinking through our options, the simplest solution would be to leverage the existing B2C Commerce storefront for logging in. Customers are already logging in to that system with their username and password, so we just need to add support for employee login using Active Directory. B2C Commerce does support using an external OAuth2 provider for customer registration and authentication, which includes support for Microsoft Active Directory, so that seems like a promising direction!

> **Further reading**
>
> You can read more about using OAuth2 providers for B2C Commerce authentication at `https://sforce.co/3za4gRX`.

However, the final requirement is to have seamless login capability across both systems. While B2C Commerce could support the employee login requirement directly, that would leave the Experience Cloud portal to implement its own authentication mechanism. If they both integrated with SSO through Active Directory, we'd be close to seamless for employees, but what about our customers?

For customers who log in with a username and password to the storefront, we need to be able to grant access to the storefront and the community at the same time. Although B2C Commerce can support the use of an external system to authenticate customers, it doesn't have any native capability to serve as the authentication *provider* for other systems. The Salesforce Platform, through Salesforce Identity, supports both external authentications through Active Directory and direct logins with a username and password and serving as an authentication provider for external systems (such as B2C Commerce).

> **Tip**
> This approach is similar to the one outlined in the *Seamless Identity solution kit*.
>
> As discussed in *Chapter 9, Supporting Key Business Scenarios*, whenever possible, start from an existing solution and adapt it to meet your needs. Please review the Seamless Identity solution kit at `https://sforce.co/3924L6c`.

The following diagram depicts this proposed solution:

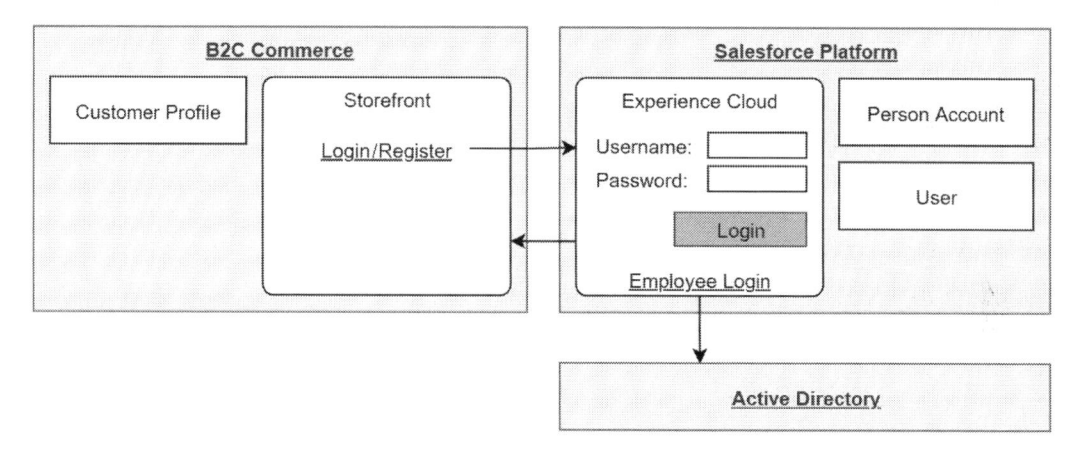

Figure 14.1 – SSO through Active Directory

This solution moves all storefront authentication into the **Experience Cloud** portion of the solution, with B2C Commerce configured to use Salesforce Identity as an OAuth2 provider. Whether customers initiate a login through the commerce storefront or the community portal, they'll be presented with the option to either log in directly with a username and password or choose the **Employee Login** option.

For **Employee Login**, you can configure Salesforce to use **Active Directory** as an identity provider. This approach allows employees to log in using their existing enterprise SSO flow without managing another set of credentials. As the **Experience Cloud** site also handles authentication for the B2C Commerce storefront, they're effectively logged into both systems.

> **Further reading**
> You can learn more about how to configure Salesforce to use Microsoft Active Directory as an identity provider at `https://sforce.co/2YRm4VJ`.

This solution appears to meet all our requirements, but we should always review the implications for licenses, quotas, governor limits, and other system constraints.

Evaluating system constraints

In the B2C Commerce portion of the solution, little is changing. Customers and employees will now log in through Experience Cloud rather than directly. However, once they're authenticated, they'll still have a customer profile in B2C Commerce as they always have. This solution doesn't rely on any new custom objects, integrations, or other data constraints, so there's no concern around quotas.

The most significant change on the Salesforce Platform side is the introduction of a new Experience Cloud-based portal. Experience Cloud is a separately licensed product from Salesforce, which will need to be purchased and provisioned. So far, we've only been planning to synchronize B2C Commerce customers with Salesforce Platform Person Account records. Person Account records consume data storage, but they don't require licenses. However, for a customer to log in to the Experience Cloud site, they also need a User record in the Salesforce Platform, which *does* require a license.

This means that, now, every B2C Commerce customer and every employee accessing the new portal will need not just a Person Account record but also a User record in Salesforce. To evaluate the impact here, review how many total customer records exist in B2C Commerce and how many employees will require access to determine the total number of licenses this will consume.

Experience Cloud licensing is a complex topic, so work with a Salesforce Platform technical architect who is familiar with Experience Cloud to determine the correct license to use. In this scenario, a **Customer Community** license will likely be the best choice, so review the available license count in the **Company Information** section of Salesforce Setup against the number of new user records being introduced to determine what gaps you have.

> **Further reading**
>
> You can learn more about Experience Cloud licensing at `https://sforce.co/3hsmnwx`.

Although there are some implications to licensing, the solution still seems viable! Existing integrations that synchronize customer (and now employee) data between B2C Commerce and the Salesforce Platform could be impacted as well. Moving the login and registration to Experience Cloud would also lend itself to moving the **My Account** section, where customers can review and change their personal information, into the Experience Cloud solution. When introducing changes, be sure to review the implications for existing solutions as well as new requirements!

In the next section, we'll tackle a novel customer service requirement and take a similar approach to evaluate potential solutions.

Customer service scenarios

Customer service is at the heart of strong customer relationships and should be considered at every customer touchpoint. We primarily covered Service Cloud in *Chapter 2, Supporting Your Customers with Service Cloud*. Service Cloud is the primary tool for your **customer service representatives** (**CSRs**), but much of the data they need to work effectively is going to come from outside systems.

When evaluating customer service-oriented scenarios in a B2C solution architecture, think about how you'll bring the tools that a CSR needs into the Service Console experience. CSRs need to work efficiently, often supporting multiple customers at a time, and they need to be able to make each individual feel as though they're an important part of your business. They should know who they're talking to, how that person has interacted with the brand, and have the tools to help them.

Just as we did in the last section, we're going to start by presenting a new requirement for the Packt Gear solution that includes a customer service element. We'll work through the requirement by looking for keywords and clues regarding what's needed to meet their requirement and then check the proposed solution against the system constraints.

Example customer service scenario

As Packt Gear rolls out its guided hike capability, which was first discussed in *Chapter 1, Demystifying Salesforce, Customer 360, and Digital 360*, it's realizing that the CSRs need more capabilities to be able to fully realize the potential of this offering.

The business has come back with the following new requirement:

Our CSRs can manage hiker signups, but customers are asking what type of gear they need for a hike, and we don't have a great way to help them. Agents should be able to view the recommended gear for a hike and either purchase it for a customer directly or add it to their wish list so that they can purchase it themselves later.

In this example, the key requirements can be summarized as follows:

- Agents should be able to see recommended products for a planned hike.
- Agents should be able to purchase products for a customer.
- Agents should be able to add products to the customer's wish list.

Let's practice developing a solution that meets the stated requirements just as we've interpreted them.

Scenario solution development

This is a simple B2C Commerce and Service Cloud scenario; none of these requirements necessitate an additional product purchase. We already have the basic guided hike data model outlined in *Chapter 1, Demystifying Salesforce, Customer 360, and Digital 360*. This data model stores the hikes and hiker registrations in the Salesforce Platform as custom objects.

In the following sections, we're going to take these requirements one at a time.

Supporting agents viewing recommended products for a hike

Based on that, the obvious solution for the first requirement is to extend the guided hike data model to include recommended products, as shown in the following diagram:

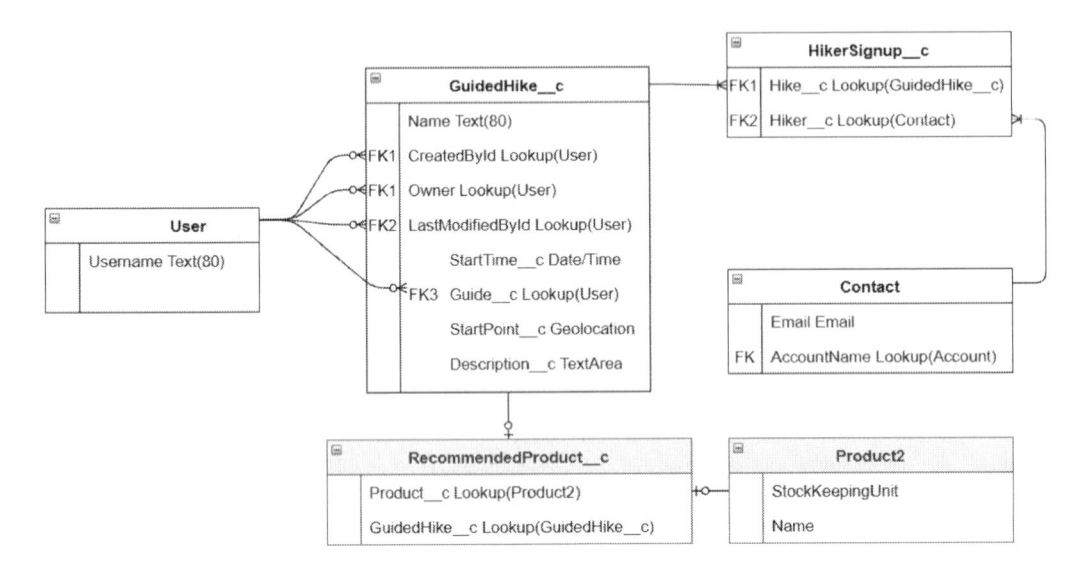

Figure 14.2 – The revised guided hike data model

In the preceding data model, a new junction object, **RecommendedProduct__c**, is being used to link the **Product2** standard object to the existing **GuidedHike__c** custom object. This allows us to model many-to-many relationships between hikes and products. We know the **GuidedHike__c** records in the Salesforce Platform are the system of record for planned hikes, but what is the **Product2** object being used for?

Remember that in the Packt Gear solution, B2C Commerce is hosting product data to display on the storefront, support search, and transact commerce. The Order Management integration will synchronize orders placed in B2C Commerce to the Salesforce Platform, which will create `Product2` records automatically to represent purchased products, but it won't contain full product details, and it won't help at all for products that haven't been purchased on the storefront yet.

> **Further reading**
> To learn more about how the native integration between B2C Commerce and Order Management maps data between the two systems, please review the following documentation: `https://sforce.co/2VBooip`.

To support the solution that was proposed earlier, we need all the product data for the Packt Gear catalog available in the Salesforce Platform. This is so that it can be associated with the Guided Hike records. Let's review a few ways in which to accomplish that.

Option 1 – synchronizing product data

The first option is to ensure that all product data in B2C Commerce is synchronized to the `Product2` object in the Salesforce Platform. Essentially, that's the approach we take between the customer in B2C Commerce and the person account on the Salesforce Platform.

There are a few challenges with this approach:

- Custom attributes on products would need to be kept in sync between systems.
- Product data is loaded into B2C Commerce via XML files from PIM, but the same format is not natively supported via the Salesforce SOAP API (which also uses XML format). If we wanted to use these files in Service Cloud, we would need customization using APEX.
- Product data changes in B2C Commerce are done via Business Manager, not the storefront, and there's no way to trigger custom code to update the Salesforce Platform from Business Manager.
- Product data loaded into the Salesforce Platform would not be used. This unnecessarily consumes data storage space and API requests against platform limits. For larger datasets, this might be a concern.

Based on these challenges, a custom integration solution would almost certainly be required, and it would not be completely in sync since B2C Commerce can't trigger updates.

Option 2 – virtualizing product data

The second option would be to create a new **external object** for B2C Commerce products and fetch the data on demand with **Salesforce Connect**. Please review *Chapter 1, Demystifying Salesforce, Customer 360, and Digital 360*, for a refresher on external objects and Salesforce Connect. This approach does not require you to synchronize data between systems, but it still ensures that we always have the latest version of the full product data available in the Salesforce Platform.

There are several advantages to this approach:

- Product data in the Salesforce Platform is always up to date with B2C Commerce.
- No storage space is consumed in the Salesforce Platform.
- No integration middleware is required.

We still need to ensure the external object in the Salesforce Platform is created with attributes that match the custom attributes on the product in B2C Commerce, just as we would if we were synchronizing data. The primary difference is that, in this model, data is retrieved on demand, so we avoid the need for middleware synchronization.

> **Important note**
> Not all native Salesforce Platform features normally work with Salesforce Connect and external objects. Please review the *General Considerations for Salesforce Connect* article at `https://sforce.co/3zCOQ9e` for more details.

The revised approach looks very similar to the previous approach, but it replaces the standard **Product2** object with a new external object, as shown in the following diagram:

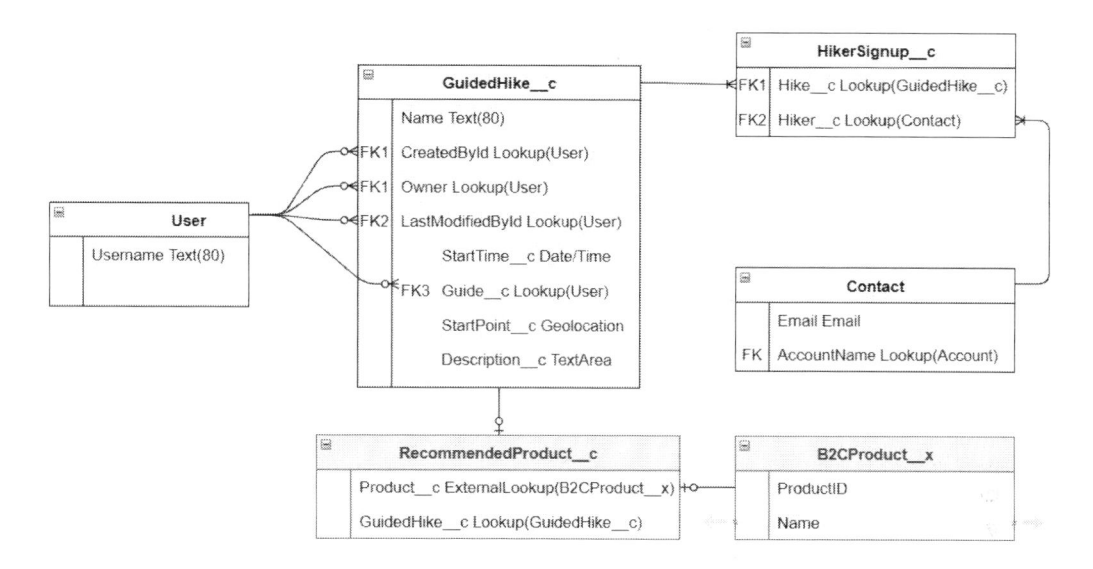

Figure 14.3 – The external object approach

We're using the Salesforce Platform data model and creating an **External Lookup** relationship from the **RecommendedProduct__c** custom object to the new **B2CProduct__x** external object. This helps you to streamline the solution in several ways instead of building something entirely custom. The guided hike record detail page in Salesforce will be able to display related records, including recommended products, and will support adding and removing related products.

This means that we can use a primarily declarative solution that builds on our existing users with permission to create and manage guided hikes and adds support to set up recommended products. Since record-level sharing is not available for external objects, one drawback to this approach is that all products for all brands and geographies will be visible to employees. Filtering on a brand or product list attribute can help to mitigate this, but it is not a security solution.

> **Important note**
>
> Using Salesforce Connect in this way requires you to implement a custom adapter since the only natively supported adapters are cross-org (to another Salesforce org) or OData. The custom adapter will consume either OCAPI or Commerce APIs from B2C Commerce to support retrieving product data on demand and mapping it to the external object.
>
> You can learn about Salesforce Connect custom adapters at `https://sforce.co/3k6Rm3c`.

Supporting CSR product purchasing

Leveraging B2C CRM Sync, we already have support for the CSR **orders on behalf of** (**OOBO**) functionality. That means an agent can open the B2C Commerce storefront and shop as a customer. A minimal solution would be to simply leverage this capability and search for the product that the customer needs, adding it to the cart and checking out using existing B2C Commerce functionality.

However, a step up from this solution would be to extend the existing OOBO functionality in B2C CRM Sync to allow the agent to directly add products to the customer's basket from the recommended product-related list. At that point, they'd just need to launch OOBO and complete checkout (or the customer could do so on their own).

As it turns out, this can be accomplished quite easily using the OCAPI baskets resource, which allows a REST API POST call to add a product to an existing basket. To enhance the solution in this way, you'd need to create and track an agent basket for the current customer, then add products to that basket when they click on the corresponding button on the recommended products-related list.

> **Further reading**
>
> Please review the capabilities of the OCAPI baskets resource at `https://sforce.co/3EbUXVt`.

So, why choose OCAPI as opposed to the newer Commerce APIs? The Commerce APIs have the same capability to add products to the current basket, but B2C CRM Sync is, at least at the time of writing, implemented with OCAPI. So, continuing to leverage OCAPI will be more consistent and efficient.

Supporting CSR managing wish list

This requirement is something of a cross between the previous two. We want to add something to a data structure in B2C Commerce; in this case, a wish list rather than the storefront basket, but we also want to embed a view of that data into the Salesforce Platform.

For much of the same reasons discussed in the preceding section on product data, we'll leverage a new external object to track customer wish lists and wish list entries. We can enhance the custom adapter we created to use with Salesforce Connect between B2C Commerce and the Salesforce Platform to also support wish list data for a given customer. This allows us to retrieve, display, and update wish list entries in B2C Commerce as though they were records in the Salesforce Platform without the requirement that we synchronize them in advance.

To sum it up, we're going to use external objects and Salesforce Connect to represent product and wish list data in the Salesforce Platform. Then, we'll extend the B2C CRM Sync OOBO capability to add support for adding products to the basket directly from the recommended products-related list either from the Person Account or Guided Hike record detail page.

This solution should give customer service agents the support they need. However, let's review any licensing or quota concerns before we commit.

Evaluating system constraints

In this case, again, we're not changing much in B2C Commerce, so there are no new concerns on that side. For the Salesforce Platform, there's some new custom code to write to enhance OOBO and build a new Salesforce Connect custom adapter. The biggest change here is the use of Salesforce Connect itself.

Salesforce Connect requires a separate license to be enabled, which must be purchased through Salesforce. Each Salesforce Connect license supports one OData or custom adapter *or* five cross-org adapter connections. In this case, we need one new custom adapter, so we need one Salesforce Connect license.

> **Further reading**
>
> Please review the cost of a Salesforce Connect license at `https://sforce.co/3Ee4riX`.

Based on this, the solution seems feasible but will have an increased cost for Packt Gear.

In the next section, we'll expand upon this example with a marketing viewpoint to ensure that we're capitalizing on the recommended gear for each hike that we've developed.

Marketing-focused scenarios

Marketing scenarios are those where customer communication at scale, especially with the intent to nurture relationships and drive increases in purchasing, is the primary goal. That could take the form of email or SMS campaigns, advertising, in-app notifications, or a variety of other channels. The foundation of successful marketing campaigns is data. Without understanding customers, it's impossible to design an effective communication strategy to engage them.

When evaluating marketing-focused scenarios, bear in mind two important considerations:

- What system or systems will be responsible for interpreting the available data and driving the customer touchpoints?
- What data do we need to drive this engagement, and how will we make it available to the marketing system?

In most cases within the Salesforce Customer 360 ecosystem, the first system will be Marketing Cloud, but the exact combination of licenses and tools could vary. Salesforce CDP is the primary solution for customer insight across known and unknown data, Marketing Cloud's core messaging and journeys platform is the primary driver for email or mobile engagement, and Salesforce Interaction Studio is the best option for personalizing customer experience touchpoints such as the content on the commerce storefront.

Please review *Chapter 4, Engaging Customers with Marketing Cloud*, for a refresher on the capabilities and component products of Marketing Cloud. In many cases, you'll be able to lean on your Marketing Cloud technical architect counterpart for details of how to leverage the available data. However, the B2C solution architect is responsible for making the right data available to deliver the desired experience.

The scenario we're going to use here is an extension of the previous one into the marketing domain. We'll examine the requirements of the business, ensure we have the right tools to meet their needs, and evaluate integration options along with system design constraints.

An example marketing scenario

Packt Gear's customer service representatives are now able to recommend the right products to their customers when a customer reaches out to schedule a hike or has a question about what to wear; great! However, that only helps with customers who proactively contact an agent, so how can we scale this model?

This brings us to the newest requirement for Packt Gear:

We need to be able to send our customers reminder emails about upcoming hikes that they're signed up for. When we do, we'll include recommended gear for the hike, but we want to make sure it's not something our customers have already purchased. We should also keep an eye on the weather on the day of the hike and ensure recommendations make sense.

By now, you should already be starting to observe the key points hidden in this simple statement. We can see that the primary communication mechanism is going to be *email*, which means core Marketing Cloud. We can gather that the email needs to include *recommended gear for the hike*, which is data stored in the Salesforce Platform, but with the twist that we need to avoid sending them recommendations for things they've *already purchased*. That means we need purchase data from **Order Management**. Finally, we need to check the *weather* for the scheduled hike and use that to adjust our *recommendations*.

The net result, restated as a series of required capabilities, is the following:

- Expose guided hikes, guide hike signups, and recommended products from the Salesforce Platform in Marketing Cloud.

- Expose the customer purchase history from Order Management in Marketing Cloud.

- Retrieve weather data for a planned hike and make it available in Marketing Cloud.

- Leverage Marketing Cloud Journey Builder to develop a communication strategy that reminds customers of upcoming hikes and recommends appropriate products.

Let's work together to develop a solution that will support the Packt Gear business.

Scenario solution development

While there appears to be a lot of requirements here, the first two boil down to synchronizing data from the Salesforce Platform into Marketing Cloud, and we have a powerful tool in our arsenal for that: **Marketing Cloud Connect**. Leverage Marketing Cloud Connect so that you can synchronize objects from the Salesforce Platform into Marketing Cloud as data extensions declaratively.

> **Further reading**
>
> Instructions regarding how to set up synchronized data sources in Marketing Cloud Contact Builder can be found at `https://sforce.co/3nuKbnk`.

Since the first three requirements are closely related, we'll cover all of those together before solving for the weather element.

Exposing Salesforce Platform data in Marketing Cloud

So, what would happen if we synchronized the following objects from the Salesforce Platform into Marketing Cloud using Marketing Cloud Connect? Take a look at the following:

- `GuidedHike__c`
- `HikerSignup__c`
- `RecommendedProduct__c`
- `OrderSummary`

The first three will give us the information we need about planned hikes, including their date and location, as well as the products that are recommended for that hike and who has signed up for them. Since the `Contact` object from Salesforce is already synced to Marketing Cloud, we can build journeys for subscribers who have upcoming hikes.

> **Tip**
>
> External objects cannot be synchronized to Marketing Cloud with Marketing Cloud Connect. If there are specific attributes from the `B2CProduct_x` record that are required, use declarative automation to copy those attributes to the `RecommendedProduct__c` junction object so that they will be available. Additional product data can be queried based on the product ID directly in Marketing Cloud if the product catalog is stored in a data extension.

The `OrderSummary` object is an Order Management object that describes the current state of an order after any modifications post-purchase. Support for synchronizing Order Management objects was added to Marketing Cloud Connect in the Salesforce Summer '21 release, so we can now build journeys directly off Order Management records instead of pushing order data from B2C Commerce, which will not provide the full picture of returns, cancelations, and other sales channels.

Note that we're not trying to synchronize the products themselves from the Salesforce Platform; that information already comes from B2C Commerce in a nightly catalog feed to Marketing Cloud. Instead, we just need to know which products are recommended for a given hike. Additionally, we'll need to extend the existing Salesforce Platform objects to support the weather requirement, which we'll discuss in the next section.

The following diagram shows a revised data model that includes Marketing Cloud:

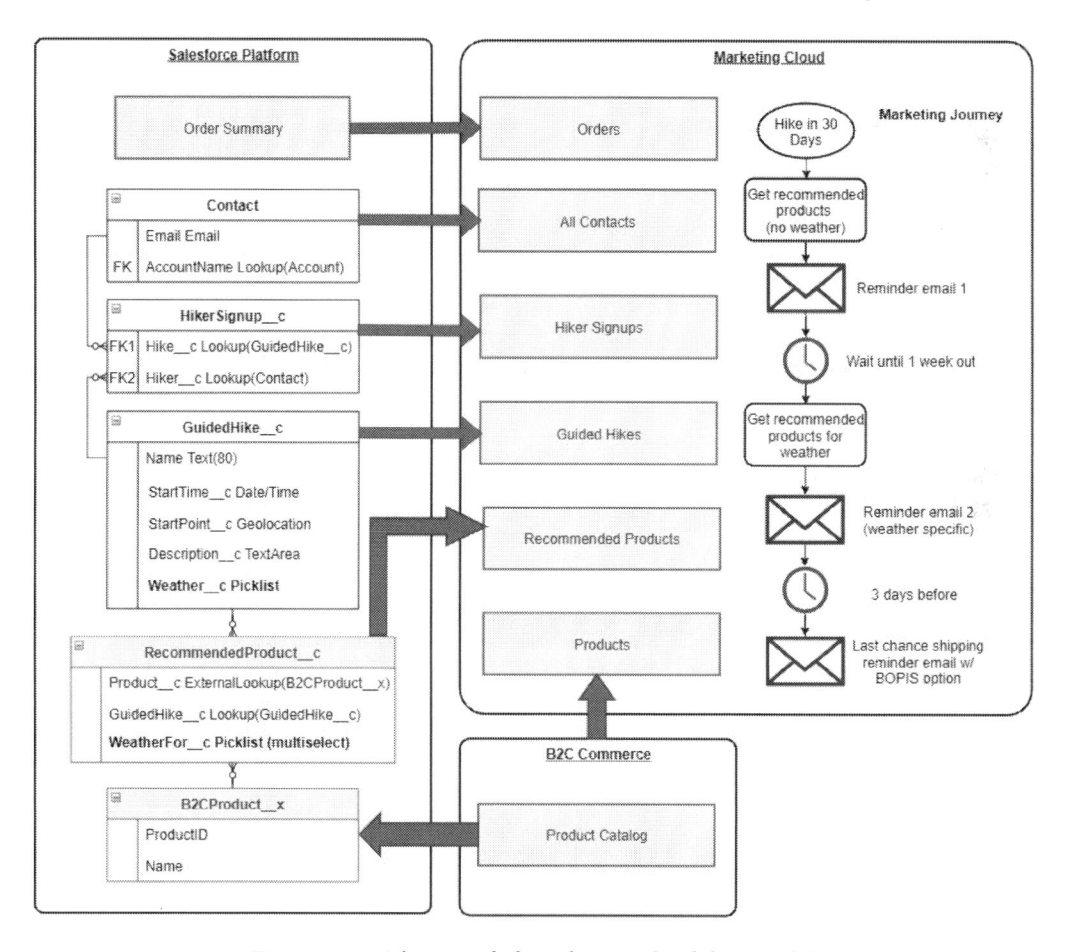

Figure 14.4 – The extended Marketing Cloud data model

That just leaves us with the question of how to integrate with weather data effectively.

Leveraging weather data for marketing journeys

For this requirement, first, we need to figure out where we're going to get weather data in the first place. When we're trying to figure out how to meet a new requirement, our general approach should be the following:

1. Is there a current product in our solution that does what we need?
2. If the answer is no, is there another Salesforce product that would integrate efficiently to fill the gap?
3. If the answer is no, is there an AppExchange or B2C Commerce partner marketplace solution that would help?
4. If the answer is no, is there a third-party product that we could integrate into the solution using a declarative approach such as Salesforce Connect?
5. If the answer is no, is there a third-party product we could integrate with custom APIs or feeds?
6. If the answer is no, it appears we need to either build something from scratch, leverage a manual process, or purchase a separate product.

For our weather data needs, none of our current products will help, and there's no other Salesforce product that's specifically designed to meet this need. AppExchange has a few options for displaying weather data in Salesforce with a Lightning web component, but that's not quite what we need here.

Fortunately, there are plenty of web services that provide weather data on demand and are simple to consume. Because we need weather data for a specific location and date, the most obvious place to store it would be on the guided hike record in the Salesforce Platform. That would also ensure it's available in Marketing Cloud since that object is already synchronized.

The **AccuWeather** API supports a simple REST-based interface where a `GET` request is used with an API key appended as a query string parameter. To keep it simple, use a scheduled flow or Apex Scheduler to retrieve and store the weather for each upcoming hike once per day.

> **Further reading**
>
> The AccuWeather API reference is available at `https://bit.ly/3Eancno`.

You might have gathered that, in our data model, we've represented weather as a picklist on the Guided Hike object and as a multi-select picklist on the Product Recommendation object. This allows us to specify the weather in simple terms (for example, rainy, cold, snowy, or hot) for the hike and filter the recommended products on the same values when we generate the email in Marketing Cloud.

> **Important note**
>
> So, is the B2C Solution Architect exam really going to expect me to know the AccuWeather API?
>
> *No*, but it's going to expect you to know when to look outside of Salesforce for the solution to a problem and how to seamlessly integrate the result back into the experience.

With this in place, we've covered all of the requirements to get the necessary data into Marketing Cloud. From there, Marketing Cloud's Journey Builder can be used to design a series of emails leading up to the planned hike. These emails will remind the customer of the location, date, and time of their hike, telling them what weather to anticipate, and what equipment they'll need to make the most of it!

All that remains for this scenario is to verify that we're not running afoul of any licensing constraints, governor limits, or quotas.

Evaluating system constraints

The biggest consideration for this scenario is the introduction of an external system in the form of the AccuWeather service. Access to that API will have to be licensed separately and support for it will need to be implemented in the core Salesforce Platform solution.

Outbound Apex REST calls are not constrained by licenses in the same way that inbound calls are, but the number of outbound calls made in a single transaction is capped at 100, and the maximum cumulative wait time for callouts in a single transaction is 120 seconds. If the Salesforce Platform process to update weather data on scheduled hikes respects these limits, there should be no issues with this integration.

> **Further reading**
>
> These values are from the *Callout Limits* documentation, which is located at `https://sforce.co/3lcQbhQ`.

The new data synchronization between Marketing Cloud and the Salesforce Platform won't impact limits or quotas on either side, and we're not making any changes in B2C Commerce, so we should be safe!

In the final section, we're going to tackle an example of data integration with requirements beyond the Salesforce ecosystem.

Data integration scenarios

As we learned with the weather example in the previous section, there are times we need to broaden our perspective from just the core B2C solution. The B2C solution architect role and the certification process expect the solution architect to be the contact between the platform's technical architects who specialize in individual components and the enterprise architect. For data and integration scenarios, be especially aware of the integration capabilities and best practices for the component products.

Within this book, we primarily covered integration in *Chapter 7, Integration Architecture Options*, and data modeling in *Chapter 8, Creating a 360° View of the Customer*. I suggest you review both chapters as refreshers on this area. However, you also need to remember the integration options and design constraints of each component product, which are covered in the first part of the book.

To keep things consistent, we're going to continue to expand on the Packt Gear example that we've been using throughout this book in our example data integration scenario.

An example data integration scenario

The Packt Gear guided hike program has really hit its stride! We've got happy campers all over the US, Canada, and Europe testing out Packt Gear in all sorts of conditions. Sometimes, things go well and sometimes not so much, and our business would love to be able to learn more about that to improve its products. Additionally, we need to make sure our guides can keep everyone safe and together in some unforgiving terrain.

This has led to the final business requirement:

We need to enhance our Packt Gear mobile app to allow hikers who are signed up for a hike to share their location so that the guide can keep everyone safe. Additionally, we also need a way for our guides to map out a full hike, not just the starting location. For hikers who purchased our recommended gear, we'd like to send a follow-up email to ask how it went. We can use this information to fine-tune our recommendations in the future.

There's quite a lot of scope hidden in these few short sentences. As always, the solution is to break things down and take them one piece at a time. It sounds as though Packt Gear already has a mobile app that they're using; that's great, as we don't have to start from scratch.

The requirement we need to fulfill is to *share their location data so the guide can keep everyone safe* and provide *guides to map out a full hike*. That means passing GPS data points in near real time from the hiker's mobile device through a cloud service to the guide's mobile device. It also means having a solution that allows you to establish a hike using waypoints on a map. This sounds complicated! Finally, we just need to collect feedback on recommended gear used in the hike.

We have the following new requirements:

- Capture GPS data points and share them between mobile devices.
- Allow guides to create maps for hikes and share them with hikers.
- Follow up with customers who used the recommended gear on a hike to get their feedback.

Let's work through a potential solution to incorporate this into our B2C solution architecture.

Scenario solution development

The first requirement, and potentially the most complex, is to track mobile GPS data and share it securely between devices and to support the design of new maps. We'll certainly need to rely on our mobile app development team to handle that portion of the work; our role is to figure out how this integrates with the ecosystem. We need to know the location of the hike itself, which is available in Salesforce. But we also need to track the real-time locations of each of the hikers.

One of the most important trade-offs you'll evaluate in this type of solution is build versus buy. None of our Salesforce ecosystem products support designing hiking routes and sharing them between users. Additionally, we don't have a native way in which to share and store high-volume data such as GPS location information within the Salesforce Platform. We could look to build something custom using Heroku or another application, but what we're looking for sounds an awful lot like commercially available software.

Just to be sure, let's review what it would take to use a new type of custom object in Salesforce to track hiker location data. With a GPS-provided latitude and longitude, along with a timestamp, it would certainly be possible to track the hiker's journey and overlay that on a map of the region where the hike is taking place. This could be rendered back to the guide's mobile device so that he knows where his hikers are.

However, let's think about the API request volume. Here, we'll make some assumptions, but in the real world, you'd need to gather data from the business team to drive this type of decision:

- ~40 guided hikes per day worldwide.
- The average hiker group is 15 hikers + 1 guide.
- The average hike duration is 1.75 hours.
- GPS data should be updated once per minute.

Based on this, we can say that *40 hikes x 16 total participants x 1 request / minute x 60 minutes / hour x 1.75 average hours = 67,200 total API requests / day.*

In addition to this, each request will create a new record in Salesforce, creating 67,200 total new records/day. Each record in Salesforce consumes 2 KB of storage, resulting in about *135 MB of storage consumed daily* for this feature alone. Evidently, we're taking a pretty big chunk out of our Salesforce limits and allocations to meet this use case, and Salesforce doesn't even use the data! That's not even taking into consideration where we'll get the map information or how we'll design the hikes themselves.

Based on this, we should look at other options. Working through our checklist for feature gaps, as shared in the previous section, there's nothing in the current solution that works. However, some market research tells us that the majority of Packt Gear customers also use a standalone hike tracking app called Hike Mapper. With this app, registered users can design their own hikes, share them with their friends, and hike together safely by temporarily sharing their location.

Based on this market research, you review the capabilities of Hike Mapper. As it turns out, Hike Mapper has a REST API that supports external integrations. It also allows customers to authorize third-party applications to access their data using an OAuth2 flow.

Based on this, we need to allow guides to link their Hike Mapper accounts to their Salesforce User records. From there, they can associate any Hike Mapper route they create with a `GuidedHike__c` record in Salesforce. Also, customers can link their Hike Mapper accounts to their Salesforce accounts through the Packt Gear mobile app. If they do, our application should automatically add the guide to their friends list to facilitate secure location sharing during the hike.

The final step, that is, capturing hiker feedback, can be accomplished by extending the existing Marketing Cloud journey to trigger another feedback email for hikers who clicked on any of the product recommendations in the previous emails to purchase. If hikers had a good experience with the product on their hike, we should note that on the recommendation record in Salesforce, so we know it's a good recommendation. If not, we can note that too but also open a customer service case on their behalf so that an agent can reach out and get more information.

The solution that has been outlined is depicted in the following diagram:

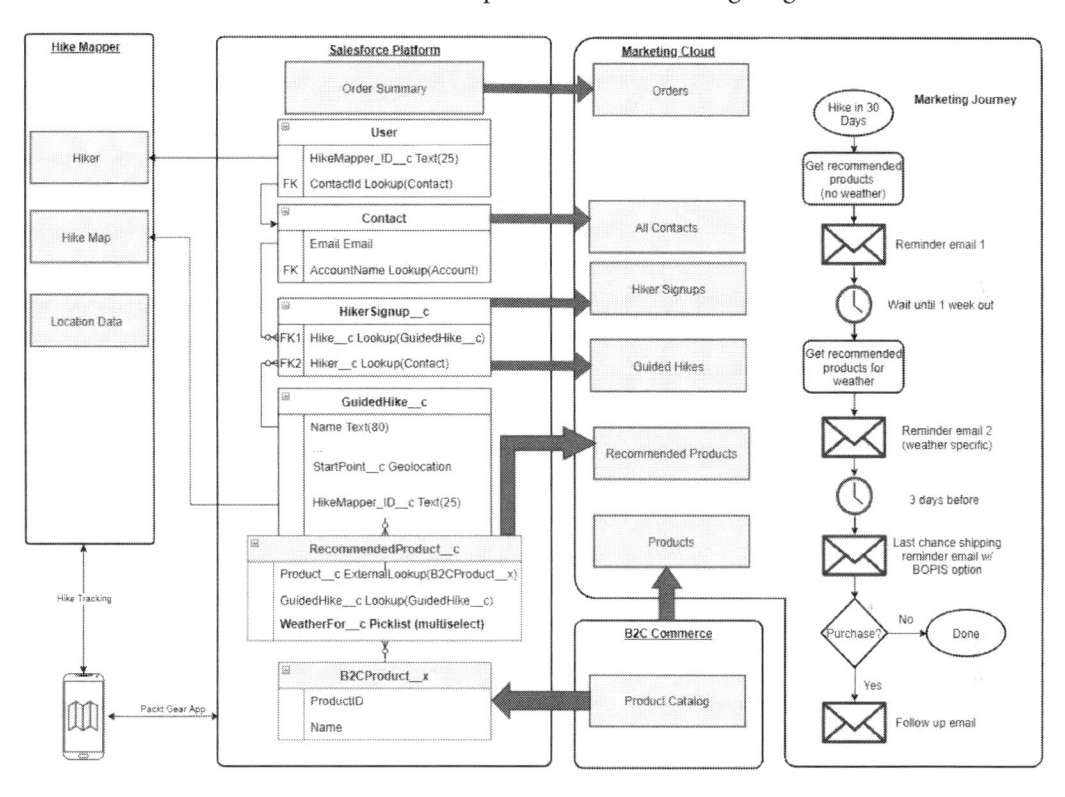

Figure 14.5 – The extended data model with the external data source

In this solution, we can see that Hike Mapper hosts GPS data from mobile apps and handles mapping requirements. Salesforce references Hike Mapper data by storing the relevant external IDs on the Salesforce objects. This minimizes the impact to the Salesforce solution for the new high-data volume requirements of the mobile device and avoids having to custom build a mapping solution. Additionally, we've extended the marketing journey on the right-hand side to include the new post-purchase email, which will be triggered based on hike completion.

There's a lot we could do on top of this, but that's a solid foundation! With your new B2C solution architecture skills, you've got everything you need to continue to develop this solution or whatever solution you encounter in your business.

Summary

In this chapter, we practiced the skills learned throughout the book by evaluating four realistic cross-cloud scenarios to develop a solution. These scenarios mimic the length and complexity that you'd see on a certification exam. So, you should start to practice taking them apart and looking for clues that will guide your solution. In a certification scenario, the options will be multiple choice; in the real world, you won't have that advantage!

At this point, you should know the capabilities, integration models, and data architecture of primary products in a Salesforce B2C solution architecture. You should understand best practices for integrating them and be able to make recommendations around the customer data model. Faced with unique business requirements, you have the process you need to break them down into specific features and evaluate products, integrations, and customizations that will meet that need.

Being a B2C solution architect is a mix of product-specific technical knowledge, enterprise architecture knowledge, and business acumen. It's a lifelong journey that will constantly require you to review the latest features and functionality of Salesforce products, adapt your approaches to match evolving best practices, and strive to understand what your current client or company needs. You've got all the tools you need, so enjoy the journey.

Questions

1. When faced with a capability gap in your current solution, what should you look for as solutions?
2. What role do governor limits, quotas, and license constraints play in evaluating a solution?
3. Which system in the B2C solution architecture ecosystem can use an external identity provider for authentication and serve as an identity provider for other systems?
4. When should you prefer data virtualization solutions such as Salesforce Connect over data synchronization solutions?
5. When should you look to an external software product to fill a gap in your solution?

Assessments

Chapter 1

1. Service Cloud
2. False, a Salesforce object is analogous to a database table containing many records.
3. False, AppExchange distributes managed and unmanaged packages for the Salesforce Platform; B2C Commerce runs on a separate technology.
4. Custom objects reside in the Salesforce Platform database; external objects are retrieved on-demand from an external system.
5. Tabular report
6. Workflow
7. Flow Builder
8. B2C Commerce, Experience Cloud, Marketing Cloud

Chapter 2

1. Professional Edition does not support API-based integrations by default, which are required in a B2C integration. The client must either enable API integration for Professional Edition or upgrade to Enterprise or Unlimited.
2. Service Console – this is where agents work with customers. The service app is for managing the Service Cloud instance.
3. Omni-channel routing.
4. Knowledge articles.
5. Pre-chat variables stored in a hidden form field.
6. A REST API for individual record updates and queries, a Bulk API for large-volume data exchange, and a Connect API for building external user experiences.

7. Service Cloud API limits would not support tracking data as high-volume as storefront page views, nor would they have appropriate performance characteristics. Since most commerce browsing is for anonymous users, it's also unlikely that this data can be accurately correlated with known customers, making it of limited use. An analytics solution, or **Customer Data Platform** (**CDP**), would be a better choice.

8. Connected app.

9. Build a custom app that retrieves the file, converts it to a CSV file, and uses the Data Loader CLI to update the Service Cloud. You could also evaluate third-party integration solutions such as MuleSoft.

Chapter 3

1. SFRA provides the fastest time to value and is mobile-optimized. Reasons for choosing a headless experience (custom or PWA kit) include increased flexibility and the de-coupling of responsibilities, but not implementation time.

2. Service Cloud for the CSR functionality, and an order management solution for order modification requirements. B2C Commerce is not a system of record for orders. Order modifications should be performed in a downstream system such as Salesforce Order Management.

3. Service agents could be making changes directly in Production, which is not the system of record for content, and those changes are getting wiped out by the scheduled nightly replication from Staging.

4. Storefront changes can be supported by modifying the SFRA code base, but Commerce APIs do not allow for custom code extensions; only the Open Commerce API (OCAPI) allows for that, so additional work will be required in a middleware layer between the mobile app and B2C Commerce to ensure mobile app changes are also pushed to Service Cloud.

5. Create a non-replicable custom object to store the results of the form submission on the storefront and a background job to call the service, using the data from the custom object, and deleting the custom object instance when it's successfully submitted to the RMA service.

6. Either the OCAPI Shop APIs or the Commerce API Shopper APIs would work for this use case.

7. B2C Commerce can access FTP, SFTP, or WebDAV file transfer systems. Given that this file contains potentially Personally Identifiable Information (PII), SFTP would be the best choice. Since the file contains customer data, it needs to be sent to Production directly.

8. Only OCAPI can support customization of the response without the use of middleware.

Chapter 4

1. Salesforce CDP.
2. Mobile Studio.
3. AMPscript supports simple programmatic customization of emails and CloudPages.
4. Marketing Cloud Data Extensions support data volumes and, unlike lists, do not require an associated subscriber for records.
5. Without a Salesforce Platform-based product, such as Service Cloud, in the solution, the customer is likely using their email address as their Subscriber Key, which is not compatible with Marketing Cloud Connect. This will necessitate a subscriber key migration, which is performed by Marketing Cloud professional services.
6. False. While it's true that the REST API is newer and should be preferred where it meets a customer's needs, the SOAP API and the REST API support different feature sets, so both may be needed in new implementations to meet all use cases.
7. Marketing Cloud Connect is the productized integration between the Salesforce Platform and Marketing Cloud and supports several use cases, including synchronizing contacts, leads, and accounts with Marketing Cloud subscribers.
8. Marketing Cloud Basic does not support Marketing Cloud Connect for contact synchronization and does not provide API calls without extra costs.

Chapter 5

1. This is an ideal use case for a blended B2C Commerce and Experience Cloud solution leveraging Salesforce Identity for seamless customer authentication on the storefront. B2C Commerce can power the shop flow and transactional needs, while Experience Cloud can power the social and content needs with potential support from Salesforce CMS.
2. This is a description of a combination of B2C Commerce, Service Cloud, and OM. B2C Commerce alone can handle canceling an order within a few minutes using retention periods. Once an order has been exported from B2C Commerce, however, it can only be canceled in a downstream system such as OM. Service agents would interact with OM within the Service console to handle cancelations, returns, and refunds. B2C Commerce can expose OM statuses in real time on the storefront.

3. Heroku Connect provides high-scale synchronization from the Salesforce Platform to a Heroku PostgreSQL database. Leveraging Heroku reduces the organization's need to design a custom cloud infrastructure to house its new data lake.

4. B2C Commerce is not the best choice for highly custom pricing or unique products and deals supported by a sales agent. With customization, B2C Commerce can support customized products for an individual purchase, but this use case would be a better fit for B2B Commerce with CPQ.

5. Salesforce CMS has native integration to B2C Commerce and Marketing Cloud, which can support most touchpoints, and can be integrated with APIs to additional touchpoints such as the mobile app to ensure that everyone is using the same consistent and brand-approved assets when building their experiences.

6. This is an ideal use case for Tableau, since it includes data from third-party systems not connected to the core Salesforce Platform. Tableau CRM would be an option if the data was primarily resident within the Salesforce Platform.

Chapter 6

1. False, the platform technical architects provide platform-specific technical expertise. An enterprise architect oversees the entire architecture for an organization or enterprise, including the B2C solution components.

2. Stakeholder interviews help inform the business needs, which will then be mapped to technical solutions required to meet those business needs.

3. A system overview diagram is used for this purpose.

4. Foundational components of a solution should always be prioritized over quick wins because they are decisions that will cause expensive rework or data problems later if they aren't implemented correctly up-front.

5. Ultimately, technology solutions are what will be used to deliver the business use cases so the role of the B2C Solution Architect is to help bridge this gap from the theoretical to the concrete.

6. True, it's important to understand how each data point relates to data in other systems and how it moves between them up-front.

Chapter 7

1. Developing and testing features that have cross-cloud dependencies may require moving those changes between environments in a coordinated fashion.

2. Marketing Cloud Connect is a supported product, the other two are development frameworks. The B2C Commerce and Order Management integration is part of the product and does not rely on custom code.

3. The Salesforce Platform should serve as the customer data master.

4. B2C CRM Sync is primarily focused on synchronizing customer data between B2C Commerce and Service Cloud.

5. False, Marketing Cloud Connect can only use the Contact, Lead, or User ID as the Subscriber Key in Marketing Cloud.

6. Order on behalf of from the Service Console into the B2C Commerce storefront.

7. Because the SaaS products that comprise this solution cannot be modified to use an external data source in all cases. Instead, data should be synchronized and the product data models should be leveraged.

Chapter 8

1. Account ID and Contact ID.

2. Customer ID and Customer Number, Site ID, and Customer List ID.

3. The platform-specific identifiers are required to support API-based integrations.

4. Existing records using an email as the Contact Key, which requires a Subscriber Key migration from Salesforce.

5. When B2C Commerce and Experience Cloud are being used together to deliver a storefront experience.

Chapter 9

1. False. The solution kits are provided as a reference solution by Salesforce, but they are not maintained with the product documentation and are not guaranteed to be up to date.

2. The solution architecture, with the workflow diagrams walking through step-by-step user interactions with the system.

3. Solution kits are high level and cover only the most common use cases. Adding your organization's needs and developing the solution kits to the level of detail required for your implementation is a necessary next step.

4. Packt Gear is using Salesforce Order Management, which is part of the Salesforce Platform, so that orders can be queried and modified directly from the Service Cloud.

5. Catalog and product data is sent from B2C Commerce Staging because it's mastered there. Order information is sent from B2C Commerce Production because that's the only place real customer information exists.

6. Collect.js.

Chapter 10

1. B2C Commerce customer lists are the scope for customer uniqueness, so aligning BUs with customer lists allows filtering all subscribers to just the customers that are in each audience for marketing purposes. Creating a separate BU for each site is more granular and supports things such as behavioral tracking and unique product catalogs per site, even when multiple sites share the same customer list.

2. The Salesforce Platform is the customer data master within the Salesforce ecosystem, so it is usually the best integration point for external customer data systems.

3. False, BUs can filter the All Subscribers list but that list always contains all contacts in the instance.

4. The customer lists used in B2C Commerce must have unique IDs to successfully leverage B2C CRM sync.

5. Having the external IDs on the Contact record supports leveraging Salesforce Connect and external objects to incorporate external data sources into the Salesforce Platform data model without synchronizing data.

Chapter 11

1. The official exam guide on Trailhead provides an overview of the exam's structure, target audience, and purpose.

2. Platform App Builder, Integration Architecture Designer, and Marketing Cloud Email Specialist (B2C Commerce Architect is not required but complimentary).

3. There are great resources on Trailhead, Partner Learning Camp, and the Solution Architecture Guidebooks that you can leverage.

4. Look for opportunities to review or contribute to integration and data mapping documentation between your area of expertise and a related system, effectively taking one more step out of your comfort zone.

Chapter 12

1. B2C Commerce is not represented in the prerequisite certifications.
2. The other two certifications are both focused on Salesforce Platform and have more transference, so taking them back-to-back is helpful. You might also choose to take both Salesforce Platform exams first and then take the Marketing Cloud Email Specialist exam last.
3. False – each exam has a minimum of 60 score questions, but many have additional unscored questions mixed in that are not identified in the exam. The pass rate is also different for each exam.
4. Each certification has an associated trailmix on Trailhead curated by Salesforce with relevant preparation materials.

Chapter 13

1. False; it's helpful but not required.
2. B2C Commerce Architect is a platform-specific technical architecture within the B2C Commerce system. B2C Solution Architect is a cross-platform solution architecture across B2C Commerce, Marketing Cloud, Service Cloud, and beyond.
3. SRA, or Site Readiness Assessment, is a process in which Salesforce works collaboratively with the customer and with the implementing partner to review the design and implementation of the new commerce experience to help ensure that it's scalable, efficient, and maintainable.
4. Target instances, interdependencies, server loads, storefront performance, and marketing/merchandising activities.
5. Separate sites allow for separate customer data, integrations, replication schedules, merchandising activities, data and analytics, and inventory tracking.
6. Turn on and off by category, control the log levels from debug to failure, and control which log levels are written to files.
7. MuleSoft is an integration solution.

Chapter 14

1. Other Salesforce products, AppExchange solutions, declarative integrations, custom integrations, then fully custom or manual solutions.

2. These aspects can make or break a solution; they are required for long-term scalability and performance. Always review system constraints before validating a solution.

3. The Salesforce Platform.

4. When the data is used infrequently, has a high data volume, or is not required to reside in the Salesforce Platform.

5. When there's no Salesforce ecosystem product that meets your needs since Salesforce products are generally faster and simpler to integrate into the ecosystem than third-party solutions.

Packt>

Packt.com

Subscribe to our online digital library for full access to over 7,000 books and videos, as well as industry leading tools to help you plan your personal development and advance your career. For more information, please visit our website.

Why subscribe?

- Spend less time learning and more time coding with practical eBooks and Videos from over 4,000 industry professionals
- Improve your learning with Skill Plans built especially for you
- Get a free eBook or video every month
- Fully searchable for easy access to vital information
- Copy and paste, print, and bookmark content

Did you know that Packt offers eBook versions of every book published, with PDF and ePub files available? You can upgrade to the eBook version at packt.com and as a print book customer, you are entitled to a discount on the eBook copy. Get in touch with us at customercare@packtpub.com for more details.

At www.packt.com, you can also read a collection of free technical articles, sign up for a range of free newsletters, and receive exclusive discounts and offers on Packt books and eBooks.

Other Books You May Enjoy

If you enjoyed this book, you may be interested in these other books by Packt:

Becoming a Salesforce Certified Technical Architect

Tameem Bahri

ISBN: 978-1-80056-875-4

- Explore data lifecycle management and apply it effectively in the Salesforce ecosystem
- Design appropriate enterprise integration interfaces to build your connected solution
- Understand the essential concepts of identity and access management
- Develop scalable Salesforce data and system architecture
- Design the project environment and release strategy for your solution
- Articulate the benefits, limitations, and design considerations relating to your solution
- Discover tips, tricks, and strategies to prepare for the Salesforce CTA review board exam

Architecting AI Solutions on Salesforce

Lars Malmqvist

ISBN: 978-1-80107-601-2

- Explore the AI components available in Salesforce and the architectural model for Salesforce Einstein
- Extend the out-of-the-box features using Einstein Services on major Salesforce clouds
- Use Einstein declarative features to create your custom solutions with the right approach
- Architect AI solutions on marketing, commerce, and industry clouds
- Use Salesforce Einstein Platform Services APIs to create custom AI solutions
- Integrate third-party AI services such as Microsoft Cognitive Services and Amazon SageMaker into Salesforce

Salesforce Data Architecture and Management

Ahsan Zafar

ISBN: 978-1-80107-324-0

- Understand the Salesforce data architecture
- Explore various data backup and archival strategies
- Understand how the Salesforce platform is designed and how it is different from other relational databases
- Uncover tools that can help in data management that minimize data trust issues in your Salesforce org
- Focus on the Salesforce Customer 360 platform, its key components, and how it can help organizations in connecting with customers
- Discover how Salesforce can be used for GDPR compliance
- Measure and monitor the performance of your Salesforce org

Packt is searching for authors like you

If you're interested in becoming an author for Packt, please visit `authors.packtpub.com` and apply today. We have worked with thousands of developers and tech professionals, just like you, to help them share their insight with the global tech community. You can make a general application, apply for a specific hot topic that we are recruiting an author for, or submit your own idea.

Share Your Thoughts

Now you've finished *Salesforce B2C Solution Architect's Handbook*, we'd love to hear your thoughts! Scan the QR code below to go straight to the Amazon review page for this book and share your feedback or leave a review on the site that you purchased it from.

`https://packt.link/r/1801817030`

Your review is important to us and the tech community and will help us make sure we're delivering excellent quality content.

Index

A

abandoned cart data model 278, 279
abandoned cart workflow 277, 278
abandonment journeys
   revenue, capturing 275
A/B testing 342
Account Manager 69, 81
Accreditation
   versus Certification 380
AccuWeather API
   about 400
   reference link 400
Adobe Experience Manager 133
Advertising Studio 103
agent 261
agent-supported chats
   integrating 265
Amazon Simple Storage Service (S3) 116
Amazon Web Services (AWS) 148
AMPscript 48, 103, 108
Analytics REST API 49
Apex callout 53
Apex REST API 50
Apex SOAP API 50

Apex triggers 316
API
   using 51
API quotas 88
AppExchange
   about 22
   solutions 22
Application Architect 329
application server 378
approval processes
   about 22
   reference link 22
apps 17, 18
architect certifications, Salesforce
   reference link 329
architecture deliverables
   about 172
   data mapping 174-176
   sequence diagram 176-178
   system overview diagram 173, 174
   technical specification document
       (TSD) 178-180
asynchronous 49
Audience data extension entry source 114

422 Index

authentication scenarios
  about 384
  example 385
  reviewing, consideration 385
  solution development 386, 387
  system constraints, evaluating 388
Authorization Code Grant type 117
automated testing 372
Automation Studio 101, 343

B

B2B Commerce
  reference link 93
B2B Commerce Lightning 49
B2C Commerce
  about 28, 92, 261, 262, 304-306
  Account Manager 81
  admin tools 70
  APIs and integrations 80
  capabilities 64
  Commerce APIs 86
  Commerce Payments 93
  customer experience options 65
  feed-based integration support 80
  integration points 87, 88
  job framework 80, 81
  merchant tools 69, 70
  Omni-Channel Inventory 92
  Open Commerce API (OCAPI) 82
  quotas and governance 88
  roles and access 69
  Salesforce Commerce Cloud family 91
  Salesforce Loyalty Management 93
  Salesforce Order Management 91
  study materials 366
B2C Commerce application
    development life cycle 186

B2C Commerce Architect 329
B2C Commerce Architect
    certification 328, 360, 361
B2C Commerce Architect exam
  topic outline 330
  topic weighting 330, 331
B2C Commerce Architect topic
  about 363
  build 365
  discovery/design 364
  integrations and customizations 365
  launch 366
  monitoring and troubleshooting 365
B2C Commerce cartridge
  about 90
  structure 371, 372
B2C Commerce Cloud Shop Connector
  about 215
  reference link 216
B2C Commerce, customer
    experience options
  headless commerce 66
  Packt Gear 68
  Storefront Reference
    Architecture (SFRA) 65
B2C Commerce customer identifiers
  about 231
  customer data access 233, 234
  customer data model 233
  data events 231, 232
B2C Commerce customer uniqueness 297
B2C Commerce Data Connector
  about 215
  reference link 216
B2C Commerce data model
  about 71
  Custom Objects 77, 78
  data sharing solutions, designing 74, 75

instances 71, 72
merchandising 72
Packt Gear 79
realms 71, 72
replication 72
Sandboxes 72
Secondary Instance Group (SIG) 72
sites 71-73
B2C Commerce data model,
  system objects
  access 76
  extending, with custom attributes 77
  inheritance 77
B2C Commerce Developer
  certification 328, 362
B2C Commerce infrastructure
  components
  reference link 378
B2C Commerce instance
  infrastructure 376, 377
  shared data structures 74
B2C Commerce log files
  reference link 376
B2C Commerce logging 375, 376
B2C Commerce Marketplace
  about 90
  reference link 90
B2C Commerce multi-realm
  structure 289, 290
B2C Commerce quotas
  API quotas, overview 88, 89
  categories 88
  designing, solutions 89, 90
  object quotas, overview 88, 89
  severities 88
B2C Commerce server 270
B2C Commerce Staging 279

B2C Commerce supplemental topics
  about 367
  build topics 371
  discovery/design 367
  launch topics 378
  monitoring/troubleshooting topics 375
B2C Commerce testing 372, 373
B2C CRM Sync
  about 191, 193, 194
  capabilities 195
  chat modifications 274
  configuration 196
  data model 196, 197
  installation 194
  implications 301
  limitations 198
B2C CRM Sync B2C Commerce
  implications 302, 303
B2C CRM Sync Salesforce Platform
  implications 303
B2C Solution Architect
  about 360
  prerequisite certifications 328
  related certifications 329
  required non-technical skills 327
  role 156
  target audience 327
  team responsibilities 157, 158
B2C Solution Architect Exam Guide
  reference link 326
B2C solution architecture
  about 6, 8
  key aspects 8
  merchant tools, capabilities 69, 70
  role 73, 74
Backend for Frontend (BFF) 66, 221
Bayeux protocol 48

BFF integration pattern
  reference link 221
billing 143
Bulk API 50
BU scenarios 286
Business Account 15
Business Manager 69
business process layer 211
business units (BUs) 99, 109, 111, 187

C

CAN-SPAN 342
capabilities, Commerce and
    Marketing Connector
  behavioral analytics 208
  data sync 205, 206
  email management 207
case email auto-response 38
case escalation queues 38
case escalation rules 38
case management tools
  about 35
  case auto-assignment 36
  email-to-case tools 36-38
  web-to-case tools 37, 38
CCPA 342
Certification
  versus Accreditation 380
Certified Technical Architect (CTA) 329
chat bots
  integrating 265
chat configuration
  extensions 273
chat design
  considerations 272, 273
chat modifications
  for B2C CRM Sync 274

Chat plugin 261
chat solution architecture
  extending 268-270
chat support
  about 38
  approach, planning 40
  foundational chat experience 39
  improved chat experience 39
  intelligent chat experience 40
chat supported use cases
  about 265
  extending 266-268
Chatter 49
chat workflow
  extending 271, 272
Classic Encryption 202
Client Credentials Grant type 117
Client Secret 84
CloudCraze 28, 93
Cloud Information Model (CIM) 104
cloud pages 107
collect.js
  about 277
  for abandonment scenarios 279
collect.js setUserInfo 279, 280
collect.js trackCart 280, 281
collect.js trackConversion 281
collect.js trackEvent 282
collect.js trackPageView 282
command-line interface (CLI) 52, 194
Commerce and Marketing Connector
  about 191, 203, 204
  capabilities 205
  configuration 208
  data model 209
  installation 204, 205
  limitations 209, 210

Index   425

Commerce APIs
  about 86
  authentication 86
  categories 86
  families 87
Commerce Cloud
  components 136
Commerce Cloud Partner Marketplace 90
Commerce Payments
  about 93
  reference link 94
Community Cloud 28, 132, 253
complementary component topics 379
Computer Telephony Integration
    (CTI) 32, 43
Configure, Price, Quote (CPQ) 143
connected apps
  use cases 57
Connect REST API 49
Content Assets 42
Content Builder 100
Content Delivery Network (CDN) 66, 135
Content Management System
    (CMS) 70, 100, 132
continuous integration (CI) 72
Core 5, 9
core B2C solution technologies 26
create, update, and delete (CRUD)
    operation 17, 216
cross-cloud application
    development life cycle
  about 184
  B2C Commerce application
    development life cycle 186
  Integrated B2C solution application
    development life cycle 187-189

Marketing Cloud application
    development life cycle 187
Service Cloud application
    development life cycle 185
cross-cloud customer identification
  about 237, 238
  customer data, in additional system 241
  progressive identity resolution 238-240
CSR managing wish list
  supporting 395
CSR product purchase
  supporting 394
customer
  about 261, 262
  identifying 226, 227
Customer 360
  about 7
  concept 6
  evolution 6
Customer 360 Audiences (C360
    Audiences) 104
Customer 360 component products,
    for B2C solutions
  B2C Commerce 7
  Marketing Cloud 7
  Service Cloud 7
Customer 360 Guide for Retail
  about 258
  goals, mapping 259
  needs, assessing 259
  reference link 258, 333
  solutions, delivering 259
  starting resources 259
customer cart
  rebuilding 283
Customer Community license 388

426   Index

customer data
  business needs, evaluating 242, 243
  cross-cloud customer data
    mapping 243, 244
  data privacy and consent
    management 245
  mastering 241
customer identity scenarios
  about 384
  example 385
  reviewing, consideration 385
  solution development 386, 387
  system constraints, evaluating 388
Customer Process API 310, 311
customer service representatives
    (CSRs) 8, 195, 310, 389
customer service scenario
  about 389
  example 389
  solution development 390
  system constraints, evaluating 395
customer support
  Digital Engagement 40
customer view
  about 248
  duplicate records, recognizing 251, 252
  experience delivery maturity 249
  global identifiers, adding 252
  global identifiers, using 253
  recognizing 250, 251
custom fields 11
Custom Metadata Types 196
Custom Objects 11, 12, 77, 78
custom solution 321

D

dashboards 24
data
  aggregating, through services 308
data access
  virtualizing, at scale 307, 308
Data API 83
Data Designer 110, 111
Data Extensions (DE) 236
data federation service 308
Data Filter 113
data framework architecture 309, 310
data import and export capabilities
  about 52
  Data Loader 52
  report export 53
data import volumes 128
Data Import Wizard 52
data integration scenarios
  about 402
  business requirement 402
  example 402, 403
  solution development 403-405
data layer 212
Data Loader 52
Data Manipulation Language (DML) 76
data model
  about 6, 10
  Custom Objects 11, 12
  external object 15
  fields 10
  objects 10
  relationships 13, 14
data routing rules 310, 311

data segmentation
  about 113
  Data Extension, segmenting 113
  lists, segmenting 113
data strategy 8
Data Warehouse 195
Datorama 98, 100
declarative automation tools
  about 19
  reference link 19
  workflows 19
Demandware 28
design/discovery 364
DevOps 10
Digital 360 8
Digital Asset Management (DAM) 133
Digital Engagement 35
Distributed Denial-of-Service
    (DDoS) 377
Distributed Marketing 125
Distributed Marketing from Salesforce
  reference link 203
Docker 67
Drupal 133

E

ECMAScript 48
Einstein Analytics 145
email management 106
Email Studio 102
email-to-case tools 36-38
Embedded CDN (eCDN) 377
Encrypted Data Sending (EDS) 202
enterprise analytics
  with Tableau 143

Enterprise customer data 297
Enterprise data management 296
enterprise integration
  with middleware tools 306
Enterprise Resource Planning
    (ERP) 138, 313
Entity Relationship Diagram (ERD)
  about 14
  reference link 140
ExactTarget 28, 98
exclusion list
  about 112
  reference link 344
Experience API 310, 311
Experience Builder 66
Experience Cloud
  about 41, 49, 132, 253
  design constraints 134
  differentiators 133, 134
  features 133
Experience Cloud licensing
  about 388
  reference link 388
Experience Page Time (EPT) 354
external customer data sources 313, 314
external data source 15
external object
  about 15, 392
  reference link 15
external system integration
  about 315
  inbound data options 317
  outbound data options 315
  with MuleSoft 318

F

feature and functionality mapping 8
feed-based integration support 80
Field Level Encryption 202
file-based integrations 51
firewall 377
Flow Builder 136
Flow Builder-created flows 21
Force.com 5
foundational multi-system 165

G

General Data Protection
    Regulation (GDPR)
  about 342
  data privacy legislation 245
  right to be forgotten 246
  right to data portability 247
  right to stop processing 247
Google Analytics 360 connector 101
Google Remote Procedure
    Call (gRPC) 316
GroupConnect 103
guided hike abandonment tracking 282
Guide Template Language (GTL) 108

H

headless commerce
  about 66
  custom 66, 67
  hybrid approaches 68
  PWA Kit and Managed Runtime 67
Heroku
  about 26, 51, 148
  using 220, 221

Heroku Connect 148, 307, 308
Heroku, in Customer 360 148
hike
  agents viewing recommended
    products for 390, 391
Hike Mapper 404
hybrid headless 133

I

inbound data options 317
incremental multi-system 166
Independent Software Vendor (ISV) 90
Individual Email Result (IER) record 201
Integrated B2C solution application
    development life cycle 187-189
Integration Architecture Designer
  about 328
  exam overview 352
  study materials 356
Integration Architecture Designer
    topic overview
  about 352-354
  build solutions 356
  business needs, evaluating 354, 355
  current system landscape, evaluating 354
  design integration solutions 355
  integration, maintaining 356
  needs, translating into integration
    requirements 355
integration-focused technologies 26
integration middleware
  about 210-214, 320
  exploring 212
Integrations and Customizations 364
integration topics 374
integration workflows 8
Interaction Studio 98, 102

Interactive Development Editor (IDE) 50
invocable Apex 136

J

JavaScript Object Notation (JSON) 48
job scheduling 369, 370
Job Steps 80, 81
joined reports 23
Journey Builder 101, 279, 343
journey orchestration 107
journey segmentation 114
JSON Web Token (JWT) 83

K

Kubernetes 67

L

Launch Readiness Bootcamp (LRBC) 379
Lean Governance Framework 355
legacy data
   handling 247, 248
Lightning flow 20
Lightning Performance Dashboard 354
Lightning Platform 5
Lightning Web Component (LWC) 171
LINK cartridges 90
load balancer 377
log file aggregation 320

M

machine learning (ML) 42
Managed Orders 193

Marketing Cloud
   about 98, 277
   Salesforce Platform data,
      exposing 398-400
Marketing Cloud APIs 106
Marketing Cloud APIs and integrations
   about 115
   Cloud SDKs, marketing 126, 127
   data, importing into Data Extension 126
   feed file-based integrations 116
   productized integration 122
Marketing Cloud APIs authentication
   about 117
   server-to-server integrations 118, 119
   Web and Public App
      integrations 119, 120
Marketing Cloud APIs integration 117
Marketing Cloud application
      development life cycle 187
Marketing Cloud BU structure 290, 291
Marketing Cloud capabilities
   about 105, 106
   cloud pages 107
   email management 106
   journey orchestration 107
   programmatic customization 108
Marketing Cloud component
   about 98, 99
   Advertising Studio 103
   Automation Studio 101
   Content Builder 100
   Datorama 100
   Email Studio 102
   Google Analytics 360 connector 101
   Interaction Studio 102
   Journey Builder 101
   Mobile Studio 103

Pardot 105
Salesforce CDP 104
Social Studio 104
Marketing Cloud Connect (MC Connect)
  about 115, 122, 191, 198, 199, 398
  capabilities 199
  configuration 200
  data model 201, 202
  features 124
  installation 199
  integration 124
  limitations 202, 203
  prerequisites 123
  reference link 216
  used, for configuring multi-org 300, 301
Marketing Cloud connector 216, 304-306
Marketing Cloud Contact Builder
  reference link 398
Marketing Cloud customer identifiers
  about 235
  customer data access 236, 237
  customer data model 235, 236
Marketing Cloud customer
    uniqueness 299
Marketing Cloud data model
  about 109
  business units (BUs) 111
  Data Designer 110, 111
  Data Extension 109
  list 109
  suppression 112
Marketing Cloud decision splits
  reference link 114
Marketing Cloud design
    considerations 127
Marketing Cloud edition
    constraints 127, 128

Marketing Cloud Email Specialist
  about 328
  exam overview 340
  study materials 345
Marketing Cloud Email Specialist
    certification 340
Marketing Cloud Email
    Specialist Exam Guide
  reference link 340
Marketing Cloud Email Specialist topic
  content creation and delivery 343
  email marketing best practices 342
  email message design 342
  marketing automation 343
  overview 341, 342
  subscriber and data management 343
  tracking and reporting 344
Marketing Cloud Field-Level Encryption
  reference link 202
Marketing Cloud file transfer options
  reference link 117
Marketing Cloud journey filters
  reference link 114
marketing-focused scenarios
  about 396
  evaluating, considerations 396
  example 397
  solution development 398
  system constraints, evaluating 401, 402
marketing journeys
  weather data, leveraging for 400, 401
Master Data Management (MDM)
    195, 218, 219, 313
matrix reports 23
Member ID (MID) 115
Merchant Identification
    Numbers (MIDs) 138

Meta API 83
Metadata API 50
Minimum Viable Product (MVP) 165
MobileConnect 103
MobilePush 103
Mobile Studio 103
Model-View-Controller (MVC) 372
MuleSoft
  about 26, 51, 145
  reference link 214
  using, in B2C solution 219
MuleSoft Accelerator for B2C
    Commerce 217, 218
MuleSoft Accelerator for Retail
  about 218
  reference link 218
MuleSoft, advantages
  about 214
  B2C Commerce Cloud Shop
      Connector 215
  B2C Commerce Data Connector 215
  Marketing Cloud Connector
      (MC Connect) 216
  MuleSoft Accelerator for B2C
      Commerce 216, 217
  MuleSoft Accelerator for Retail 218
  Salesforce Connector 215
MuleSoft Composer 147, 148
MuleSoft data federation 310
MuleSoft, in Customer 360 145
MuleSoft value proposition 146, 147
multi-cloud use case solution kits 258
multi-org
  about 286
  configuring, with Marketing
      Cloud Connect 300, 301

N

NodeJS SDK 66
non-replicable 78

O

OAuth2 134
OAuth 2.0 57
object quotas 88
OCAPI hooks 85
Omni-Channel 43
Omni-Channel Inventory (OCI)
  about 92, 296
  reference link 92
Omnichannel Inventory
    Service (OIS) 193
Omni-Channel routing
  about 32, 43, 45
  configurable components 43-45
Omni-Channel supervisor 45
Open Commerce API (OCAPI)
  about 76, 82, 196
  access control 82
  authentication 83, 84
  categories 83
  Data API 83
  hooks 85
  Meta API 83
  resources and documents 84, 85
  Shop API 83
Open CTI 43
OpenID Connect 57
Open Web Application Security
    Project (OWASP) 377
Order Management 263, 397
Order Management System (OMS) 65, 72

Order On Behalf Of (OOBO)
  about 195, 394
  capability 261
org 10
Organizational Change
    Management (OCM) 164
org-wide defaults 16
outbound data options 315-317
out-of-scope technologies 27

P

Packt Enterprises org chart 286
Packt Enterprises Salesforce
    ecosystem 295
Packt Gear 7, 68
Packt Gear B2C Commerce data model 79
Packt Gear chat support
  needs 266
Packt Gear solution 149, 150
Page Designer 66, 133
Parallel solution architectures 293
Pardot 105
Partner Learning Camp (PLC) 333
Payment Card Industry (PCI) 69
payment gateway 90
permission sets 16
Person Account 14
Personally Identifiable
    Information (PII) 245
Platform App Builder
  about 328
  exam overview 346
  study materials 351
Platform App Builder Exam Guide
  reference link 346

Platform App Builder topic overview
  about 346-348
  app deployment 350
  business logic and process
    automation 349
  data modeling and management 348
  Salesforce fundamentals 348
  user interface 350
Platform-as-a-Service (PaaS) 26, 148, 306
Point of Delivery (POD) 71
point-of-sale (POS) 68
point-of-view (POV) 134
point-to-point connectors 213, 214
point-to-point integrations
  about 189-191
  B2C CRM Sync 193
  Commerce and Marketing
    Connector 203, 204
  Marketing Cloud Connect (MC
    Connect) 198, 199
  prescriptive approach 191, 192
  productized point-to-point
    integrations 192
pre-chat form 270
pre-chat variables 261
prescriptive approach 191, 192
Primary Instance Group (PIG) 71
Process Builder-created processes 20, 21
product data
  synchronizing 391
  virtualizing 392, 393
Product Detail Pages (PDPs) 133
Product Information
    Management (PIM) 69
productized integration
  about 122
  distributed marketing 125

Index   433

Marketing Cloud Connect
   (MC Connect) 122
productized point-to-point
   integrations 193
product-specific knowledge
   gaining 336
program manager 160
programmatic customization 108
progressive identity resolution 238
Progressive Web App (PWA) 67
Progressive Web SDK 67
project sequencing
   about 167
   business case 170, 171
   evaluation 169, 170
   firm foundation, building 167-169
publication lists
   about 112
   reference link 344
Pub/Sub API 316
PWA Kit and Managed Runtime 67

Q

quote-to-cash 143

R

realm 286
record type 14
relationship 13
relationship, types
   external lookup relationship 13
   lookup relationship 13
   many-to-many relationship 13
   Master-Detail relationship 13
replicable 78
replication scheduling 369, 370

report export 53
reporting in Marketing Cloud, Salesforce
   reference link 344
reports
   about 23
   types 23
reports and dashboards
   reference link 25
REST APIs 121, 312
REST protocols 48
revenue
   capturing, with abandonment
      journeys 275

S

Safehouse 116
Sales Cloud 142
Salesforce 4
Salesforce B2B Commerce
   Lightning 140, 141
Salesforce B2C Commerce
   Technical Architects
   reference link 364
Salesforce Call Center 43
Salesforce CDP
   about 98, 104, 114, 115
   reference link 114
Salesforce certification exam
   structure 326
Salesforce CMS
   about 135
   design constraints 135
   differentiators 135
   features 135
Salesforce.com 5
Salesforce Commerce Cloud family 91
Salesforce Commerce Cloud (SFCC) 28

Salesforce Connect
    about 15, 296, 392
    reference link 288
Salesforce Connect custom adapters
    reference link 394
Salesforce Connector 215
Salesforce Content Management
        System (CMS) 49
Salesforce Data Event 243
Salesforce data security
    reference link 17
Salesforce ecosystem 6
Salesforce Experience Cloud 132
Salesforce Extensions for Visual
        Studio Code 50
Salesforce Functions 51
Salesforce Identity 134
Salesforce Knowledge
    about 41
    solutions, tracking 41
Salesforce layered approach
    reference link 212
Salesforce Loyalty Management
    about 93, 139
    reference link 93
Salesforce materials
    about 332
    Partner Learning Camp 333
    solution architecture guidebooks 332
    trailhead resources 333
Salesforce Object Query
        Language (SOQL) 50
Salesforce Order Management (OM)
    about 91, 136
    design constraints 138
    differentiators 137
    features 136, 137
    reference link 92

Salesforce orgs 10
Salesforce Payments 138
Salesforce Platform
    about 9, 26, 261
    advantages 392
    reference link 10
Salesforce Platform API options
    about 47, 48
    capabilities 49, 50
    communication mechanisms 49
    data format 48
    protocols 48
Salesforce Platform, categories
    function-specific 5
    industry-specific 5
Salesforce Platform customer
        data access 230, 231
Salesforce Platform customer
        data model 229, 230
Salesforce Platform customer
        uniqueness 298
Salesforce Platform data
    exposing, in Marketing Cloud 398-400
Salesforce Platform data events 228, 229
Salesforce Platform multi-org
        structure 287, 288
Salesforce security model 16
SAML 2.0 57
Sandboxes 72
Scope of Work (SOW) 170
scratch orgs 10
seamless identity 253, 254
Seamless Identity solution Kit 387
Secondary Instance Group (SIG) 71, 72
segmentation
    about 112
    data segmentation 113
    journey segmentation 114

Salesforce CDP 114, 115
senior developer 160
sensitive data
  movement and access, minimizing 245
server-side JavaScript (SSJS) 48, 108
server-to-server integrations 117
Service Agent 262
Service App 34
Service Cloud 11, 262, 263, 270
Service Cloud APIs and integrations 47
Service Cloud application
    development life cycle 185
Service Cloud capabilities 32
  computer-telephony
    integration (CTI) 43
  Omni-Channel 43
  Salesforce Knowledge 41
  service contracts and entitlements 42
Service Cloud customer identifiers
  about 228
  Salesforce Platform customer
    data access 230, 231
  Salesforce Platform customer
    data model 229, 230
  Salesforce Platform data events 228, 229
Service Cloud customer support
  about 34, 35
  case management tools 35
  chat support 38
Service Cloud data model
  about 45
  additional objects 46
  Salesforce Platform data
    model review 46
Service Cloud editions 33
Service Cloud request limits
    and allocations
  about 54

API access 57
API usage monitoring 56
capability capacity limitations 55
connected apps 57
data and file storage allocations 58, 59
enforcement 56
feature allocation limits 58
Salesforce licenses and editions 54
total API allocations 55, 56
Service Console 34
Service Framework
  about 374
  components 374, 375
Service-Level Agreement (SLA) 42
SFDX 350
SFRA Testing Technologies
  reference link 373
Shield Platform Encryption 202
Shop API 83
single sign-on (SSO) 57, 68
single source of truth
  architecting 219
  incorporating 220
single system 165
site architecture 367, 368
SiteGenesis 65
Site Readiness Assessment (SRA) 366
SOAP API 120, 121
SOAP protocols 48
Social Studio 104
Software Development Kits (SDKs) 126
Software Development Lifecycle
    (SDLC) 355
solution
  monitoring 319-321
Solution Architect Pocket Guide
  reference link 332

solution architecture methodology 27
solution design
  considerations 292, 293
  topics 381
solution kits
  about 260
  configurations 264
  design considerations 264
  reference link 260
  solution architecture 260, 261
  workflow 262, 263
SSH File Transfer Protocol (SFTP) 115
stakeholders
  about 158
  alignment on goals 160
  business needs, mapping to
     technology solutions 165
  full team 158
stakeholders interview
  about 161
  questions 162, 163
  results, assessing 163, 164
standard fields 11
standard objects 11
Storefront Reference Architecture
    (SFRA) 65, 362
Streaming API 48, 50
Stripe public APIs 139
Structured Query Language (SQL) 113
Subscriber Key migration
  about 123, 248
  reference link 248

summary reports 23
suppression 112
suppression lists
  about 112
  reference link 344
synchronous 49
System APIs 310, 312
System Architect 329

T

Tableau
  enterprise analytics 143
Tableau CRM 49, 145
Tableau integration 144
tabs 18
tabular reports 23
technical specification document
    (TSD) 172, 178
technology stacks 25
Tooling API 50
Total Lifetime Value (TLV) 139
Trailhead 35
Trailhead superbadges 351
Transactional Messaging API 122

U

Unmanaged Orders 193
User Acceptance Testing (UAT) 10, 72
user experience customization 17
User Interface API 49
user interface layer 211

V

value-added features
  categorizing 166

W

weather data
  leveraging, for marketing
    journeys 400, 401
Web Adapter 378
Web and Public App integrations 117
Web Application Firewall (WAF) 377
webdriver.io 373
Web Service Definition Language
    (WSDL) 51, 121
web-to-case tools 36-38
workflows 19

Printed in Great Britain
by Amazon